# THE SIERRA CLUB
# GUIDE TO
# THE NATURAL
# AREAS OF OREGON
# AND WASHINGTON

## The Sierra Club Guides to the Natural Areas of the United States

# The

# Sierra Club

# Guide

# to the

# Natural Areas of

# Oregon and
# Washington

John Perry and Jane Greverus Perry

with revisions by Roger Rapoport,
Linda Cohen, and Nancy Madway

SIERRA CLUB BOOKS    SAN FRANCISCO

The Sierra Club, founded in 1892 by John Muir, has devoted itself to the study and protection of the earth's scenic and ecological resources—mountains, wetlands, woodlands, wild shores and rivers, deserts and plains. The publishing program of the Sierra Club offers books to the public as a nonprofit educational service in the hope that they may enlarge the public's understanding of the Club's basic concerns. The point of view expressed in each book, however, does not necessarily represent that of the Club. The Sierra Club has some sixty chapters coast to coast, in Canada, Hawaii, and Alaska. For information about how you may participate in its programs to preserve wilderness and the quality of life, please address inquiries to Sierra Club, 85 Second Street, San Francisco, CA 94105.

http://www.sierraclub.org/books

The revised edition of this book was prepared by Roger Rapoport and his staff at RDR Books, Berkeley.

Library of Congress Cataloging-in-Publication Data
Perry, John, 1914–
The Sierra Club guide to the natural areas of Oregon and Washington.

Includes bibliographical references and index.
1. Outdoor recreation—Washington (State)—Guide-books. 2. Natural history—Washington (State) 3. Natural areas—Washington (State)—Guide-books. 4. Washington (State)—Description and travel—1981- —Guide-books. 5. Outdoor recreation—Oregon—Guide-books. 6. Natural history—Oregon. 7. Natural areas—Oregon—Guide-books. 8. Oregon—Description and travel—1981- —Guide-books.
I. Perry, Jane Greverus. II. Title.
GV 191.42.W2P47 1983      917.97      82-16937
ISBN 0-87156-939-6

Production by Janet Vail
Cover design by Bonnie Smetts Design
Book design by Mark Ong
Maps by Tom Camara

Printed in the United States of America on acid-free paper containing a minimum of 50% recovered waste paper, of which at least 10% of the fiber content is post-consumer waste

10 9 8 7 6 5 4 3 2 1

# CONTENTS

# THE NATURAL AREAS OF WASHINGTON   213

# INTRODUCTION

This is a guide to the quiet places, where plants grow, birds sing, and the signs of humans are few.

Western friends warned that the quiet places were overrun. One must make reservations weeks ahead to enter a wilderness. Beach parking is full by midmorning. Noisy off-highway vehicles have driven off wildlife and hikers.

Certainly the western landscape has been much changed since we first saw it more than 60 years ago. The forests are a giant patchwork, great openings formed by clear-cutting. Some trails have been trampled into muddy ditches. Many hillsides show the scars of ORVs. Campground Full signs are common.

Yet we had no difficulty finding quiet places. In the last phase of our research, we traveled 11,500 miles in these two states, camping every night in our motor home or in a tent beside a trail. On most nights we were alone or with few neighbors.

People tend to congregate. Most seem to prefer the developed recreation sites, the publicized trails. Most come at certain seasons. Those who seek solitude can find it, often nearby. One night we had a 17-mile-long river canyon all to ourselves, on another a splendid valley dotted by small lakes.

In the East, less than 10% of the land is publicly owned. Most federal and state parks, forests, and wildlife areas occupy land that was once private. Much of it was abused and abandoned, surrendered in lieu of the tax payment or sold for a few dollars per acre. Today most eastern states are paying high prices for remaining fragments of wetlands and undeveloped coast.

More than half of Oregon and almost a third of Washington remain in federal ownership, and both states also have extensive landholdings. Most of these public lands are in the mountains and deserts, although Oregon has kept much of its seacoast in public ownership.

## How We Selected Sites

We use the term "natural area" broadly, generically. A few specialists have objected. They have appropriated the term and devised narrow definitions. "Federal Research Natural Areas," for example, are "lands on which various natural features are preserved in an undisturbed state solely for research and educational purposes."

We look for places where a visitor can enjoy nature. Most such places are not pristine. Some have been logged, farmed, mined, or otherwise disturbed, but the healing processes of nature are at work. Most wildlife refuges are not "natural" since their ponds and marshes are maintained by dikes, and crops are planted to support waterfowl. Without such places few waterfowl would travel the flyways. When tens of thousands of geese and ducks endorse these places, they're good enough for us.

Large National Forests and National Parks were automatic selections. We studied smaller sites more critically. We would not include a State Park planned for intensive recreation. If, in addition to a developed area, it also had a few hundred roadless acres of interest to hikers and birders, we would consider it.

In studying a small site, we considered its setting. A small seaside park may provide access to a dozen miles of uncluttered ocean beach. A park with little more than a campground may be a wilderness trailhead. A site that is intolerably crowded on the Fourth of July may offer splendid solitude in December.

The revised edition of our book was researched and prepared for publication by Roger Rapoport and his staff at RDR Books in Berkeley, California.

## The Public Domain

When we had screened every National Park, National Forest, and National Wildlife Refuge, we had 16 million acres left over, what remains of the original public domain. Because of the different terms negotiated when these two states entered the Union, all but 310,000 acres are in Oregon. These acres sprawl over the landscape, sometimes in huge, solid blocks, sometimes in a checkerboard of 1-mi. squares, alternating with state and private land. The acreage includes mountains, deserts, plains, canyons, rivers, lakes, and wetlands.

The boundaries are not marked. This land is not divided into neat packages, like parks and forests. We could not write a single entry for, say, the 15.7 million acres of public domain in Oregon. We looked for outstanding features, such as a mountain or canyon, then studied the surrounding area. Finally, we fixed arbitrary boundaries enclosing areas that seemed to fit together.

The Bureau of Land Management (BLM) was then engaged in a prodigious task mandated by Congress: identifying each roadless area of 5,000 or more acres, then gathering data to judge its suitability for wilderness status. This data and other documents in BLM District files were invaluable to us, as were our many talks with BLM specialists. We knew where to look when our fieldwork began.

BLM sites may have unmarked boundaries. Generally, the visitor will find no signs, no gates, and—except at a few recreation sites—no facilities. Only by chance will a BLM staff member be present.

These millions of acres are yours to enjoy. Here you can drive, hike, backpack, ride horseback, and camp almost anywhere, hunt and fish subject to state laws. Except in a few developed recreation areas, you are unlikely to meet other visitors.

Much of this land has been leased, usually for grazing, and some has been fenced by ranchers. This does not shut you out. Where public land is fenced and gated, you have the right to enter—and to close the gate behind you.

How do you know you are on public land? In some areas, private and public lands are intermixed. Our entries are for areas with few private inholdings. If you have doubts or concerns, visit or telephone the BLM District Office.

What if a rancher tells you to get off his place? Go quietly. You could have strayed onto private land. But some ranchers have used the public land for so long they consider it their own. Perhaps previous visitors have misbehaved. However, such confrontations are rare even on private land. Should you have one, the BLM office would like to know about it.

## Other Public Lands

We reluctantly decided to omit county and regional parks. Inquiries convinced us that few could supply the data we needed. Some we were advised, would refuse our request, holding that their parks are for local taxpayers, not outsiders. At best, a large task would have a small yield.

We have included no military reservations. Some of these are large, and many permit limited use. However, the limits are usually strict, and they often change from day to day. The base nearest our home has a special number you call to hear whether visitors are permitted that day. Most public use of these reservations is by hunters and fishermen, but if there is one near you, inquire. Some reservations have naturalists or wildlife managers who can tell you what's there and who may even offer a guided tour.

## Private Lands

Some of the largest private holdings are those of timber companies. In the past some companies permitted or invited public use. We wrote to the largest and asked if this were still the case. Only two replied. Both asked that we not mention their lands. Neither answered our question.

Off the record, company officials said, "We allow public use, but we don't want publicity. If many more people come, we'll have to close the gates. And we must be able to close them at any time, without notice, for operating reasons."

A state wildlife official confirmed this. Most timber company lands are used by hunters and fishermen, he said, and sometimes by hikers. Some owners require permits. A few charge fees. He advised prospective visitors to inquire at the nearest federal or state forestry office. Our advice: Forget it, unless you have a special interest in an area.

# How We Gathered Information

Roughly a third of the information assembled here is available somewhere in print: leaflets, booklets, maps, technical reports, species checklists, and various official documents. We gathered over a thousand items.

Another third is in the files of state and federal agencies, much of it in district and local offices. When our friends imagined we were hiking on mountain trails, we were often combing through hundreds of file drawers.

The final third we could obtain only by questionnaire, interview, and observation. The response to our 8-page questionnaire was unbelievably good. Our talks with managers and specialists filled many notebooks. Our own field notes went into a cassette recorder as we hiked or drove.

Have we visited every site? Many, not all. We have been frequent visitors to this region since 1929. We planned our 11,500-mile itinerary to visit sites we hadn't seen before.

Gathering so much information at first hand would require several lifetimes. Just compiling a decent bird list for one site would require monthly visits for a year. We had to rely on what others had observed over past years.

Good data are available for most National Parks, Forests, and Refuges, and the BLM has greatly expanded its data on the public domain. State agencies tend to have less, but their local managers usually have knowledge of nature. And most were helpful to us in obtaining information they didn't already have.

This method does not assure scientific accuracy. We checked what we could, deleted some obvious errors, deleted some improbables. Errors doubtless remain. And phone numbers will change more often than we wish!

## Checking

Every entry was sent to the site or to its district or state headquarters. Response was excellent. Entries came back with corrections and additions. The data were revised in 1996, using the same procedure.

## What's Not in the Entries

Entries do not include information about:

*Picnic grounds.* One can picnic almost anywhere.

*Campground facilities.* Excellent directories are published.

*Cabins, inns, lodges.* We could not distinguish among lodgings on public land, lodgings on private inholdings, and lodgings just outside.

*Restaurants* and *snack bars* presented the same difficulty. Also, many close when crowds are absent.

*Playgrounds, golf courses,* and so on.

*Admission fees.* Most Parks charge fees. And the fees change from year to year. Also, toll booths are often closed when visitors are few.

At the National Parks, frequent Park users should ask about the Golden Eagle pass, which allows unlimited access for a year to all National Parks for a small fee. Senior citizens can purchase a Golden Age Pass, which offers lifetime free access, also for a small fee. The Golden Access Pass is free to blind or permanently disabled U.S. citizens and permanent residents. State Parks may have discounted fees for seniors, disabled persons, and veterans.

*Rock climbing, rockhounding, spelunking,* and *scuba diving* are too specialized for a general guide.

## Changes

These are hard times for the public lands. For years budgets failed to keep pace with increasing public use. Now federal and state agency budgets have been cut, in some cases savagely. The permanent damage thus inflicted on precious natural resources is of deep concern to us, but beyond the scope of this book. Readers will encounter many reductions in opportunities and services:

- Publications may be out of print. Others, once free, will be sold.
- Campfire programs, guided walks, and other interpretive programs may be curtailed.
- Some campgrounds may be closed, others operated for shorter seasons. Facilities may be reduced. Broken or vandalized equipment may not be replaced.
- Some Wildlife Refuges may be closed, perhaps seasonally or on certain days. Visitors may be restricted to smaller portions of refuges.
- Maintenance of hiking trails may be reduced.
- Snow plowing may be discontinued on some Park roads.

## How to Use This Book

Each state is divided into zones. Zone boundaries follow county lines, with minor exceptions. A map showing these zones appears at the beginning of each state section, together with an alphabetical list of all sites within that state.

At the beginning of each zone section is a zone map on which sites are spotted, with key numbers. Sites are listed in numerical order.

- If you plan to visit an area, find the corresponding zone and see what other sites in the zone would interest you.

- If you plan to visit—say—a National Park, locate its key number on the zone map and see what other sites are nearby.
- Entries are arranged alphabetically within zones. Information in entries is presented in a standard sequence.

## Site Name

*Parks* are for people. Most Parks have formal entrances. Most are closed to logging and hunting. Most have developed recreation sites. Parks have more facilities, more supervision, more rules, and more visitors than Forests or Refuges.

*Forests* are for trees and water. National Forests are managed for wood, water, wildlife, and recreation, although critics charge imbalance. Timber is often harvested on the more humid western slopes, vegetation maintained in semiarid areas. Hunting and fishing in National Forests are governed by state law. Recreation has a high priority in many National Forests. While there are campgrounds, one can camp almost anywhere.

*Wildlife management areas,* state operated, are for birds and beasts, fishes included. In the past, most visits were by hunters and fishermen, whose license fees supported the state systems. Now, visits by "nonconsumptive users," such as hikers and birdwatchers, are welcomed, especially outside hunting season.

*National Wildlife Refuges* are also for birds and beasts, but many have visitor facilities: auto tour routes, exhibits, information centers. Hunting is usually permitted, though often restricted to certain parts of the Refuge and with special rules.

*Public domain lands,* managed by the BLM, have many uses, including grazing, mining, forestry, and geothermal development. Most areas are open to public use. Large areas are far from any paved roads, and access often requires 4-wheel drive or a sturdy pickup truck. In the many roadless areas, travel is by foot or horseback. Most BLM lands are arid or semiarid.

*Multiple Use Areas* are peculiar to Washington and described in the state preface.

The *Pacific Crest National Scenic Trail* (PCT) is a 2,638-mi. wildland route connecting Mexico with Canada, while holding carefully to the crest of the mountain ranges of Washington, Oregon, and California. Authorized by Congress in 1968, it is largely routed over public lands, crossing or touching 33 federally designated wildernesses, 243 National Forests, and 7 National Parks as well as 5 State Parks and county lands. The PCT also crosses some private lands, but landholders have made the route available by agreement with the federal government. The hiker, biker, or equestrian on the trail may travel through elevations ranging from 140 to 13,200 ft. The U.S. Forest Service and the Pacific Crest Trail Association work together on trail-related matters.

The *Oregon National Historic Trail* was created by Congress in 1978 to raise public awareness of the historic wilderness route over which some 400,000 persons traveled to settle the western portion of the United States. Today, the trail is administered by the National Park Service in partnership with the BLM, the U.S. Forest Service, state and local governments, and private organizations. Road builders later followed the deeper, more permanent traces of the trail because these marked the best route. Today, a 2,170-mi. *Auto Trail* may be followed from Independence, MO, to Oregon City, OR. However, for people interested in tracing portions of the Oregon Trail on foot, quiet areas remain.

## Administering Agency

Entries name the agencies with management responsibility, not parent departments. Addresses of state agency headquarters appear in state prefaces, those of federal regional offices in this main preface.

## Acreage

Many National Forests and some other sites have "inholdings," privately owned land within their boundaries. If these are significant, the entry gives both the acreage within the boundaries and the acreage of publicly owned land.

## How to Get There

Routings begin from points easily found on ordinary highway maps. For large sites, the route is the one most visitors use.

Don't rely on written directions. You need maps. When a routing leaves the main routes shown on your map, make local inquiries. You'll hear about road conditions and perhaps learn more about the area.

Both states have thousands of miles of unpaved roads, many of them not shown on highway maps. National Forest maps show the

Forest roads. The public domain has BLM-maintained roads and "ways," vehicle tracks not officially recognized or maintained as roads. Visit the BLM District Office before venturing far on these back-country routes.

## Open Hours

Most National Parks are open 24 hours. Many State Parks are closed at night, though campers may be able to leave or enter. National Wildlife Refuges and many state wildlife management areas are closed at night. Forests don't have gates.

## Symbols

Symbols tell at a glance if a site offers camping, swimming, etc. Most symbols have obvious meanings:

 We use this sign to indicate both day-hiking and back-packing.

 In addition to canoeable and kayakable waters, this symbol is used for white water requiring rafts.

 Used for ski touring, usually includes snowshoeing

 We used this symbol for birding and wildlife viewing.

In many cases, the symbols correspond to items in the "Activities" part of the entry. If there is no useful information to report, the symbol stands alone.

## Description

Each site is briefly characterized: terrain, main physical features, climate, vegetation, wildlife. Subheads such as **"Plants"** and **"Birds"** do not appear in all entries, usually because no one has studied these areas.

Even if complete flora and fauna lists were available, reproducing them would require a library rather than a volume. Using whatever data we could gather, we have made selections of species, attempting to characterize the principal plant and animal communities. In some cases this has seemed best achieved by listing the most common species. In others it seemed useful to mention rarities.

Comprehensive mammal lists were less often available than bird lists. Information on reptiles and amphibians was scarce.

In entries, the singular is used to signify single species. Plurals signify more than one species. Example: ". . . mountain bluebird, woodpeckers . . ."

*Note:* Authorities often decree changes in common names. "Myrtle warbler" and "Audubon's warbler" have become "yellow-rumped warbler." But "Traill's flycatcher" has been split into "willow flycatcher" and "alder flycatcher." Most species checklists supplied to us included some of the old names. We changed these to the names most readers now use.

## Features

Noted first are wilderness areas, primitive areas, and other large and noteworthy portions of sites. Also mentioned are waterfalls, canyons, major rivers, caverns, and the principal recreation sites.

Because our concern is with natural areas, we give little or no attention to forts and other historical features.

## Interpretation

Here we note visitor centers, museums, nature trails, campfire programs, guided hikes, and other naturalist programs, if present.

## Activities

*Camping:* Entries note numbers of sites, seasons of operation, and whether reservations are required. (But remember that reservation requirements and systems often change from year to year.)

Camping in Parks is usually limited to campgrounds. Check on site.

One can camp almost anywhere in National Forests. Along some heavily traveled routes, camping is restricted to campgrounds. In some Forest areas, camping is prohibited during periods of high fire danger.

One can camp almost anywhere in public domain lands.

Most National Wildlife Refuges prohibit camping. Some state wildlife areas permit it. In some cases, hunters are allowed to park RVs overnight in parking areas.

Can one "camp"—park an RV overnight—in highway rest stops or roadside pullouts? In both Oregon and Washington, only where posted.

*Hiking, backpacking:* The backpacking symbol is used where hiking with trailside camping is permitted and attractive. It is used for some small sites that serve as trailheads.

Trails in Parks are more likely to be marked and maintained than trails in Forests, although many National Forests have extensive trail systems. National Parks and Forests often have connecting trails.

Over most of the public domain, you're on your own, although there are numerous unmapped trails and tracks.

If you plan a backcountry trip, visit the nearest ranger station or BLM District Office for useful advice on routes, trail conditions, and whether many hikers are on the trail. You may be shown trail maps, even photographs of your destination.

The hiking season in the high country is relatively short, though it varies from place to place and year to year. Some of the National Parks and National Forests publish trail bulletins. From Oct. into July, it's advisable to get the current bulletin, or to call the nearest ranger station before undertaking a long hike. Snow and ice are not the only problems. The melt and runoff create hazards. The June 21 Trail Report from North Cascades National Park begins:

> Stream crossings continue to be hazardous and difficult . . . shouldn't be attempted unless hikers are sure of their safety . . . Use a good sturdy stick or rope, and unfasten the waistband on your backpack.

Mud is an obstacle until the ground dries, and until then trail crews won't come in to clear away downed trees and repair washouts.

While the high country is splendid, the Northwest offers delightful trails in every season. Winter is the best time to explore desert canyons. The lower slopes and valleys are at their best in spring and fall.

*Hunting:* Except for the Parks, portions of some Wildlife Refuges, and recreation areas, public lands are generally open to hunting. State regulations apply everywhere, as do federal regulations on migratory species. Wildlife management areas often have special rules limiting the number of hunters or permitting hunting only on certain days.

*Fishing:* Entries report whether fishing is possible and name the principal species. In some National Parks, stocking has been discontinued, in keeping with the policy of maintaining near-natural conditions.

*Swimming:* Swimming from many Pacific beaches can be cold, rough, and dangerous, and if a site reported dangers, we include them in the entry. In some State Parks, swimming is permitted only when lifeguards are present. Responses from Forests and BLM sites often failed to mention swimming even though lakes and rivers are present. Management is permissive: Swim where you wish, at your own risk.

*Boating:* The symbol is not used for bodies of water smaller than 100 acres.

*Canoeing, kayaking, drift boating, rafting:* It seemed impractical to have symbols for each, although each is the choice for certain streams. Usually the text makes the distinction.

*Horse riding:* The symbol is used where pack trips and other trail riding were reported. Horses can be ridden in many other places: on any suitable trail in a National Forest, for example, or anywhere on BLM land. If horse rentals were said to be available, this is noted, but be aware that such enterprises come and go.

*Skiing:* Downhill ski areas are mentioned when they are on public land. Many ski areas are concessioner-operated.

*Ski touring:* Usually one can ski cross-country wherever there's enough snow. We note where this was reported as a popular activity.

*Snowmobiling:* Noted where reported. Many National and State Parks restrict or prohibit snowmobiles. They are banned in wilderness areas.

## Rules and Regulations

All sites have them. Parks have the most.

*Pets:* In Parks, the general rule is that pets must be leashed. They are often prohibited on trails and beaches and in buildings.

Refuges and wildlife areas generally require that dogs be leashed, except while used in hunting.

Some sites ban pets altogether, and entries note this.

## Cautions

Some site managers thought you should be warned—about ocean currents, summer thunderstorms, rattlesnakes. We report their warnings. But keep in mind that other managers didn't mention similar hazards.

## Publications

Entries list publications issued by sites or about sites. If a site has a descriptive leaflet, you may be able to have it sent to you, but fewer and fewer sites have sufficient staff to respond to such requests. Most leaflets, species checklists, nature trail guides, etc., are available only on site.

National Forests will send maps by mail. When we checked, the price was $3.25. All prices listed are subject to change.

"Checklist available" usually means copies can be obtained. Not always. At some sites supplies were exhausted, but we were allowed to study file copies.

## References

In the original Introduction to this guide, we included a list of books offered by commercial publishers for readers who might like general information, say, on camping, or backpacking, or on plants and animals of the Pacific Northwest region. Since 1983, however, the number of such references has mushroomed. There seem to be multitudes in virtually every category of "outdoor" book. Given such numbers of books, we were sure we would overlook many good ones, so it seemed prudent not to include references in this edition.

We suggest that readers utilize their public library, local bookstores, and also local outfitting specialists to see what books they have available about camping, hiking, skiing, fishing, climbing, kayaking, and so on. Most of the above establishments are very sensitive these days to the increased demand for and availability of outdoor publications.

Finally, as we worked on our revision, many a ranger or naturalist said to us, in effect, "Tell them to come visit us first and THEN read the books." They repeatedly spoke of the "discovery" experience as an important part of the outdoor experience overall, and we concurred. How-to or general background references that might be beneficial, sometimes necessary, ahead of time are available for browsing or purchase in the places just mentioned, as is more specific information by area, locality, or topic. Specific information, however, is also available on-site.

These are very difficult times financially for most federal and state agencies. In the course of this revision, we watched several large agencies "contract" severely. The variety of their publications has been substantially reduced too, but the ones remaining support both the agencies and the well-being of our Parks, Forests, Refuges. We hope you will take a good look at these—before you get there perhaps (pub-lications/sources are under each agency, below) and once there, to enhance your "discovery" on-site, as suggested.

Agency publications pertaining to an entire state are listed in the state preface.

# Agency Offices and Publications

## Federal: U.S. Department of Agriculture

U.S. Forest Service
Pacific Northwest Regional Office
333 S.W. First Ave.
P.O. Box 3623
Portland, OR 97208-3623
National recreation reservations: (800) 280-CAMP; (800) 879-4496
(TTY)

### Publications include:

*Camping at Selected National Forests* (information, reservations).

*A Guide to Your National Forests* (Forests listed by state, map).

*Land Areas of the National Forest System* (acreage).

*Pacific Crest National Scenic Trail.*

*Recent Publications of the Pacific Northwest Research Station* (quarterly).

U.S. Forest Service and National Park Service
Outdoor Recreation Information Center
Northwest Interpretive Association
915 Second Ave., Suite 442
Seattle, WA 98174
(206) 220-7450

### Publications include:

Almost 100 titles on recreation in the Pacific NW, including nature information, guides for hiking/camping, snow travel, mountain biking, camping/backpacking, boating/canoeing, and for explor-ing specific natural areas of OR and WA. Free brochures on the

National Forests and National Parks. (Request a catalog and order form.)

The Northwest Interpretive Assoc. supports interpretive and visitor services programs of the National Park Service, the U.S. Forest Service, the BLM, and the Army Corps of Engineers, in 5 western states. The Association is a nonprofit corporation chartered by Congress. Activities include the sale of books and maps, as well as the publication of sales and free material. Memberships are available and members receive a 15% discount on most purchases. The main office is listed above. There are Association sales outlets in most of the National Parks and Forests in OR and WA. We found staff helpful in answering questions about natural areas in the 2 states.

## U.S. Department of the Interior

Bureau of Land Management OR/WA State Office
P.O. Box 2965
1515 S.W. Fifth Ave.
Portland, OR 97208
(503) 952-6001

*Publications include:*

*Facts, Oregon and Washington* (booklet outlining programs in detail).

*National Recreation Guide* (sites and facilities listed, map of U.S. sites).

*Oregon Recreation Guide* (facilities and description by district, trail sites, map showing OR sites).

*Oregon Wilderness Study Report,* Vols. I and II, with overview.

*Rediscover Your Public Lands* (pamphlet, general information on BLM).

*Research Natural Areas in Washington and Oregon,* 2nd ed.

*State of Oregon Wilderness Status map,* U.S. Geological Survey (designated wilderness and wilderness study areas by government agency; Indian reservations).

National Park Service
Pacific West Information Center
600 Harrison St.
San Francisco, CA 94107
(415) 556-0560
(Serves OR, WA, ID, NV, CA, HI, and the Pacific Islands)

National Park Service
Columbia Cascades Cluster
909 First Ave.
Seattle, WA 98104
(206) 220-7450

### Publications include:

See U.S. Forest Service and National Park Service, Northwest
Interpretive Association (above). The Assn. will also supply free
pamphlets with maps for Crater Lake, John Day Fossil Beds,
Oregon Caves, and the Oregon National Historic Trail.

National Park Service
Long Distance Trails Office
324 S. State St., Suite 250
P.O. Box 45155
Salt Lake City, UT 84145-0155
No phone. Contact by mail for information on the Oregon National
Historic Trail.

U.S. Fish and Wildlife Service, Region 1
911 N.E. 11th Ave., Eastside Federal Complex
Portland, OR 97232-4181
(503) 231-6121

### Publications include:

*National Wildlife Refuges, A Visitor's Guide* (pamphlet listing
facilities and map of Refuge locations).

*Visitor Directory, Pacific Region* (lists Refuges and hatcheries in OR,
WA, CA, ID, NV, HI, and support services by federal and state
agencies).

## Federal and State

U.S. Forest Service and Oregon State Department of Geology and
Minerals
Nature of the Northwest Information Center, Suite 177
800 N.E. Oregon St.
Portland, OR 97232
(503) 872-2750

*Publications include:*

Oregon National Forests maps (individual, include campsite
information), $3.25.

Oregon National Forest Wilderness and Special Area maps
(include Wild and Scenic Rivers, National Scenic Areas, National
Recreation Areas), $0.50–$3.25.

Pacific Crest Trail maps by section (3), $2.25 each.

*Rogue River Float Guide,* $10.70.

All prices are subject to change. Query before sending a check.

# THE SIERRA CLUB GUIDE TO THE NATURAL AREAS OF OREGON AND WASHINGTON

# OREGON

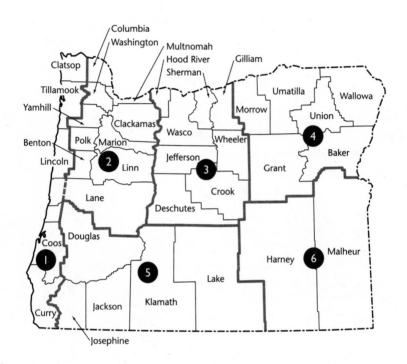

Columbia
Washington
Clatsop
Multnomah
Hood River
Sherman
Gilliam
Tillamook
Umatilla
Wallowa
Yamhill
Morrow
Union
Clackamas
Wasco
Benton
Polk
Wheeler
Baker
Marion
Jefferson
Lincoln
2
Linn
3
Grant
Crook
Lane
Deschutes
Coos
Douglas
1
6
Malheur
Harney
5
Jackson
Klamath
Lake
Curry
Josephine

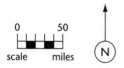

0       50
scale       miles

N

# OREGON

Oregon's principal geographic features are conspicuous: the Pacific Ocean on the W, the Columbia River Gorge on the N. Three principal mountain ranges dominate the skyline: the Coast Range near the sea, the Cascade Mountains about 75 mi. to the E, and the Blue Mountains in the NE corner, extending SW. The SE portion of the state is high desert.

Between the ocean and the Coast Range is a narrow marine shelf, seldom more than 4 mi. wide. The coast itself, sometimes rocky, sometimes sandy, is largely owned by the state. The Coast Range is not high, generally 2,000–3,000 ft. in the N, 3,000–4,000 ft. in the S, but it intercepts moist sea air, producing some of the heaviest annual rainfalls in the nation.

Most of the state's population lives in the fertile Willamette Valley, between the Coast Range and the Cascades. The Cascade Range has an average height of 5,000 ft., a few peaks rising over 10,000; Mount Hood, highest in the state, reaches 11,245 ft. Near the CA border, the two ranges merge, forming the rugged Rogue River Mountains.

The two ranges successively strip much of the moisture from E-moving air masses. The eastern two-thirds of the state is relatively dry. Only high mountains, such as the Steens, catch much precipitation.

The Blue Mountains extend SW to the valleys of the John Day and Deschutes Rivers in central Oregon. Part of the chain extends SE to the Snake River Valley, at the Idaho border; in the NE a separate branch is called the Wallowa Mountains.

The Columbia Basin, on the OR side of the Columbia River from the Cascades to the Wallowas, is the state's major wheat-producing region. The SE, a vast area bounded by the Cascades on the W, the Blue Mountains on the N, is dry, some sections receiving as little as 8 in. of precipitation per year, most of this in the winter months.

Most of the mountainous and desert areas are public land. Indeed, over 50% of the state's land area is in federal ownership. The 13

National Forests include over 15 million acres, more than a third of the federal land. Most of the rest is high desert, part of the public domain.

The state is endowed with exceptional natural diversity, from sea level to snowcapped mountains, from rain forest to desert. Often there are dramatic contrasts: mountains rising steeply from the sea, flatlands terminating in near-vertical escarpments, waterfowl congregating in wetlands surrounded by miles of desert.

It is not pristine. Of the state's 30 million forested acres, less than 5% are closed to logging. Elsewhere only scattered old-growth stands remain, and their days are numbered. Clear-cutting is standard practice, and many forest landscapes are patchworks in shades of brown and green. Chronic overgrazing has inflicted costly damage on grasslands. The great Columbia River is now a succession of impoundments.

Even so, much of OR still resembles what the early settlers saw, and you can still see the ruts made by their wagon wheels. Large areas are true wilderness, roadless, uninhabited, isolated. On foot or horseback, or in a pickup or four-wheel-drive vehicle, you can leave the paved roads, strike out cross-country, and travel for miles in solitude.

# Federal and State Agencies

## Federal Agencies

U.S. Forest Service
Pacific Northwest Region
333 S.W. First Ave.
P.O. Box 3623
Portland, OR 97208-3623
National Recreation reservations: (800) 282-camp; (800) 879-4496
(TTY)

The Siuslaw National Forest occupies the central portion of the Coast Range. In several places it includes Pacific shoreline, notably the extensive Oregon Dunes National Recreation Area. The Siskiyou National Forest is in the SW corner of the state, near but not touching the coast, extending E along the CA border to meet a part of the Rogue River National Forest.

Seven National Forests—Mount Hood, Willamette, Deschutes, Umpqua, Winema, Fremont, and Rogue River—form a huge block of land in the Cascade Range, from the Columbia River to CA. In the NE, the Wallowa-Whitman, Umatilla, and Ochoco National Forests are not so solid a mass, but their several large blocks occupy much of the Blue Mountains. The Wallowa-Whitman includes the OR side of the Hells Canyon National Recreation Area.

Publications are listed in the Introduction.

National Park Service
See Introduction for locations, phone numbers, and publications.

Crater Lake is Oregon's only National Park. It has National Forests on all 4 sides. Oregon Caves National Monument is within the Siskiyou National Forest. The John Day Fossil Beds National Monument has 3 separate units in N central OR.

Bureau of Land Management OR/WA State Office
P.O. Box 2965
1515 S.W. Fifth Ave.
Portland, OR 97208
(503) 952-6001

District Offices: Burns District, HC 74-12533, Hwy 20W, Hines, OR 97738; (541) 573-4400. Coos Bay District, 1300 Airport Lane, North Bend, OR 97459-2000; (541) 756-0100. Eugene District, 2890 Chad Dr., P.O. Box 10226, Eugene, OR 97440; (541) 683-6600. Lakeview District, 1000 Ninth St. S., P.O. Box 151, Lakeview, OR 97630-0055; (541) 947-2177. Medford District, 3040 Biddle Rd., Medford, OR 97504; (541) 770-2200. Prineville District, 3050 N.E. Third St., P.O. Box 550, Prineville, OR 97754; (541) 416-6700. Roseburg District, 777 N.W. Garden Valley Blvd., Roseburg, OR 97470; (514) 440-4930. Salem District, 1717 Fabry Rd. S.E., Salem, OR 97306; (503) 375-5646. Spokane District, 1103 N. Fancher Rd., Spokane, WA 99202; (509) 536-1200. Vale District, 100 Oregon St., Vale, OR 97918; (541) 473-3144.

The BLM manages the public domain, almost 16 million acres in Oregon, 25% of the state's land area. BLM lands constitute most of the state's SE quarter, with arms extending NW beyond Bend, Redmond, and Prineville, and NE beyond the Oxbow Dam on the Snake River. Smaller but interesting tracts are in the valleys of the lower Deschutes and John Day Rivers. Most of this land is high desert.

Much BLM land is scattered through the Willamette Valley in a checkerboard pattern, more in the S than in the N. Most of this is forest land managed for timber production. The BLM maintains a number of pleasant campsites here, but we found few tracts suitable for entries.

We had often driven across SE OR, aware of little more than endless expanses of sagebrush, a monotonous landscape we felt no impulse to explore on foot. We should have remembered that road builders choose the easiest routes, avoiding deep canyons, steep cliffs, lakes, marshes, and other obstacles. The most interesting terrain is well off the main roads.

As in other states with BLM lands, our task was to identify sites with noteworthy qualities. The public domain does not come in discrete packages like Parks and Refuges. We had first to find an interesting central feature, such as a mountain, butte, escarpment, canyon, lava flow, or marsh, then fix arbitrary boundaries defining the area one might explore from a single base or access route. We relied heavily on data gathered by the BLM for its wilderness inventory. The names attached to these sites are those used in the inventory. They have local meanings, but don't expect to find many of them on maps.

Nor do they appear on road signs. These sites are not like Parks. They have no visitor facilities, no resident personnel. In most cases you won't know you're there unless you have studied a BLM map, had local advice, or recognized a landmark.

Are they worth exploring? The desert is a harsh environment, but many people find it fascinating. We do. A small but growing number of people are backpacking in canyons, camping with pickup trucks, studying desert flora. Part of the fascination is knowing that not much has changed here since the first settlers came.

Before going far off main roads, a visit or phone call to the nearest BLM District Office is advisable. Each has a recreation specialist as well as specialists in wildlife, plant life, and geology. They're glad to help you choose a route, tell you what to expect, warn of any current problems, show you their maps.

Publications are listed in the Introduction.

U.S. Fish and Wildlife Service, Region 1
911 N.E. 11th Ave., Eastside Federal Complex
Portland, OR 97232-4181
(503) 231-6121

The Malheur National Wildlife Refuge in SE OR is one of the nation's principal nesting, feeding, and resting areas for waterfowl. Another channel of the Pacific Flyway comes through the Klamath marshes, three important fragments of which are units of the Klamath Basin Refuges. (Other units are in CA.) The largest federal Refuge is for an upland mammal: the Hart Mountain National Antelope Range, not far N of the Charles Sheldon Antelope Range in NV. Smaller but important federal Refuges are on the Columbia River, in the Willamette Valley, and on the coast.

Publications are listed in the Introduction.

## State Agencies

Oregon Parks and Recreation Department
1115 Commercial N.E.
Salem, OR 97310-1001
(503) 378-6305

Oregon Parks and Recreation Department
Information Center
2501 S.W. First Ave., #100
Portland, OR 97201
(800) 551-6949
State Park camping reservations: (800) 452-5687

Oregon has more than 200 State Parks, recreation areas, and areas of related use. Yet the entire State Park system occupies less than 100,000 acres. The system was once a unit of the Dept. of Transportation, and many of the "parks" are small but attractive roadside rest areas.

One of OR's great achievements is the chain of Parks, beach-access points, overlooks, and other state lands beside the sea. No other state has had the foresight and political courage to keep so much of its seacoast in public ownership. True, much of the land just above the beach is open to development. Also, many beaches are open to off-road vehicles, and the ORV groups are demanding more. The popular beaches are often crowded. But one can find long, quiet stretches where storm and tide have erased all signs of prior visits.

We judged 50 Parks suitable for entries. More than half are on the coast, offering or giving access to extensive open beaches. The Parks have 50 campgrounds with 5,686 sites. Campground opening and closing dates are announced each year; those in the entries are approximate. All Parks are open all year, but only 11 campgrounds have no closed season. Reservations are accepted for 26 of the campgrounds. Visitors without reservations get whatever is left. We noted yurts under camping because they are unusual and the Department asked us to mention them. It means that yurts are available, not that all sites have them.

Primitive hiker-biker camps are available at 20 coastal Parks.

As this edition went to press, we learned that 65 of OR's smaller State Parks had been listed for closure unless additional funding could be obtained. We included these as entries if they met our criteria. The consensus seemed to be that most of these areas are dear to the public heart and thus would probably not remain out of operation for long. All concerned seemed eager to find a way to keep them open.

### Publications include:

*Great News for Campers, Reservations Northwest* (camping reservations)

*Oregon Coast Lighthouses*

*Oregon Coast Trail Guide*

*Oregon State Parks Directory* (list, facilities, activities, map)

*Oregon State Parks Guide* (annual; send $1 plus postage to above address)

*Oregon State Parks/Washington State Parks* (reservations and information)

*Rates and Dates* (State Park campground fees and permits)

*Summer Events* (annual listing)

*Yurt Camping*

Oregon Tourism Commission
775 Summer St., N.E.
Salem, OR 97310
(800) 547-7842

### Publications include:

*The Official Oregon Travel Guide*

*Official State Map, 1996*

Oregon Department of Forestry
600 State St.
Salem, OR 97310
(503) 945-7200

This Department manages more than 785,000 acres of state-owned forests. 670,000 acres are in 5 State Forests, the balance scattered in smaller tracts. Most was logged or burned before coming into state ownership in the 1930s. Under state management, the forests have come back, providing improved wildlife habitat and recreation opportunities. However, the Department's mandate is to produce and harvest for revenue. The Department's major responsibility is to oversee forest practices and to provide fire protection for both state and private lands (16 million acres altogether). We looked at the 5 State Forests and included all as entries.

### Publications include:

*Forest Log* (magazine, published 6 times per year, free)
*Tillamook State Forest Recreation Resources*

Oregon Department of Fish and Wildlife
2501 S.W. First Ave.
P.O. Box 59
Portland, OR 97207
(503) 229-5403

Management of state-owned game lands is to benefit wildlife, hunters, and those who fish. However, most areas are open to hikers and other nonconsumptive users. We selected the sites where visits outside hunting season could be interesting.

### Publications include:

*Visitor's Guide: Oregon's Fish Hatcheries and Wildlife Management Areas*

Oregon Marine Board
435 Commercial St., N.E.
Salem, OR 97310
(503) 378-8587

*Publications:*

Information on river recreation

For publications on animals and plants, on a specific Park, Forest, or natural area, on hiking, camping, boating, rafting, cross-country skiing, rockhounding, etc., in OR we suggest you visit your local bookseller, library, or outfitter to browse their selection of Pacific NW literature and to inquire about current favorites. Such information may also be available at the site or sites you choose for your outdoor venture in OR. (See site entries for specific publications.) In addition, contacting area chapters of the National Audubon Society, the Sierra Club, and other environmental organizations, as well as consulting their periodicals, can be useful in identifying good references. Local chambers of commerce in or near a specific OR area that interests you may be reached by phone for information. Very useful to us were two publications sources we included in the general Introduction under the U.S. Forest Service and National Park Service: the Northwest Interpretive Association, and under the U.S. Forest Service and Oregon State Department of Geology and Minerals: the Nature of the Northwest. Their publication catalogs are extensive. They also have free publications, as do the other federal and state agencies we've listed.

Z O N E 1

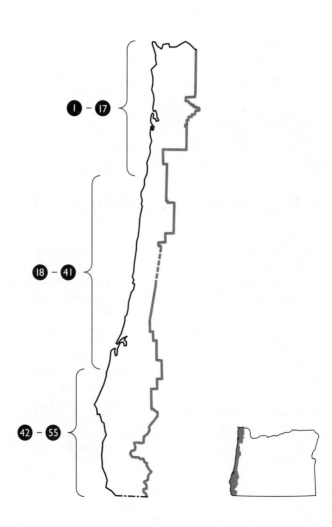

1 - 17

18 - 41

42 - 55

11

*Note:* This is a long, narrow zone with many small sites. Rather than clutter the map with numbers, we have used brackets to divide the zone into three parts. The zone preface lists sites in this zone in geographic sequence, N to S.

| Sites 1–17 | WA boundary to Lincoln City |
| Sites 18–41 | Lincoln City to Bandon |
| Sites 42–55 | Bandon to CA boundary |

Includes these counties:

| Clatsop | Lane (W portion only) | Coos |
| Tillamook | Douglas (W portion only) | Curry |
| Lincoln | | |

In OR zone 1, many Parks are arranged along the N–S coast road (US 101). It seems useful to provide a special listing of these, in linear order. Sites are listed from N to S, in three sections. Sites in the left column have ocean frontage. Those in the right column are inland but can be reached conveniently from US 101.

**Washington boundary to Lincoln City**

1. **Lewis and Clark National Wildlife Refuge**
2. **Fort Stevens State Park**
3. **Clatsop State Forest**
4. **Jewell Meadows Wildlife Area**
5. **Tillamook State Forest**
6. **Saddle Mountain State Natural Area**
7. **Ecola State Park**
8. **Hug Point State Recreation Site**
9. **Oswald West State Park**
10. **Nehalem Bay State Park**
11. **Cape Meares National Wildlife Refuge**

12. **Cape Meares State Scenic Viewpoint**
13. **Three Arch Rocks National Wildlife Refuge**
14. **Cape Lookout State Park**
15. **Siuslaw National Forest**
16. **Cape Kiwanda State Natural Area**
17. **Nestucca Spit State Park**

**Lincoln City to Bandon**

18. **Fogarty Creek State Recreation Site**
19. **Boiler Bay State Scenic Viewpoint**
20. **Otter Crest State Scenic Viewpoint**

13

# Z O N E 1

The Coast Range parallels the ocean shore from N to S, never far inland. Elevations are 2,000–3,000 ft. in the N, 3,000–4,000 ft. in the S, with occasional peaks 1,000–1,500 ft. higher. This range, intercepting the E flow of moist air from the ocean, produces heavy rainfall, in places well over 100 in. per year.

At some points along the coast, mountains rise directly from the sea, and rocky promontories extend beyond the general shoreline. Elsewhere, a marine terrace extends inland for ½ mi. to 4 mi. Most beaches are broad and sandy. Often they are backed by dunes, some low, others a few hundred feet high. And often an area of small trees, brush, and wildflowers lies back of the dunes; here, too, are a number of freshwater lakes and marshes.

Ample moisture and fine soils combine to make the forests of the Coast Range among the world's most productive. Western hemlock, Sitka spruce, western red cedar, and Douglas-fir are the most prominent species. Clear-cutting, the prevailing logging method, has seriously marred the coastal landscape. Great brown patches show where logging was fairly recent. Cultivation of even-aged stands of single species replaces brown patches with shades of green.

US 101 is the Coast Hwy except for a few intervals where local roads are closer to the ocean. Inevitably, sections of it have become congested and cluttered with the garish commercialism that defaces many seaside communities. These sections are usually near the ends of routes from the E.

More such development is occurring, but many segments of US 101 are still breathtakingly scenic. At times the highway is notched into towering cliffs, far above the sea. A few miles later it may run just back of low outer dunes or beside an estuary. Now and then it passes through forest, and one can occasionally glimpse the sea through the trees.

One seldom drives more than a few miles without seeing a place to park and walk to the seaside. Although the road was not planned as a scenic route, overlooks are numerous. Indeed, it seems that wherever the view is splendid there's a place to stop and park.

Because of the almost unbroken chain of beaches, we include as entries a number of State Parks that are not in themselves natural areas—sites we would not include if they stood alone. We have omitted a number of State Waysides and smaller State Parks either because they are within developed areas or because they seem less interesting.

Motor vehicles are allowed to drive on the beach, a policy that doubtless seemed innocent when first adopted, but each year adds more noise, trash, and hazards. However, not all beaches are motorways. The official state highway map shows where vehicles are prohibited altogether and where they are prohibited at certain times. Unfortunately, although the Oregon Dunes National Recreation Area is federal, its beaches are state controlled, and vehicles are allowed on most of them.

Islands are scattered along the coast, some just bits of rock rising above the waves, others a few acres in size. Many have odd shapes: spires, haystacks, arches. Many are included in the Oregon Islands National Wildlife Refuge. We have not made this Refuge an entry because its elements, most of them very small, extend over 290 mi., and landing is prohibited. Together with other islands, promontories, and cliffs, they provide safe nesting and resting areas for countless gulls, terns, cormorants, puffins, guillemots, and other seabirds, as well as haven for seals and sea lions. During their migrations, gray whales are commonly seen from many vantage points on shore. Jetties, sand spits, mudflats, and salt marshes attract great numbers of shorebirds and waterfowl.

The sea-tempered climate is equable; seldom is it uncomfortably hot or cold. However, rain and fog are frequent from late Oct. to mid-May. Half of the very large annual precipitation falls from Dec. through Feb., most of the rest in spring and fall. Coastal summers are clear and cool.

One can expect the more popular sites to be crowded on summer weekends. However, we had no difficulty finding quiet places on a midsummer visit. The busiest Parks are, of course, those with the most campsites; those that accept reservations have done so in self-defense.

Such is the appeal of beaches that most visitors ignore the coastal forests. Yet these forests, because of the ample moisture, are quite unlike forests E of the mountains. Although only a few fragments of the original forest remain, these are well worth visiting. The 1-mi. trail through the rain forest at Cape Meares offers a memorable experience. Two National Forests and three State Forests are in this coastal zone. Timber is harvested in all of them, but there are areas where trees have grown to respectable size and are not yet scheduled for cutting.

*Hiking, backpacking:* The Oregon Coast Trail is not completed. We were advised that it can be hiked from the Columbia River to Lincoln City, roughly 110 mi. of the projected 370. A number of our entries S of Lincoln City include the statement "on the Oregon Coast Trail." Most of these sites have primitive hiker-biker camps. Many beaches S of Lincoln City can be hiked, but the segments are not yet linked.

*Swimming:* An official publication noted "swimming" at a certain State Park. Responding to our questionnaire, the local manager said "no swimming." It's a judgment call. Swimming is forbidden on few beaches but inadvisable on many. The water is cold. Strong currents and tricky waves are common. Here and there are sheltered coves where the water is quiet and a few degrees warmer. Many people splash in the surf, in shallow areas; few venture into deep water for actual swimming.

*Boating:* Entries attempt to note which sites have ramps, whether on rivers or freshwater lakes.

## Agate Beach State Recreation Site

Oregon Parks and Recreation Department
18 acres.

1 mi. N of Newport off US 101.

Beach access 1 mi. S of Yaquina Head. Viewpoint. Short trails. Usually a broad sandy beach. Agate hunting is significant when wave action exposes the gravel bed below the sand.

**Birds:** Common murre and Brandt's cormorant nest at nearby Yaquina Head Refuge. Species often seen include surfbird, rhinoceros auklet, tufted puffin, pigeon guillemot, loons.

## Bandon State Natural Area

Oregon Parks and Recreation Department
15 acres.

½ mi. S of Bandon off US 101

Beach access. Sand dunes. Viewpoint: numerous tall, slender offshore rocks. A massive offshore rock that displays a profile resembling a head is known locally as Face Rock.

## Bandon State Park

Oregon Parks and Recreation Department
879 acres.

From Bandon, 4 mi. S on US 101. Right 1 mi. on Bradley Lake Rd.

Beach access. Entrance road crosses vegetated dunes. Large and small offshore rocks to N, extensive stretch of broad sand beach to S. A small creek cuts through the N end, a popular wading area for children.

## Beachside State Park

Oregon Parks and Recreation Department
17 acres.

On US 101, 4 mi. S of Waldport.

½ mi. of hard sand beach. Partially wooded site; pine and spruce, salal in understory.
  *Camping:* 80 sites. Reservations.

**Headquarters**
OR Parks and Recreation Dept., 5680 S. Coast Hwy, South Beach, OR 97366; (541) 563-3220.

## Beverly Beach State Park

Oregon Parks and Recreation Department
130 acres.

On US 101, 7 mi. N of Newport.

Large, heavily used campground on E side of US 101. Passage under highway to wide sand beach, partly sheltered by headlands, backed by fossil-bearing cliffs.

**Interpretation:**
*Nature trail. Evening slide programs.*

**Activities**

*Camping:* 278 sites. Yurts. All year. Reservations.

*Hiking, backpacking:* Primitive hiker-biker camp. Hiking on beach.

**Headquarters**
OR Parks and Recreation Dept., 198 N.E. 123rd St., Newport, OR 97365; (541) 265-9278.

## Boiler Bay State Scenic Viewpoint

Oregon Parks and Recreation Department
33 acres.

From Newport, 15 mi. N on US 101.

Rocky coast; waves sending spray high. Blowhole on promontory has waterspout in storms, sometimes at high tide.

## Bullards Beach State Park

Oregon Parks and Recreation Department
1,226 acres.

1 mi. N of Bandon on US 101.

Attractive, popular Park on the ocean and Coquille River. Entrance road passes among vegetated dunes, past campground, along river, to parking area near jetty and old lighthouse. Area back of foredunes is grassy, many wildflowers, some groves of shore pine. 4 mi. of wide sand beach. 3 mi. of river frontage. Historic 1896 lighthouse.

**Birds:** Surfbird, oystercatcher, turnstone, other shorebirds often seen on jetty, which is open to foot traffic. Good birding along river's mudflats.

### Activities

*Camping:* 192 sites. Yurts. All year. Reservations required.

*Hiking, backpacking:* Primitive hiker-biker camp. Pleasant hiking along beach and river, back of dunes.

*Boating:* Ramp on river.

*Horse riding:* Designated area for parking and unloading horse trailers. 7-mi. trail. Horse camp.

### Headquarters

OR Parks and Recreation Dept., Box 25, Bandon, OR 97411; (541) 347-2209.

## Cape Arago State Park; Shore Acres State Park; Sunset Bay State Park

Oregon Parks and Recreation Department
Total 1,272 acres.

SW of Coos Bay on Cape Arago Hwy; Cape Arago State Park is about 14 mi. from Coos Bay.

Closely related Parks, not quite adjacent. Much of the land was part of an estate including fine botanic gardens, now maintained at Shore Acres. Cape Arago projects ½ mi. into the sea, with rocky cliffs up to 100 ft.

*Sunset Bay State Park:* 395 acres. A small bay almost entirely enclosed by precipitous sandstone cliffs. Conifers grow to edge of bluffs. Small rock islands at the bay's opening. Sheltered from wind and wave. Wide sand beach. Water usually warmer than at the open beaches outside.

*Shore Acres State Park:* 743 acres. 1 mi. beyond Sunset Bay. The former owner employed talented landscape designers, imported many varieties of exotic plants. The state now maintains the gardens. The shoreline features huge sandstone slabs, so tilted that breaking waves send spray high into the air.

*Cape Arago State Park:* 134 acres. 2 mi. beyond Shore Acres. A small, neatly kept day-use area offering fine views of the scenic coast. Steller sea lions often seen. Sand beaches N and S of Cape, not suitable for swimming. Tide pools.

**Birds:** Many shorebirds, including occasional rarities. Some nesting species on the cliffs. Seen from the headlands: red-necked grebe, red-throated loon, pigeon guillemot, rhinoceros auklet, shearwaters, tufted puffin, scoter, gulls, terns. Many passerine species at Shore Acres.

## Activities

*Camping:* At Sunset Bay. 137 sites. Yurts. Reservations.

*Hiking, backpacking:* On the Oregon Coast Trail. Primitive hiker-biker camp at Cape Arago. Trail links the 3 units.

*Swimming:* At Sunset Bay.

*Pets are prohibited at Shore Acres.*

## Headquarters

OR Parks and Recreation Dept., Sunset Bay State Park, 13030 Cape Arago Hwy, Coos Bay, OR 97420; (541) 888-4902.

## Cape Blanco State Park

Oregon Parks and Recreation Department
1,880 acres.

From Port Orford, 9 mi. N on US 101, then left to Park.

Cape Blanco is the most westerly point in OR. The road crosses low-lying meadows and marshes, then climbs to the Park, 200 ft. above sea level. Site of a historic lighthouse. Sweeping views of coast to N and S. Park is largely forested, Sitka spruce and alder. 2½ mi. frontage on Sixes River. Road and trails down to ocean beaches. Offshore rocks. Many wildflowers, including yellow head, cone flower, coral bells, yellow sand verbena, Douglas's dune tansy.

**Birds:** Lighthouse area offers opportunity to observe migrating warblers in fall. Noted on visit: northern flicker, tree and cliff swallows, goldfinch, robin, cormorant, gulls.

### Activities

*Camping:* 58 sites. Open mid-April–Nov.

*Hiking, backpacking:* Primitive hiker-biker camp. Beach hiking.

*Fishing:* River: chinook, cutthroat, steelhead.

*Horse riding:* 1 trail, but can ride off trail in open areas. Horse camp.

### Headquarters

OR Parks and Recreation Dept., P.O. Box 299, Sixes, OR 97476; (541) 332-6774.

## Cape Kiwanda State Natural Area

Oregon Parks and Recreation Department
185 acres.

From Pacific City, 3 mi. N on Sand Lake–Pacific City Rd.

Cape Kiwanda juts seaward about 1,500 ft. Rugged sandstone headland up to 220 ft. above the sea. 1½ mi. of ocean beach. Some areas of
sand dunes. Site is 80% forested: shore pine, Douglas-fir, Sitka spruce,
western hemlock. Rhododendron, wildflowers on the Three Capes
Scenic Dr., linking Capes Meares, Lookout, and Kiwanda.

*Boating:* Dory fishing fleet launches here.

## Cape Lookout State Park

Oregon Parks and Recreation Department
1,974 acres.

12 mi. SW of Tillamook, on Three Capes Scenic Dr.

Basalt headland extends 2 mi. into the ocean; ridge 800 ft. above sea
level. S face has nearly vertical cliffs. Lower N face is indented with
coves. From the base of the headland, Netarts Sand Spit extends 5 mi.
to N, enclosing Netarts Bay. Marshes fringe the bay. Beach along the
spit is broad, sandy.

**Plants:** Coastal rain forest; annual rainfall about 90 in. Sitka spruce,
western hemlock, western red cedar, with red alder along clearings.
Understory of salal, box blueberry, salmonberry, Pacific wax myrtle.
Forest groundcover includes sword fern, skunk cabbage, trillium, lily-
of-the-valley, other wildflowers.

**Birds:** 150 species identified. Diverse habitats attract bay ducks,
shorebirds, seabirds, passerines.

### Features

*Netarts Sand Spit:* one of the least developed sand spit–estuary sites in
OR. N third is dune system partially stabilized by vegetation. Middle
third is a dense forest of Sitka spruce. S third partially forested with
shore and maritime pines. Salt marshes along bay side. The N 3 mi. of
the spit has been proposed for permanent preservation as a natural
area.

*Three Capes Scenic Dr.* links Capes Meares, Lookout, and Kiwanda.

### Interpretation:

*Campfire programs.* June–Aug.

## Activities

*Camping:* 245 sites. Yurts. All year. Reservations.

*Hiking, backpacking:* Primitive hiker-biker camp. 5-mi. trail from main campground to tip of Cape. Trailhead at midpoint, junction of park road and Scenic Dr. From here trail passes through mature rain forest, along ridge with fine views on both sides. Another trail, 2 mi. long, descends from the trailhead down the S side of the Cape. Beach hiking on Spit.

## Headquarters

OR Parks and Recreation Dept., 13000 Whiskey Creek Rd. W, Tillamook, OR 97141; (503) 842-4981.

## Cape Meares National Wildlife Refuge; Three Arch Rocks National Wildlife Refuge

U.S. Fish and Wildlife Service
138 acres/17 acres.

Refuges 10 mi. W of Tillamook, on Three Capes Scenic Dr. off US 101. Follows signs to gravel parking lot. Access to Cape Meares Refuge is from the parking lot. Three Arch Rocks Refuge, offshore, can be seen from the Cape.

*Cape Meares National Wildlife Refuge* is 138 acres of old-growth forest with vertical sea cliffs. Largely forested with Sitka spruce and western hemlock, all old-growth. Ocean cliffs, rocky outcroppings, and rolling headlands. Refuge for colonial seabirds and other coastal species.

**Birds:** Include bald eagle, black oystercatcher, double-crested, Brandt's, and pelagic cormorants, surfbird, black turnstone, common murre, tufted puffin, red and northern phalaropes, pigeon guillemot. Gulls include glaucous-winged, western, Thayer's, ring-billed, mew, Bonaparte's, Heermann's. Also peregrine falcon, pygmy owl, Vaux's swift, swallows, chickadees, thrushes, and warblers.

*Hiking:* 2 hiking trails. One trail loops through old-growth forest to a giant Sitka spruce; the other is part of the Oregon Coast Trail from the town of Cape Meares to the Refuge. Both start from parking lot.

*Three Arch Rocks National Wildlife Refuge* is 17 acres located ½ mi. offshore from Oceanside. The Refuge is part of the Oregon Islands Wilderness and is closed to the public. The best way to observe the seabirds is from the mainland with a high-powered scope or from a boat at least 500 ft. away.

The Refuge is home to the largest seabird colony S of Alaska with 226,000 nesting birds. The common murre colony, estimated at 220,000, is of international importance. The Refuge also has the largest tufted puffin colony, with an estimated 2,000 to 4,000 birds. Other birds are Brandt's, pelagic, and double-crested cormorants, western, glaucous-winged, Thayer's, ring-billed, mew, Bonaparte's, and Heermann's gulls, rhinoceros auklet, pigeon guillemot, bald eagle, brown pelican.

Three Arch Rocks also serves as a pupping area for threatened Steller sea lions. A 500-ft. buffer zone was established in 1994 to protect the seabird and marine mammals. The zone is effective May 1–Sept. 15.

## Headquarters

U.S. Fish and Wildlife Service, c/o Western Oregon Refuge Complex, 26208 Finley Refuge Rd., Corvallis, OR 97333; (541) 757-7236.

## Cape Meares State Scenic Viewpoint

Oregon Parks and Recreation Department
233 acres.

10 mi. W of Tillamook, on Three Capes Scenic Dr., off US 101.

Promontory overlooking cliffs and offshore rocks with many nesting seabirds. Parking area, lighthouse, and several good viewpoints at the tip. "Octopus Tree," an exceptionally large, oddly branched spruce, diameter near base between 9 and 10 ft. On Three Capes Scenic Dr., linking Capes Meares, Lookout, and Kiwanda.

*Hiking, backpacking:* Primitive hiker-biker camp. Trail from park entrance to lighthouse, about 1 mi., through exceptionally fine rain forest. Also trail to beach, National Wildlife Refuge. Short section of Oregon Coast Trail.

**Adjacent**
Capes Meares National Wildlife Refuge (see entry this zone).

## Cape Sebastian State Park
Oregon Parks and Recreation Department
1,104 acres.
From Gold Beach, 7 mi. S on US 101.

Cape Sebastian is a precipitous headland 700 ft. above the sea. The Park is chiefly a fine viewpoint, vistas up and down the coast, up to 50 mi. on clear days. Trails. Azalea, rhododendron, and ceanothus along roadside. Sitka spruce forest covers a portion of the headland where a steep trail leads to the beach.

## Carl G. Washburne Memorial State Park
Oregon Parks and Recreation Department
1,209 acres.
14 mi. N of Florence on US 101.

2 mi. of ocean beach backed by dunes and large, rolling hills that are old dunes, now covered with vegetation, including fir, Sitka spruce, shore pine, cedar, hemlock. Prominent understory of evergreen huckleberry and rhododendron. Tide pools at base of rocky cliffs. Agates often found.

### Activities
*Camping:* 66 sites.
*Hiking:* Beach available well beyond site boundaries. 4-mi. nature trail loop.

### Nearby
Siuslaw National Forest (see entry this zone).

## Cherry Creek Research Natural Area

U.S. Bureau of Land Management
590 acres.

From Coquille on old Hwy 42, turn N (just W of Coquille High School) onto Fairview-McKinley Rd. At Fairview, 9 mi. N, turn right onto Coos Bay Wagon Rd. Go 7 mi. to Cherry Creek Park and turn left on Cherry Creek County Rd. Proceed (road becomes BLM Cherry Creek Access Rd.) for 6 mi. to Big Tree Recreation Site, at edge of natural area.

Complex ridge-and-valley topography bordering Cherry Creek. Lower and middle slopes moderate to steep; gentle to moderate along ridgetops. Elevations range from about 680 to about 1,480 ft.

**Plants:** Established for scientific research as a typical example of old-growth Douglas-fir and hemlock forest. Average age of Douglas-fir, over 300 years. Western hemlock somewhat younger. Red cedar and tan oak also present; bigleaf maple and California bay laurel common in streamside areas. Dense understory, mostly sword fern, with thickets of huckleberry, Oregon grape, rhododendron, vine maple.

**Mammals:** Elk, mule deer, black bear, mink, raccoon, ringtail, skunk, marten, weasel, snowshoe hare, many small rodents and bats.

*No camping here or at the Big Tree Recreation Site.*

*Hiking:* ½ mi. nature trails, else cross-country.

## Headquarters

Bureau of Land Management, Coos Bay District, 1300 Airport Lane, North Bend, OR 97459; (503) 756-0100.

## Clatsop State Forest

Oregon Department of Forestry
154,000 acres.

E side of Clatsop County with small portions in Columbia County. SE of
Astoria. Crossed by US 30, US 26, Hwy 202.

Forest land cut over and abandoned, now managed by the Dept. of
Forestry under a mandate to produce revenue for the counties.
Chiefly Douglas-fir and western hemlock. Mountainous terrain,
rounded ridges, steep to moderate slopes. Highest point 3,020 ft.
Annual precipitation about 90 in.

No campgrounds, long trails, or other recreation developments
except as noted in Activities. Managed for timber production, with
concern for wildlife habitat, water quality, and recreation. Most recreational use is by hunters and fishermen. However, mountain biking,
hiking, and sightseeing are increasing. The Forest has lakes, waterfalls,
and streams in areas seldom visited outside hunting season. Vigorous
wildlife population. It's well worth exploring. A map is available and
HQ will advise where to go.

**Plants:** Principal tree species are Douglas-fir, western hemlock, Sitka
spruce, western red cedar, noble and grand firs, red alder. Prominent in
understory: sword fern, thimbleberry, salal, Oregon grape, salmonberry. Flowering species include red elderberry, devil's club, Indian
thistle, red huckleberry, Oregon iris, white trillium, fireweed, Oregon
anemone, paintbrush, penstemon, phlox.

**Birds:** 40 species recorded, including bald eagle, osprey, turkey vulture, kestrel, blue grouse, mountain quail, band-tailed pigeon, owls,
rufous hummingbird, flycatchers, gray and Steller's jays, red-breasted
nuthatch, western tanager, red crossbill.

**Mammals:** Include Roosevelt elk, mule deer, bobcat, spotted skunk,
coyote, mountain beaver, Townsend chipmunk, chickaree, deer
mouse, snowshoe hare, bats. Mountain lion and black bear present,
seldom seen.

## Activities

*Hiking:* Service roads and fire trails. 1.3-mi. interpretive trail through mature and young forest areas, past meadows frequented by elk.

*Hunting:* Deer, elk, bear.

*Fishing:* Trout, salmon, steelhead.

*Swimming:* No developed sites. Some streams have deep places.

*Mountain biking:* No developed trails, but many forest roads to ride near Astoria.

### Nearby

Jewell Meadows Wildlife Area (see entry this zone).

### Publications

Forest leaflet.

Astoria District, Forestry Dept., map, ½ in. = 1 mi.

### Headquarters

OR Dept. of Forestry, Rt. 1, Box 950, Astoria, OR 97103; (503) 325-5451.

## Darlingtonia State Natural Area

Oregon Parks and Recreation Department
18 acres.

From Florence, 5 mi. N on US 101.

Remarkable display of *Darlingtonia,* the insectivorous "cobra plant," so called because of its colorful cobralike hood. Boardwalk into bog. Exhibit.

## Devil's Elbow State Park

Oregon Parks and Recreation Department
485 acres.

From Florence, 13 mi. N on US 101.

Bay with sandy beach. To N is rocky point with 2 huge rocks at tip. Trail to Heceta Head lighthouse and viewpoint.

**Adjacent**
Carl G. Washburne Memorial State Park (see entry this zone).

## Devil's Punchbowl State Natural Area
Oregon Parks and Recreation Department
8 acres.

From Newport, 8 mi. N on US 101.

On a point of land. Viewpoint. Bowl-shaped rock formation has tunnel entrances from the sea through which waves thunder. Access to extensive sand beach. Marine gardens.

## Doerner Fir Recreation Site
U.S. Bureau of Land Management
400 acres.

From Coos Bay travel S on US 101 to Hwy 42. Continue S on Hwy 42 to Coquille. Turn left onto Fairview-Coquille Rd. to Four Corners in Fairview. Turn right onto Coos Bay Wagon Rd. for 3.9 mi. to Middle Creek Access Rd. Turn left and drive 13.6 mi. to a four-way intersection. Turn right onto Burnt Mtn.–Middle Creek Tie Rd. and drive 4.8 mi. to Burnt Mtn. Access Rd. At a T-intersection turn left and drive approximately 4.9 mi. to East Fork Brummitt Creek Rd. Then 4.6 mi. over gravel to the well-marked trailhead.

The Doerner fir is the largest known Douglas-fir in the world and stands 329 ft. tall and 11.5 ft. in diameter. The ½ mi. trail leading to the fir takes you through one of the coast's finest old-growth forests, and, according to the BLM, one of the most interesting you will ever see. The trail is steep in spots and sturdy footwear is recommended.

## Interpretation

*Growing Forest Auto Tour.* A 60-mi. journey through 500 years of forest growth, from tiny seedling to the Doerner fir. Stop by HQ and pick up a copy of the driving booklet or call ahead of time and they will mail it to you.

## Headquarters

Bureau of Land Management, Coos Bay District, 1300 Airport Lane, North Bend, OR 97459; (541) 756-0100.

........................................................................................................................................

## Ecola State Park

Oregon Parks and Recreation Department
1,299 acres.

From Cannon Beach, 2 mi. N on US 101.

Outstanding scenic area. 6 mi. of ocean frontage. Tillamook Head is a huge basalt promontory, spur of the Coast Range, highest point 1,200 ft. Large rocks offshore attract sea lions, seabirds. Annual precipitation about 82 in.

**Plants:** Upland area rolling to steep, largely forested. Some fine old-growth, immense Sitka spruce, western hemlock, with red alder, western red cedar. Understory: red huckleberry, salmonberry, red elderberry, sword fern, deer fern, lady fern. Flowering plants include seaside tansy, lily-of-the-valley.

**Birds:** No list available, but diverse habitats attract good variety of sea, shore, and upland species.

**Mammals:** Include elk, mule deer, sea lion.

**Reptiles and amphibians:** Include northern alligator lizard, Pacific tree frog, western toad.

*Hiking:* On the Oregon Coast Trail.

## Elliott State Forest

Oregon Department of Forestry
93,000 acres.

Umpqua River, E of Reedsport, is N boundary. From Hwy 38, secondary roads lead S into the Forest, notably Loon Lake and Scholfield Rds.

Includes some of the steepest terrain in OR: deep canyons, knifelike ridges. Highest point: 2,097 ft. Although there are some disconnected tracts, most of the acreage is a solid block. Most of the forest was burned in 1868, but growing conditions are good and recovery was excellent. Public use has increased gradually; most visitors are those who prefer a primitive environment. We were told there is little hiking because of the steep terrain. However, more than 450 mi. of roads, most unpaved, some abandoned, offer hiking opportunities. This is an active tree farm; drivers should be alert for log and rock trucks.

**Plants:** 90% of area in Douglas-fir. 45% is 80–130 years old, most of the rest under 40 years. Other species include red alder, hemlock, cedar, maple. Understory: sword fern, salal, evergreen and red huckleberries, rhododendron, Oregon grape. Flowering plants, limited under tree canopy, include trillium, sweet-scented bedstraw, oxalis.

**Birds:** No data. Common loon seen on Loon Lake. Also spotted owl, marbled murrelet.

**Mammals:** Roosevelt elk, black bear, black-tailed deer.

### Features

*10-mi. scenic corridor* along S bank of Lower Umpqua River.

*Loon Lake,* popular recreation area.

### Activities

*Camping:* BLM campground on Loon Lake, 30 sites. Memorial Day–Labor Day. Primitive camping elsewhere.

*Fishing:* Salmon, steelhead, in streams.

*Boating:* Dock, ramp, rentals at Loon Lake. Also boating on Umpqua River.

**Headquarters**

OR Dept. of Forestry, Coos Management District, 300 Fifth St., Bay Park, Coos Bay, OR 97420; (541) 267-4136. (S of Coos Bay, off US 101, at top of Bunker Hill.)

## Floras Lake State Natural Area

Oregon Parks and Recreation Department
1,361 acres.

From Port Orford, N 10 mi. on US 101; follow signs to Lake. Site is not well marked. Advised to park at airport, hike in.

Undeveloped site between lake and ocean. 1 mi. frontage on lake, 2½ mi. on ocean. Vertical sandstone bluffs, over 200 ft. Forest of Sitka spruce, shore pine, western hemlock, with understory of salal, rhododendron, evergreen huckleberry.

## Fogarty Creek State Recreation Site

Oregon Parks and Recreation Department
142 acres.

From Depoe Bay, 2 mi. N on US 101.

Popular beach, wide and smooth. Fogarty Creek winds through. Wooded area back of beach: shore pine, alder, spruce.

## Fort Stevens State Park

Oregon Parks and Recreation Department
3,763 acres.

From Astoria, 10 mi. W on US 101.

Attracts the most visitors of any OR State Park, and parts of the site are highly developed. Historic area, but the site includes outstanding natural features.

Bounded on the N by the Columbia River, on the W by the ocean. Access to over 5 mi. of broad beach, 3 mi. of river frontage. Elevations to 100 ft. Includes Coffenbury Lake, about 1 mi. long, several smaller, shallow lakes. Narrow sand dune ridges, swampland, tidal marshes. W half of Park consists of extensive sandflats that accreted after construction of the Columbia River jetties.

**Plants:** Botanists have identified 10 plant zones, from human-planted sand stabilization areas near the sea to native old-growth forest in the E interior. Foredunes have beach grass, seashore lupine, yellow sand verbena, sea lymegrass, dune bluegrass. Shore pine planted back of dunes. Ground cover of the stabilized sandflats include beach grasses, lupine, kinnikinnick, salal, Scotch broom, twinberry. Ridge and swale vegetation is largely natural coastal forest: large red alder, Sitka spruce, shore pine, Douglas-fir, with western red cedar, hemlock, willow, Oregon crab apple, cascara, elderberry, salmonberry, ocean spray, huckleberry, blackberry, sword fern.

**Birds:** Checklist on file. Trestle Bay tidal zone is a major stopover for migrating waterfowl. Nesting species include mallard, pintail, baldpate, teal, scaup, bufflehead. A few snowy plovers nest on the beach. Clatsop Spit is known to birders as a place to spot rarities such as gyrfalcon, golden plover, sharp-tailed and buff-breasted sandpipers, Buller's shearwater. Spit is also a good area for migrating warblers.

**Mammals:** In the old-growth marshy spruce forest and lake areas, include mule deer, nutria, mink, beaver, raccoon, opossum, chickaree, chipmunk.

**Features**

*Historic area:* gun batteries, building foundations, *visitor center.*

*Columbia River Beach,* via Jetty Rd. About 1 mi. of frontage.

*Bay area,* also via Jetty Rd. Bay is about 2 mi. wide, much used by migrating waterfowl.

*Fire Control Hill,* reached by trail. Viewpoint.

*Peter Iredale Beachfront,* named for a wrecked ship. Miles of wide, sandy beach.

*Natural vegetation area* at the S end of Coffenbury Lake.

## Activities

*Camping:* 605 sites. Yurts. All year. Reservations. *Campground is generally full on peak holidays and late summer weekends.*

*Hiking, backpacking:* Oregon Coast Trail begins here. Primitive hiker-biker camp. 5 mi. of trails within site.

*Fishing:* Salmon, flounder, bass, perch, ling cod, from jetty and N end of Spit. Fishing fair in the lakes.

*Swimming:* Lake, supervised mid-June–Labor Day. Surf swimming is inadvisable.

*Boating:* Ramps on Coffenbury, Crabapple, and Creep and Crawl Lakes.

*Bicycling:* 8.5 mi. of bike trails.

## Publications

Park leaflet with map.

Site map.

Bicycle and hiking trail map.

## Headquarters

OR Parks and Recreation Dept., Hammond, OR, 97121; (503) 861-1671.

---

## Harris Beach State Recreation Area

Oregon Parks and Recreation Department
171 acres.

Near CA border. From Brookings, 2 mi. N on US 101.

Sandy beach with occasional rock outcroppings. Back of beach, land rises to moderately level bench, an ancient beach, about 160 ft. above sea level. Offshore sea stacks and Goat Island, seabird rookery.

## Activities

*Camping:* 151 sites. Yurts. All year. Reservations.

*Hiking, backpacking:* Primitive hiker-biker camp. Nature trail.

**Headquarters**
OR Parks and Recreation Dept., 1655 US 101, Brookings, OR 97415; (541) 469-2021.

## Hug Point State Recreation Site

Oregon Parks and Recreation Department
131 acres.

From Cannon Beach, 4 mi. S on US 101.

Small, attractive, sheltered ocean beach.

## Humbug Mountain State Park

Oregon Parks and Recreation Department
1,842 acres.

From Port Orford, 6 mi. S on US 101.

On one of the most scenic sections of US 101. Forested hills come down almost to the ocean's edge. At Humbug Mountain, the highway (traveling S) turns into Brush Creek Canyon and passes the mountain on the inland side. Mountain rises from the beach to 1,756 ft. Park has 4 mi. of ocean frontage; only 2 mi. are accessible because of the steep bluffs.

**Plants:** Mountain slopes and canyon floor partially forested: Sitka spruce, western hemlock, Douglas-fir, alder, bigleaf maple. Virgin stand of Oregon myrtle.

**Activities**

*Camping:* 106 sites. Mid-April–Nov.

*Hiking, backpacking:* Primitive hiker-biker camp. 5.5-mi. loop trail to top of mountain. Beach hiking. Segment of Oregon Coast Trail.

*Fishing:* Surf and creek.

*Swimming:* Surf. We saw people swimming in the creek.

**Headquarters**
OR Parks and Recreation Dept., Port Orford, OR 97465; (541) 332-6774.

---

## Jessie M. Honeyman Memorial State Park

Oregon Parks and Recreation Department
522 acres.

From Florence, 3 mi. S on US 101.

Within the Oregon Dunes National Recreation Area (see entry this zone), on both sides of US 101. Within the area of high dunes, but 2 mi. from the ocean beach. Frontage on Woahink and Cleawox Lakes. One of the most popular Parks; campground often crowded on weekends.

**Plants:** Some forested land on E, with fir, spruce, hemlock, cedar; understory of salal, rhododendron, huckleberry, thimbleberry, salmonberry. Park borders on a bog with insectivorous plants.

### Activities

*Camping:* 382 sites. Yurts. All year. Reservations.

*Hiking, backpacking:* Primitive hiker-biker camp. Oregon Coast Trail passes through Oregon Dunes National Recreation Area.

*Swimming:* All lakes.

*Boating:* 3 lakes. Ramps.

*Fishing:* In the lakes: lunker bass, crappie, bluegill, perch, catfish, trout.

### Publication
Leaflet.

### Headquarters
OR Parks and Recreation Dept., 84505 US 101, Florence, OR 97439; (541) 997-3641.

## Jewell Meadows Wildlife Area

Oregon Department of Fish and Wildlife
1,123 acres.

From Portland, W on Hwy 26 to Jewell Junction, about 55 mi. Continue
N on unmarked highway beside Nehalem River 9 mi. to Jewell. W 1½
mi. on Hwy 202.

Three parcels of land and a privately owned buffer. Area is maintained
to provide for wintering Roosevelt elk, habitat for elk and other
wildlife. Hunting is prohibited. Elk can usually be seen Nov.–April,
75–200 animals, feeding and resting in the meadows. Other elk use
the meadows along Beneke Creek. When the elk move to higher
ground for the summer, mule deer can often be seen early morning
and evening.

Habitats include mixed-age stands of conifers, hardwood forest of
red alder and bigleaf maple, streamside trees and shrubs, abandoned
orchards, grassy meadows, sedge wetlands, small ponds, clear streams.
Wildflowers April–May. The Beneke Creek–Crawford Ridge loop is a
pleasant, low-key, scenic drive on gravel roads.

### Nearby
Clatsop State Forest (see entry this zone).

### Publication
Folder with map.

### Headquarters
OR Dept. of Fish and Wildlife, Region 1, Rt. 5, Box 325, Corvallis, OR
97330; (503) 757-4186.

## Lewis & Clark National Wildlife Refuge

U.S. Fish and Wildlife Service
35,000 acres total; 8,313 acres of land.

Islands in the Columbia River E of Astoria. Access by private boat only.

Slow-moving river water has deposited silt in the estuary, forming marshy islands and sandbars. The Refuge, on the OR side of the main channel, includes 20 named islands and far more bars, mudflats, and tidal marshes. Most of the islands are flooded at high tide. Trees and shrubs on some of the higher islands upstream. The area, extending 15 mi. along the river, is the largest natural marsh in W OR, a major stopover for waterfowl on the Pacific Flyway.

**Birds:** In Feb. and March some 3,000 tundra swan, 2,000 dusky Canada geese, and 50,000 ducks may be present, the ducks mostly mallard, pintail, wigeon, green-winged teal, with lesser number of scaup and canvasback. Bald eagle often seen. Many shorebirds on exposed flats.

**Mammals:** Beaver, muskrat, raccoon, mink, weasel. Deer and seal sometimes seen.

### Activities

*Hunting:* Waterfowl. Some portions may be closed. Inquire.

*Fishing:* Salmon, trout, sturgeon, warm-water game fish.

*Boating:* Those unfamiliar with this area should consult HQ before a visit. Some tidal channels are navigable only at high tide. HQ can also suggest launching points. Hunting leaflet says facilities are available at Aldrich Point and John Day Point.

### Nearby

Julia Butler Hansen Refuge for the Columbian White-Tailed Deer (WA).

### Publications

Leaflet with map.

Bird checklist.

Hunting regulations.

### Headquarters

U.S. Fish and Wildlife Service, c/o Julia Butler Hansen Refuge for the Columbian White-Tailed Deer, 46 Steamboat Slough Rd., Cathlamet, WA 98612; (360) 795-3915.

## Loeb State Park

Oregon Parks and Recreation Department
320 acres.

From Brookings, 8 mi. NE on local road, along Chetco River.

In the Chetco River Canyon; ½ mi. of river frontage. Noted for a grove of virgin Oregon myrtle, a tree species with limited range. Also what is said to be the northernmost grove of Coast redwoods, diameters 5–8 ft.

### Activities

*Camping:* 53 sites, mid-April–Oct.

*Hiking, backpacking:* Primitive hiker-biker camp. Trails in Siskiyou National Forest.

### Adjacent

Siskiyou National Forest (see entry this zone).

### Headquarters

OR Parks and Recreation Dept., c/o Harris Beach State Park, 1655 US 101, Brookings, OR 97415; (541) 469-2021.

## Nehalem Bay State Park

Oregon Parks and Recreation Department
878 acres.

From Manzanita, 3 mi. S on US 101; right 1½ mi. on entrance road.

Sand spit with dunes between Nehalem Bay and ocean. Entrance road passes among old dunes, fully vegetated, mostly shore pine with some Douglas-fir, spruce, hemlock, oak, none large. Then area of scrub with stunted shore pine, broom, gorse. 6 mi. of fine ocean beach.

## Activities

*Camping:* 292 sites. Mid-April–Oct.

*Hiking, backpacking:* Primitive hiker-biker camp. On Oregon Coast Trail.

*Swimming:* Sand beach on bay. Also surf.

*Boating:* Ramp on bay.

*Horse riding:* Beach trail.

## Headquarters

OR Parks and Recreation Dept., 9500 Sandpiper Lane, Nehalem, OR 97131; (503) 368-5154.

## Neptune State Scenic Viewpoint

Oregon Parks and Recreation Department
302 acres.

From Yachats, 3 mi. S on US 101.

Scenic area. About 2½ mi. of rugged, rocky ocean front. Terrain is rough. Salal, huckleberry, Sitka spruce. At N end is a deep, long fissure through which waves roll, breaking spectacularly.

## Nestucca Spit State Park

Oregon Parks and Recreation Department
484 acres.

Just W of Pacific City.

Stabilized sand spit. 2¼ mi. of ocean frontage, 3 mi. on estuary. Some shore pine with Scotch broom, beach grass. Tide flats. For shore- and seabirds, this offers as good birding as better-known sites N and S.

*Boating:* Ramp on estuary of Nestucca River.

## New River

U.S. Bureau of Land Management
1,168 acres (land).

Located between Bandon and Boice Cope County Park at Floras Lake.
Vehicle access points are Croft and Floras Lake Rds.

Designated an Area of Critical Environmental Concern (ACEC), New River is managed to maintain biodiversity and quality habitat for native communities of plants, birds, animals, and fish. Varied ecosystems along the river include meadows, deflation plains, forests, estuary, open sand dunes, brackish and freshwater wetlands. Public beach access points are at Floras Lake and at Storm Ranch off Croft Rd., where you must wade across the river to reach the actual beach. Additional public beach is broken up by private landholdings and is only seasonally accessible by nonmotorized craft. New River was formed approximately 100 years ago. It meanders N parallel to the coast for approximately 9 mi. before entering the ocean.

**Birds:** Include bald eagle, peregrine falcon, brown pelican, many shorebirds nesting and rearing young in spring and summer; also neotropicals and wintering waterfowl.

### Activities

*Hiking:* Beach access at Floras Lake limited March 15–Sept. 15 for wildlife protection.

*Fishing:* Seasonally restricted by OR Dept. of Fish and Wildlife.

### Headquarters

Bureau of Land Management, Coos Bay District, 1300 Airport Lane, North Bend, OR 97459; (541) 756-0100.

## Ona Beach State Park

Oregon Parks and Recreation Department
237 acres.

From Newport, 8 mi. S on US 101.

Broad, sand ocean beach. Boat ramp on Beaver Creek. Wooded hill-side on S side.

## Oregon Dunes National Recreation Area

U.S. Forest Service
27,450 acres/31,500 acres within boundaries; additional 1,450 acres of National Forest lands outside of boundary at S end. Within and part of Siuslaw National Forest (see entry this zone).

N, Siuslaw River to Coos River S. Several access roads from US 101. Foot trails to beach from 3 campgrounds.

The area extends 40 mi. along the ocean. Up to 2½ mi. wide. Largely W of US 101 but includes frontage on Siltcoos Lake, Tahkenitch Lake, and Umpqua River E of the highway. The most extensive sand dune area on the West Coast, dunes up to 300 ft. high moving slowly E in the prevailing wind, gradually burying trees, in places coming close to the highway.

10 vehicle and foot access points in the 40 mi. The beach is state land, and motor vehicles are allowed on about half of it. In three large sections, the dunes and the area back of the dunes are also open to ORVs.

A number of small lakes and wetlands have formed E of the dunes. The principal plant species are shore pine, Sitka spruce, wax myrtle, evergreen huckleberry, coast willow, and salal. Nonnative species, becoming very pervasive, include European beach grass and Scotch broom.

About a third of the area within boundaries is privately owned. Much of the private land is along the highway.

Because each vehicle access route leads to an area open to ORVs, many visitors assume the entire area is an ORV playground. However, implementation of a recently approved management plan has restricted ORV use within specific areas of the Oregon Dunes, such as environmentally sensitive areas and areas managed for nonmotorized uses. Thus, there are many quiet and isolated areas where one can go to experience the dunes' unique beauty. In addition, the state has recently closed significant portions of beaches to vehicles, particularly between Siltcoos and Tahkenitch Creeks.

**Birds:** Checklist available. Many sea- and shorebirds are seen, especially at river mouths. Eagle, blue heron, osprey around lakes.

**Mammals:** Mule deer, raccoon, and beaver common.

### Features

*North Dunes:* The best backcountry for hikers is between the Siltcoos and Umpqua Rivers. Less open sand, more natural diversity. Access from Siltcoos Rd. (Stagecoach Trailhead), Waxmyrtle, Lagoon, and Carter Lake Campgrounds (Taylor Dunes Trailhead), Oregon Dunes Overlook, Tahkenitch Campground, and Tahkenitch Creek Trailhead.

*Umpqua Dunes Scenic Area:* 3,000 acres. From Umpqua Lighthouse to Tenmile Creek. Includes the largest dunes. Much of the area is open to foot traffic only. Access from Eel Creek Campground or Umpqua Lighthouse State Park.

*Honeyman Dunes:* SW of Cleowax Lake. Access from Jessie M. Honeyman State Park (see entry this zone).

*South Jetty, Siuslaw River:* Vehicle access to parking areas. Dunes closed to ORVs. Beach closed to vehicles May 1–Sept. 30. One of the good birding spots.

*Horsfall Corridor:* S of Horsfall Rd. is now closed to ORVs. Offers additional hiking opportunities from Bluebill Trailhead.

### Interpretation

*Visitor center* on US 101 at Reedsport. Exhibits, literature, information.

*Evening programs, other interpretive activities* are planned. Inquire.

*Oregon Dunes Overlook* staffed by volunteers during summer months.

### Activities

*Camping:* 13 campgrounds, about 500 sites. Some open all year.

*Hiking, backpacking:* Part of the Oregon Coast Trail. Beach and dune camping permitted. Over 35 mi. of trails within the dunes, many leading to beaches along scenic creeks. Threemile Lake is a popular destination for overnight backpackers (trailhead at Tahkenitch Campground). Trails are usually well marked with posts in the open sand dunes. Spring and early summer hikes may encounter standing water when crossing through wetland areas.

*Fishing:* Surf, jetties, lakes.

*Swimming:* Unsupervised. Strong undertows and riptides. Occasional large waves.

*Boating:* Ramps on the 8 largest lakes and on Siuslaw and Umpqua Rivers.

*ORVs must comply with state and federal regulations. Special equipment required.*

*Occasional high waves. Near the water, don't turn your back on the surf; avoid logs and piles of driftwood.*

## Publications

Oregon Dunes NRA map.

*Hiking Trails in the Oregon Dunes National Recreation Area.*

*Off-Highway Vehicle Guide.*

*Sand Tracks* (leaflet).

## Adjacent or Nearby

Jessie M. Honeyman Memorial State Park, Umpqua Lighthouse State Park, William M. Tugman State Park (see entries this zone).

## Headquarters

U.S. Forest Service, 855 Highway Ave., Reedsport, OR 97467; (541) 271-3611.

## Oswald West State Park

Oregon Parks and Recreation Department
2,474 acres.

From Cannon Beach, 10 mi. S on US 101.

The Coast Range meets the ocean here. Most of Neahkahnie Mountain (1,661 ft.) is within the Park. Scenic section of Coast Hwy, high above the sea, many overlooks. Numerous small streams. The largest, Short Sands Creek and Necarney Creek, converge and enter the sea at Short Sands Beach. Except for this small beach, the coast has vertical basaltic cliffs rising as much as 700 ft. Rock promontories extend into the ocean; the largest is Cape Falcon.

**Plants:** Dense vegetation, in places resembling rain forest. Principal trees: western hemlock, western red cedar, Sitka spruce. Along Short Sand and Necarney Creeks, exceptionally large old-growth hemlock and spruce. Understory of salal, red huckleberry, salmonberry, thimbleberry, blackberry, red elderberry. Wildflowers include lily-of-the-valley, trillium, monkeyflower, wood sorrel, skunk cabbage.

**Birds:** Most common: 8 gull species, shorebirds, Steller's jay, raven, crow, swallows, robin. Brown pelican in migration.

**Mammals:** Often seen: chickaree, Townsend chipmunk, brush rabbit. Present but seldom seen: striped and spotted skunks, raccoon, mule deer, Roosevelt elk.

### Activities

*Camping:* 37 primitive walk-in sites. Mid-Mar.–Nov.

*Hiking, backpacking:* 15 mi. of trails within the Park. On the Oregon Coast Trail. Scenic trails: Cape Falcon, Neahkahnie Mountain. Trails from parking areas to beach. Camp only at campground.

*Fishing:* Some trout in streams. Perch and greenling in surf.

*Swimming:* Limited by cold water. Unsupervised.

### Headquarters

OR Parks and Recreation Dept., 8300 Third St., Nehalem, OR 97131; (503) 368-5943.

### Otter Crest State Scenic Viewpoint

Oregon Parks and Recreation Department
1 acre.

From Newport, 10 mi. N on US 101.

On Cape Foulweather, a flat-topped rock bluff 453 ft. above the sea. Shoreline here has steep rock cliffs.

## Pistol River State Park

Oregon Parks and Recreation Department
440 acres.

From Gold Beach, 11 mi. S on US 101.

Wide sand beach. Large sand dunes. At S end, a 160-ft. rock knoll;
viewpoint. At N end, Pistol River.

## Rogue Wild and Scenic River

U.S. Bureau of Land Management/U.S. Forest Service
84 mi.

From the mouth of the Applegate River, 6 mi. W of Grants Pass to
Lobster Creek Bridge, about 12 mi. upstream from Gold Beach. A Forest
road parallels the lower portion, a BLM road the upper. The middle
portion is roadless.

Designated a Wild and Scenic River in 1968, with three zones: the
"Wild" zone is free-flowing, accessible only by trail. "Scenic" sections
have road access points. "Recreational" sections have some shoreline
development and many roadside access points. The 47 mi. above Marial are administered by the BLM, the 37 below Marial by the Siskiyou
National Forest. Visitors can travel the 84 mi. by boat, the wild portion on foot. The foot trail is closed to bicycles, vehicles, and horses.
The float trip requires special boats and skills.

The river flows from NW of Crater Lake National Park, passing
through the Umpqua and Rogue River National Forests in its upper
reaches. Float trips through the Wild and Scenic portion usually begin
at sites between Grants Pass and Grave Creek. From here the river cuts
through dissected plateaus exposing serpentine, greenstone, granite,
sandstone, slate, and shale. Many rapids, riffles, and falls. The canyon
is narrow in places. Between Grants Pass and the sea, the river drops
almost 1,000 ft.

**Plants:** Vegetation in and above the canyon is diverse because of the varied terrain, soils, and microclimates. On the upper reaches, willow along the banks, Oregon ash and bigleaf maple in moist places, Pacific madrone, California black ash, and Oregon white oak on dry ridges. Downstream, western red cedar, Port Orford cedar, Pacific yew, canyon live oak, golden chinquapin, tan oak, Oregon myrtle, with stands of Douglas-fir, western hemlock, grand fir, sugar pine. Rarities include weeping spruce, knobcone pine, and pitcher plants in remote sites. Many side streams lined with rhododendron, azalea, Pacific dogwood, Oregon grape, salal, salmonberry. Many ferns.

**Birds:** Species likely to be seen in proper season include pied-billed grebe, mallard, wood duck, great blue heron, osprey, bald eagle, kingfisher, Virginia and sora rails, common snipe, mourning dove, common nighthawk, goshawk, acorn woodpecker, western wood pewee, 4 swallows, plain titmouse, common bushtit, white-breasted nuthatch, winter and Bewick's wrens, western bluebird, solitary vireo, yellow warbler, yellow-breasted chat, northern oriole, lazuli bunting, lesser goldfinch, sparrows.

**Mammals:** Deer, bear, otter, raccoon, mink, chickaree, ring-tail.

### Activities

*Camping:* 19 Forest Service, BLM, and county campgrounds, 1,315 sites. But only 6 of the campgrounds have road access. Also trailside camping. Seasons vary; generally May–Oct.

*Hiking, backpacking:* A 40-mi. trail follows the N bank from Grave Creek to Illahe. Intermediate road access at Marial. Most hikers take 5 days for the trip. The trail is not difficult, but ask about current conditions. No vehicles, bikes, or horses. Be prepared to purify the water.

*Fishing:* The Rogue is a famous fishing stream. Salmon, steelhead, cutthroat, rainbow, shad, and sturgeon.

*Boating:* Special Rogue-type drift boats are generally used. Also rubber rafts. The river is wild and treacherous. Professional river guides take parties on 3- to 5-day float trips. Only people with considerable wild river experience should attempt the run without a guide. They should obtain detailed information and travel in groups of two or more boats. Individual float permits are required May 15–Oct. 15, obtainable from BLM's Rand visitor center, 14335 Galice Rd., Merlin, OR; (541) 479-3735. Commercial jet boats make daily trips from Gold Beach to Agness and return, as well as from Grants Pass to Grave Creek and back.

## Adjacent
Wild Rogue Wilderness of Siskiyou National Forest.

## Publication
*Rogue River Float Guide* (map, description, information).

## Headquarters
Bureau of Land Management, Medford District, 3040 Biddle Rd., Medford, OR 97504; (541) 770-2220. Bureau of Land Management, Coos Bay District, 1300 Airport Lane, North Bend, OR 97459; (541) 756-0100. U.S. Forest Service, P.O. Box 440, 1501 N.W. 6th St., Grants Pass, OR 97526; (541) 479-5301.

......

# Saddle Mountain State Natural Area
Oregon Parks and Recreation Department
2,882 acres.

15 mi. inland from the sea. From Necanicum Junction on US 26 (9 mi. E of Seaside on US 101), 7 mi. N on entrance road.

W portion relatively flat, with young trees and shrubs. Larger area is occupied by steep cliffs and slopes of Saddle Mountain; three main peaks over 3,200 ft. Sweeping views from top include snowcapped mountains, miles of shoreline, mouth of Columbia River.

**Plants:** Most of the site is forested. Old-growth stands include some of the largest western hemlock in the Coast Range, a forest of Sitka spruce and hemlock, and some ancient Pacific silver fir. About 300 plant species have been identified, more are thought to be present. Those identified include several rare or endangered species, some occurring only here, and some dating as far back as the Ice Age. Outstanding array of wildflowers includes nodding onion, Oregon lily, yellow and pink fawn lilies, alpine lily, false Solomon's seal, lily-of-the-valley, Oregon purple iris, wood buttercup, columbine, bleeding heart, wallflower, saxifrages, goatsbeard, cinquefoil, redwood sorrel, violets, starflower, Saddle Mt. bittercress, hairystem sidalcea, trillium, penstemons, paintbrush. Many of the plant species found here are difficult to identify because they differ from typical forms of the species, a consequence of the mountain's isolation.

**Birds:** Include turkey vulture, Cooper's and sharp-shinned hawks, blue and ruffed grouse, mountain quail, screech and great horned owls. Vaux's swift, kingfisher, northern flicker, pileated, hairy, and downy woodpeckers, western wood pewee, black-capped and chestnut-backed chickadees, varied and Swainson's thrushes, golden-crowned and ruby-crowned kinglets, western tanager, pine siskin. Warblers: orange-crowned, yellow, yellow-rumped, hermit, MacGillivray's, Wilson's.

**Mammals:** Presumed to include 3 shrews, shrew-mole, coast mole, several bat species, brush rabbit, snowshoe hare, mountain beaver, chickaree, deer mouse, white-footed vole, coyote, black bear, raccoon, short-tailed and long-tailed weasels, mink, bobcat, elk, mule deer.

## Activities

*Camping:* 6 primitive sites. Spring opening depends on weather.

*Hiking:* Trail to mountaintop. Rocky and steep. Often windy, chilly at top. Don't attempt this unless you're an experienced hiker and in good shape.

## Headquarters

OR Parks and Recreation Dept., c/o Fort Stevens State Park, Hammond, OR 97121; (503) 861-1671.

## Samuel H. Boardman State Scenic Corridor

Oregon Parks and Recreation Department
1,473 acres.

From Brookings, N about 6 mi. on US 101. Park extends N 9 mi.

Rugged coastline: cliffs, crags, promontories, offshore rocks. Also sand beaches. 4 areas developed for day use. Trails to beaches. Viewpoints. Seabirds and marine mammals often seen offshore. Offshore rocks include wave-carved arches and islands covered with spruce trees. House Rock, 400 ft. above the sea, offers view of the shoreline S for 25 mi. to Point St. George in CA. Vegetation includes azalea, rhododendron, ceanothus, hillsides of Oregon iris.

## Seal Rock Wayside

Oregon Parks and Recreation Department
8 acres.

From Newport, 10 mi. S on US 101.

One of the best places to see seals, sea lions, and seabirds. Rugged coast; many offshore rocks.

## Shore Acres State Park

See Cape Arago State Park this zone.

## Siskiyou National Forest

U.S. Forest Service
1,093,542 acres/1,163,583 acres within boundaries.

SW OR; 39,688 acres in NW CA. W of Grants Pass. Principal access routes from US 101, US 199, I-5.

Near the coast, but no ocean frontage. Covers a major portion of the Siskiyou Mountain Range, which links the Cascade Mountains on the E and Coast Range on the NW. Includes a small section of the Coast Range. Grayback Mountain, 7,055 ft. elevation, is highest point. Area is mountainous, steep, rough, with short drainages. Crossed by Rogue River (see entry this zone). Five rivers originate within the Forest. Timberlands, open grass and brush areas, large outcrops of serpentine.

**Plants:** Area has unique botanical diversity, mingling of species characteristic of regions to N, S, E, and W. Also many relict species. Principal trees: Douglas-fir, ponderosa and sugar pines, Port Orford cedar, white, noble, and Shasta firs. Some old-growth stands. Among the rare species: weeping spruce. Prominent in understory: madrone, California black oak, tan oak, manzanita, bigleaf maple, buckthorn. Estimated 2,000 species of flowering plants, but no checklist.

**Birds:** Checklist of over 150 species. Common species include great blue heron, mallard, wood duck, common merganser, turkey vulture, red-tailed hawk, blue grouse, California quail, band-tailed pigeon, 4 owls, rufous hummingbird, kingfisher, northern flicker, western wood pewee, swallows, Steller's jay, chestnut-backed chickadee, common bushtit, red-breasted nuthatch, wrens, robin, varied thrush, golden-crowned kinglet, 4 warblers, 4 sparrows, western tanager, pine siskin, American goldfinch, rufous-sided towhee.

**Mammals:** Checklist available. Include mule deer, Roosevelt elk, black bear, chipmunk, gray squirrel, shrews, moles, bats, snowshoe hare, brush rabbit, mountain beaver, beaver, ground squirrels, pocket gophers, several mice, porcupine, gray fox, coyote, marten, fisher, mink, weasels, skunks. Seldom seen: mountain lion, bobcat.

**Reptiles and amphibians:** Include several salamander species, tree frog, western toad, northern red-legged and foothill yellow-legged frogs, fence, sagebrush, and alligator lizards, and snakes: rubber boa, ringneck, racer, gopher, garter, California and mountain kingsnakes, western rattlesnake, various garter snakes.

## Features

*Kalmiopsis Wilderness:* 179,862 acres. In S central region. Two principal access routes: (1) from US 199 near Kerby, Eight Dollar Mountain Rd. N across Illinois River, up to parking area on ridge above Onion Camp; (2) from Brookings on US 101, E and N on local road beside Chetco River, then up past Long Ridge and Quail Prairie lookout to Vulcan Peak area. Both routes normally can be traveled by cars in good condition. Also off Forest Rd. 4103, Illinois River Rd., about 10 mi. W of Selma. Includes most of Chetco River headwater basin. Harsh, rugged country; rocky, brushy, low elevation canyons; rushing streams. Area has special interest for botanists, both because of great variety of species and presence of rarities, including *Kalmiopsis leachiana,* an extremely rare rhododendron.

*Wild Rogue Wilderness:* 36,038 acres, including 8,971 acres of BLM land. In N central region. (See entry for Rogue Wild and Scenic River this zone.) Very steep terrain; essentially a canyon. The wilderness serves chiefly as a buffer zone for the Wild section of the river. Only one developed trail. Brush and cliffs make cross-country travel next to impossible.

*Grassy Knob Wilderness:* 17,200 acres. Near Powers, 7 mi. E of Port Orford. 2 roads lead into rugged, forested canyon terrain. Dense underbrush with only one developed trail. Broad views of wilderness and ocean.

*Red Buttes Wilderness:* 3,400 acres in Siskiyou National Forest. Additional acreage in Rogue River and Klamath National Forests. SE of Cave Junction, extending N from CA border. Elevations 3,600–6,300 ft. This is subalpine terrain, with characteristic meadows and wildflowers. 11 mi. of trails, including the Boundary National Recreation Trail.

Also, 5 *Wild and Scenic Rivers:* the *Chetco, Elk, Illinois, N Fork of Smith River,* and the *Rogue.* Whitewater opportunities for both rafters and kayakers. Commercial river outfitters can be hired.

Several *botanical areas* and *research natural areas* have been established. These are of interest primarily to specialists, not the general public. Those interested should inquire at HQ or at any ranger office.

### Includes
*Oregon Caves National Monument* (see entry zone 5).

### Activities
*Camping:* 30 campgrounds, 270 sites. A few are inaccessible except by water. Last part of May–Labor Day. Some campgrounds are primitive: pit toilets, only some with water. Also several nearby BLM campgrounds. *Valley of the Rogue State Park,* 12 mi. E of Grants Pass, is open all year for camping.

*Hiking:* Over 600 mi. of trails. Trail along Rogue River. (See also Rogue Wild and Scenic River entry this zone.) Forest and wilderness maps show trail system. Some hikers camp in the wilderness areas, but demand has not been sufficient to require a permit system. Watch out for poison oak at lower elevations.

*Hunting:* Deer, elk, bear, grouse, quail, pigeon, dove.

*Fishing:* Rogue and others rivers are well known for excellent fishing: chinook, steelhead, coho, cutthroat.

*Boating:* See entry this zone for Rogue Wild and Scenic River. Also, the Illinois River, for about 35 mi. above its junction with the Rogue, is attracting whitewater enthusiasts. Check with rangers about float permits.

*Horse riding:* Outfitters in nearby communities provide pack and saddle stock, guides.

*Bicycling:* Check with rangers for trails that accommodate bikes. Mountain bikes are prohibited in wilderness areas.

## Publications

Forest map, $3.25.

Wilderness map, $2.00.

## Headquarters

U.S. Forest Service, 200 N.E. Greenfield Rd., P.O. Box 440, Grants Pass, OR 97526; (541) 471-6500.

## Ranger Districts

Chetco R.D., 555 5th St., Brookings, OR 97415; (541) 569-2196. Galice R.D., 200 N.E. Greenfield, Box 440, Grants Pass, OR 97526; (541) 471-6500. Gold Beach R.D., 1225 S. Ellensburg, Box 7, Gold Beach, OR 97444; (541) 247-3600. Illinois Valley R.D., 26558 Redwood Hwy, Cave Junction, OR 97523; (541) 592-2166. Illinois Valley visitor center, 201 Caves Hwy, Cave Junction, OR 97523; (541) 592-2631. Powers R.D., Powers, OR 97466; (541) 439-3011.

## Siuslaw National Forest

U.S. Forest Service
630,000 acres/840,000 acres within boundaries.

On or near coast. N portion from Cape Lookout to Lincoln Beach. S portion from near Yaquina River to Coos Bay. Access from US 101, US 20, Hwys 22, 18, 34, 126, 38.

43 mi. of ocean frontage, the only National Forest with much seacoast. The coastal part of the Forest has been designated the Oregon Dunes National Recreation Area. We have made it a separate entry.

As the acreage figures indicate, the Forest has many inholdings. The largest solid blocks of Forest land are in the S. The N portion is more fragmented but has several blocks of significant size.

The Forest extends inland over the Coast Range. It includes two prominent peaks: Mount Hebo in the N, 3,147 ft.; and Mary's Peak to the E, 4,097 ft., highest in the Coast Range, offering splendid vistas. Steep slopes, sharp ridges, deep-cut canyons, open areas, sheer rock faces, cascades, waterfalls. Climate is moist, an average of 90 in. of rain each year, mostly in the winter. Snowfall is rare except on the peaks.

Inland hiking opportunities are limited. Dense vegetation may make off-trail travel difficult. Trails often lead into roadless wilderness areas. Here, indeed, are quiet places—if one is able and equipped to reach them. When in doubt check with rangers ahead of time.

**Plants:** Much of the Forest is in the western hemlock zone. Near the coast there are dense stands of Douglas-fir, western hemlock, and Sitka spruce—some of the largest trees on earth—along with lesser amounts of western red cedar. These give way to areas of shorter red alder, which in turn give way to bogs too wet to support trees. Draping everything are ferns, mosses, and lichens. (The Forest Service notes that while the Amazon rain forest has 185 tons of plants per acre, the Siuslaw has just under 400 tons per acre!) At higher elevations noble and Pacific silver fir. Thick undergrowth of salmonberry, vine maple, salal, Oregon grape, blackberry; many varieties of wildflowers occur throughout. After fires and logging, only fragments of old-growth forest remain.

**Birds:** Over 200 species recorded. The variety of habitats—ocean shoreline, estuaries, dunes, meadows, streams, and dense forest—offers good birding opportunities. Species noted include loons, gadwall, pintail, shoveler, canvasback, bufflehead, grebes, scoter, mergansers, surfbird, yellowlegs, golden and bald eagles, various hawks and owls, blue and ruffed grouse, western tanager, pine siskin, mountain quail, Steller's jay, common bushtit. Endangered or threatened species include bald eagle, peregrine falcon, northern spotted owl, snowy plover, marbled murrelet.

**Mammals:** Roosevelt elk, black-tailed deer, black bear, mountain lion, mountain beaver, river otter, muskrat, mink, marten, nutria, bobcat, raccoon, red and gray foxes, wolverine, brush rabbit, snowshoe hare, bats, shrew-mole.

## Features

*Cascade Head Scenic Research Area:* 6,600 acres. Off US 101 S of Neskowin, in the N portion of Forest. Cascade Head is a 1,770 ft. promontory. About 2½ mi. of ocean frontage, estuary, floodplain, river, forest. Cliffs and offshore islands have nesting seabird colonies, seals, sea lions. Rain forest. Trails.

*Cummins Creek Wilderness Area:* 9,173 acres. Reached from US 101 on W. Ten Mile Rd. 100 to 2,400 ft. elevation. Heavily forested and completely surrounded by roads. Steep and broken terrain. Contains the only remaining old-growth Sitka spruce in OR's wilderness system. 2

principal streams drain directly into the Pacific and support important runs of fish. Only 4.5 mi. of trails; recreation use is still minimal,
mostly for hunting. A 3-mi. gravel road at the W end will be con-
verted to a trail in the future.

*Drift Creek Wilderness Area:* 5,798 acres. N of Waldport. Access is by
trails. Steep forested slopes, dense tree canopy, small meadows. Sea
level to 2,200 ft. elevation. Dominated by stands of old-growth Douglas-fir in which several pairs of endangered northern spotted owl
have recently been located. Drift Creek supports runs of chinook and
coho salmon and steelhead trout. Recreation use is associated with
fishing, hunting, or hiking. 7.5 mi. of trails; access from Harris Ranch
and Horse Creek N and S Trailheads.

*Mount Hebo area:* 1,700 acres. E of Pacific City. Pockets of mature trees.
Includes headwaters of several rivers. *Hebo Lake* is a "fishing hot spot,"
say the rangers. The Mount Hebo Campground facilities have recently
been closed because of problems associated with over-use.

*Mary's Peak,* summit 4,097 ft. Highest point in the OR Coast Range.
Take US 101 to Hwy 34 at Waldport or Hwy 20 at Newport, to Hwy 30.
10 mi. of easy to moderate trails. Wildflowers, bird-watching, and
panoramic views of the Willamette Valley, the Cascade peaks, and, on
clear days, the Pacific. A few campsites. Cross-country skiing and
managed snowplay area.

*Rock Creek Wilderness Area:* 7,486 acres. Access from US 101 on Forest
Rd. W 56 (unpaved). Sea level to 2,200 ft. Rock Creek and Big Creek
drain into Pacific. These are managed as a wild fishery by the OR
Dept. of Fish and Wildlife. Area is most notable for its coniferous forest and dense ground cover. No trails presently; cross-country travel is
difficult due to steep slopes and dense brush. Present recreation use is
light. When completed, the Oregon Coast Trail will pass adjacent to
the area.

### Interpretation

*Cape Perpetua visitor center,* on US 101 3 mi. S of Yachats. *Exhibits, film,
information, publications, nature trails.* Open 7 days a week in summer.
Points of interest reached by nature trails include tide pools, Devil's
Churn, Spouting Horns, Cape Cove Beach, 500-year-old "Giant
Spruce" along Cape Creek, and Cummins Creek Trailhead. Cook's
Ridge/Gwynn Creek Loop Trail and Cummins Creek Loop are longer,
more difficult trails through old-growth forest, with some ocean
views.

*Cape Perpetua overlook,* 2 mi. off US 101, the highest point on the OR coast, offers a fine view of the coast. Camping available.

## Activities

*Camping:* 18 campgrounds, including 2 large group campgrounds, with 567 sites. (480 additional sites available at Oregon Dunes National Recreation Area.) Some open all year. Trailside camping permitted in many areas; check with rangers. Due to heavy winter rains, some roads, bridges, trails, campgrounds may wash out by spring. Call Ranger Districts ahead of time for travel information.

*Hiking:* Total trail mileage (including Oregon Dunes National Recreation Area) is presently 121.8. Access to inland areas, limited because of thick vegetation and steep terrain, is being improved.

*Hunting:* Deer, elk, bear, grouse, quail, dove, pigeon.

*Fishing:* Surf, lakes, streams.

## Publications

*Recreation Guide* (camping and trails).

*Recreation Report* (update for current season).

*Accessible Sites of the Siuslaw National Forest.*

*Cape Perpetua Hiking Trails.*

*Come and Discover Mary's Peak.*

*If This Is a Rainforest, Where Are the Toucans?*

*1996 Forest Facts.*

Wilderness Areas (Waldport R.D.).

## Headquarters

U.S. Forest Service, Siuslaw National Forest, Supervisor's Office, 4077 Research Way, P.O. Box 1148, Corvallis, OR 97333; (541) 563-3211/750-7246 (TDD).

## Ranger Districts

Alsea R.D., 18591 Alsea Hwy, Alsea, OR 97324; (541) 487-5811. Hebo R.D., 31525 Hwy 22, Hebo, OR 97122; (503) 392-3161. Mapleton R.D., 10692 Hwy 126, Mapleton, OR 97453; (541) 268-4473. Waldport R.D., 1049 S.W. Pacific Hwy, Waldport, OR 97394; (541) 563-3211. Cape Perpetua Visitor Center, 2400 US 101S, Yachats, OR 97498; (541) 547-3269. Oregon Dunes National Recreation Area, 855 Hwy Ave., Reedsport, OR 97647; (541) 271-3611.

## South Beach State Park

Oregon Parks and Recreation Department
433 acres.

From Newport, 2 mi. S on US 101.

About 1 mi. of broad, sandy beach backed by 20-ft. dunes partly stabilized by beach grass, small pines. Back of the dunes, dense growth of salal, box blueberry. Rhododendron, shore pine planted in developed area. About 40 acres of rhododendron, pine and spruce.

### Interpretation
*Nature trail,* about ½ mi.

### Activities
*Camping:* 257 sites. Mid-April–Oct. Reservations.

*Hiking, backpacking:* 4 mi. of beach, beyond Park limits. On Oregon Coast Trail. Hiker-biker primitive camp.

*Fishing:* Surf: sea bass, cod, perch.

*Swimming:* Surf, unsupervised.

### Headquarters
OR Parks and Recreation Dept., 5580 S Coast Hwy, South Beach, OR 97366; (541) 867-4715.

## Sunset Bay State Park

See Cape Arago State Park this zone.

## Three Arch Rocks National Wildlife Refuge

See Cape Meares National Wildlife Refuge this zone.

## Tillamook State Forest

Oregon Department of Forestry
363,000 acres.

NW OR, about 25 mi. W of Portland. Crossed by Hwy 6, Glenwood to
Tillamook, and local road NE from Mohler.

Steep mountain slopes. Highest point about 3,680 ft. Some ridges
extremely sharp. More rounded mountains and gentler slopes near
the coast. Steep river gradients and occasional waterfalls in upstream
areas. Rivers: Nehalem, Salmonberry, Miami, Kilchis, Wilson,
Tualatin, Trask. Numerous smaller streams. Precipitation as much as
130 in. per year.

Site of the Tillamook Burn, fires in 1933, 1939, and 1945 that
destroyed 356,000 acres. Much of the burned area was abandoned by
private owners. A state bond issue financed a major reforestation program. Significant timber harvesting is now possible from this once
barren landscape.

**Plants:** 95% of the area is forested, much in even-aged stands. Principal tree species: Douglas-fir, western hemlock. No old growth. Other
species include Sitka spruce, western red cedar, noble fir, red alder,
bigleaf maple. Understory includes vine maple, sword fern, California
hazel, red huckleberry, bracken fern, thimbleberry, salmonberry, salal,
trailing blackberry, Oregon grape, snowberry, huckleberry. Flowering
species include starflower, trillium, lotus, elderberry, oceanspray, foxglove. A number of plant species found on King Mountain occur only
on a few isolated peaks in the Coast Range.

**Birds:** 71 species recorded; more probably present. Noted: bald eagle,
hawks, grouse, rufous hummingbird, northern flicker, woodpeckers,
wood pewee, Steller's jay, golden-crowned kinglet, western tanager,
pine siskin, rufous-sided towhee.

**Mammals:** Include roosevelt elk, mule deer, coyote, beaver, mountain
beaver, rabbits, wood rat, raccoon, black bear, mink.

## Interpretation
New *education program* being developed. Emphasis on aspects of reforestation.

## Activities
*Camping:* 3 campgrounds open along Wilson River Hwy 6 to Tillamook. *Gales Creek Campground:* walk-in tent and drive-in sites. *Elk Creek Campground:* walk-in camping only. *Jones Creek Campground:* walk-in tent and drive-in sites. All 3 are semideveloped, with toilets and pumps for water. Each has signboard with camper information, a Tillamook State Forest map, and interpretive information.

*Hiking, backpacking:* 24 mi. of trails. Hikers can travel the entire system or use any of 4 intermediate access points.

*Hunting:* Deer, elk, bear.

*Fishing:* Streams: trout, salmon, steelhead.

*Swimming:* Informal. Pools in streams. Unsupervised.

*Horse riding:* Trail section from Browns Camp to Elk Creek Park. (Portions on roads with vehicle traffic.)

*Mountain biking:* 20 mi. of developed trails and many forest roads to ride; trailhead at Rogers Camp.

*Motorcycling:* 100 mi. of developed trails. Keep to designated trail system.

*Browns Camp is a center for motorcycling. Cycles permitted on designated trails nearby.*

## Publications
Forest leaflet (no map).

*Tillamook Forest Trails* (includes trail map).

Auto tour guide.

## Headquarters
OR Dept. of Forestry, 4907 E. Third St., Tillamook, OR 97141; (503) 842-2545. (1 mi. E of Tillamook, E of county fairgrounds.) Or: 801 Gales Creek Rd., Forest Grove, OR 97116; (503) 359-7470.

## Umpqua Lighthouse State Park

Oregon Parks and Recreation Department
2,715 acres.

From Reedsport, 6 mi. S on US 101.

At mouth of the Umpqua River, 2½ mi. of ocean beach, ½ mi. on Lake Marie. Sand dunes to 500 ft., said to be highest in U.S. Islands of dead trees show how dunes have been moving E. Old dunes now partially stabilized by vegetation. Rhododendrons prominent, especially at Lake Marie. Nearby is jetty at mouth of Winchester Bay.

### Activities

*Camping:* 63 sites. Mid-April–Oct.

*Hiking, backpacking:* On Oregon Coast Trail. Primitive hiker-biker camp.

*Swimming:* Lake and surf.

### Adjacent

Oregon Dunes National Recreation Area (see entry this zone).

### Headquarters

OR Parks and Recreation Dept., Box 94, Winchester Bay, OR 97467; (541) 271-4118.

## William M. Tugman State Park

Oregon Parks and Recreation Department
560 acres.

From Coos Bay, 19 mi. N on US 101.

On the inland side of US 101; no ocean frontage. On Eel Lake, scenic area, surrounded by low forested hills. 5 mi. of lake frontage.

## Activities

*Camping:* 115 sites. Also hiker-biker camp.

*Fishing:* Trout. Dock accessible to people with disabilities.

*Swimming:* Lake. Unsupervised.

*Boating:* Large paved ramp and trailer parking. Boat speed limit 10 mph.

## Adjacent
Oregon Dunes National Recreation Area (see entry this zone).

## Headquarters
OR Parks and Recreation Dept., c/o Umpqua Lighthouse State Park, P.O. Box 94, Winchester Bay, OR 97467; (541) 271-4118.

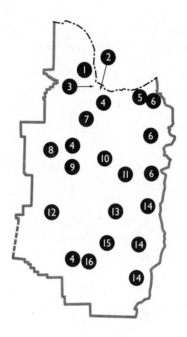

1. Sauvie Island Wildlife Area
2. Milo McIver State Park
3. Tryon Creek State Park
4. Willamette River Greenway
5. Columbia River Gorge National Scenic Area
6. Mount Hood National Forest
7. Champoeg State Heritage Area
8. Baskett Slough National Wildlife Refuge
9. Ankeny National Wildlife Refuge
10. Silver Falls State Park
11. Santiam State Forest
12. William L. Finley National Wildlife Refuge
13. Cascadia State Park
14. Willamette National Forest
15. Ben and Kay Dorris State Recreation Area
16. Elijah Bristow State Park

# ZONE 2

Includes these counties:

| | | |
|---|---|---|
| Columbia | Clackamas | Linn |
| Washington | Marion | Multnomah |
| Lane (central and E portions) | | Benton |
| Polk | Yamhill | |

The Willamette Valley lies between the Coast Range and the Cascade Mountains. This zone includes the valley and the W slope of the Cascades. It extends from the Columbia River to the Calapooya Mountains S of Eugene.

A majority of Oregonians live in this fertile valley. Soil and climate support a richly productive and diversified agriculture. Industry and commerce are also concentrated here.

Before all this development, the valley supported large wildlife populations. Each spring and fall, vast numbers of waterfowl came through. Some spent the winter here, some were all-year residents. The flocks are smaller now, and their future depends in large measure on the few Refuges that have been set aside.

As one might expect, the public Parks near Portland, Salem, and other population centers are heavily used. Most of them could not be considered quiet natural areas. We have, though, included several that still have relatively undisturbed portions, to be enjoyed chiefly midweek or off-season.

More than a dozen State Parks are strung along the Columbia River Gorge. In 1986 the Columbia River National Scenic Area was established. While the gorge retains some of its original grandeur, and is now further protected, we did not think any of the Parks suitable for an entry. The Columbia River Gorge NSA, however, is described.

Two National Forests include 97% of the acres in the entries that follow. Almost all of this Forest land is in the mountains to the E of the valley. These Forests are units of a huge block of National Forest land extending from the Columbia River to the CA border.

Snow and rainfall are heavy on the W slopes. Many of the rivers flowing down from the mountains have been dammed, the U.S. Army Corps of Engineers being responsible for 10 of the principal impoundments. These reservoirs are much used for water-based recreation: water skiing, sailing, fishing, swimming, power boating. We have noted those that are within National Forests, not those surrounded by privately owned land.

## Ankeny National Wildlife Refuge

U.S. Fish and Wildlife Service
2,796 acres.

From I-5, 10 mi. N of Albany, Talbot exit. Then 2 mi. W on Wintel Rd.

In the fertile Willamette Valley. Bottomlands near the confluence of the Santiam and Willamette Rivers. One of three Refuges in the valley providing wintering grounds for the dusky Canada goose, a race with a restricted range. Feed crops are cultivated. Hedgerows of hawthorn, wild rose, ash, and berry species surround most fields. Several dense deciduous woods.

Several miles of paved county roads cross the Refuge, providing good viewing. The entire Refuge, including a 1½-mi. trail through fields and woods, is open to foot travel May 1–Sept. 30.

**Birds:** 193 species recorded. Chief waterfowl species: Canada goose, mallard, wigeon, pintail, green-winged teal. Also grebes, herons, hawks, quail, band-tailed pigeon, shorebirds, woodpeckers, many songbirds.

**Mammals:** Mule deer, red fox, opossum, nutria, raccoon, skunk, coyote.

*Hunting:* Band-tailed pigeon, dove. Special regulations.

*Refuge is closed to all use Oct. 1–April 30. Otherwise, open daylight hours. Leashed dogs permitted only in designated parking areas.*

**Publications**

Leaflet with map.

Checklists of birds, mammals, plants.

**Headquarters**

Not on-site. U.S. Fish and Wildlife Service, Western OR Refuge Complex, 26208 Finley Refuge Rd., Corvallis, OR 97338; (541) 757-7236.

## Baskett Slough National Wildlife Refuge

U.S. Fish and Wildlife Service
2,492 acres.

12 mi. W of Salem. From intersection of Hwy 99W and Hwy 22, W 1½ mi. on Hwy 22.

Near the center of fertile Willamette Valley. In open farm country near foothills of the Coast Range. An ancient lakebed surrounded by rolling, forested hills. One of three Refuges in the valley providing wintering grounds for the dusky Canada goose, a race with a restricted range. Feed crops are cultivated. General elevation about 200 ft.; Baskett Butte is 414 ft. Morgan Lake, 65 acres, and other wetlands and associated fields are the primary feeding and resting areas.

**Birds:** Seasonally common or abundant species include tundra swan, Canada goose, mallard, pintail, green-winged teal, wigeon, shoveler, wood duck. Also great blue heron, red-tailed hawk, kestrel, northern harrier, California quail, pheasant, killdeer, snipe, greater yellowlegs, great horned owl, northern flicker, downy woodpecker, swallows, chikadees, jays, wrens, kinglets, cedar waxwing, several warblers.

**Mammals:** Common species include opossum, shrews, Townsend mole, little and big brown bats, raccoon, striped skunk, ground squirrel, giant pocket gopher, deer mouse, nutria, brush rabbit, black-tailed deer.

### Activities

*Hiking:* Main trail, 3 mi.; closed Oct. 1–May 1 for benefit of wintering waterfowl. Baskett Butte Trail, 1 mi., open all year.

*Bird-watching:* Waterfowl can be seen, fall and winter, from both sides of Coville and Smithfield county roads and parking areas on Coville Rd., and from wildlife viewing kiosk on Hwy 22.

*Dogs must be leashed and are only permitted in parking areas.*

## Publications
Leaflet with map.

Checklists of plants, birds, mammals.

## Headquarters
U.S. Fish and Wildlife Service, 10995 Hwy 22, Dallas, OR 97338; (503) 623-2749. Open by appointment only. No visitor center.

## Ben and Kay Dorris State Recreation Area
Oregon Parks and Recreation Department
92 acres.

From Eugene, 31 mi. E on Hwy 126.

Forested site on McKenzie River. Boat ramp.

### Nearby
Willamette National Forest (see entry this zone).

## Cascadia State Park
Oregon Parks and Recreation Department
258 acres.

On US 20, 14 mi. E of Sweet Home.

Highway and S Santiam River Gorge bisect the site. River terrace and mountain slopes. Open meadows, old-growth timber stands. Much Pacific dogwood in the understory.

*Camping:* 26 primitive sites. Opening date determined by winter weather.

## Nearby

Willamette National Forest (see entry this zone).

## Champoeg State Heritage Area

Oregon Parks and Recreation Department
587 acres.

N of Salem. From I-5, exit 278, 27 mi. S of Portland.

Wooded setting on Willamette River. Although not an outstanding natural area, it has interest because of an arboretum and botanical garden featuring flora native to OR. *Visitor center* depicts aspects of OR history.

### Activities

*Camping:* 48 sites. Yurts. All year.

*Hiking:* 10 mi. of trails.

*Mountain biking:* Can use hiking trails.

### Headquarters

OR Parks and Recreation Dept., 7679 Champoeg Rd. N.E., St. Paul, OR 97137; (541) 633-8170.

## Columbia River Gorge National Scenic Area

(See also zone 3 entry.)
U.S. Forest Service/States of Oregon and Washington/4 tribal governments/6 local counties
300,000 acres in OR and WA.

OR section extends from the Sandy River near Troutdale for 80 mi. E to the Deschutes River. Along I-84 E of Portland.

A National Scenic Area (NSA) is an area in which rural and scenic areas are protected while community growth and development are encouraged. The Columbia River Gorge NSA was created by Congress in 1986.

The Columbia River Gorge itself is a deep canyon between WA and OR, a water route through the Cascade Mountains. Slopes rise steeply to 1,500 ft. and more, close to the river, with nearby mountains to over 4,000 ft. The w portion, near Portland, has many spectacular waterfalls and sections of rain forest. This is the world's greatest concentration of waterfalls, 11 in total, including the famous 620 ft. Multnomah Falls, one of the highest in the U.S. Beyond the mountains, E of Hood River, the gorge opens on a landscape of oaks and grasslands, blending into sagebrush desert. This is drier, warmer climate. Wildflower enthusiasts may want to visit *McCall Nature Preserve* and *Rowena Plateau*.

This was originally one of the continent's most scenic areas. However, only scattered bits of shoreline remain in public ownership. I-84, close to the river, is the quickest route on the OR side along the gorge, and is heavily traveled. The older and more leisurely Historic Columbia River Hwy, running parallel to I-84, still offers some lovely cliffside panoramas. Three bridges, at Cascade Locks, Hood River, and The Dalles, will take you across to the WA side.

The gorge is the only sea-level passage through the Cascade Range, yet it also reaches 4,055 ft. at Larch Mountain. The differences between sea level and subalpine environments create great diversity of plants and wildlife. Here one can find Barrett's penstemon and the Columbia Gorge daisy.

In the gorge as a whole, there are 200 mi. of maintained trails at many hiking levels.

The river's flow has been blocked by dams. Mining, industrial and commercial development, and suburban sprawl had threatened the remaining natural areas. The National Scenic Area was established in hopes of guiding rather than halting further development.

See also OR entry in zone 3, and WA entry in zone 2.

### Headquarters

U.S. Forest Service, Pacific NW Region, 902 Wasco Ave., Suite 200, Hood River, OR 97031; (541) 386-2333.

## Elijah Bristow State Park

Oregon Parks and Recreation Department
848 acres.

15 mi. SE of Eugene on Hwy 58.

On S bank of the Middle Fork, Willamette River, just below Dexter Dam; at SE end of the Willamette Valley, close to the Cascade Range foothills. Scenic river shore forest, largely undeveloped; most of the site will remain in its natural condition. An area ¾ mi. downstream from the dam has tall cottonwoods, some Douglas-fir, western red cedar. W side of river is an island, nesting for herons, osprey. Mainland portion has 2 water areas, Channel Lake and Lost Creek, and the greatest variety of trees in the Park—and active beavers.

**Plants:** Tree species also include grand fir, western hemlock, western yew, incense cedar, western hazel, bigleaf maple, river willow. Shrubs include Oregon grape, salal, Scotch broom, blackberry, snowberry, poison oak. Wildflowers include trillium, fringe cup, buttercup, larkspur, bleeding heart, lupines, iris, camas lily.

**Birds:** Include osprey, turkey vulture, red-tailed hawk, kestrel, mallard, pintail, wood duck, kingfisher, great blue heron, killdeer, rufous-sided towhee, scrub jay, solitary vireo, fox sparrow. Bald eagle seen occasionally.

**Mammals:** Include black-tailed deer, red fox, cottontail, beaver, muskrat, coyote, black bear, ground squirrel, chickaree, pocket gopher. The ranger also told us: "There's got to be mountain lions with as many deer as we have, but no sightings as yet."

## Activities

*Hiking:* 1-mi. loop trail. 10 mi. of multiuse trails along the banks of the Willamette River and within the Park.

*Horse riding, mountain biking:* 10 mi. of multiuse trails (see above).

*Canoeing, kayaking:* Beginning of 208-mi. canoe trail down Willamette River Greenway (see entry this zone). Park is located at River Mile 200.5 on the Middle Fork of the Willamette River.

**Nearby**

Dexter Lake and Lookout Point Lake (U.S. Army Corps of Engineers); both within Willamette National Forest (see entry this zone). Camping, fishing, swimming, boating.

**Headquarters**

OR Parks and Recreation Dept., 38263 Wheeler Rd., Dexter, OR 97431; (541) 726-7997.

## Milo McIver State Park

Oregon Parks and Recreation Department
951 acres.

5 mi. NW of Estacada, off Springwater Rd.

Broad rolling meadows and wooded areas on natural terraces above the Clackamas River. Panoramic view includes Mounts St. Helens, Adams, and Hood. Trees include Douglas-fir and western red cedar; understory of Oregon grape, ferns.

**Activities**

*Camping:* Campground has 44 sites; also group camp.

*Hiking:* 4 mi. of trails.

*Fishing:* Chinook salmon. State fish hatchery located within Park bounds.

*Horse riding:* Equestrian trail.

*Boating:* Current is swift, may be treacherous; should be navigated only by the skilled.

**Headquarters**

OR Parks and Recreation Dept., 24101 S. Entrance Rd., Estacada, OR 97023; (503) 636-9886/630-7150.

## Mount Hood National Forest

U.S. Forest Service
1,060,253 acres.

From the Columbia River S. Crossed by US 26 and Hwy 35.

Many windows in Portland offer views of 11,235-ft. Mount Hood. The Forest is one of the most popular resorts in the NW, summer and winter. Within the Forest boundaries are ski resorts, lodges, golf courses, restaurants, shops, private residences, and other developments. Half a million people a year come just to drive the main roads and see the sights. Cattle graze, timber is harvested, Christmas trees cut.

But visitors tend to congregate. It's a big Forest, and it's not difficult to find quiet places away from the main roads, trails where meetings with other hikers are infrequent.

The Forest straddles the Cascade Range. The area is mountainous, moderate to steep slopes, with over 4,500 mi. of streams, 161 lakes, 6 reservoirs. Snowfall is heavy in the high country. The skiing season begins in Nov. and ends about April, although one can still ski on the upper glaciers through the summer.

Over 3,000 mi. of Forest roads, mostly unpaved, varying conditions. Most were built for logging access. A Forest map is necessary.

**Plants:** 85% of the area is forested. Principal tree species are Douglas-fir, western hemlock, Pacific silver, noble, and grand firs, ponderosa pine. Old-growth stands can be seen in several areas, notably Bagby Hot Springs and Bull of the Woods. Understory species include rhododendron, salal, Oregon grape, vine maple, huckleberry, bear grass, sword fern. Many wildflowers, but no list available. Reported above timberline: sulphur flower, penstemon, Jacob's ladder, arnica, paintbrush, Cascade aster, yarrow.

**Birds:** Checklist of 132 species limited to Mount Hood's S slope, a transition zone with 9,000-ft. altitude range. Species noted include pied-billed grebe, great blue and green-backed herons, tundra swan, Canada and white-fronted geese, mallard, wood duck, Barrow's goldeneye, harlequin duck, hooded and common mergansers, sharp-shinned, Cooper's, and red-tailed hawks, golden and bald eagles, osprey, kestrel, gray and Steller's jays, band-tailed pigeon, rock and mourning doves, barn, screech, and great horned owls, mountain bluebird, dipper, cedar waxwing. Also 7 woodpeckers, 8 flycatchers, 5 swallows, 3 chickadees, 3 nuthatches, 5 wrens, 9 warblers, 4 finches, 2 crossbills.

**Mammals:** No checklist available. Species reported include marmot, porcupine, northern flying squirrel, chickaree, golden-mantled ground squirrel, pika, chipmunk, shrew, coast mole, many bats, snowshoe hare, short- and long-tailed weasels, marten, spotted skunk, mule deer, mountain lion, bobcat, black bear.

## Features

*Mount Jefferson Wilderness:* 99,600 acres. Dominated by 10,497-ft. Mount Jefferson. Lowest point in the area is 3,000 ft. 5 glaciers on the mountain. Alpine meadows, lakes seen only by hikers, many streams. Area is a volcanic plateau with several large, steep-sided extinct or dormant volcanos, small younger cones, lava flows. About 62% forested. More than 160 mi. of trails, including 36 mi. of the Pacific Crest Trail. Numerous lakes, about 60 offering opportunity for fishing. About 75 in. of precipitation annually, more than half as snow. Snowfall may begin in Oct., snow cover lasts into summer. The area includes portions of the Deschutes (zone 3) and Willamette (zone 2) National Forests (see entries). *Wilderness permit required. Special regulations govern use of horses.*

*Mount Hood Wilderness:* 47,100 acres. Includes the peak of Mount Hood and slopes on the W, N, and E, extending W almost to Zigzag. About half alpine, high meadows with thin soil, fragile vegetation. *Wilderness permit required. Horses prohibited on many trails.*

*Bull of the Woods Wilderness:* 22,000 acres. Numerous small lakes. Bull of the Woods peak, central portion of area, 5,523 ft. Timbered slopes and valleys.

*Columbia Wilderness:* 40,900 acres. Above the sheer cliffs of the Columbia River Gorge. Shown on some maps as "Columbia River Gorge National Scenic Area." For about 28 mi. E of Multnomah Falls, the Forest boundary comes close to I-80N and the river. Most of the land along the river is privately owned, and much of it has been developed. The Interstate is OR's principal W–E route. Along the route are many parking areas and trailheads. This is a popular hiking area, only a few miles from Portland on the Interstate, scenic, with mild winters. However, most hikers are day-trippers. With trail information, a backpacker should have little difficulty finding reasonable solitude in the backcountry.

The area has broad, flat ridgetops; deep, steep-sloped drainages; mountain peaks; lakes; waterfalls; cliffs; chasms. Elevations from 100 ft. near the river to 4,900 ft. on Mount Defiance. Special bird and mammal lists for the gorge have been prepared by the Skamania County Resource Agent and are available from the Columbia River Gorge NSA. *Forest Trails of the Columbia Gorge* (see Publications) lists 32 trails, from 0.6 to 21.1 mi. in length, with the elevation change for each. Loop trails range from 1.2 to 11.2 mi. The Pacific Crest Trail crosses the area.

Hikers should be aware that the Bull Run Watershed Management unit, on the SW of this area, is closed to public use, except for a segment of the PCT.

*Multnomah Falls,* a major feature on the gorge, is also part of the NSA.

*Salmon-Huckleberry Area:* 68,000 acres. SW of Mount Hood, directly S of Zigzag. Forested slopes and ridges of the South Fork of the Salmon River and Mack Hall Creek. Salmon Butte, 4,877 ft., is a landmark and viewpoint; reached by trail linking 2 Forest roads. Rain forest; dense stands of Douglas-fir, true firs, western red cedar, western hemlock, with dense understory. Hiking on moderate slopes.

*Olallie Scenic Area:* 10,798 acres on the crest of the Cascade Range, adjoins Mount Jefferson Wilderness and Warm Springs Indian Reservation. Not classed as wilderness, but most of it is reached only by trail. Features include *Breitenbush Cascades,* river dropping 1,600 ft. in 0.8 mi. into a deep canyon; *Breitenbush Lake,* 60 acres, at 5,500 ft. elevation; *Olallie Meadow,* once a lake, now a marshy area slowly becoming forested; many wildflowers; *Olallie Butte,* 7,215 ft., highest cinder cone in the Cascade Range. *Olallie Lake,* 238 acres, is largest of several lakes in the area. More than 45 mi. of trails, including 15 mi. of Pacific Crest Trail. *Oregon Skyline Rd., S-42,* is scenic but primitive—not for trailers.

*Columbia River Scenic Hwy,* US 30, about 52 mi. from Wahkeena Falls to Mount Hood Loop Hwy, S-35. The National Forest boundary is close to the road and river. Indeed, a few small parcels are on the river but across railroad tracks. Many falls and other scenic features along the way. Parking areas and trailheads.

Combined with the *Mount Hood Loop* and US 26, this offers a 170-mi. auto tour from Portland. A leaflet describes features along the way and interesting side trips.

## Activities

*Camping:* 107 campgrounds, over 2,000 sites. Seasons vary with elevation and weather, some campgrounds opening March and April, others not until July. Informal camping except where posted. Reservations accepted.

*Hiking, backpacking:* 1,170 mi. of established trails, plus many more mi. of little-used Forest roads. High country trails may not be open until July, but good hiking is available at lower altitudes. Wilderness hiking requires permit and observance of special rules. In addition to the maps listed under Publications, trail information sheets are available at HQ and Ranger Districts.

*Hunting:* Elk, deer, black bear, blue and ruffed grouse, quail, wild turkey.

*Fishing:* 1,500 mi. of trout streams, 277 mi. of salmon and steelhead streams. Also lake fishing.

*Boating:* Only 6 of the lakes and reservoirs exceed 100 acres. Ramps are indicated on 3. Boats with motors are prohibited on some lakes. Boats are used chiefly by fishermen.

*Horse riding:* Horse trails in all Ranger Districts. Outfitters may change from year to year; inquire.

*Skiing:* Several commercial ski areas operate within the Forest. HQ will supply leaflets.

*Ski touring, snowmobiling:* Winter sports map shows trails suitable for ski touring, snowmobiling, as well as closed routes.

## Publications

Maps: Forest, $3.25; *Forest Trails of the Columbia Gorge,* $6.95; *Lakes of the Mt. Hood National Forest;* Mt. Hood Wilderness, $6.95; Mt. Jefferson Wilderness, $6.95; Olallie Scenic Area, $0.50.

Trail guides: Castle Canyon Trail; Cool Creek Trail; Day Hikes Around Mt. Hood; Eagle Creek Trail; Flag Mountain Trail; Horse Trails on the Zigzag District; Huckleberry Trail System; Mountain Meadows Loop Trail; Salmon Butte Trail; Salmon River–Hunchback Trail System; Veda Lake Trail; Zigzag Mountain Trail System.

Leaflets: *Bagby Hot Springs; Birds of Mt. Hood's S. Slope* (checklist); *Bull of the Lake* (includes map); *Camping Outside a Campground; Climbing Mt. Hood; Lost Lake; Multnomah Falls; Oregon Scenic Highway Drive, Mt. Hood Loop* (includes map); *Rock Lakes Basin* (includes map); *Timberline Wildlife.* Mimeo information pages: Big Slide Lake; Columbia Gorge District Scenic Drive; Hideaway Lake; Mother Lode Lakes; Pansy Lake; Round Lake; Welcome Lakes.

**Headquarters**
U.S. Forest Service, 2955 N.E. Division St., Gresham, OR 97030; (503) 666-0771.

**Ranger Districts**
Barlow R.D., Dufur, OR 97021; (541) 467-2291. Bear Springs R.D., Rt. 1, Box 222, Maupin, OR 97037; (541) 328-6211. Clackamas R.D., 61431 E. Hwy 224, Estacada, OR 97023; (503) 630-6861. Columbia River Gorge National Scenic Area, 902 Wasco Ave, Suite 200, Hood River, OR 97031; (541) 386-2333. Hood River R.D., 6780 Hwy 35, Mt. Hood, OR 97041; (503) 352-6002. Zigzag R.D., Zigzag, OR 97973; (503) 622-3191.

**Santiam State Forest**

Oregon Department of Forestry
47,700 acres.

From Salem, SE on Hwy 22. Much of the Forest land is near the Santiam River between Mill City and Detroit Dam. Access is by unpaved Forest roads; advisable to consult map at HQ.

Gentle to very steep slopes on Willamette Valley side of the Cascade Mountains. Elevations from 830 to 5,012 ft. Climate is moist: about 75 in. of precipitation annually. Much of the Forest was logged off and abandoned before 1940. In 1951, fire destroyed 21,400 acres of prime timber. Timber was salvaged and the land reforested. Now managed chiefly for timber production. North Santiam River is a whitewater stream. Several creeks, waterfalls.

**Plants:** 95% forested. No old-growth stands. Timber is harvested as it matures. Principal species: Douglas-fir, western hemlock, western red cedar at lower elevations; Douglas-fir, western hemlock, noble fir above. Red alder, bigleaf maple, black cottonwood along creeks. Understory of vine maple, salal, Oregon grape, sword fern, blackberry, thimbleberry. Flowering species include rhododendron, mountain ash, dogwood, salmonberry.

**Birds:** Common species include pileated woodpecker, nighthawk, junco, grosbeak, robin, bushtit, wood pewee, California quail, rufous hummingbird, northern flicker, pine siskin.

**Mammals:** Black-tailed deer, beaver, California ground squirrel, chickaree, snowshoe hare, chipmunk, mountain beaver, coyote. Seldom seen: elk, river otter, marten, bobcat, black bear, mountain lion.

## Interpretation
*Maples Wayside Nature Trail,* 35 mi. E of Salem on Hwy 22. Self-guiding, ¼ mi.

## Activities
*Camping:* Scattered primitive sites.

*Hiking:* Only 2 mi. of established trails, to Shelburg Falls and Butte Creek Falls. Those interested in hiking elsewhere are advised to consult HQ.

*Hunting:* Deer, bear, elk.

*Fishing:* Trout, salmon, steelhead.

*Canoeing/kayaking:* River is for experts only. Detailed information necessary.

## Nearby
Willamette National Forest (see entry this zone).

## Publications
Forest leaflet.

Nature trail guide.

## Headquarters
OR Dept. of Forestry, 22965 N. Fork Rd., S.E., Lyons, OR 97358; (503) 859-2151.

## Sauvie Island Wildlife Area

Oregon Department of Fish and Wildlife
13,000 acres.

About 1 mi. N of Portland city line on US 30, turn E on Sauvie Island
Bridge. Cross bridge, then N 2 mi. on Sauvie Island Rd. to HQ.

*Open:* 4 A.M.–10 P.M.

Large, irregularly shaped island in the Columbia River. S portion and
several tracts in N portion are private land. Much of the N portion is
low-lying, with lakes, channels, seasonal impoundments, marshes.
Also oak-ash woodlands, grasslands, and cultivated fields. Embankment and sand beach along the Columbia River.

Chiefly for migrating and wintering waterfowl. About half of the
area is open to hunting seasonally; the balance is wildlife refuge. Several roads lead to parking areas and trailheads. (See map available at
HQ.) Some wildlife viewing is possible from autos, but limited during
hunting season, when access by nonhunters is restricted.

**Birds:** Seasonally, large numbers of tundra swan, sandhill crane, mallard, pintail, wigeon, green-winged teal. In late November, flights of
as many as 150,000 waterfowl can be seen. Other common species
include great blue heron, Canada goose, cinnamon teal, shoveler,
wood duck, bufflehead, ruddy duck, common merganser. Common
raptors: turkey vulture, red-tailed hawk, northern harrier, kestrel. Bald
eagle late Nov. through the winter. California quail and pheasant
both common. Also shorebirds: Virginia rail, sora, coot, killdeer,
snipe, sandpipers. Also northern flicker, hairy and downy woodpeckers, willow flycatcher, wood pewee, barn swallow, scrub jay, crow,
black-capped chickadee, bushtit, white-breasted nuthatch. 2 wrens,
robin, varied thrush, kinglets, many warblers, sparrows, finches,
black-headed grosbeak, Bullock's oriole.

**Mammals:** Among those known or believed to be present are opossum, shrews, moles, little brown and big brown bats, brush rabbit,
Townsend chipmunk, northern flying squirrel, ground squirrel,
beaver, nutria, muskrat, pocket gopher, wood rat, voles, coyote, red

fox, raccoon, striped skunk, mink, mule deer. Occasional Columbian white-tailed deer on N end of island.

### Features

*Oak Island,* with oak groves, offers access to Sturgeon Lake, largest body of water on the island. Fishing, swimming. Closed to all entry except by permit during waterfowl hunting season.

*Rentenaar Rd.,* reached from Reeder Rd. on E side, is favored observation area to see late-afternoon flights of waterfowl during hunting season. Access to lower dike, foot route to McNary Lakes, Pete's Slough, other interior points, except in waterfowl hunting season.

*Steelman Rd.,* continuation of Sauvie Island Rd., goes N to Crane Lake. From here, foot access to several points on W side of island. Closed except by permit from waterfowl hunting season to April 15.

*Walton Beach,* on Columbia River, on Reeder Rd. Fishing, swimming. Open year-round.

### Activities

*Hiking:* On secondary roads, dikes, trails, Columbia River beach, etc. Much of the area is accessible only on foot or by small boat. Non-hunters are excluded from some areas in hunting season.

*Hunting:* Daily permit required. By permit, limited hunting for certain nongame species in the off-season.

*Fishing:* Chiefly warm-water species, primarily catfish, bass, crappie. Trout in Halderman Pond on Oak Island.

*Swimming:* Lake, river. No supervision.

*Boating:* Several launching sites. Many narrow channels are best explored by canoe or kayak; be alert for tide changes and swift tidal currents. Sturgeon Lake is extremely shallow in summer and affected by tides.

### Publications

Leaflet with map.

Wildlife checklist.

### Headquarters

OR Dept. of Fish and Wildlife, 506 S.W. Mill St., Portland, OR 97208; (503) 229-5403. Area manager, on the island: (503) 621-3488.

## Silver Falls State Park

Oregon Parks and Recreation Department
8,700 acres.

26 mi. E of Salem on Hwy 214.    

OR's largest State Park, featuring 10 waterfalls, 5 over 100 ft. high.
North and South Forks of Silver Creek cut deep gorges in the foothills
of the Cascade Mountains. All of the falls are seen from within the
canyon; moist microclimate, moss draped heavily on tree branches,
deep moss on the ground, many ferns in the forest understory.

The Park is well known and popular. South Falls day-use area is
likely to be crowded on any fine weekend. However, the campground
and picnic areas are the places where people congregate. Canyon
trails are likely to be uncrowded early and late in the day.

**Plants:** Heavily wooded, chiefly Douglas-fir and western hemlock.
Some old-growth stands with large specimens. Understory includes
salal, Oregon grape, vine maple, salmonberry, sword and maidenhair
ferns. Wildflowers include Klamath weed, forget-me-not, buttercup,
wild ginger, foxglove, goatsbeard, coral bells, monkeyflower, lily-of-
the-valley, ox eye daisy, starflower, bleeding heart, spring beauty.

**Birds:** Species mentioned or noted are dipper, northern flicker, white-
crowned sparrow, California quail, downy woodpecker, wood pewee,
black-capped chickadee, golden-crowned kinglet, Brewer's blackbird,
rufous-sided towhee, dark-eyed junco.

**Mammals:** No data. Beaver are active in the Park.

### Features
*Silver Creek Canyon Trail,* 6½-mi. circuit with optional shorter hikes.
Canyon can be entered at several points, and trail has shorter loops.
10 waterfalls along the trail, highest 184 ft.

### Activities
*Camping:* 61 sites. Mid-April to end of Oct.

*Hiking:* In addition to canyon trails, 12 mi. of trails in SE half of Park.

*Swimming:* South Fork is dammed at day-use area, but water is only waist deep.

*Horse riding:* Stable near entrance. Equestrian trails.

## Publications

Leaflet with map. (May not be available.)

Map.

Canyon trail guide.

## Headquarters

OR Parks and Recreation Dept., 20024 Silver Falls Hwy, S.E., Sublimity, OR 97385; (503) 873-8681.

## Tryon Creek State Park

Oregon Parks and Recreation Department
635 acres.

SW Portland, off I-5 on Terwilliger Blvd.

Small Park, a logging site in the late 1800s. The forest has naturally regrown into a mixture of red alder, Douglas-fir, bigleaf maple, and western red cedar. Many small mammals, including beaver, and over 50 species of birds make this Park their home.

## Interpretation

A *nature center* provides general Park information and educational exhibits and programs.

3½-mi. loop *nature trails* surround the center.

## Activities

*Hiking:* 8 mi. of trails, including Trillium Trail for people of all abilities.

*Horse riding:* 3.5 mi. of trails.

*Bicycling:* 3 mi. of paved trail (part of Portland's biking system).

## Headquarters

OR Parks and Recreation Dept., 11321 S.W. Terwilliger Blvd., Portland, OR 97219; (503) 636-9886.

## Willamette National Forest

U.S. Forest Service
1,675,157 acres.

Midway between Eugene and Bend, about 110 mi. N to S, 40 mi. wide.
Crossed by US 20, Hwys 22, 126, 58.

On the W slope of the Cascade Mountains. Largest National Forest in
OR; with adjacent Forests forms a block of over 9 million acres covering most of the OR Cascades.

Precipitation is heavy, 50–120 in. a year, much as snow piling deep
on the high slopes each winter. Moisture and favorable soils make this
an outstanding timber-producing area. The runoff flows through over
1,500 mi. of rivers and streams, into 335 natural lakes and many reservoirs.

The Forest includes some of the highest country in the Cascades.
Elevations range from 10,497 ft. at the top of Mount Jefferson in the
NE corner down to 935 ft. at the W edge. The steepest slopes are in the
many deeply cut stream canyons.

Closeness to population centers and outstanding scenery have
made the Willamette one of the most popular Forests. Many visitors
come just to drive around one of the several scenic loops. Others congregate at the reservoirs just inside the W boundary. The several large
wilderness areas and other roadless areas offer hikers and backpackers
ample opportunities for solitude.

**Plants:** Densely forested, chiefly Douglas-fir, with noble fir, mountain
hemlock, grand fir, and lodgepole pine at higher elevations. Although
many variations occur, depending on the situations and histories of
stands, a typical pattern has Douglas-fir as the dominant species, with
associated western hemlock and western red cedar, the understory
including Oregon grape, vine maple, salal, trailing blackberry, rhododendron, golden chinquapin, ferns. Wildflowers include: Oregon
oxalis, inside-out flower, twinflower, vanilla leaf, evergreen violet,
sweetscented bedstraw, fairybells. Nonforested areas include rock outcrops and scree slopes, mountain meadows, bogs.

**Birds:** Checklist available. Species reported include 3 grebes, great blue heron, common egret, Canada and white-fronted geese, mallard, pintail, green-winged and cinnamon teals, wigeon, shoveler, wood duck, common goldeneye, hooded merganser. Also goshawk, sharp-shinned, Cooper's, red-tailed, and rough-legged hawks, bald eagle, osprey, blue and ruffed grouse, California and mountain quail, band-tailed pigeon, 5 owls, 3 hummingbirds, northern flicker, Williamson's sapsucker, 7 woodpeckers, 3 chickadees, 8 warblers.

**Mammals:** No checklist. Species reported include brush rabbit, snowshoe hare, mountain beaver, chipmunk, marmot, gray squirrel, pocket gopher, beaver, deer mouse, porcupine, coyote, red and gray foxes, raccoon, marten, fisher, weasel, mink, wolverine, spotted skunk, river otter, mountain lion, bobcat, Roosevelt elk, mule deer, black bear.

## Features

*Mount Washington Wilderness:* 52,738 acres, including 14,116 in the Deschutes National Forest (see entry zone 3). Rugged country topped by jagged peaks. Separated from Three Sisters Wilderness by Hwy 242. The 7,802-ft. mountain is a dissected volcano, the summit scraped bare by ice floes. Nearby is the "Black Wilderness," one of the largest lava sheets in the U.S. Near the center, Belknap Crater, 6,872 ft., is a cinder and ash cone, source of much of the lava flow. The Pacific Crest Trail enters the area at McKenzie Pass, crosses part of the lava field, skirts Belknap Crater, and proceeds N on the W slopes of Mount Washington to a region of dense forest and high lakes. A lower-altitude trail loops around 6,116-ft. Scott Mountain, passing near many small lakes. Hiking season begins June or July, depending on snow cover.

*Three Sisters Wilderness:* 286,708 acres, including 94,370 acres in the Deschutes National Forest (see entry zone 3). The Three Sisters are snowcapped high peaks. 14 glaciers. Volcanic landscape. Forests, alpine meadows, many lakes, waterfalls. Separated from Mount Washington Wilderness by Hwy 242. Includes about 40 mi. of Pacific Crest Trail, plus a network of other trails. Area is usually accessible by July, snow remaining on some trails until Aug. Cool evenings; snow can fall in summer. Good trout fishing.

*Mount Jefferson Wilderness:* 107,008 acres, including 32,734 acres in the Deschutes National Forest and 5,021 acres in the Mount Hood National Forest (see entry this zone). 5 glaciers on the 10,497-ft.

mountain. Much of the high country is open and parklike, with scattered trees, scree slopes, patches of snow remaining through most of the summer. Lowest elevation is 3,000 ft. Most lakes and meadows are between 5,000–6,000 ft. About 150 lakes, most of them tiny, about 60 offering fishing. 36 mi. of the Pacific Crest Trail, more than 120 mi. of other trails.

*Diamond Peak Wilderness:* 54,185 acres, including 34,413 acres in the Deschutes National Forest (see entry zone 3). Area surrounds 8,744-ft. Diamond Peak, highest point in this area along the Cascade Crest. Boundaries are within 1 mi. of Odell, Summit, and Crescent Lakes. Many smaller lakes within area. About 50 mi. of trail, including a section of the PCT. Bushwhacking is feasible with map and compass.

*Wilderness permits are required for entry to the preceding areas.*

*Waldo Lake Recreation Area:* 48,993 acres. A 6,700-acre lake, 6 mi. long, at 5,414 ft. elevation. The area lies between the Three Sisters and Diamond Peak Wildernesses just W of the Cascade Crest. Not a wilderness, because paved roads lead to developments on the E side, but the W and N shores are primitive, reached only on foot or by boat, and developments are set back from the E shore. Many miles of trails lead to countless small lakes, 286-ft. Salt Creek Falls, various peaks, and the Pacific Crest Trail. A 20-mi. loop trail circles Waldo Lake. Boating, but speed limited to 10 mph. Three campgrounds, 208 sites.

*McKenzie Pass* on Hwy 242 offers an extraordinary vista of recent volcanic activity from Mount Hood to the Three Sisters. Exhibits and leaflet at the *Dee Wright Observatory.* The pass is usually open July–Oct., otherwise closed by snow.

*Detroit, Blue River, Cougar,* and *Hills Creek Lakes* are U.S. Army Corps of Engineers lakes lying wholly or partially within the National Forest, on or near the W boundary. These and several Corps lakes nearby, outside the Forest, are popular recreation areas, chiefly for water-based activities. The Forest Service has campgrounds at the lakes. The lakes are subject to considerable drawdown in dry weather.

### Interpretation

*Lava River Interpretive Trail* at McKenzie Pass on Hwy 242 W of Sisters. ½-mi. loop.

*Evening programs* are scheduled at some larger campgrounds in summer. Look for posted notices.

## Activities

*Camping:* More than 80 campgrounds, 1,200 sites. Seasonal openings range from April 15–July 1, closings from Sept. 15–Nov. 30.

*Hiking, backpacking:* 1,400 mi. of trails, including trails in the wilderness areas and Waldo Lake Recreation Area. McKenzie River National Recreation Trail, 28 mi., follows the McKenzie River and Hwy 126 from Fish Lake, near US 20, S to McKenzie Bridge. Sections available from the road for short hikes. Fall Creek National Recreation Trail, 13 mi., begins just inside the Forest's W boundary, SE of Eugene, E of Fall Creek Lake, on Forest Rd. 18. Follows Fall Creek. Usually snow-free in winter. Suitable for short or overnight hikes.

*Hunting:* Deer, elk.

*Fishing:* Brook, rainbow, cutthroat trout.

*Swimming:* Chiefly at Waldo Lake and Corps of Engineers lakes.

*Boating:* Waldo Lake (10 mph limit) and Corps of Engineers lakes.

*Canoeing, kayaking:* Whitewater on McKenzie River.

*Horse riding:* Pack trips into wilderness areas. Pack and saddle stock, guide service, available at Stayton, OR.

*Skiing:* Willamette Ski Area. Dec.–March.

*Ski touring:* Trails S from Waldo Lake to Odell Lake and Crescent Lake in Deschutes National Forest, continuing to and into Crater Lake National Park.

## Adjacent or Nearby

Mount Hood National Forest (zone 2), Deschutes National Forest (zone 3), Umpqua National Forest (zone 5), Cascadia State Park (zone 2). See entries.

## Publications

Maps: Forest, $3.25; Diamond Peak Wilderness, $5.25; Mt. Jefferson Wilderness, $6.25; Mt. Washington Wilderness, $6.25; Three Sisters Wilderness, $6.25; Waldo Lake Recreation Area, $2.25.

Trail guides: *Fall Creek National Recreation Trail; McKenzie River National Recreation Trail; Willamette Pass Ski Tours,* $1.50; *Willamette Trails.* Bird checklist.

*Lakes of the Willamette National Forest.*

*McKenzie Pass* (leaflet).

*Santiam Pass Winter Recreation Area,* $2.50.

## Headquarters

U.S. Forest Service, 210 E. 11th Ave., Eugene, OR 97401; (541) 465-6521.

## Ranger Districts

Blue River R.D., Blue River, OR 97413; (541) 822-3317. Detroit R.D., Star Rt., Box 320, Mill City, OR 97360; (541) 854-3366. Lowell R.D., P.O. Box 325, Lowell, OR 97452; (541) 937-2129. McKenzie R.D., McKenzie Bridge, OR 97401; (541) 822-3381. Oakridge R.D., 46375 Hwy 58, Westfir, OR 97492; (541) 782-2291. Rigdon R.D., 48458 Hwy 58, Oakridge, OR 97463; (541) 782-2283. Sweet Home R.D., 4431 Hwy 20, Sweet Home, OR 97386.

## Willamette River Greenway

Oregon Parks and Recreation Department
4,212 acres (state land).

From Cottage Grove Reservoir, near Cottage Grove, and Dexter Reservoir, near Dexter, to Multnomah Channel and Columbia River at Sauvie Island.

The Willamette River flows for over 200 mi. through the Willamette Valley. More than half the state's population lives within 10 mi. of the river. Most lands bordering the river are privately owned. The river flows through towns and past factories, mills, warehouses, farms, and homes.

The Greenway Program is a cooperative state and local effort to maintain and enhance the remaining natural qualities of lands along the river. At intervals are state and local parks, river-access points, and other public sites.

Average river flow is 2–4 mph. Some upstream sections are swift and shallow, limiting use to rafts, canoes, and drift boats. Campgrounds are too infrequent to permit boat camping from end to end, but trips of a few days can be planned.

## Publication

*Willamette River Recreation Guide,* $1.00 (available on mailed request).

**Headquarters**
OR Parks and Recreation Dept., 1115 Commercial St. N.E., Salem, OR
97310-1001; (503) 378-6305.

## William L. Finley National Wildlife Refuge

U.S. Fish and Wildlife Service
5,325 acres.
From Corvallis, 10 mi. S on Hwy 99 W. W to entrance.

*Open:* Daylight hours.

Near the S end of the Willamette Valley. Mild, rainy winters provide
good environment for waterfowl. Mostly cleared farmland in ryegrass
and sudan grass. Hedgerows of rose and blackberry. Many artificial
ponds and marshes; water levels down substantially in summer.
Meandering creeks. Highest point: Pigeon Butte, 546 ft.

Best seen on foot. Two roads cross the site, which offer several
viewpoints. Summer visits are least rewarding.

**Plants:** About 700 acres of woodland: Oregon oak, maple, fir. Thickets
of Oregon ash. Many ferns, orchids, lilies in moist areas. In and
around impoundments: cattail, bur-reed, pondweeds, arrowhead,
water plantain. Great variety of grasses and sedges. Flowering species
include buttercups, columbine, larkspur, Oregon grape, poppy, bleeding heart, fringe cup, serviceberry, clovers, geraniums, hollyhocks,
violets, starflower, forget-me-not, daisy, thistles.

**Birds:** Entire population of dusky Canada goose winters in this
region. Seasonally common and abundant species include great blue
heron, tundra swan, mallard, pintail, green-winged teal, wigeon,
shoveler, wood duck, coot, dunlin, common snipe, turkey vulture,
northern harrier, red-tailed hawk, kestrel, California quail, pheasant,
killdeer, band-tailed pigeon, mourning dove, great horned owl, rufous
hummingbird, northern flicker, downy woodpecker, swallows, jays,
black-capped chickadee, bushtit, nuthatches, brown creeper, marsh
wren, robin, Swainson's and varied thrushes, kinglets, starling, 3 warblers.

**Mammals:** Include opossum, shrews, little brown and big brown bats, raccoon, striped skunk, red fox, ground squirrel, chipmunk, chickaree, giant pocket gopher, deer mouse, woodrats, nutria, brush rabbit, black-tailed deer, and Roosevelt elk.

## Interpretation

*Woodpeck Loop Trail,* self-guiding, passes several types of habitat.

*Current information* on bulletin boards and at *self-guiding kiosks.*

## Activities

*Hiking:* 10 mi. of trails. Cabell Marsh, Mill Hill, Pigeon Butte, other points of interest reached only on foot.

*Hunting:* In designated area. Special rules. Inquire.

*Fishing:* Marginal. Cutthroat trout.

*Much of the goose habitat is closed Nov.–May 1.*

## Publications

Refuge leaflet.

Checklists of birds, mammals, plants.

Nature trail guide.

Hunting information.

## Headquarters

U.S. Fish and Wildlife Service, Western Oregon Refuge Complex, 26208 Finley Refuge Rd. Corvallis, OR 97330; (541) 757-7236.

Z O N E

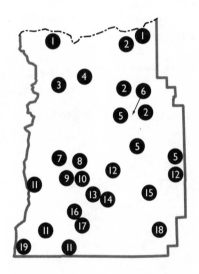

1. Columbia River Gorge National Scenic Area

2. John Day River (Mainstream, North Fork)

3. White River Wildlife Area

4. Deschutes River Recreation Lands

5. John Day Fossil Beds National Monument

6. Shelton State Park

7. Cove Palisades State Park

8. Crooked River National Grassland

9. Peter Skene Ogden State Scenic Viewpoint

10. Smith Rock State Park

11. Deschutes National Forest

12. Ochoco National Forest

13. Crooked River Canyon

14. Prineville Reservoir; Prineville Reservoir State Park

15. Crooked River, North and South Forks

16. Badlands

17. Dry River Canyon; Horse Ridge

18. Sand Hollow; Gerry Mountain; Logan Butte; Redman Rim; Sears Creek; Hampton Butte; Cougar Well; Hampton; Stockpile

19. LaPine State Park

Z O N E

Includes these counties:

| | | |
|---|---|---|
| Hood River | Gilliam | Crook |
| Wasco | Wheeler | Deschutes |
| Sherman | Jefferson | |

The N zone boundary is the Columbia River. The Hood, Deschutes, and John Day Rivers, flowing through the zone, empty into the Columbia, as do numerous lesser streams. The W boundary is the E slope of the Cascade Mountains. Part of Mount Hood and a substantial portion of the Mount Hood National Forest are in zone 3, but the entry appears in zone 2, which has the larger portion.

The Blue Mountains intrude into the zone from the NE; this is the high country of the Ochoco National Forest, the E central part of the zone. S of these mountains begins the extensive high desert country.

Three National Forests within the zone include more than 2 million acres, by far the largest part of the public lands. Some relatively small tracts of public domain, lands administered by the BLM, are along the John Day and Deschutes Rivers; still smaller tracts are around Lake Billy Chinook, the White River, and lesser streams. Much of the high desert country in the SE part of the zone is public domain, partly as large blocks with many inholdings, partly as checkerboard.

Except in the mountains, rainfall is scanty in the zone: less than 14 in. per year at The Dalles, about 12 at Bend, less than 10 at Prineville, still less in the high desert. Wheat and other field crops are grown in the NE region, both with and without irrigation. Cattle ranching is somewhat more common in the central region.

The larger rivers of the zone have interesting possibilities. Several entries describe sections of the Crooked River: the N and S Forks near the headwaters, a canyon S of Prineville, and a longer canyon downstream, partly within the Crooked River National Grassland. The John

Day River attracts whitewater boaters in the spring, but its flow drops sharply in summer; then its canyon can be explored on foot. The Deschutes River has many aspects: fearsome white water, placid stretches, a large lake; it flows through grassy meadows and deep, rugged canyons.

The zone includes magnificent ponderosa forests, extensive stands of juniper, and sagebrush deserts. Wildlife varies with the habitats. Mule deer are common in several sectors; elk and pronghorn occur in some localities, in relatively small numbers. The zone has no extensive wetlands to attract vast numbers of waterfowl, but both residents and migrants can be seen on many lakes and streams.

About a dozen State Parks are along the Columbia River within this zone. They are mentioned, collectively, in the entry for the Columbia River Gorge National Scenic Area, but none met our criteria for natural areas. About a dozen State Parks are clustered in the region around Prineville and Bend. Of these, several are noted because of their scenic qualities or their proximity to natural areas.

In the high desert region, as explained in the state introduction, we have described a few places that have exceptional features.

## Badlands

U.S. Bureau of Land Management
33,172 acres.

9 mi. E of Bend. N of US 20; S of Alfalfa.

About 10 mi. E–W, 9 mi. N–S, with many rolling hills and jagged dark reddish-brown and black basalt escarpments and outcroppings. Wind-blown sand has formed many small basins and valleys. Dense western juniper forest, including old stands, covers almost the entire area. Portions have been used for grazing, woodcutting, and a bombing range; now reverting to natural state. 58 mi. of primitive, unmaintained vehicle routes, most unused and reverting. Camping is at large.

**Plants:** Understory species include big sage, gray and green rabbitbrush, bitterbrush, Idaho fescue, wheatgrass, phlox, cheat grass.

## Headquarters

Bureau of Land Management, Prineville District, 3050 N.E. 3rd St., P.O. Box 550, Prineville, OR 97754; (541) 416-6700.

## Columbia River Gorge National Scenic Area

(See also zone 2 entry.)

Along I-84 close to the river from Bonneville to the zone boundary E of the intersection with Hwy 74.

The Columbia River Gorge still has scenic qualities: forested hillsides, massive canyon walls, striking rock formations, waterfalls, valleys of tributary streams. The Columbia River Gorge National Scenic Area was established 10 years ago in part to protect these qualities. But Bonneville Dam, The Dalles Dam, and John Day Dam have formed consecutive impoundments. Nowhere within this zone does the river flow free. A narrow strip along the shore includes heavily traveled I-84, railroad tracks, towns and cities, commercial and industrial establishments.

Trailheads at several points near I-84 exits give access to forested areas. Also near exits are a number of small State Parks, waysides, parking areas, and boat-launching facilities. Some have campgrounds. None met our criteria for entries. However, a trip through the gorge can be quite pleasant.

### Publications

*Bonneville Lock and Dam* (leaflet with information on parks and other facilities); *John Day Lock and Dam* (leaflet); *The Dalles Lock and Dam* (leaflet). All available from U.S. Army Corps of Engineers, Portland District, P.O. Box 2946, Portland, OR 97208-2946.

## Crooked River Canyon

U.S. Bureau of Land Management
13,586 acres.

From Prineville, 7 mi. S on Hwy 27.

The road first enters a steep-walled, narrow canyon: columnar basalt, cliffs, ledges, talus slopes. Here the river is swift and shallow, about 20 ft. wide. After 2 mi. the valley widens, the stream meandering through hayfields. 3 mi. farther the canyon again narrows. The BLM land is on both sides of the river, the larger portion extending W about 6 mi. Above the canyon, the land is relatively flat, sloping downward to the W, with some low rolling hills, occasional outcroppings of brown basalt.

Hwy 27 is on the E side of the river, often close to the stream, occasionally climbing to points offering good views. Access to the W side is offered by primitive BLM and county roads not shown on highway maps. Inquire locally or at the BLM's Prineville office. At the S end of the canyon, Hwy 27 crosses the dam impounding Prineville Reservoir.

**Plants:** A few large ponderosa along the river. Scattered clusters of juniper along the valley floor and slopes, with dense stands to the W. Big sagebrush, bitterbrush, green rabbitbrush, native bunchgrass. In W portion, areas of crested wheatgrass.

## Activities

*Camping:* Primitive campgrounds with designated sites are scattered along Hwy 27. Several, maintained by the BLM, have latrines, tables. There are also places where one can park beside the river. Another primitive campground is just beyond the dam, on the shore of the reservoir.

*Hiking:* The canyon is the most interesting portion of this site; side canyons and some moderate slopes offer opportunities. More than 10 mi. of primitive, unmaintained vehicle routes in the W portion.

*Boating:* Light boats can be launched on the reservoir S of the dam. However, the access track is steep and rough with a near-hairpin turn. Anything larger than a rowboat should be launched at Prineville Reservoir State Park (see entry this zone). The river is not suitable for canoeing, being shallow and rocky.

## Adjacent
Prineville Reservoir (see entry this zone).

## Headquarters
Bureau of Land Management, Prineville District, 3050 N.E. 3rd St., P.O. Box 550, Prineville, OR 97754; (541) 416-6700.

## Crooked River National Grassland

U.S. Forest Service
106,136 acres/151,138 acres within boundaries.

NW of Prineville. Largest block, irregular in shape, roughly a right triangle, mostly E of US 97, bisected by US 26, extending N from Jefferson County line. Other blocks around Lake Billy Chinook, extending SW around Crooked River Gorge and Deschutes River to Jefferson County line.

Land homesteaded around 1900. Included in submarginal farmlands acquired by government in 1930s. Now managed chiefly as grazing land. Elevations from about 2,200 to 5,108 ft. In the largest block, much of the area is relatively flat, rising to high buttes in the S. Numerous intermittent streams. Haystack Reservoir, 180 acres, offers boating, fishing.

The land around Lake Billy Chinook has more interesting features. Round Butte Dam backed water up three principal streams—the Metolius, Deschutes, and Crooked Rivers—forming a 4,000-acre lake consisting of three long, narrow arms in spectacular deep canyons. The Cove Palisades State Park is a popular resort with marina, cafe, store, campgrounds, and other developments, mostly on the E side of the E arm. The access road W from Culver on US 97 descends into the canyon to the marina, with fine vistas, loops S along the shore, crosses one arm of the lake to The Peninsula, then another to the Lower Desert.

### Features

*Lower Crooked River:* 9.8 mi. of designated Wild and Scenic River. This stretch, running from near Ogden State Wayside on US 97 to Lake Billy Chinook, is a winding river with rock walls 600–700 ft. tall. The stretch is extremely dangerous and for experts only.

*Middle Deschutes River:* 20 mi. of designated Wild and Scenic River. This section, from Odin Falls to Lake Billy Chinook, offers many recreational opportunities, including camping, hiking, fishing, swimming, and expert kayaking.

## Activities

*Camping:* Campground at Haystack Lake, 24 sites. Also camping at State Parks. Informal camping elsewhere on Forest Service land, unless posted.

*Hiking:* Primitive roads near and SW of Lake Billy Chinook. Bush-whacking feasible.

*Swimming:* Lake Billy Chinook.

*Boating:* Lake Billy Chinook and Haystack Reservoir.

*The National Grassland is administered by the Ochoco National Forest.*

## Publication

Forest map, $3.25 (includes Ochoco National Forest).

## Headquarters

U.S. Forest Service, Ochoco National Forest, P.O. Box 490, Prineville, Oregon 97554; (541) 475-9272.

## Crooked River, North Fork

U.S. Bureau of Land Management
11,080 acres.

E of Prineville, on S boundary of Ochoco National Forest (see entry this zone). No easy access and roads are not signed, but a Forest road is nearby. Consult the BLM's Prineville Office or Ochoco National Forest HQ.

Narrow canyon up to 900 ft. deep winds S from National Forest boundary. Almost vertical basalt walls. Steep hills W of canyon; basalt flows to E. Many side canyons. Upper Falls is near Forest boundary on private land. Lower Falls 11 mi. downstream. Upper Falls, unique in this desert country, drops 15–20 ft. into a pool.

**Plants:** Ponderosa pine forest at upper end of canyon, juniper-sage-brush toward lower end. Hills to W have juniper, Douglas-fir, pon-derosa, as well as sagebrush and associated desert species.

## Activities

*Camping:* At large. No facilities.

*Hiking:* The canyon can be hiked, with difficulty; be sure to get current local advice and permission from private landowners. Elsewhere, no maintained trails but 19 mi. of primitive ways, now reverting. Look out for rattlesnakes.

*Swimming:* Pool below Upper Falls.

## Adjacent

Ochoco National Forest (see entry this zone).

## Headquarters

Bureau of Land Management, Prineville District, 3050 N.E. 3rd St., P.O. Box 550, Prineville, OR 97754; (541) 416-6700.

........................................................................................

## Crooked River, South Fork

U.S. Bureau of Land Management
19,600 acres.

19 mi. NE of US 20 at Hampton. Access is from Camp Creek Rd. on the S or off Crooked River Hwy on the N end. E of Prineville. Inquire at the BLM's Prineville Office.

River has cut a steep-walled canyon up to 800 ft. deep in Twelvemile Table Mesa. Main canyon about 6 mi. long. E of canyon, mesa is relatively flat, open, offering miles of vistas. W of river are some low rolling hills, with steeper terrain the NW portion. Area lies between the Ochoco Mountains to the N and high lava plains to S. Wildlife is said to be abundant.

Canyon is open and relatively wide, with colorful pinnacles, caves, alluvial slopes and terraces. Several dirt tracks in or out. Several side canyons.

**Plants:** On N-facing slopes: juniper, big sagebrush, Idaho fescue, wheatgrass, needlegrass. Dense juniper stands in W portion; small, isolated juniper on mesa. Many wildflowers along river.

*Hiking, backpacking:* Easier access and easier hiking through this canyon than in North Fork Canyon. Hikers often start at Pickett Canyon, travel 12 mi. downstream to Crooked River Hwy. Best hiking seasons are late spring, early fall. River flow dwindles in summer. Look out for rattlesnakes.

## Headquarters

Bureau of Land Management, Prineville District, 3050 N.E. 3rd St., P.O. Box 550, Prineville, OR 97754; (541) 416-6700.

## Deschutes National Forest

U.S. Forest Service
1,602,809 acres/1,852,282 acres within boundaries.

On both sides of US 97 S and NW of Bend. Also crossed by US 20, and Hwys 242, 58, and 31.

This is the third-largest National Forest in OR, part of a huge block of National Forest land extending from the WA border to CA. On the E slope of the Cascade Mountains. Elevations from about 2,000 to 10,358 ft., most between 4,000 and 5,000 ft. Snowcapped peaks, craters, cinder cones, and other volcanic formations, some formed as recently as 1,400 years ago. Over 200 lakes and reservoirs, many of them more than 1 mi. high. 730 mi. of streams, including the headwaters of the Deschutes and Metolius Rivers. Forest slopes and valleys, high meadows. In 1990, Newberry National Volcanic Monument was created within the Forest. It is also administered by the Forest Service.

The Forest is popular in all seasons, recording over 3 million visitor-days per year. However, it has extensive roadless areas, and those who travel on foot or horseback can easily find isolation.

**Plants:** Ponderosa predominates through most of the area and is the chief species harvested. Lodgepole pine also common. Whitebark pine, usually found at altitudes over 5,000 ft., and sugar pine are widely distributed. Species occurring in more limited areas include Douglas-fir, incense cedar, Engelmann spruce, western larch, mountain hemlock, and six firs: grand, noble, Pacific silver, white, Shasta red, and subalpine. Juniper in drier E sections. Although conifers predominate, deciduous species include willows, black cottonwood, quaking aspen. Understory includes serviceberry, elderberry, mountain mahogany. Wildflowers are most abundant in mountain meadows, along forest edges and roadsides, and in moist places. Species include asters, lupines, cinquefoils, false lily-of-the-valley, calypso orchid, alpine pyrola, Indian pipe, lady's slipper, narrowleaf and roundleaf sundews, paintbrush, penstemons, monkeyflowers.

**Birds:** Checklist available. Large variety. Residents include great blue heron, Canada goose, mallard, ring-necked duck, Barrow's goldeneye, bufflehead, hooded and common mergansers, cormorant, goshawk, Cooper's, red-tailed, Swainson's, and ferruginous hawks, golden and bald eagles, prairie falcon, kestrel, blue, ruffed, and sage grouse, California and mountain quail, killdeer, 6 owl species, northern flicker, 6 woodpecker species, horned lark, 3 jays, 3 nuthatches, dipper, winter and canyon wrens, mountain bluebird, evening grosbeak, pine siskin, red crossbill, dark-eyed junco. Many others in migration.

**Mammals:** Checklist available. Mule deer, spring until late fall. A few Roosevelt elk. Pronghorn on desert fringe. Black bear, coyote, beaver, mink, otter, marten, skunk, badger. Also porcupine, pika, marmot, cottontail, black-tailed jackrabbit, snowshoe hare, flying squirrel, ground squirrels, chipmunk, deer mouse.

### Features

*Cascade Lakes Hwy,* also known as Century Dr., 76 mi. long, begins at Bend, extends W and S though the heart of the Forest, returning to US 97 at a point 25 mi. S of Bend. Fine views of snowcapped Three Sisters, Bachelor Butte, Broken Top, and other peaks. The road passes near many high mountain lakes, beside the Deschutes River, through tall conifer forest. Spur roads, paved and unpaved, lead to other lakes, campgrounds, and viewpoints. Along the way are well-marked trailheads with parking areas. Highest section often closed by snow until June or July.

Other scenic drives include *US 20,* NW from Sisters, over Santiam Pass. *Hwy 242,* W from Sisters, to McKenzie Pass. Closed in winter.

*Crane Prairie Reservoir:* 3,850 acres. Shallow, with many stumps and snags. Elevation 4,445 ft. Protected nesting area for osprey and bald eagle. Many waterfowl in fall. 5 campgrounds; boat launching; information center. Good place for wildlife observation. Road access.

*Crescent Lake:* 4,000 acres. Deep natural lake dammed to increased water storage. Elevation 4,580 ft. Surrounded by forest with stands of Douglas-fir, white fir, lodgepole, ponderosa. 12 mi. of shoreline. Campgrounds; boat launching; swimming. Fishing best in spring, early summer. Road access. Trails into nearby *Diamond Peak Wilderness.*

*Davis Lake:* 3,000 acres. Elevation 4,390 ft. Formed behind a rugged lava dam. Moderate depth. Boat launching, but motors can be used only to and from fishing sites, speed limited to 10 mph. A good lake for canoeing. Shoreline marshes, grass and bulrush. Surrounded by pine forests. Good area for birding: waterfowl and songbirds. Fishing for rainbow, coho, kokanee, whitefish. Campgrounds. Road access.

*Diamond Peak Wilderness:* 54,185 acres (including acreage in Willamette National Forest). Diamond Peak, 8,744 ft., is a popular climb, as is 7,128-ft. Mount Yoran. About 50 mi. of trails, including part of the Pacific Crest Trail. Usually accessible July–Oct. Many small lakes. Fishing streams. Mosquitoes a nuisance until Sept.

*Mount Jefferson Wilderness:* 107,008 acres (including acreage in Mount Hood and Willamette National Forests). Many peaks, lakes. Extensive trail system. Popular hiking area, day and overnight. Mount Jefferson, 10,497 ft., is second-highest peak in OR; perpetual glaciers. Nearly 100 lakes, many good for fishing. Season: July–Oct.

*Mount Washington Wilderness:* 52,738 acres (including acreage in Willamette National Forest). Adjoins Three Sisters Wilderness. Rugged volcanic landscape. Mount Washington, 7,802 ft., is a challenging climb, for the experienced. 66 lakes and potholes; good fishing. Pacific Crest Trail passes through. Season: July–Oct.

*Mount Thielson Wilderness:* 54,267 acres (including acreage in Umpqua and Winema National Forests). On Cascade Crest, elevations 4,200–9,182 ft. Headwaters of the Deschutes and North Umpqua Rivers, Cottonwood Creek. Vegetation representative of both E and W sides of the Cascades. About 70% forested: Douglas-fir, mountain hemlock, lodgepole, some ponderosa. Pacific Crest Trail passes through.

*Newberry National Volcanic Monument:* 56,000 acres. Includes *Lava Butte,* a 500-ft. cinder cone 6,000 years old. Extending W and N is a 6,117-acre lava field. Road access. *Newberry Caldera* is S of Lava Butte. Largest dormant volcano of the region, 8,000 ft. high, 25 mi. at base. The top has collapsed and enlarged repeatedly for hundreds of thousands of years. Cinder cones, lava, and pumice erupted as recently as

1,400 years ago. 2 lakes within the caldera at over 6,300 ft. elevation. Large obsidian flow also within caldera. Road access. Camping, trails, horse camp, boating, ski touring, snowmobiling. *Lava Cast Forest,* N of Newberry Caldera, is an ancient forest invaded by lava. *Lava River Cave,* 12 mi. S of Bend, off US 97. Main tunnel inside lava flow extends almost 1 mi. Visitors need sweaters, can rent lanterns. Nominal admission fee. *Paulina Peak,* on the edge of the caldera rim, at 7,984 ft. offers a stunning view of the caldera and the surrounding geologic landscape.

*Odell Lake:* 3,500 acres. Elevation 4,790 ft. Occupies an old glacial valley. About 6 mi. long, 1½ mi. wide, deep. Surrounding forest of firs: Pacific silver, Shasta red, subalpine, white, with Engelmann spruce, western and mountain hemlock, Douglas-fir, ponderosa, lodgepole, and white pines. Annual precipitation of over 70 in. supports luxuriant understory. Abundant wildlife. Kokanee and lake trout. 4 campgrounds; marina, boat launching. Road access.

*Three Sisters Wilderness:* 286,708 acres (including acreage in Willamette National Forest). Snowcapped Three Sisters are high peaks in Cascade Range. 14 glaciers. Area usually accessible July–Oct., snow remaining on some trails until Aug. Pacific Crest Trail crosses, about 40 mi. Volcanic landscape; many notable geologic features. Forests, alpine meadows, many lakes, waterfalls. Snow can occur in summer. Mosquitoes are a nuisance until mid-Aug. Good fishing.

### Interpretation

*Lava Lands visitor center,* on US 97 SW of Bend. Open daily 10–4. Phone: (541) 593-2421. Exhibits, slide shows. *Naturalist* on duty. Near many of area's geologic features. Number of short *nature trails.*

*Newberry Caldera Rim Trail* is a 21-mi. loop. 4 other hiking trails within the Monument of approximately 8 mi. in length.

### Activities

*Camping:* 125 campgrounds, including 8 within Newberry Caldera, over 2,000 sites. Campgrounds differ in size, accessibility, and facilities. Many are on or near lakes or stream, but *camping is prohibited within 100 ft. of the high-water line around many lakes. Some setback zones are greater than 100 ft. Look for postings.*

*Hiking, backpacking:* 550 mi. of trails. Also 10,000 mi. of roads, including dirt and primitive roads good for hiking. Many relatively short, undemanding trails to small lakes and other attractive camping locations. Also trails at lower elevations that can be used in winter.

Although many hikers use the Forest, only a minority of trails are heavily traveled. Ask a ranger to suggest a lightly used trail if you seek solitude.

*Hunting:* Mule deer is principal game. Elk are summer residents, bear scarce. Waterfowl on the larger lakes. Upland game birds include blue and ruffed grouse, quail, chukar.

*Fishing:* 158 lakes and reservoirs, elevations 1,940–7,240 ft., have stocked trout and salmon. Pools from less than 1 acre to over 5,000 acres. 247 mi. of fishable streams.

*Swimming:* Designated swimming areas on a number of lakes, usually at campgrounds. Elsewhere at your discretion.

*Boating:* Ramps on larger lakes. Special restrictions on many lakes: no motors, 10 mph limit, etc.

*Canoeing, kayaking, rafting:* Deschutes River is popular. Several dangerous falls and cascades; get information before launching. Metolius River is for experts; here, too, current conditions should be ascertained. Good canoeing and canoe camping on several lakes.

*Horse riding, pack trips:* Pack and saddle stock, guide services available; list of packers available. Some trails are closed to horses. In wilderness areas, horses are prohibited within 200 ft. of lakes and streams. Horse camp in Newberry Caldera.

*Skiing:* Bachelor Butte Ski Area, elevation 6,200 ft. Usual season Nov.–May. Willamette Pass Ski Area, elevation 5,120 ft., usual season Dec.–April.

*Ski touring, snowmobiling:* Abundance of dry snow; many sunny days in winter. Snowmobile route at Bachelor Butte, Cascade, Newberry Crater, Paulina Lake. Many areas suitable for ski touring.

### Adjacent
Fremont, Winema, and Umpqua National Forests (see entries zone 5). Willamette National Forest (see entry zone 2).

### Publications
Maps: Deschutes National Forest, $3.25; Mount Jefferson Wilderness, $6.95; Mount Washington Wilderness, $6.95; Newberry National Volcanic Monument; Three Sisters Wilderness, $6.95.

Bird, wildlife checklists.

Leaflets: *Cascade Lakes Highway, Crane Prairie Osprey Management Area, Deschutes National Forest, Fishing Directory, Floating on the Deschutes*

*River, Lakes of the Deschutes National Forest, Lava Butte Geological Area, Lava Cast Forest, Lava River Cave, Native Trees of the Deschutes, Newberry National Volcanic Monument: 101 Facts.*

Mimeo information pages: Bend River District Trails, Drifting on the Waters of the Deschutes National Forest, Fishing on the Deschutes National Forest, Headwaters of the Metolius River, Hiking Trails South of Crescent Lake, Hunting on the Deschutes National Forest, Sisters Ranger District Trails, Snow Guide.

### Headquarters
U.S. Forest Service, 1645 Hwy 20E, Bend, OR 97701; (541) 388-2715.

### Ranger Districts
Bend R.D., 1645 Hwy 20E, Bend, OR 97701; (541) 388-2715. Crescent R.D., P.O. Box 208, Crescent, OR 97733; (541) 433-3224. Fort Rock R.D., 1230 N.E. 3rd St., Bend, OR 97701; (541) 388-5664. Sisters R.D., P.O. Box 249, Sisters, OR 97759; (541) 549-2111.

### Deschutes River Recreation Lands
U.S. Bureau of Land Management

From US 197 at Tygh Valley, E about 8 mi. on Hwy 216.

We consider this site one of our most pleasant discoveries. Approaching the river, Hwy 216 descends into a winding canyon to a modern bridge that replaced Sherar's Bridge, built in 1860. This was a traditional Indian crossing, and pioneers floated their wagons across. Here the river drops over falls and enters a narrow cut. When we visited, Indians were fishing from high platforms with long-handled nets. A state biologist was monitoring the fish ladder.

½ mi. E of the bridge, a BLM road enters the scenic canyon, following the river downstream for 17 mi. The road is unpaved, rough in places but not difficult. The canyon is 600–800 ft. deep, walls generally steep to vertical, some talus. Occasional small side canyons. Basalt, shades of brown and tan with hints of red. Sparse desert vegetation. The river is wide, moderately swift, generally shallow but—at the time of our visit—deep enough for floating, with sections used by fishermen with outboards.

The BLM land is a relatively narrow strip along the river. Some of the private land along the rim is posted. The road dead-ends, with private land beyond. Occasional trains use the tracks across the river from the road.

Local fishermen and -women know about the canyon, but on a July visit only one other camping couple shared the canyon with us overnight.

## Activities

*Camping:* Primitive, informal campground at Sherar's Bridge, used by fisherwomen and -men. Camping also in designated sites along the 17-mi. road. 2 other primitive campgrounds, with restrooms, managed by the BLM.

*Hiking, backpacking:* It may be possible to hike to the river's junction with the Columbia, but this would require permission to cross several private landholdings.

*Fishing:* Steelhead, rainbow trout.

*Boating:* Rafting, kayaking, and canoeing from US 26 to Sherar's Bridge, 53 mi., *experts only.* Don't run falls at Sherar's Bridge. Put-in there for 45-mi. run to Columbia River. Rapids class II–IV, one portage around Sherar's Falls, a class VI. Fishermen and -women use powered jet boats in river, launching near end of the canyon road. *Motorized water craft are not allowed above Sherar's Bridge.* They are allowed below the bridge except on alternating Thursdays through Fridays from about mid-June to July. (Contact OR State Marine Board or the BLM about these and other river closings.) Avoid using the Lower Deschutes from Trout Creek to Sandy Beach during weekends from mid-July through first weekend in Sept.

## Headquarters
Bureau of Land Management, Prineville District, 3050 N.E. 3rd St., P.O. Box 550, Prineville, OR 97754; (541) 416-6700.

....................................................................................................

## Dry River Canyon; Horse Ridge
U.S. Bureau of Land Management
11,076 acres.

On both sides of US 20, from about 16 mi. SE of Bend to 1 mi. NW of Millican.

Dry River drained an Ice Age lake, spilled over Horse Ridge, cut a canyon through lava. Canyon is about 2½ mi. long, N of the highway, roughly paralleling it. N are two low ridges. Scattered clusters of juniper, a few ponderosa, with Idaho fescue, wheatgrass, mountain mahogany, rabbitbrush, yarrow. In the canyon, some trees used by nesting raptors.

S of the highway, Horse Ridge and Horse Ridge Summit are steep basalt hills. Vegetation is similar to the N side, except for a 600-acre Research Natural Area established to preserve a nearly pristine western juniper–big sagebrush–threadleaf sedge plant community.

### Adjacent
On N, Badlands (see entry this zone).

### Headquarters
Bureau of Land Management, Prineville District, 3050 N.E. 3rd St., P.O. Box 550, Prineville, OR 97754; (541) 416-6700.

................................................................................................................

## John Day Fossil Beds National Monument
U.S. National Park Service
14,014 acres.

Three widely separated units. (1) Sheep Rock: from Dayville on US 26, W 5 mi. (2) Painted Hills: from US 26 W of Mitchell, 6 mi. NW on marked county road. (3) Clarno: from Fossil on Hwy 19, 20 mi. W on Hwy 218.

Sedimentary strata of the John Day Basin contain one of the longest continuous records of plant and animal fossils, tracing evolution of life forms for 45 million years, from the near-subtropical climate of the Eocene Epoch through the Pliocene.

High desert region. The John Day River flows through the Sheep Rock Unit. The exposed strata are colorful, bands in shades of red, yellow, and green. Also around the valley are high buttes, escarpments, and pinnacles of basalt. Scattered juniper with sagebrush and bunchgrass. Cottonwood and willow beside streams. Many wildflowers in May. Surrounding mountains have forests of Douglas-fir, true firs, larch, pines.

**Birds:** Species include Canada goose, ducks, great blue heron, California quail, chukar, pheasant, magpie, red-tailed hawk, golden eagle.

**Mammals:** Include coyote, bobcat, badger, mule deer, jackrabbit, cottontail, rodents.

**Reptiles:** Rattlesnake common.

## Features

*Sheep Rock Unit:* 8,913 acres. Strata sharply tilted, eroded into picturesque forms; cliffs, peaks, gorges, canyons. Colors from brick red and brown to bronze, bluish-green, buff, white. High viewpoint.

*Painted Hills Unit:* 3,132 acres. Dramatically eroded landscape, strikingly colorful layers: pale yellow to rich brick red, green, white. Sagebrush desert.

*Clarno Unit:* 1,969 acres. Hills, bluffs, towering palisades and pinnacles of brown to bronze rock.

## Interpretation

*Headquarters* and *visitor center* in Sheep Rock Unit is a restored ranch house with outbuildings. Information, exhibits, publications. Good birding spot.

    *Wayside exhibits* at overlooks along roads.

## Activities

*Hiking:* 10 hiking trails in the 3 units, some with self-guided information.

*Fishing:* John Day River.

## Publications

Leaflet with map.

Trail guides at several trailheads.

## Headquarters

National Park Service, HC 82, Box 126, Kimberly, OR 97848; (541) 987-2333.

## John Day River (Mainstream, North Fork)

U.S. Bureau of Land Management, state, and private land.
147 river mi.

From near Dale on US 395 on the North Fork of the John Day to
Tumwater Falls 10 mi. upstream from the confluence with Columbia
River. Principal access points: bridge at Service Creek; Hwy 218 at
Clarno; Hwy 206 at Cottonwood. Other access points are on private
land, and landowner permission is needed.

The John Day River has been designated a National Wild and Scenic
River and a State Scenic Waterway from Service Creek to Tumwater
Falls, 10 mi. above its mouth. From the headwaters on the North
Fork, nearly 140 mi. upstream from Service Creek, the river flows
through the Umatilla National Forest to Dale, and then through BLM
and private land to Tumwater Falls. Public access to the John Day is
limited downstream of Service Creek to bridge crossings at Clarno and
Cottonwood. Scenic Waterway designation limits further developments within ¼ mi. of the river.

BLM recreation specialists estimate that the 100-mi. lower segment
of the Deschutes River attracted 140,000 visitors in 1995, but only
10,000 visited the John Day. One reason is limited access. Also, river
flow has extreme seasonal variations. Aug. flow may be less than ⅟₃₀ of
the April–May flow. ("You can wade it without getting your shoes
wet," said a BLM man.) April and May are the best months to float the
river.

Travel by small raft or shallow-draft boat is the preferred way to see
the canyon. A few people can and do hike the canyon in the dry season, we were told, but the extremely rugged terrain, summer heat,
and limited access discourage most hikers.

N of Clarno the river flows through a rugged canyon, generally
1,500 ft. deep. Elevations from 1,650 ft. at Clarno to 535 ft. at the end
of the canyon. Reddish-brown basalt with a great variety of formations: cliffs, pillars, columns, isolated escarpments, blocks, small
stepped plateaus. Many scenic side canyons. Vegetation is dominated
by Idaho fescue and wheatgrass, with some scattered juniper. Also big
sagebrush, hackberry, rabbitbrush, cacti, lupines, cheat grass.

Upstream, from Service Creek to Clarno, the terrain is somewhat less rugged but still wild and scenic, with few sightings of ranch houses or other development.

## Activities

*Camping:* No designated sites. Certainly no facilities. Firepan use is required. No ground fire or fire rings. Carry out human waste.

*Boating:* Motorized boats are prohibited between Clarno and Tumwater Falls May 1–Oct. 1.

*Canoeing, kayaking, rafting:* Best in April–May. 3 major rapids. Few people run the river N of Clarno, but those who do say it's outstanding; one class IV rapids. Most run from Service Creek to Clarno, 48 mi. Last take-out is above Tumwater Falls, 10 mi. above the Columbia. The falls drop into the slack water of the John Day Dam pool. Boaters usually take out at Cottonwood Canyon, Hwy 206.

*Whether traveling by boat or on foot, check at HQ for maps, conditions, advice. The BLM emphasizes that one must obtain permission before crossing private land.*

## Headquarters

Bureau of Land Management, Prineville District, 3050 N.E. 3rd St., P.O. Box 550, Prineville, OR 97754; (541) 416-6700.

## LaPine State Park

Oregon Parks and Recreation Department
3,000 acres.

27 mi. SW of Bend off US 97.

Home to "Big Tree," 191 ft. tall and 326 ft. around, the largest ponderosa pine in OR. The Park is an ideal base camp while exploring OR's "lava lands," including Newberry National Volcanic Monument (see entry for Deschutes National Forest this zone) and the wilderness areas of nearby Cascade Mountains. Don McGregor Memorial Viewpoint offers views of the winding Little Deschutes River, and also of the work of the mountain pine beetle.

## Activities

*Camping:* 145 sites, including fuel and electrical hookups and group sites.

*Hiking:* 0.5-mi. trail.

*Swimming:* With care, river has slight current.

## Headquarters

OR Parks and Recreation Dept., c/o High Desert Management Unit, 62976 O.B. Riley Road, Bend, OR 97701; (541) 388-6055.

## Ochoco National Forest

U.S. Forest Service
843,644 acres/978,470 acres within boundaries.

In 3 blocks. Largest block E and N of Prineville, crossed by US 26 and secondary roads. Second block NW of Burns, crossed by secondary roads only. Smallest block, about 22 mi. by 7 mi., SE of Prineville, S of Post on Crooked River Hwy.

Many visitors come in search of thunder eggs, moss agate, petrified wood, vistaite, and other prizes.

Much of the Forest is over 5,000 ft., highest point over 7,000. Terrain varied, from flat and slightly rolling to broken topography with cliffs and river canyons to mountains. Numerous creeks. Small lakes, the largest 90 acres.

**Plants:** Mostly forested. Ponderosa pine with Douglas-fir, lodgepole pine, white and grand firs, western larch. Some old-growth stands. Some high desert scrub. Flowering species include mariposa lily, wyethia, balsamroot, paintbrush. Best flowering season is May–July.

**Birds:** No checklist. Species reported include great blue heron, Canada goose, bittern, red-tailed hawk, owls, magpie, flycatchers, meadowlark, golden eagle, pheasant, chukar, ruffed grouse, quail, pileated woodpecker, lazuli bunting.

**Mammals:** No checklist. Species reported include pronghorn, mule deer, elk, porcupine, chipmunk, ground squirrels, coyote, badger, bobcat, skunk, raccoon.

## Features

*Black Canyon Wilderness:* 13,400 acres. Elevations from 2,853 ft. at the mouth of Black Canyon Creek to 6,372 ft. at Wolf Mountain. Canyon rim about 5,700 ft. Steep slopes, rock slides, bluffs, timbered and open areas, relatively level benches and mesas. Mesas and benches generally forested with ponderosa, Douglas-fir, other conifers. Several perpetually flowing streams, tributaries of John Day River system. In Paulina Ranger District.

*Bridge Creek Wilderness:* 5,400 acres. Elevations range from 5,200 to 6,607 ft. According to rangers, this is the place for solitude. Steep, rugged terrain, old, unmaintained trails, so experience is a must.

*Mill Creek Wilderness:* 17,400 acres. In Prineville Ranger District. Variable terrain, some rugged, steep areas; some meadows, prairies. Ponderosa and lodgepole.

*Lookout Mountain Recreation Management Area.* In Big Summit Ranger District. Some of the most rugged terrain, elevations from 3,793 to over 6,900 ft. Parklike stands of ponderosa with Douglas-fir on steep N slopes. Open, grassy top; vistas. It is a favorite spot for winter activities. Both cross-country skiing and snowmobiling are popular.

*Cottonwood Creek Area.* Includes the headwaters of Cottonwood, Brown, Deep, and Battle Creeks. Ridges and canyons form a steep, deeply dissected landscape.

*Rock Creek Area.* Includes the headwaters of Rock Creek and W Birch Creek. The area is thought to support wintering and breeding bald eagles and also wolverines. Historians may find the old China Ditch of interest (built by Chinese laborers in the 1800s), as well as the native American artifacts located at various sites.

*Steins Pillar.* Near Mill Creek and Forest Rd. 33. Stone monolith rising 350 ft. above base.

*Wild Horse Range.* Small bands of wild horses often seen in central and W half of Big Summit Ranger District.

*Silver Creek.* Remote stream surrounded by steep slopes. Narrow riparian corridor gives one a sense of enclosure when hiking along the creek. Fish include redband trout and mottled sculpin. Long-bearded mariposa lily, thought to grow only in the Ochoco Mountains, occurs here.

*Deep Creek,* permanent stream, with best fishing in spring and early summer. Wildflowers plentiful spring through midsummer. Area closed from late Sept. to mid-Nov. during hunting season. Limited access in winter, except by snowmobile.

*Spanish Peak,* 6,871 ft., in Paulina Ranger District, highest point in District, accessible by road. Vistas.

*Snow Mountain,* 7,163 ft., at NE edge of Snow Mountain Ranger District. Lookout station; viewpoint.

### Activities

*Camping:* 25 campgrounds, 196 sites. Open April 20–Nov. 15. Informal camping elsewhere except as posted.

*Hiking, backpacking:* 121 mi. of trails, chiefly in N unit (largest block). Many miles of roads, most unpaved, some little used. Bushwhacking feasible in many areas.

*Hunting:* Mule deer, elk, upland game birds.

*Fishing:* Streams and lakes. Trout, bass.

*Horse riding:* Considerable use of trails. Pack trips uncommon.

*Snowmobiling:* Large sections of Forest are deer winter range, and special areas are closed.

### Publications

Forest map, $3.25 (includes Crooked River National Grassland).

*Off-Road Vehicle Travel Map* (includes National Grassland).

### Headquarters

U.S. Forest Service, Ochoco National Forest, P.O. Box 490, Prineville, OR 97754-0490; (541) 416-6500.

### Ranger Districts

Big Summit R.D., 33700 N.E. Ochoco Ranger Station, Prineville, OR 97754; (541) 416-6645. Crooked River R.D., 813 S. Hwy 97, Madras, OR 97741; (541) 475-9272. Paulina R.D., 171500 Beaver Creek Rd., Paulina, OR 97751; (541) 477-3713. Prineville R.D., P.O. Box 687, Prineville, OR 97754; (541) 416-6500. Snow Mountain R.D., H.Q. 74 Box 12870, Hines, OR 97738; (541) 573-7292.

## Peter Skene Ogden State Scenic Viewpoint

Oregon Parks and Recreation Department
98 acres.

9 mi. N of Redmond on US 97.

Another view of the Crooked River Gorge, also seen at Smith Rock
State Park and Crooked River National Grassland (see entries this
zone). Here the canyon is 400 ft. wide, over 300 ft. deep. Not as spectacular as at Smith Rock, but worth a brief stop.

## Prineville Reservoir; Prineville Reservoir State Park

U.S. Bureau of Land Management/Oregon Parks and Recreation
Department/Oregon Department of Fish and Wildlife
3,010 acres of water; about 5,500 acres of public land around the
reservoir administered by the Water and Power Resources Service;
additional BLM lands nearby.

For State Park: from Prineville 1 mi. E on US 26, then 16 mi. S on
marked county road. For dam: from Prineville, 19 mi. S on Hwy 27.

Reservoir formed by damming Crooked River. State Park is a popular
resort occupying a peninsula on the N shore. Chiefly water-based
recreation. Lake is surrounded by dry hills, sparse juniper and sagebrush. Interesting lava rock formations: columns, pillars, blocks. Some
private land on the lakeshore, but development is limited chiefly to
the N shore. Much of the remaining shoreline is undeveloped, without road access. Popular rockhounding area.

Much of the land outside the Park and near the lake is known as the
Prineville Reservoir Wildlife Area. The Department of Fish and Wildlife
has game management responsibility, not ownership. Deer are relatively abundant. Some waterfowl nest at the inlet April–May, which is
also the best time for desert wildflowers, depending on rainfall.

### Activities

*Camping:* At State Park, 70 sites, mid-April–Oct. Reservations. Informal BLM campsites along Hwy 27 (see entry, Crooked River Canyon).

*Hiking:* No trails, but bushwhacking is feasible. Few people hike, we were informed, but it's possible to hike around the lake, about 14 mi. of difficult hiking.

*Hunting:* Not within the State Park, but on BLM land.

*Fishing:* Rainbow trout, bass, catfish.

*Swimming:* Lake.

*Boating:* Ramp and other facilities at State Park. Informal ramp, poor access road, near dam; suitable for light boats only.

### Adjacent
Crooked River Canyon (see entry this zone).

### Publication
Park leaflet.

### Headquarters
OR Parks and Recreation Dept., Prineville Lake Rt., Box 1050, Prineville, OR 97754; (541) 447-4363. Bureau of Land Management, Prineville District, 3050 N.E. 3rd St., P.O. Box 550, Prineville, OR 97754; (541) 416-6700.

---

### Sand Hollow; Gerry Mountain; Logan Butte; Redman Rim; Sears Creek; Hampton Butte; Cougar Well; Hampton; Stockpile
U.S. Bureau of Land Management
100,000 acres.

These are contiguous units of a block of BLM land about 30 mi. N–S, 8 mi. E–W. Just N of US 20. W boundary is about 1 mi. N of Hampton; E boundary meets US 20. Names read N to S.

High desert, above 4,200 ft., with buttes and mountains rising as much as 1,100 ft. above surrounding land. Juniper occurs throughout the area, sometimes in dense stands, more often well scattered. Principal plant species: low and big sagebrush, rabbitbrush, lupine, Idaho fescue, wheatgrass, bitterbrush. Portions once seeded with crested wheatgrass.

*Sand Hollow:* Low, rolling hills; higher hills extending E–W forming part of Steen Ridge. In W and N, rugged dark brown basalt escarpments. Boundaries are county and BLM roads.

*Gerry Mountain:* Mountain is butte-shaped, elevation 5,200 ft., offering sweeping vistas. Two smaller mountains, rolling hills. NE portion relatively flat. N, E, and S boundaries are county roads.

*Redman Rim:* Rim rises about 1,000 ft. above surrounding land, about 1½ mi. long, up to 1¼ mi. wide. Rimmed with dark brown basalt escarpments and outcroppings. Steep slopes. 650-ft. Ibex Butte is nearby. Also shallow basins, high rolling hills. County road on part of N boundary, BLM roads on S and E.

*Logan Butte:* A scenic outcropping of John Day clay formations covering nearly 2 sq. mi. (Public access not available. Landowner permission must be obtained.)

*Sears Creek:* Low rolling hills dissected by deep drainages. Canyon about 160 ft. deep extends E–W for 1½ mi., rimmed with reddish-brown basalt. NE and SW portions have more varied terrain: hills and small ravines. Roads along parts of all boundaries.

*Hampton Butte:* Foothills rising to a rugged basalt rim, edge of a 600-acre plateau, part of the scenic Hampton Buttes. To the N, smaller plateaus, rolling hills, a shallow canyon. Primitive routes on portions of N, S, and W boundaries.

*Cougar Well:* E half is relatively flat desert plain, sloping gradually up to W; a small N–S canyon bisects this portion. To the W, low rolling foothills join a large butte, offering sweeping vistas. W flank of butte drops sharply, forming a small, secluded valley. Part of E boundary is county road; W boundary is BLM road.

*Hampton:* Divided by N–S ridge of reddish-brown basalt about 4 mi. long. To E, low rolling hills and desert plain. To W, low hills slope downward to shallow valley. Small escarpments in NW. County road on E, BLM routes on W and S.

*Stockpile:* Dry river bed in central portion with reddish-brown basalt outcroppings. Tributary dry river bed in E. In W, low rolling hills sloping down to E. County roads on W and E. S boundary is US 20.

Much of the area has been used for grazing, signs of which are ways, fences, and small reservoirs, many now reverting to nature. Most of the area is in a natural state. Utility power lines cross, but no residences or other developments.

**Adjacent**
Crooked River, South Fork (see entry this zone) on the N.

**Headquarters**
Bureau of Land Management, Prineville District, 3050 N.E. 3rd St., P.O. Box 550, Prineville, OR 97754; (541) 416-6700.

## Shelton State Park

Oregon Parks and Recreation Department
30 acres.

10 mi. SE of Fossil off Hwy 19.

Towering pines and a winding creek make this Park ideal for those who seek a quiet, remote spot to camp and also want to fish, hunt, bike, rockhound, or look for fossils in nearby areas. *(Note: It is illegal to dig or remove fossils on most public lands.)*

### Activities
*Camping:* 36 primitive sites. Mid-April–Oct., weather permitting.
*Hiking:* 2 mi. of trails for foot traffic only.

### Nearby
John Day River (see entry this zone), with bass and trout fishing, swimming, boating and rafting, and John Day Fossil Beds National Monument (see entry this zone).

### Headquarters
OR Parks and Recreation Dept., c/o John Day Management Unit, P.O. Box 9, Canyon City, OR 97820; (541) 575-2773.

## Smith Rock State Park

Oregon Parks and Recreation Department
623 acres.

From Redmond, 6 mi. N on US 97 to Terrebonne, then E 3 mi.

Scenic area on Crooked River. Winding canyon cut 300 ft. deep through colorful layers of sedimentary rock, contrasts with flat lands surrounding. Cliffs on N side considerably higher than observation area on S. Spires, columns, vertical cliffs.

From observation area, one can hike down trail to canyon floor, cross river on footbridge. Trails on both sides of river. Day-use area.

### Headquarters
OR Parks and Recreation Dept., c/o Cove Palisades State Park, 7300 Jordan Rd., Culver, OR 97734; (541) 546-3412.

............................................................................................................................

## Cove Palisades State Park
Oregon Parks and Recreation Department
4,130 acres.
From Culver on US 97, 5 mi. W.

Round Butte Dam formed Lake Billy Chinook, backing up water in canyons of Deschutes, Crooked, and Metolius Rivers, forming lake with 3 long, narrow arms. State Park is chiefly on E side, a popular resort with marina, cafe, store, campgrounds, and other facilities. Activity at the Park is almost entirely water-based. Several scenic overlooks. Desert region. Juniper-sagebrush community.

Those interested in exploring surrounding land areas will find them scenic and uncrowded. Much adjacent area is within the Crooked River National Grassland (see entry this zone).

### Activities
*Camping:* 2 campgrounds, 272 sites. Mid-April–Oct. Reservations.
*Fishing:* Kokanee, rainbow, brown trout, bass.
*Swimming:* Usual season April–Oct.
*Boating:* Ramps, marina, rentals.

*Crowded most summer weekends, all holiday weekends.*

### Publication
Leaflet.

**Headquarters**
OR Parks and Recreation Dept., 7300 Jordan Rd., Culver, OR 97734;
(541) 546-3412.

## White River Wildlife Area

Oregon Department of Fish and Wildlife
25,000 acres.

From The Dalles, S on US 197 about 33 mi. to Tygh Valley, then W past
Wamic.

An irregularly shaped area 50 mi. long from Pine Grove, N to 15 Mile
Creek, between US 197 and the Hood River National Forest. Farming,
timber, and rangeland area. Established to provide deer and elk an
alternative to feeding on farmers' crops. Several thousand deer and
several hundred elk are attracted here in winter, as they come down
from the high country in the National Forest. Stop at site HQ to ask
where viewing is best. In spring and fall this is a good birding area,
between farms and forest. Elevation 1,500–2,000 ft.

**Headquarters**
OR Department of Fish and Wildlife, Region III, 61374 Parrell Rd.,
Bend, OR 97701; (541) 382-5113.

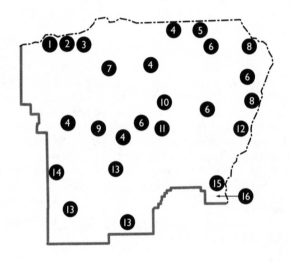

1. Umatilla National Wildlife Refuge
2. McNary Wildlife Park
3. Cold Springs National Wildlife Refuge
4. Umatilla National Forest
5. Wenaha Wildlife Management Area
6. Wallowa-Whitman National Forest/Wallowa Lake State Park
7. McKay Creek National Wildlife Refuge
8. Hells Canyon National Recreation Area
9. Bridge Creek Wildlife Area
10. Ladd Marsh Wildlife Area
11. Elkhorn Wildlife Area
12. McGraw Creek; Homestead; Sheep Mountain
13. Malheur National Forest
14. Murderers Creek Wildlife Area
15. Brownlee Reservoir
16. Farewell Bend State Recreation Area

Z O N E 4

Includes these counties:

| | | |
|---|---|---|
| Morrow | Wallowa | Grant |
| Umatilla | Union | Baker |

Dominant feature of the area is the Blue Mountains range, extending from the NE corner to the John Day Valley in the SW. Part of the chain projects SE to the Snake River Valley, OR's border with ID in this zone. The mountains are generally from 5,000 to 6,000 ft. with numerous peaks over 7,000, the highest point being 10,033 ft. Much of this high country is within the 3 National Forests of the region.

Even in the mountains, annual precipitation is only moderate, but much of it falls as snow, providing good skiing. The lower country is dry, including the broad plateau of the Columbia River and the other river valleys. Snowmelt provides reliable water flow for many good trout and salmon streams. The zone has many lakes and reservoirs, most of them small. Reservoirs used for irrigation are often well down in summer.

Route I-84 cuts across the zone, NW to SE. US 395 is a N-S highway in the W portion of the zone, US 26 E-W along the John Day River in the S. A few good state and county roads also tend to follow river valleys. Large sections of the zone are either roadless or served by roads to be used with caution, especially in winter. The official highway map's designation of "all-weather roads" is, in some cases, optimistic.

The Hells Canyon National Recreation Area straddles the Middle Snake River in OR and ID. Publicity has focused on the river canyon and the popularity of rafting through the impressive rapids. However, the area is huge, 662,000 acres in the two states, much of it wilderness. Each of the National Forests has substantial wilderness acreage, offering almost unlimited opportunities for backpacking and pack trips.

Elk and deer take to the high country in summer, seek the valleys when snow falls, often invading farmers' fields. Several wildlife management areas provide limited alternatives. Most of the natural wetlands of the zone have been obliterated, so the refuges that provide good wintering grounds are well patronized by ducks and geese.

In the SE corner of the zone, below Hells Canyon, the Snake River has been dammed. The Brownlee Reservoir, in a scenic desert canyon, is easily accessible but lightly used.

## Bridge Creek Wildlife Area

Oregon Department of Fish and Wildlife
13,086 acres.

From US 395 at junction with Hwy 244, E a short distance to Ukiah, then S on unpaved Forest Service Rd. 52 about 3 mi. Continue straight where road turns E toward Granite. Unimproved road runs S through the Wildlife Area to a point overlooking the North Fork, John Day River. Road best suited to pickups and 4-wheel-drive vehicles. Advisable to hike.

W boundary is canyon of Camas Creek. Forested valley, open grassland. Bridge Creek crosses E–W at about midpoint. Elevation about 4,000 ft. Wintering ground for deer and elk that summer in Umatilla National Forest. The entire area is open to public entry by permit only Dec. 1–April 30, when the animals may be viewed. Nonhunters should know that camping is permitted within 100 yds. of designated roads during hunting season. Nonhunters would be well advised to limit their visits to the period Dec. 1–Sept. 14.

### Adjacent

*Ukiah-Dale Forest Wayside,* 2,987 acres, along the Camas Creek Canyon, US 395, between Ukiah and Dale. Scenic. Campground, 25 sites. Season depends on winter weather.

*Umatilla National Forest* (see entry this zone).

### Headquarters

OR Dept. of Fish and Wildlife, 2501 S.W. 1st Ave., P.O. Box 59, Portland, OR 97207; (503) 872-5276.

## Brownlee Reservoir (OR side only)

Idaho Power Company/U.S. Bureau of Land Management

Access from I-84 near Huntington. From Huntington, Snake River Rd. runs close to reservoir for about 30 mi., N to Richland on Hwy 86.

The Idaho Power Company Dam on the Snake River, 12 mi. S of Copperfield on Hwy 86, has backed up a 58-mi. pool, to a point 10 mi. W of Weiser, ID. Desert valley; brown, rounded, largely treeless mountains on both sides. Cliffs, slides, boulders; a few sand dunes on ID side. Snake River Rd. is gravel, reasonably well maintained, with sections of washboard. Land along the road is a patchwork of private holdings and BLM sites, but there has been little development. We saw a number of informal campsites and boat-launching places. The BLM's *Spring Recreation Site* is quiet, scenic.

River and upper portion of reservoir are quite shallow, but small outboards were operating in Aug., with water level several feet below high point.

The section N of Huntington has few visitors other than fishermen; the road is lightly traveled. For much of the distance, there is no road on the ID side. The road offers an easy way to enjoy a scenic desert canyon in relative isolation.

**Plants:** Lower slopes along the reservoir: wheatgrass, cheat grass, bitterbrush, big sagebrush. In moist areas of draws: some Douglas-fir, white fir, huckleberry, snowberry. Higher and drier slopes have Idaho fescue, serviceberry. Wildflowers include larkspur, buttercup, arrow-leaved balsamroot, violet, penstemon, paintbrush, mariposa lily, bluebell, clarkia, lupines, phlox, fireweed.

**Birds:** No checklist. Species noted included chukar, blue grouse, Steller's jay, Clark's nutcracker, red crossbill. Wintering area for bald eagle.

**Mammals:** Mule deer wintering range. Elk, black bear, coyote, chickaree, weasel. Mountain lion reported.

### Activities

*Camping:* The BLM's Spring Recreation Site, 3 mi. N of Huntington, 14 sites, primitive, all year. Informal camping along the route.

*Hiking:* Snake River Rd. is lightly traveled, pleasant hiking. Numerous places to bushwhack into the hills.

*Hunting:* On BLM land. Deer, elk, grouse, chukar.

*Fishing:* Said to be good: bass, crappie, catfish.

*Swimming:* Local comment: "If you're hot enough."

*Boating:* Ramp at Spring Recreation Site is steep. Along the way, informal launching spots for light boats. More facilities on ID side near dam.

### Headquarters
Bureau of Land Management, Federal Building, P.O. Box 987, Baker, OR 97814; (541) 523-1256.

## Cold Springs National Wildlife Refuge
U.S. Fish and Wildlife Service
3,117 acres.

From I-84 N, exit on Hwy 207. 6 mi. N to Hermiston. E 81 mi. on Stanfield Loop Rd. Entrance on left.

About 1,550 acres of open water at full pool. Water is used for irrigation, and levels drop greatly in the summer dry season. Summer is least desirable time to visit. Large numbers of waterfowl arrive in late fall. Peak winter populations vary but usually reach 30,000 ducks, 10,000 geese. Desert environment; about 7 in. of precipitation annually. A road with parking areas is on the S shore. An information station stocked with brochures is at the entrance.

**Plants:** Cheat grass steppe community: sagebrush, rabbitbrush, mustard, buckwheat, bitterbrush, Russian thistle. Cottonwood and Russian olive at shoreline.

**Birds:** Chiefly mallard, pintail, green-winged teal, wigeon, shoveler, Canada goose. Most waterfowl species common to the Pacific Flyway are seen here at times. Bald and golden eagles in winter. Red-tailed and Swainson's hawks, northern harrier, kestrel in summer. White pelican, tundra swan, sandhill crane occasional during migration. Many shorebirds.

**Mammals:** Often seen on and near the Refuge: mule deer, cottontail, black-tailed jackrabbit, muskrat, coyote, badger, beaver.

**Reptiles and amphibians:** Often seen: short-horned, side-blotched, and western fence lizards. Great Basin spadefoot toad, Pacific tree frog, bullfrog, western yellow-bellied racer, gopher snake.

### Publications
General brochure.

Hunting information.

### Headquarters
U.S. Fish and Wildlife Service, P.O. Box 700, Umatilla, OR 97882; (541) 922-3232.

---

## Elkhorn Wildlife Area
Oregon Department of Fish and Wildlife
9,630 acres.

Exit I-84 at North Powder, then 9 mi. W on North Powder River Ln.

Wintering area and supplemental feeding grounds for elk and deer. Area is managed to minimize the loss of winter range and habitat along the N, W, and S portions of the Powder River Valley. Diversified topography and vegetation along the 8 tracts of the area.

**Plants:** Pines, firs, western larch, and juniper. Deciduous species include hawthorn, birch, alder, aspen, and cottonwood. Also Idaho fescue, pine grass, wheatgrass, meadow foxtail, clover, and burnet.

Although the area is managed primarily for elk and deer, other big game and nongame mammals, upland game birds, waterfowl, and fish also benefit and are frequently seen.

**Birds:** Blue and ruffed grouse, California quail, mourning dove, Canada goose, mallard, blue-winged and cinnamon teals, coot, great blue heron, killdeer, yellow-headed black bird, 4 swallows, rufous and calliope hummingbirds, northern flicker, yellow-bellied sapsucker, hairy woodpecker.

**Mammals:** Rocky mountain elk, mule deer, black bear, raccoon, beaver, coyote, badger, weasel, porcupine, striped skunk, Oregon ground squirrel, chipmunk, snowshoe rabbit.

### Activities

*Camping:* 2 primitive sites.

*Hiking:* ½ mi. of self-guided nature trail, 3 wildlife viewing areas.

*Horsedrawn elk-viewing excursions:* Weekends, Dec. 1–March 1.

*Fishing:* Rainbow and brook trout.

*Hunting:* Fall. Big game and game birds.

### Publication
Brochure.

### Headquarters
OR Dept. of Fish and Wildlife, 61846 N. Powder River Ln., North Powder, OR 97867; (541) 898-2826.

..............................................................................................

## Farewell Bend State Recreation Area
Oregon Parks and Recreation Department
Off I-84, 25 mi. NW of Ontario.

The Park is located near the bend in the Snake River where the Oregon Trail pioneers first set foot in OR. Large and often steep rolling hills, an abundance of wildflowers in the spring, and an interesting diversity of rocks along the banks of the scenic Snake River.

### Activities

*Camping:* 94 campsites, plus 43 primitive sites. Covered wagon and tepee camping also available.

*Fishing:* Bass and catfish—"Catfish capital of Oregon."

*Boating:* Boat ramp, boat and fishing dock.

### Headquarters
OR Parks and Recreation Dept., Farewell Bend State Park, Star Rt., Huntington, OR 97907; (541) 869-2365.

## Hells Canyon National Recreation Area

See Wallowa-Whitman National Forest this zone.

## Ladd Marsh Wildlife Area

Oregon Department of Fish and Wildlife
2,400 acres.

About 5 mi. SE of La Grande. Crossed by I-80 N; Hwy 203 is E
boundary.

Of interest chiefly because few wetlands remain in NE OR. Marsh and
cropland with small areas of open water. Canada goose, sandhill
crane, several duck species. Upland game birds are stocked. Except in
hunting season, some of the area is closed to the public. Self-guided
nature trail. (Groups of naturalists and students can arrange guided
visits.) Reasonably good viewpoints are just outside, worth checking if
you pass this way in spring or fall.

### Headquarters

Or Dept. of Fish and Wildlife, Region IV, Box 339, La Grande, OR
97850; (541) 963-2138.

## Malheur National Forest

U.S. Forest Service
1,458,055 acres/1,540,423 acres within boundaries.

Few inholdings but very irregular shape. S of John Day, on both sides of
US 395, but boundaries are 1–4 mi. away from highway. Another large
section generally N and E of John Day is connected with the S portion
by a strip 6–8 mi. wide, on the E side.

In the SW sector of the Blue Mountains, extending S to the high desert. Elevations from 3,700 to 9,038 ft. Highest country is in the Strawberry Mountain Wilderness. Elsewhere the forested mountains are rolling, with moderate slopes. Large, grassy mountain meadows, bright with wildflowers in season. The lower country, approaching the desert, is plateaulike, with open grassland and sagebrush. Precipitation is 14–30 in., increasing with altitude. Summers are dry. High country usually snow-covered Dec.–March.

Includes the headwaters of the Malheur and Silvies Rivers, major part of the John Day headwaters. Numerous creeks and intermittent streams. 8 lakes, 3–50 acres.

7,000 mi. of roads within the Forest. Most are logging roads maintained only when needed, but there are ample opportunities for backcountry driving; one seldom encounters another vehicle.

**Plants:** Chief tree species: ponderosa pine. 77% of area is commercial forest. Several forest types, depending on altitude: subalpine fir, mixed fir-pine, ponderosa, white fir, lodgepole, and sagebrush-juniper. Old-growth stands in scattered locations. Prominent understory species include huckleberry, bitterbrush. Flowering species include iris, paintbrush, elephants head, larkspur, lupines, fireweed, mariposa lily.

**Birds:** Include golden eagle, red-tailed hawk, blue and ruffed grouse, raven, gray jay, great horned owl, mountain bluebird, killdeer, upland sandpiper. Also prairie falcon, mountain quail, mourning dove, kestrel, goshawk, Canada goose, mallard, cinnamon teal, great blue heron, spotted sandpiper, sandhill crane, willet, long-billed curlew.

**Mammals:** Include mule deer, Rocky Mountain elk, pronghorn, bighorn sheep, black bear, beaver, muskrat, mountain lion, bobcat, coyote, Townsend ground squirrel, various rodents.

**Reptiles and amphibians:** Include gopher and garter snakes, western rattlesnake, short-horned and western fence lizards, Pacific tree frog.

### Features

*Monument Rock Wilderness:* 19,620 acres. On E boundary of Forest, about one-third in Wallawa-Whitman National Forest (see entry this zone). Elevations vary from about 5,200 ft. to 7,873 ft. on Bullrun Rock. Fire lookout at Table Rock, 7,815 ft. Forested at lower elevations. Vegetation gives way above treeline to high meadows.

*Strawberry Mountain Wilderness:* 68,000 acres. Almost all of the area is above 6,000 ft., several peaks over 8,000 ft., Strawberry Mountain

9,038 ft. 5 of the 7 major life zones of the U.S. are represented, roughly parallel bands, characteristic plant-animal communities changing with altitude. 5 high-altitude lakes. This is high country, but trails leading into the wilderness are, for the most part, not difficult.

Normal hiking season is July–Nov., but snow may occur until mid-July and in late Oct. Freezing night temperatures may occur in any month. Summer thunderstorms are common.

Hikers should have good maps and local information, such as availability of water. Horse travelers must carry all feed needed by their stock.

*Vinegar Hill–Indian Rock Scenic Area:* 29,077 acres. Above timberline, high in Greenhorn Mountains at N end of Forest, nearly half of it in the Umatilla National Forest (see entry this zone). Scenic views of mountain meadows, steep cliffs, timbered slopes, abundant wildflowers. Gold and silver mines dating back to late 1800s dot the countryside. Fire lookouts on Vinegar Hill, 8,131 ft., and Indian Rock, 7,353 ft.

*Scenic drive* about 70 mi., from John Day E on US 26 to Prairie City, SE and S on County Rd. 14, W on CR-16 through Logan Valley, NW on County Rd. 15 to US 395, N to John Day. Grant County Chamber of Commerce at John Day has descriptive leaflet.

*Cedar Grove,* at W end of Forest, 60 acres of Alaska cedar, isolated hundreds of miles from other Alaska cedar stands.

*Rosebud Fossil Area,* N of Izee at W edge of Forest. Marine fossil shells are embedded in soft shale of exposed road banks. Forest Rd. 16020 approaches.

*Magone Lake Slide.* The landslide that formed Magone Lake in the early 1800s can be viewed from a good trail over rough, irregular ground. It supports oddly tilted trees carried down by the slide.

### Activities

*Camping:* 20 campgrounds, 200 sites. Open to camping whenever snow-free; sump piped water June–Sept. Informal camping elsewhere, subject to regulations.

*Hiking, backpacking:* 250 mi. of trails, plus many more miles of little-used Forest roads. Trails into Strawberry Mountain Wilderness are most popular. Attractive trails in other parts of the Forest have lighter use. Ask at Ranger Districts. New Forest map shows only maintained trails. Wilderness map is better for those areas. There are also 3

National Recreation Trails, one along the Malheur River, one into Cedar Grove, and the third to Arch Rock.

*Hunting:* Mule deer, elk, some pronghorn and bighorn sheep, upland game birds, waterfowl.

*Fishing:* Streams, some lake: rainbow, cutthroat, steelhead, chinook, brook, Dolly Varden.

*Swimming:* Magone Lake. Season: July–Aug.

*Canoeing:* Magone and Yellowjacket Lakes.

*Rockhounding:* Small-scale collecting allowed throughout the Forest except in wildernesses and campgrounds: petrified wood, jasper, agate, thunder eggs.

*Ski touring:* About 200 mi. of marked snowmobile trails. High country usually has sufficient snow Dec.–March.

*Snowmobiling:* Prohibited in wilderness area.

ORV travel is permitted *except* in Wilderness, in Vinegar Hill–Indian Rock Scenic Area, on a few designated trails, and in some designated area closures.

### Adjacent
Umatilla National Forest, Wallowa-Whitman National Forest, Ochoco National Forest (see entries this zone).

### Publications
Forest map, $3.25.

Strawberry Mountain Wilderness map, $3.25.

Mimeo information pages: activities, campgrounds.

### Headquarters
U.S. Forest Service, P.O. Box 909, John Day, OR 97845; (541) 575-3000.

### Ranger Districts
Bear Valley R.D. and Long Creek R.D., same address as HQ. Burns R.D., Box 12870, Burns-Bend Star Rt., Burns, OR 97720; (541) 573-7292. Prairie City R.D., P.O. Box 156, Prairie City, OR 97869; (541) 820-3311.

## McGraw Creek; Homestead; Sheep Mountain

U.S. Bureau of Land Management
20,000 acres.

Three units, not quite adjacent; McGraw Creek and Homestead N and Sheep Mountain S of Hwy 86 at Copperfield. All have frontage on Snake River Rd.

Near but not on Hells Canyon and Oxbow Dam impoundments of Snake River. Steep sloping ridges, stream valleys, a canyon in McGraw and Sheep Mountain units. Some lava outcroppings. Elevations from 1,780 to 4,940 ft. All 3 units considered for wilderness designation. N unit adjoins proposed wilderness area in Wallowa-Whitman National Forest.

**Plants:** Ponderosa pine and Douglas-fir at higher elevations, with snowberry, bitter cherry, wild rose in understory. Pine, fir, aspen, and willow on lower NE-facing slopes and along riparian zones with understory of Oregon grape, snowberry, snowbrush. Also open grassy slopes. Botanists consider the Snake River Canyon area unique— many rare and unusual species occur.

**Birds:** No checklist for distribution. Noted: red-tailed hawk, great horned owl, chukar, magpie, Canada goose, killdeer.

**Mammals:** Deer and elk abundant. Black bear and mountain lion present.

### Activities

*Hiking, backpacking:* Generally steep, rather rugged terrain. Trail from end of Snake River Rd., N along river through McGraw Creek until to within 1–2 mi. of Hells Canyon Dam. Connecting trail leads NW at McGraw Creek to Hells Canyon National Recreation Area (see entry for Wallowa-Whitman National Forest this zone).

*Hunting:* Deer, elk, chukar, bear, mountain lion.

### Headquarters

Bureau of Land Management, Baker Resource Area, Federal Building, P.O. Box 987, Baker, OR 97814; (541) 523-1256.

## McKay Creek National Wildlife Refuge

U.S. Fish and Wildlife Service
1,836 acres.

From Pendelton, US 395, S 6 mi. Entrance on left.

*Open:* March 1–Sept. 30, 5 A.M.–1½ hours after sunset. After Sept. 30, hunting is permitted, in season, in designated areas. Wed., Sat., and Sun.; wildlife observation is permitted in these same areas, nonhunting days preferred.

An irrigation reservoir with a narrow strip of surrounding land. Desert region; about 7 in. of annual precipitation.

**Plants:** Cheat grass steppe community: sagebrush, rabbitbrush, mustard, buckwheat, bitterbrush, Russian thistle.

**Birds:** Waterfowl concentrations can be observed late fall and winter. Peak populations vary, usually reach 30,000 ducks, 10,000 geese. Primary species: mallard, pintail, green-winged teal, wigeon, shoveler, Canada goose. Bald and golden eagles common in winter. Red-tailed and Swainson's hawks and northern harrier, kestrel active all summer. White pelican, tundra swan, sandhill crane seen occasionally in spring and fall migrations. Many shorebirds.

**Mammals:** Mule deer, cottontail, black-tailed jackrabbit, muskrat, coyote, badger, and beaver often seen.

A gravel, 2-mi. wildlife observation drive with turnouts and parking areas is on W shore.

### Publications

Brochure.

Hunting Leaflet.

### Headquarters

U.S. Fish and Wildlife Service, P.O. Box 700, Umatilla, OR 97882; (541) 922-3232.

## McNary Wildlife Park

U.S. Army Corps of Engineers
500 acres.

1½ mi. NE of Umatilla, immediately below McNary Lock and Dam.

Not a natural area but an interesting effort to create viable wildlife habitat. Site was a gravel pit and disposal site during dam construction, 1947–57. Later, ponds were established and stocked with game fish. Further grading and plantings have created a variety of habitats: rabbitbrush-sage scrub, open marsh, closed marsh, open ponds and lakes, flowing streams, riparian woods, grassland, pine grove. The site is 1¼ mi. long by ¼ mi. wide, bounded by the Columbia River, a paved road, the interstate bridge, and McNary Dam. However, a corridor of riparian habitat extends 9 mi. W into the Umatilla National Wildlife Refuge (see entry this zone). The surrounding area is semiarid shrub steppe, so the richness and diversity of this site attract many species of wildlife.

On reading the site leaflet, we wondered if this were a kind of safari park. It is not; no animals are confined.

**Plants:** Checklist available. Many are native to the area, but exotic and cultivated species have also been used.

**Birds:** Checklist. About 129 species recorded. Abundant or common, seasonally: pied-billed grebe, great blue heron, black-crowned night heron, mallard, pintail, gadwall, teals, wigeon, wood duck, ring-billed gull, coot, killdeer, kestrel, California quail, pheasant, doves, nighthawk, kingbirds, 3 swallows, magpie, raven, crow, robin, cedar waxwing, starling, western meadowlark, red-winged and Brewer's blackbirds, cowbird, evening grosbeak, house finch, goldfinch, rufous-sided towhee, lark sparrow, dark-eyed junco, song and house sparrows.

**Mammals:** Checklist available. Species include mule deer, jackrabbit, cottontail, ground squirrels, marmot, pocket gopher, pocket mouse, wood rat, voles, beaver, muskrat, coyote, raccoon, weasels, badger, skunks, river otter, shrews, mink, porcupine.

**Interpretation**

*Nature trail,* ¾ mi., self-guiding, pamphlet. *Naturalist* present all year.

*Photo blinds,* chiefly for waterfowl.

**Activities**

*Fishing:* Rainbow trout, largemouth bass, bluegill, catfish.

**Publications**

Checklists of plants, birds, mammals.

Nature trail guide.

**Headquarters**

Army Corps of Engineers, 201 N. 3rd St., Walla Walla, WA 99362-1876. Resource Manager: (541) 922-3211.

---

## Murderers Creek Wildlife Area

Oregon Department of Fish and Wildlife
40,000 acres.

¼ mi. E of Dayville, or 30 mi. W of John Day, near Milepost 132 on Hwy 26.

Area is close to the South Fork of the John Day River and John Day Fossil Beds National Monument (see entries zone 3) offering many archeological and geological points of interest nearby. Excellent year-round birding. Bighorn sheep viewable during winter and early spring. Access to hike-in fishery at Aldrich Ponds, and to Black Canyon Wilderness and Aldrich Mountain Wilderness Study Area.

Primitive camping with miles of undeveloped roads and trails for hiking and horseback riding. Rivers, creeks, and 5 ponds offer 27 mi. of fishing access. Upland bird and large game hunting in season.

**Headquarters**

OR Dept. of Fish and Game, HCR 01, Box 911, Dayville, OR 97825; (541) 987-2843.

## Umatilla National Forest

U.S. Forest Service
1,402,480 acres, including 311,197 in WA.

Three principal blocks. Largest lies NE of I-84, N of La Grande. Crossed by Hwy 204. The 2 other pieces are E and W of Ukiah and US 395. Alternate I-84 summer route E–W is Blue Mountain Elkhorn Scenic Byway. I-84W terminus is Hwy 74. I-84E terminus is either Hwy 7 at Baker City (through gold country) or Forest Rd. 73 at North Powder (Anthony Lake High Country).

In the Blue Mountains. Elevations from 1,900 to 7,720 ft. Part of a large block of forest land, adjoining Malheur and Wallowa-Whitman National Forests. Diverse terrain. In the N, sharply dissected plateaus and steep slopes. The central portion is partly rolling, partly dissected, the S rolling to steeply rolling, the SW relatively flat or undulating. About two-thirds of the area is commercial forest. The balance is a mix of shrub and grassland.

Climate is generally temperate, semiarid, but with great variations depending on altitude and exposure. Annual precipitation is about 20 in. at lower elevations, up to 65 in. in high country, where snowfall averages 100 in. Summers are dry.

Headwaters of the Umatilla, North Fork John Day, Lower Snake, and Walla Walla Rivers are within the Forest. More than 1,100 mi. of fishing streams. Olive Lake, 145 acres, is the only natural lake larger than 3 acres. The largest reservoirs are under 100 acres.

Camping, hunting, and fishing are the principal visitor activities. Tens of thousands of hunters congregate in elk season. Although some campgrounds may be fully occupied at other times, few places in the Forest are heavily used, and hikers can easily find isolation. Numerous trails outside the wilderness are open to use by ORVs, but it's not difficult to observe which trails they favor.

The Forest has over 5,000 mi. of roads, of which only 78 mi. are paved and 678 mi. are improved gravel. Almost half of the road system is considered primitive. Many of these roads are closed under Access and Travel Management Plans. Open primitive roads should be approached with caution.

**Plants:** Four major vegetation zones. At 2,800–3,600 ft., western juniper with big sagebrush, wheatgrass, Idaho fescue. At 2,900–4,900 ft., more humid places, ponderosa pine forests with Douglas-fir, grand fir, lodgepole pine, western larch; understory of sagebrush, bitterbrush, mahogany, snowberry, spirea, and grasses. From 4,900–6,600 ft., grand fir is dominant, with ponderosa and lodgepole pines, western larch, and Douglas-fir. Also in this zone are twinflower, heartleaf arnica, bishops cap, huckleberry, pipsissewa, pasqueflower. From 4,500 ft. to timberline at 7,900, subalpine fir, Engelmann spruce, grand fir, western larch, and Douglas-fir, with huckleberry, heartleaf arnica, hawkweed, anemone, other subalpine flowers.

**Birds:** Checklist available. Species include goshawk, golden and bald eagles, osprey, prairie falcon, grouse, great horned, barred, and flammulated owls, 5 woodpeckers, northern flicker, Williamson's sapsucker, Steller's jay, Vaux's swift, dipper, winter wren, hermit thrush, kingfisher, Merriam's turkey, pine grosbeak, MacGillivray's and yellow warblers. Area noted for numbers and variety of woodpeckers.

**Mammals:** No checklist. Species reported include river otter, marten, mink, beaver, badger, bobcat, mountain lion, black bear, coyote, mule and Columbian white-tailed deer, elk, bighorn sheep. Exceptionally large elk population.

### Features

*Wenaha-Tucannon Wilderness:* 177,412 acres, of which 66,417 are in OR, remainder in WA. Elevations from 2,000 ft. at the Wenaha River to 6,401 ft. at Oregon Butte (WA). Rivers and streams have cut deep canyons into broad tablelands. High ridges have steep, gravelly slopes. Vegetation from bunchgrass at lower elevations to subalpine. Many streams. Wenaha River and Crooked, Rock, and Butte Creeks have good fishing. About 165 mi. of trails reached from a dozen trailheads. Saddle and pack horse use subject to special rules. Wilderness permit required.

*Vinegar Hill–Indian Rock Scenic Area:* 29,285 acres, about half in Malheur National Forest (see entry this zone). Alpine topography, over 7,000 ft. elevation. Cirque basins, steep cliffs, rocky outcrops, with views of timbered slopes, mountain meadows with abundant wildflowers. Remains of old gold mines.

*Thompson Flat* and *Potamus Creek,* in Heppner Ranger District. The Flat, about 1½ mi. sq., is semiarid, sagebrush and bunchgrass with scattered juniper and ponderosa pine. At the edge, the land drops abruptly, providing scenic views of the North Fork of the John Day

River and Potamus Creek. The creek canyon has steep, dissected side slopes, vertical rock outcrops, scattered trees.

*Kendall-Skyline Rd.,* on the crest of the Blue Mountains, extends 44 mi. from the N end of the Forest to Hwy 204. Fine views of the Wenaha-Tucannon Wilderness, Mill Creek, Walla Walla River. Segments vary from gravel surface to primitive. Check conditions.

*Scenic route:* Hwy 204, Weston to Elgin, passes Umatilla Breaks Viewpoint, fine view of rugged canyon of the Umatilla River Wilderness.

## Activities

*Camping:* 26 campgrounds, 316 sites. Earliest opening: April 20. Most open June 1–July 1.

*Hiking, backpacking:* Miles of mapped and maintained trails. Off-trail hiking is feasible in many areas.

*Hunting:* Outstanding elk hunting. Also deer, bear, turkey.

*Fishing:* 1,100 mi. of fish-bearing streams, of which over 700 mi. are capable of supporting salmon, steelhead. Fishing in lakes includes some ice fishing.

*Swimming:* At a few lakes.

*Boating:* Motors permitted only at Olive Lake. River floating between Rondowa and Troy in the gorge of the Grande Ronde River.

*Horse riding:* Outfitters in nearby communities provide pack and saddle stock, guides.

*Skiing:* Two commercial ski areas.

*Ski touring:* No special trails but many opportunities.

*Snowmobiling:* Several posted trails, but most snowmobilers use unplowed roads or travel cross-country. Banned only in wilderness area and certain winter game ranges.

## Publications

Forest map, $3.25

Information letter, sent on request.

Wenaha-Tucannon Wilderness map, $2.25.

ORV map.

Access and travel maps.

## Headquarters

U.S. Forest Service, 2517 S.W. Hailey Ave., Pendleton, OR 97801; (541) 278-3716.

**Ranger Districts**

Heppner R.D., P.O. Box 7, Heppner, OR 97836; (541) 676-9187. North Fork John Day R.D., P.O. Box 158, Ukiah, OR 97880; (541) 427-3231. Pendleton R.D., 2517 S.W. Hailey Ave., Pendleton, OR 97801; (541) 276-3811. Pomeroy R.D., Rt. 1, Box 53-F, Pomeroy, WA 99347; (509) 843-1891. Walla Walla R.D., 1415 W. Rose, Walla Walla, WA 99362; (509) 522-6290.

## Umatilla National Wildlife Refuge

U.S. Fish and Wildlife Service
8,879 acres in OR; 14,000 acres in WA zone 6; about 16,500 acres of water.

On the Columbia River. From I-84N, exit at US 730 E of Boardman. NE on US 730 about 4 mi., then left on Patterson Ferry Rd.

The closing of the John Day Dam in 1968 inundated much traditional waterfowl habitat. It also created McCormack Slough in OR and Patterson Slough in WA. The Refuge was established to maintain this new waterfowl habitat. Peak winter populations are over 80,000 geese, 325,000 ducks.

Directions above are to McCormack Slough, largest land parcel on the OR side. Signs are up and brochures are available at contact station. Ridge Rd., marked Parking A, leads to a high point overlooking pond and cattail marsh. Marsh Rd., marked Parking BCDE, leads to junction of slough and Columbia River. From the parking areas, trails and gated service roads cross fields, sagebrush flats, to shores of slough and river. The Refuge is busy during hunting season but appears to have few visitors at other times.

**Plants:** Desert region, about 7 in. of rain yearly. Cheat grass steppe community: sagebrush, rabbitbrush, mustard, buckwheat, bitterbrush, russian thistle. Cottonwood and Russian olive along shores. Cattail, rushes, other marsh vegetation.

**Birds:** Checklist available. 189 species recorded. Seasonally abundant and common species include pied-billed grebe, double-crested cormorant, great blue heron, tundra swan, Canada goose, mallard, gadwall, pintail, teals, wigeon, shoveler, goldeneye, bufflehead. Long-billed curlews are a special feature. Their return is celebrated locally as heralding spring weather. About 200 are produced on the Refuge each year. Other abundant or common species: northern harrier, kestrel, California quail, pheasant, coot, killdeer, greater yellowlegs, Baird's and western sandpipers, avocet, ring-billed gull, terns, rock and mourning doves, northern flicker, kingbirds, horned lark, bank and barn swallows, magpie, raven, crow, marsh wren, robin, cedar waxwing, house sparrow, western meadowlark, yellow-headed and red-winged blackbirds, northern oriole, cowbird, house finch, goldfinch.

**Mammals:** Often seen: mule deer, cottontail, black-tailed jackrabbit, muskrat, coyote, badger, beaver, big brown bat. Less often seen: mink, river otter, porcupine, bobcat, skunks, raccoon, opossum, various rodents.

**Reptiles and amphibians:** Often seen: short-horned, side-blotched, and western fence lizards, Great Basin spadefoot toad, Pacific tree frog, bullfrog, western yellow-bellied racer, gopher snake. Present but seldom seen: long-toed salamander, Oregon alligator lizard, western skink, striped whipsnake, Oregon rattlesnake, wandering garter snake, western painted turtle.

### Feature
*27 blinds* on the marsh can be used for photography and observation as well as hunting.

### Publications
General brochure.

Umatilla bird checklist.

Hunting information.

### Headquarters
U.S. Fish and Wildlife Service, P.O. Box 700, Umatilla, OR 97882; (541) 922-3232.

## Wallowa Lake State Park
See Wallowa-Whitman National Forest.

## Wallowa-Whitman National Forest

U.S. Forest Service
2,526,280 acres.

NE OR. Two major blocks. The larger, shaped like a backward C, lies against the ID border, close to the WA border. Access from points on Hwys 86, 203, 237, 82, and 3, the last crossing a neck of the C. The other block, irregular in shape, is largely within the triangle formed by I-84, US 395, and US 26.

Mountainous region of great diversity, elevations ranging from 875 ft. at the Snake River to 9,839 ft. atop Sacajawea Peak. Matterhorn Peak is 9,833 ft. The Wallowa Mountains, a range about 80 mi. long, are high, rugged, snowcapped, granite slopes rising above the timberline, many high lakes. The Forest also includes part of the more extensive Blue Mountains, not quite so high, forested slopes generally more moderate. Along the E border, the Snake River flows through Hells Canyon. Here 649,956 acres, including parts of the Nez Perce and Payette National Forests in ID, became the Hells Canyon National Recreation Area by Act of Congress in 1975.

Climate is as varied as the terrain. Annual precipitation ranges from desert conditions, less than 10 in., to as much as 40 in., including much snow in the high country. Many streams feed the rivers flowing from the Forest, including the Burnt, Grande Ronde, Imnaha, John Day, Lostine, Minam, Powder, and Wallowa.

The Forest is well and favorably known by many backpackers, hunters, and fishermen and -women, as well as skiers, but its distance from large cities limits crowding. The lakes are popular camping places in summer, but anyone who hikes can find as much solitude as wished.

**Plants:** Only about half of the region is forested. The balance is a mixture of alpine zone vegetation, barren slopes, grassy meadows, desert plant communities, and riparian fringes. Principal tree species: ponderosa and lodgepole pine, Douglas-fir, white fir, western larch, Engelmann spruce. Great variations of altitude, soils, and moisture produce many different plant communities. More than 500 species have been identified on the lower slopes of Hells Canyon alone. Wildflower displays peak April–June at low elevations, July–Aug. on high slopes. Among many flowering species: buttercup, lupines, fleabane, western clematis, fawn lily, monkeyflower, penstemons, phacelia, aster, spring beauty, heather, bluebell, phlox, blazing star, arrow-leaved balsamroot, evening primrose.

**Birds:** No checklist. Many habitats include wide assortment of species. Those reported include tundra swan, Canada goose, mallard, teals, wood duck, goldeneye, Virginia rail, killdeer, long-billed curlew, spotted sandpiper, avocet, goshawk, golden and bald eagles, prairie falcon, blue grouse, calliope hummingbird, white-headed woodpecker, mountain chickadee, dipper, varied and hermit thrushes, vireos, veery, marsh wren, 3 warblers, yellow-breasted chat, Cassin's and gray-crowned rosy finches, pine siskin.

**Mammals:** No checklist. Species reported include a few bighorn sheep, mountain goat, mountain lion, seldom seen. Also 3 bats, deer mouse, pika, snowshoe hare, weasel, badger, spotted skunk, bobcat, coyote, beaver, elk, mule deer, black bear.

## Features

*Hells Canyon National Recreation Area:* 649,956 acres in OR and ID, includes the 216,342-acre Hells Canyon Wilderness and the National Wild and Scenic River section of the Snake River. Hells Canyon, cut by the Snake River, is the world's deepest river gorge, averaging 6,600 ft., 20 mi. long. The upper 5 mi. is flooded by Hells Canyon Dam, but the area is now protected against further alterations.

Numerous outfitters offer float and jet boat trips. The floating season is about May 20–Sept. 10. Private parties who wish to float the river must make reservations and obtain a permit from Hells Canyon National Recreation Area, P.O. Box 699, Clarkston, WA 99403.

About 5,000 visitors travel the canyon each year by boat, by horse, or on foot. This is wild country, and one should know what to expect before setting forth.

S entry into the canyon is from Oxbow, OR, on Hwy 86, crossing into ID, N to Hells Canyon Dam, across the dam back to OR, the road ending in ¼ mi. From Enterprise on Hwy 82, roads lead to the Hat Point Viewpoint, overlooking the canyon. Ask about current road conditions from Imnaha to Hat Point. From Asotin, WA, a 23-mi. gravel road follows the Snake upstream to the Grande Ronde River.

The Wilderness Area, on the OR side, is a strip 4 to 6 mi. wide along the Snake River. This area is roadless. It is surrounded by the larger portion of the Recreation Area, which is penetrated by a few Forest roads. (Check on conditions before trying them.) Many hiking trails in the entire area. Many streams, but water should be purified for drinking; many streams are dry July–Sept. Winter weather in the canyon is usually mild. The high country is usually snow-covered until late spring or early summer.

*Hells Canyon Scenic Byway* offers some of the most dramatic scenery in the country. The 314-mi. trip, on a combination of county, state, private, and Forest roads, includes a loop road through the Wallowa Mountains. The Wallowa Mountain Loop (Forest Rd. 39) is about 54 mi. of paved 2-lane roads and 11 mi. of 1½-lane roads. A side trip off the loop should include the Hells Canyon Overlook, which offers a view of canyon country with open slopes and rolling hills visible across the entire canyon. The overlook is 3 mi. from the junction of Forest Rds. 39 and 396.

*Eagle Cap Wilderness:* 356,158 acres. Generally W and S of Enterprise. Includes the highest peaks of the Wallowas, more than 50 lakes, many in glacial cirques. The Minam, Lostine, Wallowa, and Imnaha Rivers flow from the slopes of Eagle Cap. Fishing is good to excellent; special bag limits apply on some lakes.

The wilderness map is 1:100,000 scale contour. Mileage is also marked. Usual season is July 1–Oct. 30, shorter for some of the highest lakes and passes. Saddle and pack horses can be used, subject to a few regulations. Wilderness entry points are Forest trails, though in several places a road is less than a mile away. Permits available at trailheads.

The *Minam River Gorge* enters from the present wilderness area and extends NW. Prominent ridges, deep canyons. Heavily forested stream and river bottoms; bare and rocky ridges.

*Anthony Lakes Recreation Area* lies W of North Powder off I-84. Winter ski area. Summer camping, hiking, fishing, boating. Several well-maintained trails of different levels within approximately 20 sq. mi., including Elkhorn Crest Trail, 22.6 mi.; Lakes Lookout Trail, 0.7 mi., difficult; Crawfish Basin/Elkhorn Trail Loop, 5.3 mi.; Van Patten Lake, 0.5 mi., moderate; Crawfish Lake, 1.6 mi.; Anthony Lake Shoreline Loop, 1 mi.; Hoffer Lakes Loop, 1 mi.; and Black Lake Trail, 1 mi., easy.

*Phillips Lake,* 2,450 acres, is a popular recreation area: camping, fishing, swimming, boating. *Nature trail,* ½ mi.

*Wallowa Lake,* about the same size, is just outside the Forest boundary, S of Joseph on Hwy 82. This is one of the gateways to the Forest and Eagle Cap Wilderness.

*Wallowa State Park:* 166 acres. On the lake, opens when winter weather ends. 210 campsites. Reservations. Hiking, fishing, swimming, boating. Ramp; boat rentals.

*Catherine Creek State Park:* 168 acres. Just outside the Forest on Hwy 203 about 5 mi. SE of Union. 10 primitive campsites. Access to trails and Forest roads.

*Elkhorn Dr.* is a 106-mi. loop road W of Baker, passing through a scenic part of the Forest, various plant communities. A brochure describes highlights of the trip, which include the Anthony Lakes region and Phillips Lake.

*Lostine Canyon Scenic Dr.,* 18.9 mi., follows the route of an ancient glacier. From Lostine off Hwy 82.

## Activities

*Camping:* Approximately 58 campgrounds, 461 sites. Earliest opening April 15, some as late as July 1.

*Hiking, backpacking:* No data, but Forest maps show hundreds of miles of trails, at all altitudes, plus hundreds of miles of little-used Forest roads. The Hells Canyon and Eagle Cap areas are favored by backpackers, but other parts of the Forest are also attractive, including areas accessible earlier in the year.

*Hunting:* Deer, elk, bear, pheasant, blue and ruffed grouse. Sheep subject to special permit.

*Fishing:* Brook, rainbow, cutthroat. In the Snake, smallmouth bass, sturgeon, channel catfish.

*Swimming:* Lakes.

*Boating:* Chiefly at Phillips, Wallowa, and Anthony Lakes, and above Hells Canyon Dam. Rafting on the Snake River in Hells Canyon, with licensed outfitters or by permit. Also floating trips on the Grande Ronde and its upper tributary, the Wallowa, by raft, drift boat, or kayak or canoe. Essential to obtain full information before beginning trip.

*Horse riding:* Pack trips in the Forest, especially the wilderness areas. Outfitters nearby; ask at HQ.

*Skiing:* Ski area at Anthony Lake. Wallowa Lake offers cross-country skiing. Gondola to 8,200-ft. Mount Howard open summer only, for scenic views.

*Ski touring:* Some marked trails. Many unplowed Forest roads offer opportunities.

*Snowmobiling:* 850 mi. of signed trails. Trail map with information available.

### Publications

Maps: Wallowa-Whitman Forest; Hell's Canyon National Recreation Area; Eagle Cap Wilderness; Snowmobile trails.

*Anthony Lakes Recreation Area.*

*The Elkhorn Drive* (leaflet).

*Floating the Grande Ronde.*

*Campground Directory* (leaflet).

### Headquarters

U.S. Forest Service, P.O. Box 907, Baker City, OR 97814; (541) 523-6391.

### Ranger Districts

Baker R.D., 3165 10th St., Baker City, OR 97814; (541) 523-4476. Eagle Cap R.D., 88401 Hwy 82, Enterprise, OR 97828; (541) 426-4978. Hells Canyon NRA, 88401 Hwy 82, Enterprise, OR 97828; (541) 426-4978. La Grande R.D., 3502 Hwy 30, La Grande, OR 97850; (541) 963-7186. Pine R.D., General Delivery, Halfway, OR 97834; (541) 742-7511. Unity R.D., P.O. Box 38, Unity, OR 97884; (541) 446-3351. Wallowa Valley R.D., 88401 Hwy 82, Enterprise, OR 97828; (541) 426-4978. Wallowa-Whitman R.D., P.O. Box 907, Baker City, OR 97814; (541) 523-6391.

---

## Wenaha Wildlife Management Area

Oregon Department of Fish and Wildlife
10,660 acres.

Difficult road access. Hwy 3 (Enterprise, Lewiston) to Grande Ronde River. Across river, county road SW to Troy, about 18 mi. Wildlife area is around Troy, mostly SW.

Elk winter range. The elk move to higher ground about end of May. Present acreage is very irregular in shape; many inholdings. About 8

mi. of joint boundary with Umatilla National Forest; short section of joint boundary with Wenaha-Tucannon Wilderness. About 6 mi. of frontage on Grande Ronde and Wenaha Rivers, E and W of Troy. Rivers flow through steep-sided canyons. Climate is semiarid.

**Plants:** Western juniper with big sagebrush, wheatgrass. Idaho fescue. In more humid places, ponderosa pine with Douglas-fir, grand fir, western larch; understory includes sagebrush, bitterbrush, snowberry, spirea.

**Birds:** Species include great blue heron, Canada goose, mallard, green-winged teal, shoveler, wood duck, common and Barrow's goldeneyes, hooded and common mergansers, coot, goshawk, sharp-shinned, Cooper's, red-tailed, and rough-legged hawks, golden and bald eagles, osprey, blue and ruffed grouse, California quail, chukar, common snipe, screech, flammulated, great horned, pygmy, long-eared, short-eared, and saw-whet owls, black-chinned, rufous, and calliope hummingbirds, pileated, Lewis's, hairy, downy, and white-headed woodpeckers, gray jay, black-capped and mountain chickadees, canyon and rock wrens, bohemian and cedar waxwings, northern and loggerhead shrikes, 5 warblers, 4 grosbeaks.

**Mammals:** Elk, mule deer, Columbian white-tailed deer, black bear, mountain lion, bobcat, raccoon, striped skunk, mink, beaver, weasel, badger, ground squirrel, pine squirrel, marmot.

**Reptiles and amphibians:** Long-toed salamander, western toad, tree frog, spotted frog, western fence lizard, Pacific gopher snake, rubber snake, mountain and wandering garter snakes. Great Basin rattlesnake.

## Activities

*Camping:* Primitive sites. No water.

*Fishing:* Rainbow, Dolly Varden, whitefish, steelhead, chinook, largemouth bass.

## Publication

Information sheet with map showing open roads.

## Headquarters

OR Dept. of Fish and Wildlife, Rt. 2, Box 2283, La Grande, OR 97850; (541) 963-2138.

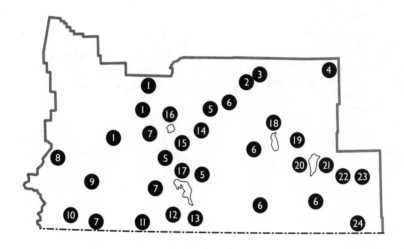

1. Umpqua National Forest
2. Fort Rock State Monument
3. Christmas Valley Area
4. Glass Butte Recreational Rockhound Area
5. Winema National Forest
6. Fremont National Forest
7. Rogue River National Forest
8. Zane Grey
9. Rogue Wild and Scenic River
10. Oregon Caves National Monument
11. Soda Mountain
12. Bear Valley National Wildlife Refuge
13. Klamath Wildlife Area
14. Klamath Marsh National Wildlife Refuge
15. Sun Pass State Forest
16. Crater Lake National Park
17. Upper Klamath National Wildlife Refuge
18. Summer Lake Wildlife Area
19. Diablo Mountain; Wildcat Mountain; Coglan Buttes
20. Lake Abert
21. Abert Rim
22. Warner Lakes
23. Hart Mountain National Antelope Refuge
24. Spaulding Reservoir

# ZONE 5

Includes these counties:

Douglas (except portion on coast)  Klamath

Josephine  Lake  Jackson

The W portion of zone 5 is mountainous. On the SW and S are parts of the Siskiyou National Forest. Parts of the Rogue River National Forest are on the S and E. The Umpqua National Forest is on the NE.

The central portion of the zone straddles the Cascade Range. Most of this area is National Forest land, plus Crater Lake National Park. It includes many peaks from 5,000 to 9,500 ft. high, many rushing streams. Just E of the Park, extending N and S along US 97, is the Klamath Basin, a region of shallow lakes and wetlands, a stopover for some 4 million ducks and geese in migration, nesting grounds for many waterfowl and wading and shorebirds. Upper Klamath Lake is the largest in OR. The basin includes several interesting Refuges.

Beyond the mountains of the Fremont National Forest, E of the Klamath Basin, is the beginning of the high desert region. Here are many shallow alkali lakes and ephemeral lakes, vestiges of a huge, ancient lake, as well as some productive marshes. The NE portion of the zone has many volcanic features. In the SE is the Hart Mountain National Antelope Refuge, above a dramatic fault scarp. This E part of the zone is predominantly public land. The high desert is mostly public domain, managed by the BLM.

Thus the zone contains a great variety of habitats: elevations from 1,000 to almost 10,000 ft., climates from humid to dry. The zone has alpine meadows, extensive forests, wetlands, rivers, lakes, and sagebrush desert. Terrain includes jagged peaks, sheer fault scarps, rolling hills, canyons, green valleys, and desert flats.

## Abert Rim

U.S. Bureau of Land Management
22,800 acres.

Above US 395 about 25 mi. N of Lakeview.

One of the highest fault scarps in North America, rising some 2,500 ft. above the valley floor, overlooking Lake Abert (see entry this zone). In the Miocene period, lava covered much of E OR. Later, fractures occurred, and great blocks were tilted. The rim is the W edge of one block; the lake is atop another.

Above the rim, terrain is generally flat, sloping slightly to the E. Low basalt cliffs in the SE. An interesting feature is Colvin Timbers, a remnant stand of ponderosa pine. Sagebrush plant community over most of the area, some juniper in the SE. Pronghorn seen occasionally. Area used for grazing; fences, stock reservoirs, vehicle ways.

Most of the area adjoining to the NE is BLM land.

*Hiking:* Best access to top of rim is from Fremont National Forest roads leading N from Hwy 140. Rim extends S into the Forest. Map and local information both needed. The view is exceptional, but the area is otherwise undistinguished.

### Headquarters

Bureau of Land Management, Lakeview District, 1000 S. 9th St., Lakeview, OR 97630; (541) 947-2177.

## Bear Valley National Wildlife Refuge

U.S. Fish and Wildlife Service
4,200 acres.

Take US 97 to just S of Worden, turn left onto access road ½ mi. to observation point. Road stops short of the Refuge.

The Refuge was established in 1978 to protect a major night roost site of wintering bald eagles. Consisting mainly of old-growth ponderosa pine, incense cedar, Douglas-fir, and white fir. The mature stands, with large limbs, make perfect landing and resting spots for the eagles. Located on a NE slope, the roost also shelters the raptors from the harsh and prevailing winter winds. As many as 300 birds have used the area in a single night. Several bald eagle pairs also nest in the Refuge.

The Refuge is closed to all public entry, *except* walk-in deer hunters in season (fall until Nov. 1), in order to reduce disturbance to the birds. Excellent opportunities Dec.–March to observe early morning fly-outs of large numbers of bald eagles and other raptors from just outside the Refuge at Bear Valley observation area.

### Publications

*Klamath Basin National Wildlife Refuges.*

*Bald Eagles of the Klamath Basin.*

*Common Wildlife of the National Wildlife Refuges.*

Checklist of wildlife.

### Headquarters

U.S. Fish and Wildlife Service, Klamath Basin National Wildlife Refuges, Rt. 1, Box 74, Tulelake, CA 96134; (906) 667-2231.

---

## Christmas Valley Area

U.S. Bureau of Land Management
210,000 acres.

From Hwy 31 (Lakeview to La Pine) about 18 mi. N of Silver Lake, E on county road to Fort Rock and Christmas Valley.

This entry describes the area generally N of the valley. From the valley, BLM roads lead to other parts of the area. Roads to Crack-in-the-Ground, Devils Garden, and Four Craters are usually in good condition. Others may be also, but inquire, especially in wet weather.

High lava plains. Elevations generally above 4,000 ft. Highest point is a 5,585-ft. lava cone. The area is of interest because of its volcanic features, fossil beds, and an unusual forest. Low, rolling terrain with shallow, dry lakebeds. Climate is dry. No permanent lakes or streams. Cool winters, hot summers. Spring and fall are the best hiking seasons.

**Plants:** Mostly big sagebrush, gray and green rabbitbrush, scattered juniper in the S, moderate to dense juniper with big sagebrush and bitterbrush to the N. Lava-associated plants include penstemon, phacelia, groundsels, biennial cinquefoil, larkspur, showy townsendia, sulphur flower, sagebrush mariposa, hoary aster. Sand dunes and fossil lake plants include prostrate amaranth, silvery lupine, salt heliotrope, saltgrass; shrubs include greasewood, spiny hopsage, shadscale saltbush.

**Birds:** Species reported include bald and golden eagles, prairie falcon, rough-legged and red-tailed hawks, loggerhead shrike, pinyon jay, magpie, Brewer's blackbird, northern flicker. Large wintering flocks of robin, mountain bluebird, Townsend's solitaire in juniper woods.

**Mammals:** Species reported include coast mole, black-tailed and white-tailed jackrabbits, cottontail, kangaroo rat, porcupine, yellow-pine chipmunk, wood rat, deer mouse, Townsend ground squirrel, coyote, mountain lion, bobcat, badger. Winter range for 25,000–40,000 mule deer.

## Features

*Devils Garden Lava Bed,* 8 mi. NE of Fort Rock. 45-sq.-mi. lava flow. S half is rather smooth-surfaced, moderate irregularities. N portion very rugged, difficult walking, some cinder cones. Considerable variety of lava formations. The "garden" is the central area, not lava-covered, with sagebrush, grasses, some juniper. In NE is *Derrick Cave,* a large lava tube, undeveloped.

*Four Craters Lava Bed,* 9 mi. N of Christmas Valley. Surrounding area has sagebrush flats and low, rolling hills. Craters area, about 5,000 acres, is recent lava flow, extremely rough surface features, with four large spatter cones. *Crack-in-the-Ground* is a unique geological feature, an extensive crack with depths up to 70 ft.

*Fossil Beds,* E of Christmas Valley. As an ancient lake dried, sand blew off, exposing a bog where fossils had been preserved. Over 7,000 acres closed to all vehicles. *Fossil collecting prohibited.*

*Lost Forest,* NE of Christmas Valley. A Research Natural Area. Sand blowing into a ponderosa forest appears to have served as a mulch, maintaining an area of forest in a region with a dry climate, generally too dry for such growth. Sand dunes to W and S.

*Squaw Ridge Lava Bed,* about 2½ mi. E of the Devils Garden Bed, 12 mi. NE of Fort Rock. Feature is *Lava Butte,* large peak, surrounded by very rugged terrain.

### Activities

*Camping:* Any suitable place on BLM land. No facilities.

*Hiking, backpacking:* No trails. Bushwhacking is feasible; country is open with numerous landmarks. Some of the lava beds offer difficult footing. Essential to carry sufficient water.

*Hiking in the lava beds is hazardous: rough footing, sharp rocks.*

*Sand dunes E of Fossil Lake are open to and much used by ORVs.*

*Advisable to consult HQ for maps, current information on roads.*

### Nearby
Fort Rock State Monument (see entry this zone).

### Headquarters
Bureau of Land Management, Lakeview District, 1000 S. 9th St., Lakeview, OR 97630; (541) 947-2177.

----

## Crater Lake National Park
U.S. National Park Service
183,180 acres.

From Klamath Falls, N on US 97 and Hwy 62, 57 mi.

About 6,700 years ago, vast quantities of lava were ejected from Mount Mazama, leaving a cavity into which the mountaintop collapsed. Rain and snow collected in the cavity, forming a lake of 21½ sq. mi., 4½ to 6 mi. across, 1,932 ft. deep, one of the world's deepest lakes. A jagged rim surrounds the lake, rising almost vertically 500 to 2,000 ft. above its surface. Back of the rim, the outward slope is gradual.

The main visitor access route enters from the south. Rim Dr., a 33-mi. auto route, circles the lake. The S and W entrance roads are open all year. Rim Dr. and the N entrance road are closed by snow, usually from mid-Oct. to early July. Although the Park has over half a million visitors a year, most are day visitors who arrive at Rim Village, travel all or part of Rim Dr. Few enter the surrounding parklands.

The Park is surrounded by National Forests. Elevations from 4,400 ft. at the S entrance to 8,926 at Mount Scott, a parasitic cone on the E side of Mount Mazama. Several treeless, pumice-covered flats recall past volcanic activity. Most of the Park is heavily forested, open and parklike except in the SE.

The lake has no inflowing streams and no outlet. A number of streams originating on the mountainside drain to the Rogue or Klamath Rivers. Most precipitation falls as snow, about 50 ft. per year at Park HQ. Only about 6% of precipitation falls June–Aug. Within the Park, precipitation varies with altitude and location. The E slopes, in rain shadow, are semiarid.

**Plants:** Four principal plant communities: ponderosa pine forest to about 5,500 ft.; lodgepole pine forest from 5,500–6,500 ft.; and mountain hemlock forest to over 8,000 ft. The fourth is pumice desert, treeless except where lodgepole is invading. Each community is a complex of species. In all, about 570 species have been identified within the Park. Common trees are Douglas-fir, Shasta red, noble, white, and subalpine firs, western white, whitebark, and sugar pines, mountain and western hemlock. The many shrubs include willows, alders, ash, California hazel, chinquapin, currant, gooseberry, spirea, thimbleberry, raspberry, serviceberry, ceanothus, dogwood, mountain heath, manzanita, snowberry, big sagebrush, rabbitbrush.

Wildflowers include phlox, western pasqueflower, sulphur flower, violets, columbine, monkeyflower, gillas, monkshood, aster, lupines, fireweed, orchids. July and Aug. have best flower displays.

**Birds:** Checklist available. About 175 species recorded. Most often seen: Clark's nutcracker, gray jay, Steller's jay. Also common: blue and ruffed grouse, red-tailed hawk, hairy woodpecker, pygmy owl, black-backed three-toed woodpecker, mountain and chestnut-backed chickadees, red-breasted nuthatch, dipper, winter wren, kinglets, Cassin's finch, pine siskin, pine grosbeak, dark-eyed junco, western tanager, 6 warblers.

**Mammals:** Checklist. Common species include vagrant shrew, shrewmole, 2 bats, deer mouse, voles, marten, weasel, badger, coyote, red fox, marmot, golden-mantled ground squirrel, Townsend chipmunk, chickaree, porcupine, pika, snowshoe hare, elk, mule deer, black bear.

**Reptiles and amphibians:** Checklist. Often seen: long-toed salamander, boreal toad, Pacific tree frog, Cascades frog. Valley garter snake is only snake reported.

## Features

*Rim Village* is the center of visitor activity: overlooks, visitor center, shops, services. Gasoline is available in summer only at Mazama Campground.

*Mazama Flats Wilderness:* 9,200 acres, including acreage in the Umpqua National Forest. Elevations from 5,000 to 6,200 ft. Includes a major part of the Rogue River headwaters and the deep canyon of Upper Mazama Creek.

*Red Blanket Wilderness:* 5,200 acres. On the SW flank of Mount Mazama. Elevations from 3,800 to 6,000 ft.; no prominent peak. N section includes Thousand Springs. S end terminates at walls of Red Blanket Canyon. Lower part of the canyon is prime winter range for elk, deer.

*Sphagnum Bog Wilderness:* 6,800 acres. NW side of Park. Separated from Red Blanket Wilderness only by Hwy 62. Also on the lower slopes of Mount Mazama. Includes the 680-acre *Sphagnum Bog Special Interest Scenic Area.*

*Sand Creek–Pinnacles Area,* in SE corner, extends into adjacent National Forest. Wide canyon with sloping walls of scoria and pumice. Branch road from Rim Dr.

*Garfield Peak,* 8,060 ft., reached by 1.7-mi. trail along rim wall.

*The Watchman,* 8,025 ft., also offers sweeping vistas. On W side of rim, reached by 0.8-mi. trail.

*Cloudcap,* 8,070 ft., E of side of rim, can be reached by auto, short spur road.

*Castle Crest Wildflower Garden,* near Park HQ, has species found in the Park.

*Sphagnum Bog and Boundary Springs* are among several unique ecological areas. Because they are fragile, they have been given special protection. Botanists and others with serious interest may inquire.

## Interpretation

*Visitor center* at Rim Village. At Sinnott Memorial Overlook, *frequent ranger talks.*

*Information counter* at HQ.

*Rim Rd.,* 33 mi., has many wayside *exhibits* and *overlooks.*

*Nature trails* at Castle Crest Wildflower Garden and near Mazama Campground. Also Godfrey Glen Nature Trail.

*Boat trips* on Crater Lake include talks by rangers.

*Evening programs* at Rim Center Building and Mazama Campground, summer months.

## Activities

*Camping:* Mazama Campground, 198 sites, mid-June to end of Sept., snow permitting. Lost Creek: 12 primitive sites.

*Hiking, backpacking:* 65 mi. of trails, including 26 mi. of Pacific Crest Trail, which crosses the Park. Many short hikes, easy to moderate. Backcountry travel is very light, partly because of the short season.

*Fishing* is permitted but not popular. Stocking the lake has been discontinued.

*Ski touring:* In area around HQ. Cafeteria and curio shop are open in winter.

*Snowmobiling:* Restricted to N entrance road, which is not plowed.

## Adjacent
Umpqua, Winema, and Rogue River National Forests (see entries zone 5).

## Publications
Leaflet with map.

Checklists of birds, mammals, amphibians and reptiles, trees.

Mimeo information pages: origin of Crater Lake, snowshoeing, ski touring, winter camping.

## Headquarters
National Park Service, P.O. Box 7, Crater Lake, OR 97604; (541) 594-2211.

## Diablo Mountain; Wildcat Mountain; Coglan Buttes

U.S. Bureau of Land Management
333,360 acres.

NE of Hwy 31 between Lake Abert and Summer Lake. Access from local roads NE from Paisley and E from town of Summer Lake.

High desert. The 2 lakes, now 25 mi. apart, were once part of a large lake. Both are shallow, too alkaline for fish, with extensive saltflats exposed in dry seasons. From Summer Lake, the land rises gradually to the E. Mount Diablo, at 6,145 ft., is part of a N–S rim, the E edge dropping vertically 1,800 ft. Other high points in the area: Wildcat Mountain, 5,560 ft.; Tough Peak, 5,625 ft.; Euchre Butte, 5,315 ft.; Coglan Buttes, 6,207 ft. Most of the area is relatively flat; some low, rolling hills; many shallow, ephemeral lake basins. Several fault block ridges with steep escarpments, basalt rims. Sand dunes near Summer Lake.

Parts of the area are grazed, and ranchers have established a few small watering places. Hikers must bring all the water they need. Spring and fall are the best hiking times.

The area is crossed by a number of BLM roads. For information on road conditions and available maps, check at the BLM office.

Mount Diablo, E of Summer Lake, is surrounded by a 113,000-acre roadless area proposed for wilderness status. Few hikers or backpackers enter this harsh area. These few favor the Diablo Rim, chiefly for its sweeping vistas.

**Plants:** Near the 2 lakes, salt-tolerant species such as shadscale, greasewood, spiny hopsage, Indian ricegrass, desert paintbrush, seablite, showy townsendia, hoary aster, common cryptantha, hairy evening primrose. Between the lakes: sagebrush, rabbitbrush, squirreltail, needlegrass, death camas, larkspur, specklepod milkvetch.

**Birds:** Nesting golden eagle; prairie falcon, kestrel, red-tailed hawk. Around Coglan Buttes, sparse, scattered nests of burrowing and short-eared owls. For water and shorebirds of the lakes, see entries this zone for Lake Abert and Summer Lake Wildlife Area.

**Mammals:** Sparse herds of deer and pronghorn. Deer mice, voles, woodrat, rabbit. Wild horses sometimes seen in N of area.

## Headquarters

Bureau of Land Management, Lakeview District, 1000 S. 9th St., Lakeview, OR 97630; (541) 947-2177.

........................................................................

## Fort Rock State Monument

Oregon Parks and Recreation Department
190 acres.

From US 97 near La Pine, about 26 mi. SE, then 7 mi. E on county road to Fort Rock.

One of OR's most spectacular geological features, an unusual crater known as a *tuff ring*. Almost ½ mi. in diameter, 325 ft. above base at highest point. Surrounded by sagebrush flats.

### Nearby

Christmas Valley Area (see entry this zone).

........................................................................

## Fremont National Forest

U.S. Forest Service
1,196,351 acres; 1,710,750 acres within boundaries.

Two areas. (1) W of Lakeview, from the CA border to Hwy 31 near junction with US 97. (2) E of Lakeview, N and S of Hwy 140.

The Forest land includes over 100 fragments of less than 1 sq. mi., as well as several large blocks. Although the blocks include numerous inholdings, these do not obstruct visitor activities. On the Forest boundaries are the Deschutes and Winema National Forests, the Modoc National Forest in CA, and much BLM land.

Generally rolling terrain with numerous mountain peaks, on the E side of the Cascade Mountains. Elevations from 4,150 ft. to Crane Mountain, 8,454 ft. Precipitation averages 22 in. per year, with considerable variation depending on location and elevation. Dry summers. Substantial snowfall on the high slopes. Forest roads in the high country may be closed by snow Dec. 1–May 1.

Part of the W area is close to Summer Lake (see entry this zone for Summer Lake Wildlife Area). Here forested slopes rise from the lakeshore to Winter Ridge, looking out over the lake and surrounding desert. This pattern is common to the region: timbered slopes rising from sagebrush flatland.

The E portion includes the S part of Abert Rim (see entry this zone), highest fault scarp in the U.S. A Forest road leads to a dramatic viewpoint overlooking Lake Abert.

Although most of the site is forested, it includes some meadows and high semidesert. Numerous small streams carry off snowmelt. Largest are the Sprague, Chewaucan, and Sycan Rivers. Thompson Reservoir, 2,600 acres, is the largest body of water, a recreation area. Dog Lake, 491 acres, is the only other lake of more than 100 acres, but the Forest includes many smaller ones.

**Plants:** Checklist available. 85% forested. Three principal forest types: ponderosa pine, mixed conifer, lodgepole. Prominent tree species include ponderosa and lodgepole pines, white fir, incense cedar. Remaining old-growth stands are about 3%–5% of the total. Understory species include bitterbrush, sagebrush, currant. In sites not forested: juniper, low sagebrush, fescues, grasses. Flowering species include arrow-leaved balsamroot, aster, bleeding heart, fireweed, foxglove, clarkia, penstemons, phacelia, spreading phlox, twinflower, western yarrow.

**Birds:** Checklist. 176 species recorded. 85 species are all-year residents. Species include grebes, white pelican, great blue and green-backed herons, black-crowned night heron, American bittern, tundra swan, Canada, white-fronted, snow, and Ross's geese, many ducks, goshawk, sharp-shinned, Cooper's, red-tailed, Swainson's, rough-legged, and ferruginous hawks, golden and bald eagles, 3 grouse, 8 owls, all woodpeckers found in the region, 3 jays, varied and hermit thrushes, both kinglets, 4 finches, 7 warblers.

**Mammals:** Checklist of 67 species. Includes numerous shrews, mice, rats, bats, pika, white-tailed and black-tailed jackrabbits, marmot, ground squirrels, porcupine, marten, fisher, weasel, mink, badger, mountain lion, bobcat, elk, mule deer, pronghorn, black bear.

**Reptiles and amphibians:** 22 species said to be present, but no checklist.

## Features

*Gearhart Mountain Wilderness:* 22,809 acres. At 8,354 ft., Gearhart Mountain is the highest of many volcanic domes in western Lake County. Cirques and U-shaped valleys are the marks of vanished glaciers. Picturesque rock formations cap most of the ridgetops, which offer sweeping vistas. High mountain meadows. Lower, lodgepole pine forests and mixed ponderosa pine-white fir forests. Blue Lake is the only lake in the area.

A singe 12-mi. trail with a 4-mi. spur crosses the wilderness, along the ridge, dropping down to Blue Lake. The terrain and open forests make bushwhacking feasible. (Snowdrifts on the trail persist until mid-June or early July.) Terrain and snow cover favor ski touring and snowshoeing in winter, but access roads are likely to be blocked by snow. Saddle and pack horses are subject to special rules.

*Crane Mountain roadless area:* 23,396 acres. Near CA border. Crane Mountain, 8,454 ft., is the highest point in the Forest.

*North Warner Viewpoint,* overlooking Crooked Creek Canyon, is also on Forest Rd. 3615 leading to the Abert Rim Viewpoint.

*Scenic drive:* Forest Rd. 290, along Winter Ridge, overlooking Summer Lake. Access from Hwy 31 N of Summer Lake (turning S) or from Hwy 31 via Forest Rd. 3313 near the S end of Summer Lake.

## Activities

*Camping:* 19 campgrounds, 181 sites. May 15–Oct. 15. Also, 3 historic fire lookouts available as rentals.

*Hiking, backpacking:* The Forest reports only 200 mi. of trails. However, it has 6,000 mi. of roads, most of them unpaved and little used. Also, most forest areas are open, inviting off-trail travel.

*Hunting:* Chiefly mule deer, blue grouse.

*Fishing:* 395 mi. of fishing streams. Brook and rainbow trout. Also lakes with bass, perch, catfish.

*Boating:* Power boats on Thompson Reservoir. 5 mph limit on Dog Lake. No motors on other lakes.

*Canoeing:* Lakes only. Canoe camping on Dead Horse Lake.

*Horse riding:* Some use of horses, but no nearby outfitters. Allowed on all trails and roads unless specifically prohibited.

*Skiing:* Ski area on summit of Warner Mountain. Usual season Dec.–March.

*Ski touring:* On unplowed roads, suitable trails. Usual season Jan. 1–April 15.

*Snowmobiling:* Forest reports about 189 mi. of suitable trails, not groomed.

## Publications

Forest map, $3.25.

Gearhart Mountain Wilderness map, $2.25.

Checklists of plants, birds, mammals.

List of recreation sites.

## Headquarters

U.S. Forest Service, 524 N. G St., Lakeview, OR 97630; (541) 947-2151.

## Ranger Districts

Bly R.D., Bly, OR 97622; (541) 353-2427. Lakeview R.D., Lakeview, OR 97630; (541) 947-3334. Paisley R.D., Paisley, OR 97636; (541) 943-3114. Silver Lake R.D., Silver Lake, OR 97638; (541) 576-2107.

## Glass Butte Recreational Rockhound Area

U.S. Bureau of Land Management
10,911 acres.

10 mi. SE of Hampton on S side of US 20.

Dominant feature is pyramidal Glass Butte, elevation 6,385 ft., about 1,500 ft. above surrounding land. To NW and E are several canyons extending from Glass Butte, forming steep-sloped valleys and low, rolling hills with massive reddish-brown and gray basaltic outcroppings and boulders. Vegetation mainly clusters of juniper, mountain mahogany, big sagebrush, rabbitbrush. Below the W and S slopes of the Butte, lower rolling hills with stands of juniper. Smaller N–S canyons to the S. Native Americans gathered obsidian here, and rockhounds still do. Site includes miles of fencing and ways, cattle troughs, reservoirs, a microwave station atop the Butte.

No facilities, primitive camping only.

**Headquarters**
Bureau of Land Management, Prineville District, 3050 N.E. 3rd St., Prineville, OR 97754; (541) 416-6700.

---

## Hart Mountain National Antelope Refuge
U.S. Fish and Wildlife Service
278,000 acres.

From Lakeview, 6 mi. N on US 395. E about 16 mi. on Hwy 140, then NE 19 mi. on county road to Plush. Follow signs 25 mi. NE to HQ. (Also see note on alternate routes, cautions.)

One of the most unusual wildlife refuges. Remote, with relatively few visitors, but usually accessible by any auto in good condition. Massive fault block ridge. W side is a scenic, rugged escarpment rising 3,600 ft. above Warner Lakes (see entry this zone); cliffs, steep slopes, knife ridges. Several canyons extend from the valley floor to the ridgetop. Entrance road passes roadless canyons well worth exploring. Highest point is Warner Peak, 8,065 ft. E side descends gradually in series of hills and low ridges.

Somewhat surprisingly, the area has a number of reliable springs, cold and "hot." Rock Creek flows from the NE, emerging from a deep canyon onto open range near HQ. Other creeks flow S and E.

The Refuge was established to provide spring, summer, and fall range for pronghorn, most of which move S to the Charles Sheldon Antelope Range (NV) in winter. Mission has been expanded to include all high desert wildlife.

Entire Refuge is open to foot and horse travel. It is one of the few federal Refuges that has a campground and that permits backcountry camping.

**Plants:** Mostly sagebrush community. Native plants important to wildlife are wheatgrass, Thurber's needlegrass, squirreltail, Sandberg bluegrass, Indian ricegrass, Idaho fescue, wild buckwheat, low and big sagebrush, bitterbrush. Isolated stands of juniper, aspen, some old-growth ponderosa. Colorful wildflower display in early summer.

**Birds:** Checklist of 264 species includes records from nearby Warner Lakes, a noted birding area. Seasonally common or abundant high desert species include turkey vulture, red-tailed, Swainson's, and rough-legged hawks, golden eagle, sage grouse (several strutting grounds), California quail, killdeer, mourning dove, great horned and short-eared owls, poorwill, nighthawk, northern flicker, western kingbird, ash-throated and Hammond's flycatchers, Say's phoebe, western wood pewee, horned lark, barn and cliff swallows, magpie, raven, crow, black-capped and mountain chickadees, white-breasted nuthatch, canyon wren, robin, mountain bluebird, Townsend's solitaire, kinglets, northern shrike, yellow-breasted chat, western meadowlark, western tanager, evening grosbeak, goldfinch, rufous-sided towhee, lark and sage sparrows.

**Mammals:** Include pronghorn, mule deer, bighorn sheep, coyote, feral horse, ground squirrel, kangaroo rat, marmot, bobcat.

### Interpretation
*Information* is best obtained at the HQ in Lakeview. The field HQ is often unmanned, but leaflets and maps are available.

### Activities
*Camping:* One campground open whenever the Refuge is accessible, 1 other open Aug. 1. Both primitive.

*Hiking, backpacking:* No trails, but cross-country hiking is said to be excellent, especially along Poker Jim Ridge to NE and on Hart Mountain to S. Permit required for overnighting. (Backcountry permit, self-issued at Refuge HQ.)

*Hunting:* Pronghorn, mule deer, bighorn. Special regulations; inquire.

*Fishing:* Small streams, pond. Trout.

*Horse riding:* Horse travel is permitted. Corrals available at Post Meadows, June 15–Nov. 1.

*Sometimes inaccessible in winter. Roads often closed because of muddy and hazardous conditions in spring. Nearest gasoline and telephone at Plush. Refuge may be unmanned.*

### Nearby
Largely surrounded by BLM land. In dry weather, other routes shown on OR's official highway map are interesting. One leads NE from field HQ to Frenchglen, another S to Hwy 140 near Guano Lake (open June 15–Nov. 1). Don't try either without local advice.

## Publications

Leaflet with map.

Bird checklist.

Native plant notes.

Public use regulations with map.

## Headquarters

U.S. Fish and Wildlife Service, P.O. Box 111, Lakeview, OR 97630; (541) 947-3315.

---

## Klamath Marsh National Wildlife Refuge

U.S. Fish and Wildlife Service
37,600
From US 97 about 45 mi. N of Klamath Falls, E 6 mi. on Silver Lake Rd.

Large natural marsh, an important nesting and feeding area for greater sandhill crane and waterfowl. The road crosses the marsh, and an unimproved side road goes S along the E side of the Refuge to Wocus Bay, where pelicans are sometimes seen. Birders say there's not much action here until May but much to see then and through Aug.

**Birds:** Most waterfowl species found at other Klamath Basin Refuges are seen here, though not in such large numbers as at the Lower Klamath and Tule Lake units of the Klamath Basin complex (CA). Unlike these units, the Klamath Marsh Refuge includes habitat for ruffed grouse, osprey, long-eared, spotted, great gray, pygmy, saw-whet, and screech owls, white-headed woodpecker, Williamson's sapsucker. Red-necked grebe sometimes seen in roadside ditches.

*Hunting:* Designated area. Inquire.

## Nearby

Winema National Forest (see entry this zone). Silver Lake Rd. continues into the Forest. The Klamath Marsh extends about 8 mi. NE of the Refuge. The Winema National Forest map shows several local roads that might reward exploration.

## Publications

Refuge map.

*Klamath Basin National Wildlife Refuges* (leaflet).

*Bald Eagles of the Klamath Basin.*

Wildlife checklist.

Beginners Checklist.

## Headquarters

U.S. Fish and Wildlife Service, Klamath Basin National Wildlife Refuges, Rt. 1, Box 74, Tulelake, CA 96134; (916) 667-2231.

## Klamath Wildlife Area

Oregon Department of Fish and Wildlife
3,390 acres.

6 mi. S of Klamath Falls on Miller Island Rd.

On the Klamath River. Not a large Refuge but, given its strategic point in the Klamath Basin, an important flyway. Midway between the Upper Klamath National Wildlife Refuge (see entry this zone), and the Lower Klamath NWR (CA).

Five habitat types: farmland, marshland, potholes, saltgrass flats, and dry brushlands. Elevation 4,100 ft.; 1,700 acres of wetland. Best time to visit is usually April–May, when Refuge serves as breeding, nesting, and rest area for migrants. Fall peak: late Oct.–early Nov.

**Birds:** Checklist available. Seasonally abundant and common species include eared and western grebes, white pelican, double-crested cormorant, great blue heron, great egret, black-crowned night heron, American bittern, tundra swan, Canada, lesser Canada, white-fronted, and snow geese, mallard, gadwall, pintail, blue-winged and cinnamon teals, wigeon, shoveler, redhead, canvasback, lesser scaup, common goldeneye, bufflehead, ruddy duck, common merganser, coot, killdeer, common snipe, spotted and least sandpipers, willet, greater yellowlegs, dunlin, long-billed dowitcher, avocet, black-necked stilt, Wilson's phalarope, California, ring-billed, and Bonaparte's gulls, Forster's, Caspian, and black terns, red-tailed hawk, bald eagle, kestrel, northern harrier, pheasant, mourning and rock doves, rufous hummingbird, barn owl, northern flicker, western kingbird, horned lark, tree, barn, and cliff swallows, marsh wren, yellow-rumped warbler, western meadowlark, red-winged, yellow-headed, and tricolored blackbirds, evening grosbeak, house finch, goldfinch, savannah, vesper, lark, and sage sparrows.

**Mammals:** Common species include mule deer, coyote, striped skunk, muskrat, black-tailed jackrabbit, cottontail, marmot, Belding ground squirrel, harvest mouse, mountain vole, Pacific shrew, little brown bat.

**Reptiles and amphibians:** Include common and Klamath garter snakes, northwestern pond turtle, spotted frog.

## Publications

Area map.

Checklist of wildlife.

## Headquarters

OR Dept. of Fish and Wildlife, 61374 Darrell Rd., Bend, OR 97701; (541) 382-5113.

........................................................................................................................

## Lake Abert

U.S. Bureau of Land Management

On US 395 about 25 mi. N of Lakeview.

A visitor unfamiliar with this region may wonder why so large and scenic a lake is unused, no shoreline development, no boats in sight. The extensive flats are a clue. The lake, once part of a far larger body of water, is shallow and too alkaline for fish. Brine shrimp and other organisms attract shorebirds, and birding along the shore is rewarding in winter and spring; swans, waterfowl, occasional gang-feeding by pelicans from Warner Valley. Eared grebe, ruddy duck on the lake all year except midwinter. Marshes to the N, reached by a county road, are also lively. Further N on US 395, about 4 mi. S of Wagontire, a small lake at the roadside was well populated in Aug.: Canada goose, Wilson's phalarope, avocet, killdeer—and a golden eagle wading at the edge.

The highway beside Lake Abert is at the foot of the Abert Rim (see entry this zone), one of the highest fault scarps in the U.S. Roadside parking is scarce along the shore, especially to the N.

## Oregon Caves National Monument

U.S. National Park Service
480 acres.
Within Siskiyou National Forest (see entry zone 1).
SW OR. From Cave Junction on US 199, 20 mi. SE on Hwy 46.

Feature is Marble Cave, a complex of chambers and passageways, dripstone and flowstone calcite formations. A 75-min. conducted tour climbs from the entrance at 4,020 ft. elevation to exit at 4,238 ft.

Above ground, mountainous forested terrain. Annual precipitation about 60 in.; wet winters, dry summers. Surrounding is a disjunct portion of the Siskiyou National Forest, E of US 199, which adjoins a disjunct portion of the Rogue River National Forest, both on the CA border, in the Siskiyou Mountains.

**Plants:** Checklist available. Site is entirely forested, a transition zone between forest types. Below 4,000 ft. is a mixed broadleaf-conifer forest: Douglas-fir and a few pines with tan oak, canyon live oak, Pacific madrone, bigleaf maple, golden chinquapin, rhododendron, manzanita. Higher is all conifers, Douglas-fir up to 6-ft. diameter, white fir, Port Orford cedar, incense cedar. Some virgin stands of Douglas-fir, largest specimen 13-ft. diameter, 182 ft. tall. Many flowering species including bleeding heart, inside-out flower, twinflower, bluebell, yarrow, pearly everlasting, St. John's wort, fawn lily, Pacific trillium. Eight orchid species. Sword, bracken, and lady ferns. Mosses, alumroot, many lichens.

**Birds:** Checklist. Prominent are Steller's and gray jays, Clark's nutcracker. Also: turkey vulture, sharp-shinned, Cooper's, and red-tailed hawks, golden eagle, kestrel, blue and ruffed grouse, mountain quail, band-tailed pigeon, mourning dove, screech, great horned, long-eared, and saw-whet owls, 4 woodpeckers, mountain and chestnut-backed chickadees, white-breasted and red-breasted nuthatches, dipper, brown creeper, 3 thrushes, mountain bluebird, both kinglets,

Hutton's and warbling vireos, many warblers, western tanager, black-headed and evening grosbeaks, lazuli bunting, pine siskin, green-tailed and rufous-sided towhees, dark-eyed junco, sparrows.

**Mammals:** Checklist. Abundant or common species include chicka-ree, California and golden-mantled ground squirrels, Townsend chip-munk, western gray squirrel, white-footed mouse, wood rat. Other species occurring in National Forest, such as black bear, occasionally enter the Monument.

### Interpretation

*Illinois Valley visitor information center* in Cave Junction, ½ block up Hwy 46.

On-site *information station* near entrance. *Naturalist* on-site June–Sept. For programs, check at information station.

*Guided tours* every day except Christmas. *Note:* Children must be at least 42 in. tall and must demonstrate ability to climb a set of test stairs unassisted. Children may not be carried through the cave, and child-care services are not available.

*Cave tour not recommended for people with heart, breathing, or walking difficulties: 550 steps; some long narrow passages.*

*Cliff Nature Trail*, self-guiding, about 45 min.

*Hiking:* 10 mi. of trails within the Monument. No Name Trail, 1.1 mi., passes mountain streams, mossy cliffs, dense forest. Big Tree Trail, 3 mi., to virgin forest. Connecting trails into National Forest. *Snow-shoes usually needed winter and spring.*

*Pets are not permitted in cave or buildings or on trails. Parking lot not shaded.*

*Last 8 mi. of Hwy 46 narrow, winding. Trailers not recommended. Trailer parking limited in summer.*

### Publications

Leaflet with map.

*Oregon Caves Underworld* (newspaper).

Checklists of plants, birds, mammals.

### Headquarters

National Park Service, 19000 Caves Hwy, Cave Junction, OR 97523; (541) 592-2100 (voice, TDD).

## Rogue River National Forest

U.S. Forest Service
638,259 acres, including 54,016 acres in CA.

In two principal blocks, from N and W boundaries of Crater Lake National Park to and across the CA border. Crossed by Hwys 230, 62, 140. S block is just W of I-5.

The larger block, about two-thirds of the Forest, is in the Cascade Mountains, on the N, W, and S boundaries of Crater Lake National Park, extending S along the boundary of the Winema National Forest. On the NW it adjoins the Umpqua National Forest. Highest point is 9,495-ft. Mount McLoughlin, lowest about 2,500 ft. The smaller block is in the Siskiyou Mountains and adjoins the Siskiyou National Forest on the W. Highest peak is Mount Ashland, 7,533 ft.; many peaks in the range are over 1 mi. high. The two blocks are about 25 mi. apart.

The N block is a high plateau with deep canyons, sloping W, many small streams gathering to form the Rogue River. Visitors who enter or leave the National Park by the W entrance can see spectacular sections of the Rogue River Gorge along Hwy 62.

Annual precipitation is moderate, ranging from 20 to 40 in., most of it Oct.–March, much as snow in the higher elevations. Snow usually limits access to the high country until mid-July. Summers are warm and dry, with occasional thunderstorms. The climate supports a dense forest of Douglas-fir and sugar pine. Alpine meadows occur on many high slopes.

The most accessible and popular lakes are Fish (350 acres), Willow (300 acres), Applegate (988 acres), and Squaw (45 acres). Many smaller lakes, chiefly in the Sky Lakes region, are reached only on foot or horseback.

**Plants:** About 90% forested: Douglas-fir, sugar pine, other conifers, including ponderosa and western white pine, white fir, incense cedar, western and mountain hemlocks, Shasta red fir. Associated in various habitats: bigleaf and vine maples, madrone, golden chinquapin, Oregon white oak. Understory species include western hazel, Oregon boxwood, baldhip rose, big huckleberry, western princes pine, vanilla leaf, Oregon grape, white-veined wintergreen, slender-tubed iris, starflower, sedges. On rock outcrops and scree slopes: pine-mat manzanita, western groundsel, collomia, great hounds tongue, larkspur. Species in open meadows include false hellebore, fawn lily, spring beauty. The E–W–oriented Siskiyous are well known to botanists because they contain numerous rare and endangered species.

**Birds:** No checklist. Some waterfowl and shorebirds occur at various lakes. Upland species reported include golden and bald eagles, sharp-shinned, Cooper's, red-tailed, and rough-legged hawks, blue grouse, California and mountain quail, band-tailed pigeon, rock and mourning doves, screech, great horned, pygmy, short-eared, northern spotted, saw-whet, and snowy owls, Vaux's swift, rufous and Anna's hummingbirds, 4 woodpeckers, western kingbird, 5 flycatchers, 6 swallows, 3 thrushes, Bohemian and cedar waxwings, 7 warblers.

**Mammals:** No checklist. Species reported include black bear, mountain lion, bobcat, mule deer, elk, mink, weasel, marten, fisher, raccoon, western spotted skunk, gray fox, coyote, mountain beaver, snowshoe hare, pika, porcupine, Townsend chipmunk, chickaree, northern flying squirrel.

**Features**

The Forest map includes a small map with sections in 5 colors, keyed to indicate degrees of isolation. The most isolated areas are on the boundaries shared with the Umpqua National Forest, Crater Lake NP, Winema and Siskiyou National Forests.

*Sky Lakes Area:* 113,500 acres, including 43,300 acres in the Winema National Forest. About 6 mi. wide, 27 mi. long, extending S from the National Park, straddling the southern Cascades. Elevations from 3,800 to 9,495 ft. More than 200 lakes and ponds. All motorized equipment is prohibited, and motorized vehicles are barred from trails leading into the area. Includes 35 mi. of the Pacific Crest Trail. Many side trails. Drinking water is scarce. Travelers should study the descriptive folder before entering the area.

*Red Buttes Wilderness:* 20,300 acres. Some acreage also in Rogue River and Siskiyou National Forests. Straddles the Siskiyou Mountains at the CA border. Terrain is highly dissected, steep slopes, scenic. Mosaic of meadows, brush fields, dense forest, small lakes, rocky areas.

The *Butte Fork Trail* accesses one of the largest remaining mixed evergreen old-growth forests in the Siskiyou Crest area. Species include sugar and ponderosa pines, Douglas-fir, incense cedar, western white pine, canyon live oak, Pacific madrone, and others.

## Interpretation

*Nature trail* at Mammoth Pines, on Hwy 62.

*Theater in the Woods* at Union Creek Campground has an exceptional schedule of summer weekend-evening programs, featuring well-known speakers.

## Activities

*Camping:* 34 campgrounds, 495 sites. Most are open May–Sept.

*Hiking, backpacking:* 450 mi. of trails. In addition to Pacific Crest Trail, many lead into high country, to secluded lakes, into adjoining National Forests and the National Park. Trail guides available, see Publications.

*Hunting:* Deer, elk.

*Fishing:* The Rogue is a famous fishing stream. Other streams, lakes. Rainbow trout, steelhead.

*Swimming:* Mostly at Squaw Lakes and Applegate Lake. Others are cold.

*Boating:* Fish Lake, Applegate Lake. 10 mph limit. The sections of the Rogue suitable for rafting and kayaking are outside the Forest, downstream.

*Horse riding:* Most pack trips are in Sky Lakes Area and to Siskiyou Crest. For outfitters, ask Klamath Falls and Medford Chambers of Commerce.

*Skiing:* Commercial area at Mount Ashland. Usual season: Dec.–March.

*Ski touring:* About 100 mi. of suitable trails.

*Snowmobiling:* About 150 mi. of suitable trails.

## Adjacent or Nearby

Crater Lake National Park (see entry this zone). Siskiyou National Forest (zone 1).

Umpqua and Winema National Forests (zone 6). Klamath National Forest (in CA).

## Publications

Forest map, $3.25.

*Sky Lakes Users Guide,* map, $2.25.

*Upper Rogue River Recreation Trails,* booklet of maps and trail guides.
*Mammoth Pines Nature Trail,* guide.
*Gin Lin Trail,* historic trail guide.

## Headquarters
U.S. Forest Service, P.O. Box 520, Medford, OR 97501; (541) 858-2200.

## Ranger Districts
Applegate R.D., 6941 Upper Applegate Rd., Jacksonville, OR 97530; (541) 899-1812. Ashland R.D., 645 Washington St., Ashland, OR 97520; (541) 482-3333. Butte Falls R.D., P.O. Box 227, Butte Falls, OR 97522; (541) 865-2700. Prospect R.D., Prospect, OR 97536; (541) 560-3400.

## Rogue Wild and Scenic River
See entry zone 1.

## Soda Mountain
U.S. Bureau of Land Management
5,640 acres.

18 mi. SE of Ashland, near CA border, E of I-5, S of Hwy 66. On Schohiem Rd., not shown on highway maps. Local information or consult BLM office.

The Pacific Crest Trail borders NW portion. Very steep terrain, from 2,800 to 5,700 ft. Camp, Dutch Oven, and Salt Creeks run through the site. Mixed conifers and hardwoods; extensive, dense brush fields; some open, grassy slopes. Surrounded largely by other BLM and private timberlands.

The BLM considers the area outstanding for backpacking, camping, (at large), horseback riding, wildlife observation, says that the site has great botanical diversity, abundant water, scenic vistas.

**Birds:** Species reported include Cooper's, sharp-shinned, and red-tailed hawks, golden eagle, kestrel, wild turkey, blue and ruffed grouse, California and mountain quail, screech, great horned, long-eared, and pygmy owls, pileated, acorn, Lewis's, hairy, and downy woodpeckers, ash-throated, dusky, and western flycatchers, horned lark, black-capped, mountain, and chestnut-backed chickadees, dipper, white-breasted, red-breasted, and pygmy nuthatches, Townsend's solitaire, 6 species of warbler, 3 finches, green, rufous-sided, and brown towhees.

**Mammals:** Include shrews, moles, brush rabbit, black-tailed jackrabbit, California and golden-mantled ground squirrels, chipmunks, chickaree, beaver, porcupine, gray fox, coyote, raccoon, ringtail, weasel, striped skunk, bobcat, mule deer, black bear.

### Headquarters
Bureau of Land Management, Medford District, 3040 Biddle Rd., Medford, OR 97504; (541) 770-2200.

## Spaulding Reservoir

U.S. Bureau of Land Management
65,720 acres.

18 mi. E of Adel on Hwy 140. Also on BLM roads.

Variety of terrain. Site is narrow at S end, on Hwy 140 near NV border, broadens considerably to N. N–S distance about 18 mi. S portion a broad sage flat above Guano Rim, a 450-ft. fault scarp running N–S in W portion for about 12 mi. Rolling topography in central portion. Sage Hen Canyon begins as a small drainage in the S, deepens in 5 mi. to Spaulding Reservoir. N and NE portions contain broken rims, plateaus. Site contains 20 ephemeral lakebeds.

Much of area grazed. Three reservoirs for cattle; Spaulding, near center of site, is associated with Spaulding Ranch, a private inholding.

The BLM judges the area to be excellent for hiking and backpacking, especially the canyons and broken country in the central and E portions.

Except on the SW, the site is surrounded by other BLM land. To the W, below Guano Rim, is a large dry lakebed. To the NW is 6,510-ft. Lone Grave Butte; this area is adjacent to Hart Mountain National

Antelope Refuge (see entry this zone) and much used by hunters and trappers. To the E is Ryegrass Valley, a broad sage basin.

**Plants:** Mostly sagebrush communities. Big sagebrush community includes squirreltail, rabbitbrush. Wildflowers: desert paintbrush, larkspur, clustered broomrape, milkvetch, desert-parsley, sand lily, long-leaved phlox, cushion buckwheat. Low sagebrush community includes bluegrass and squirreltail. Wildflowers: bitterroot, aster, mat buckwheat, scabland and line-leaf fleabane, prickly sandwort, Hood's phlox. Stands of willow and aspen below the rims on E and N.

*Hiking, backpacking:* Spring and fall best seasons. Bring all the water you need.

### Headquarters
Bureau of Land Management, Lakeview District, 1000 S. 9th St., Lakeview, OR 97630; (541) 947-2177.

---

## Summer Lake Wildlife Area
Oregon Department of Fish and Wildlife
18,000 acres.

On Hwy 31, about 75 mi. NW of Lakeview.

Summer Lake was once part of a much larger lake. It is now shallow and alkaline; broad saltflats are exposed in dry seasons. Fresh water flows into the N portion, maintaining a large wetland with marshes, streams, potholes, and ponds. Surrounded on three sides by high desert, on the fourth by a wooded ridge, this wetland attracts many species of wildlife. The high desert to the E is mostly BLM land. (See Diablo Mountain entry this zone.)

Dikes provide a pleasant auto tour route and opportunities for hiking. Pick up a map at HQ and go explore. Map is self-explanatory. Area is small enough to see birds in half a day. Roads are well-maintained gravel.

Only the N tip of the lake is within the Refuge. Pause at the pond on the W side of the highway just S of HQ. Concentrations of shorebirds are often seen on the lakeshore to the S, and it's possible to park beside the highway and walk across the flats.

**Birds:** Seasonally abundant and common species include grebes, white pelican, great blue heron, black-crowned night heron, bittern, tundra swan, Canada and snow geese, mallard, gadwall, pintail, teals, wigeon, shoveler, redhead, canvasback, lesser scaup, common golden-eye, bufflehead, ruddy duck, sandhill crane, Virginia rail, coot, gulls, terns. Red-tailed and Swainson's hawks, northern harrier, California quail, pheasant. Abundant and common shorebirds: snowy plover, killdeer, common snipe, long-billed curlew, least and western sandpipers, long-billed dowitcher, avocet, black-necked stilt, Wilson's phalarope. Also owls, nighthawk, northern flicker, many songbirds. Spring and fall are best seasons, but a visit is pleasant at any time. About 170 species have been recorded, including a number of rarities.

**Mammals:** No checklist. Deer, muskrat common.

### Activities

*Camping:* Primitive site near HQ. A Parks and Recreation Division wayside campground is nearby on Hwy 31.

*Hunting:* Designated areas; special rules; inquire.

*Public access to dikes may be restricted during hatching season, beginning about July 1; some areas may be only open to hunters in hunting season.*

### Nearby

Fremont National Forest (see entry this zone). A scenic Forest road begins about 4 mi. N of Summer Lake.

Diablo Mountain (see entry this zone).

### Publications

Map with hunter information.

Bird checklist.

### Headquarters

OR Dept. of Fish and Wildlife, Box 8, Hines, OR 97738; (541) 573-6582.

## Sun Pass State Forest

Oregon Department of Forestry
20,250 acres.

SE of Crater Lake National Park. From Hwy 62 near Fort Klamath, N
about 2 mi. on Hwy 232, which crosses site.

Hwy 232 crosses Sun Pass at 5,405 ft. Mountainous, steep to moderate
slopes with some relatively flat areas. Elevations 4,200 to 6,000 ft.
Annual precipitation 14–30 in. Pumice from eruption of Mount
Mazama (the mountain forming Crater Lake) mantles the area.

Ponderosa pine forest managed for timber production. About
11,190 acres are harvested each year under an uneven-age management plan. Forest is open for public recreation, but primary use is
wood-fiber production.

Wood River originates near here in large springs. Sun and Annie
Creeks flow through.

**Plants:** All forest. Ponderosa with lodgepole and sugar pines, Douglas-
fir, Shasta red, white, and grand firs, incense cedar. Understory species:
chinquapin, cottonwood, manzanita, snowbrush, aspen, sedge. Flowering species include aster, false Solomon's seal, penstemons, fireweed,
wintergreen, dogbane, hawkweed, pussytoes, lupines, phacelia.

**Birds:** 85 species recorded. Unpublished checklist. Those noted include
bald eagle, raven, magpie, grouse, mountain bluebird, unspecified owls,
hawks, woodpeckers, flycatchers, and warblers.

**Mammals:** Often seen: porcupine, squirrel, mule deer, badger, chipmunk. Present but seldom seen: black bear, elk, beaver, mink, weasel,
mountain lion. Unpublished checklist.

### Activities

*Camping:* Permitted; no facilities. Preferred campsites are along Sun
Creek.

*Hiking:* 2¾-mi. unimproved trail begins at Sun Creek Bridge, leads to S
boundary of National Park. Beaver ponds along trail. Also hiking on
forest roads or bushwhacking.

*Hunting:* Elk, deer.

*Fishing:* Trout.

*Ski touring, snowmobiling:* On Forest roads.

### Adjacent

Crater Lake National Park and Winema National Forest (see entries this zone).

*Jackson F. Kimball State Park,* 19 acres, on Hwy 232; has 10 primitive campsites; opening depends on end of winter weather.

### Headquarters

OR Dept. of Forestry, 3200 DeLap Rd., Klamath Falls, OR 97601; (541) 883-5681.

---

## Umpqua National Forest

U.S. Forest Service
988,149 acres.

SW OR. Between I-5 and US 97, S of Hwy 58. Crossed by Hwys 138, 227, 230.

On the W side of Cascade Range. Mountainous, deep valleys cut by streams carrying snowmelt toward the sea. Highest point is 9,182-ft. Mount Thielsen, on the boundary with Winema National Forest. Here the E arm of the Forest extends S to the N boundary of Crater Lake National Park, with the Deschutes National Forest to the E, Rogue River National Forest to the W and S. Here, too, is Diamond Lake, over 3 mi. long, 3,000 acres, at an elevation of 5,183 ft. Downstream the North Umpqua flows beside Hwy 138 toward Roseburg, making this a scenic route used by many Forest visitors.

To the N, the Calapooya Mountains separate the Umpqua from the Willamette National Forest. An arm of the Forest extends N almost to Hwy 58, W of Oakridge.

Most of the W boundary is drawn sharply along section lines. To the W are forested hills in a checkerboard pattern of public and private ownership, the public lands managed for timber production.

A scenic area close to I-5 and population centers, the Forest attracts many visitors, summer and winter. However, the irregular terrain, cut by many large and small stream valleys, enables hikers to find secluded places even on holiday weekends. The popular centers, of course, are crowded at such times.

In addition to Diamond Lake, two reservoirs, Lemolo and Toketee, have more than 100 acres. The Forest includes 46 smaller lakes, many of less than 5 acres, all open to fishing.

In sharp contrast to the semiarid environment across the ridge, the W side is humid, annual precipitation averaging about 65 in. This promotes more rapid tree growth and a denser understory with many ferns and mosses as well as shrubs.

**Plants:** 90% forested, including extensive stands of old-growth Douglas-fir. Principal tree species: Douglas-fir, mountain hemlock, white fir, western hemlock, western white, lodgepole, and sugar pines. Also Jeffrey and ponderosa pines, western red and incense cedars, shasta red fir. Associated: Pacific yew, golden chinquapin, Pacific madrone, bigleaf maple, salal, sword and bracken ferns. Rhododendron display in May. No wildflower checklist available, but species mentioned include yarrow, arnica, Canadian thistle, Oregon grape, twinflower, snowberry, pipsissewa, lupines, corn lily, bear grass, larkspur, monkeyflower, foxglove, vanilla leaf, baneberry, anemone, spreading dogbone.

**Birds:** Checklist. Species recorded include common loon, horned, western, and pied-billed grebes, double-crested cormorant, great blue and green-backed herons, Canada and white-fronted geese, other waterfowl, sharp-shinned, Cooper's, red-tailed, and Swainson's hawks, golden and bald eagles, peregrine falcon, blue and ruffed grouse, California and mountain quail, barn, screech, great horned, pygmy, spotted, great gray, long-eared, and saw-whet owls, Anna's, rufous, Allen's, and calliope hummingbirds, northern flicker, yellow-bellied sapsucker, 6 woodpeckers, 5 flycatchers, 3 jays, 5 wrens, 3 vireos, western tanager, black-headed and evening grosbeaks, lazuli bunting, pine siskin, 7 sparrows.

**Mammals:** Species recorded include several shrews, pika, brush rabbit, snowshoe hare, mountain beaver, marmot, ground squirrels, pocket gophers, beaver, muskrat, porcupine, coyote, red and gray foxes, ringtail, raccoon, marten, fisher, weasel, mink, wolverine, badger, river otter, black bear, mountain lion, bobcat, Roosevelt elk, mule deer, black-tailed deer.

**Reptiles and amphibians:** Include rough-shinned newt, 8 species of salamander, 5 frogs, 7 snakes, including western rattlesnake.

## Features

*Mount Thielsen Wilderness:* 52,738 acres, including acreage in the Deschutes and Winema National Forests. On the crest of the Cascade Mountains. Douglas-fir forest on lower slopes, alpine vegetation above. Summer habitat for deer, elk, black bear, other mammals. Trails from Diamond Lake area. Pacific Crest Trail crosses N–S through the area.

*Park Winema Roadless Area:* 5,400 acres, including acreage in the Winema National Forest. On the N boundary of Crater Lake National Park, adjoining a wilderness area within the Park. On the lower N flanks of Timber Crater. On the Pacific Crest Trail.

*Mazama Flats Roadless Area:* 9,200 acres, including acreage in the Rogue River National Forest. On the N boundary of Crater Lake NP, adjoining a wilderness area within the Park. Includes the *Boundary Springs Scenic Area,* major part of the Rogue River headwaters, the deep canyon of Upper Mazama Creek, and Lake West.

*Limpy Rock Roadless Area:* 6,700 acres. Drainages on N side of North Umpqua River. Easy access. Elevations from 1,500 to 4,500 ft., moderate to steep slopes below, gentle above. Forest of Douglas-fir, incense cedar, western hemlock, chinquapin, madrone. Moderate use by hunters. No fishing streams.

*Diamond Lake Area,* including *Lemolo Lake, Mount Thielson, Howlock Mountain.* This area attracts the largest number of visitors. Diamond Lake is developed with resorts, RV parks, campgrounds, summer residences, stores, marinas. Lemolo is somewhat less developed but has a resort, campgrounds, boat ramps. Trails connect with nearby Pacific Crest Trail, also lead to the two principal mountains, and Mount Thielsen. Mount Bailey, Rodley Butte, and Lemolo Falls are other points of interest.

*Fish Lake Area,* in the headwaters of the South Umpqua River, is reached only by trail. The nearest road is 3 mi. from the 90-acre lake. From the lake, formed by a landslide into Fish Creek Canyon, the creek cascades down the face of the natural dam. Nearby are Buckeye Lake (15 acres) and Cliff Lake (7 acres).

*Numerous waterfalls,* including Steamboat, Fall Creek, Grotto, Toketee, Watson, Lemolo, Clearwater, Shadow, South Umpqua, Cow Creek,

Canton Creek, Yakso, Con Creek, Parker, Cathedral. Watson, 272 ft,, is highest in S OR. Most have viewpoints within 1 mi. of nearest road.

## Interpretation

*Information center* at Diamond Lake.

*Evening programs* Fri., Sat. in summer.

*Nature trail,* ½ mi.

## Activities

*Camping:* 57 campgrounds, 956 sites. Earliest opening date April 15, latest closing Dec. 1.

*Hiking, backpacking:* 349 mi. of trails, 270 currently maintained. Forest map shows which are maintained. Also 3,780 mi. of Forest roads, most unpaved and lightly used. 28 mi. of the Pacific Crest Trail N of National Park. Each Ranger District has a leaflet describing popular trails: length, elevation, season, grades, points of interest.

*Hunting:* Deer, elk, grouse, quail.

*Fishing:* 49 lakes: brook, rainbow, and brown trout. Also streams. North Umpqua is famous for its summer steelhead run.

*Swimming:* Mostly the larger lakes.

*Boating:* Power boats restricted to 10 mph on Diamond Lake; 40 mph on Lemolo, with some no-wake zones.

*Canoeing:* Whitewater kayaking on North Umpqua River, spring months. Class III–IV rapids. HQ has information.

*Horse riding:* Some pack trips, some private horse use.

*Ski touring:* About 26 mi. of marked cross-country ski trails, most originating in Diamond Lake and Lemolo Lake areas. Also use of unplowed Forest roads.

*Snowmobiling:* About 130 mi. of marked and groomed trails.

## Adjacent or Nearby

Crater Lake National Park (see entry this zone).

Deschutes (zone 3), Rogue River and Winema (this zone), and Willamette (zone 2) National Forests (see entries).

*Susan Creek Park* (BLM), 176 acres, 29 mi. NE of Roseburg on Hwy 138, just outside the Forest, on a whitewater section of the Umpqua River. Camping: 33 sites.

## Publications

Forest map, $3.25.

*Umpqua National Forest Facts.*

*Pacific Crest National Scenic Trail* (Umpqua section, folder).

*Diamond and Lemolo Lake Areas.*

*Diamond and Lemolo Lake Nordic Trails.*

*Diamond Lake Snowmobile Trails.*

*North Umpqua River Recreation Guide.*

*North Umpqua Trail.*

Mimeo information pages: campgrounds, hiking trails by Ranger District.

## Headquarters

U.S. Forest Service, P.O. Box 1008, Roseburg, OR 97470; (541) 672-6601/TDD (541) 957-3459.

## Ranger Districts

Cottage Grove R.D., 78405 Cedar Park Rd., Cottage Grove, OR 97424; (541) 942-5591. Diamond Lake R.D., Toketee Route, Box 101, Idleyld Park, OR 97447; (541) 498-2531. Glide R.D., Glide, OR 97443; (541) 496-3532. Steamboat R.D., Toketee Star Route, Idleyld Park, OR 97447; (541) 498-2511. Tiller R.D., Rt. 2, Box 1, Tiller, OR 97484; (541) 825-3201.

## Upper Klamath National Wildlife Refuge

U.S. Fish and Wildlife Service
14,400 acres.

About 20 mi. NW of Klamath Falls on Hwy 140.

Marshy shallows of Upper Klamath Lake, bordering Agency Lake. Accessible only by boat; little of the waterfowl areas can be seen from shore.

The Klamath Basin is one of the great waterfowl areas. Most of the region's wetlands have been drained, but concentrations of 1 to 2 million birds still occur. Upper Klamath is one of a chain of 5 federal

Refuges in OR and CA maintained for these waterfowl. Upper Klamath is unique for its vast tule marsh, drowned stream channels with willow-lined banks.

**Birds:** Colonies of several hundred nests of double-crested cormorant, great blue heron, black-crowned night heron. Other nesting species include sandhill crane, white pelican, red-necked grebe, avocet, black-necked stilt, gadwall, mallard, redhead, cinnamon teal, ruddy duck, common merganser, shoveler, coot, Canada goose, California and ring-billed gulls, Caspian, Forster's, and black terns, Wilson's phalarope, willet. Most numerous species in migrations include pintail, mallard, wigeon, shoveler, ruddy duck, white-fronted, cackling, Canada, and snow geese.

## Activities

*Hunting:* Designated areas. Special regulations. Inquire.

*Fishing:* Limited to designated areas. Inquire.

*Boating:* Launching ramps at Rocky Point and Malone Springs: For birding, canoe would be best craft. Inquire at HQ at Tule Lake N.W.R., CA, for current regulations and directions to marked canoe trail.

## Publications

*Klamath Basin National Wildlife Refuges* (leaflet).

*Beginners Checklist.*

*Canoe Trail Guide.*

Public hunting area map.

Bird checklist.

## Headquarters

U.S. Fish and Wildlife Service, Klamath Basin National Wildlife Refuges, Rt. 1, Box 74, Tulelake, CA 96134; (916) 667-2231.

## Warner Lakes

U.S. Bureau of Land Management
About 70,000 acres in several units.

From US 395 5 mi. N of Lakeview, E about 28 mi. on Hwy 140 to Adel. Then N on county road to and beyond Plush.

The county road follows a chain of alkali lakes, some ephemeral, a few watered, all vestiges of a large ancient lake. To the E, a 3,600-ft. escarpment rises abruptly to the high ground of Hart Mountain National Antelope Refuge (see entry this zone).

Lakes at the S end of the chain—Hart, Crump, and Pelican—are largely surrounded by private land. This section has wetlands attracting large numbers of waterfowl as well as white pelicans. Birding is good along the public road.

The S BLM tract includes Lynch's Rim, a dramatic fault scarp rising 1,300 ft. above the valley. The S end of the tract drops sharply into Deep Creek Canyon. Vegetation above the rim is generally dense: juniper and aspen groves, mountain mahogany, big and sagebrush, bitterbrush, Idaho fescue, Sandberg's bluegrass, Hood's phlox, bitterroot, big-fruited desert-parsley.

**Plants:** In the Warner Valley, marsh and wet meadow communities include baltic rush, hardstem, small-fruited, and alkali bulrushes, common spike-rush, goldenrod, water hemlock, cut-leaved water-parsnip, field mint, saltwort, alkali-marsh butterweed.

Dry saltgrass communities include alkali birdbeak, greasewood, Lemon's alkaligrass, borax weed, spiny hopsage, red goosefoot.

In the N of the valley, greasewood dunes with spiny hopsage, big sagebrush, rabbitbrush, globemallow, basin wild rye, and Indian ricegrass.

Sand dunes in the S of the valley have spiny hopsage, greasewood, big sagebrush, rabbitbrush, shadscale, tansy mustard, smooth malocothrix, desert paintbrush, hairy evening primrose, and sea purslane.

**Birds:** Hart Mountain Refuge publishes a checklist including species reported from the Warner Lakes. Seasonally abundant and common species: loon, eared, western, and pied-billed grebes, white pelican, double-crested cormorant, great blue heron, common and snowy egrets, black-crowned night heron, American bittern, tundra swan, Canada goose, mallard, gadwall, pintail, teals, wigeon, shoveler, redhead, canvasback, bufflehead, ruddy duck, common merganser. For upland species, see Hart Mountain entry (this zone). In migration, large flocks of sandhill crane.

### Headquarters
Bureau of Land Management, Lakeview District, 1000 S. 9th St., Lakeview, OR 97630; (541) 947-2177.

## Winema National Forest

U.S. Forest Service
1,040,433 acres.

In several large sections, on both sides of US 97 S of its intersection with Hwy 58. Access from Hwys 140, 62, 138.

The several sections are arranged in a great, irregular oval. A section about 6 mi. wide, 38 mi. deep, extends S from Crater Lake National Park. Its W border adjoins the Rogue River National Forest. The Upper Klamath National Wildlife Refuge is on its E boundary. This section includes the Mountain Lakes Wilderness and parts of the Pacific Crest Trail.

The upper part of the oval surrounds the Klamath Marsh. On its W boundary are the National Park and Umpqua National Forest; Deschutes National Forest is on the N boundary, Fremont National Forest on the E. The S portion lies between Upper Klamath Lake and the Fremont National Forest.

Terrain is mountainous to flat and rolling. Elevations from about 4,100 ft. at the lakeshore to 9,182-ft. Mount Thielsen in the NW. W portion has typical glaciated landform features. The E portion is relatively flat, but has several peaks and buttes rising to about 7,000 ft.

Climate is semiarid, about 14 in. of annual precipitation at lower altitudes. Most of the precipitation at higher altitudes is winter snow, up to 10 ft. on the highest slopes.

Numerous lakes. Upper Klamath, largest natural lake in OR, lies between two sections of the Forest. Agency Lake, a large, shallow, marshy area providing good waterfowl habitat and fishing, is nearby. Launching ramps for both lakes are within easy reach of the Forest. Largest lakes within the Forest are Lake of the Woods (1,113 acres), Fourmile (over 900 acres), and Miller (565 acres). Of 36 other lakes, all are smaller than 100 acres, 25 less than 10 acres. Most are in the W portion of the Forest.

There are 3 major spring-fed rivers. The Sycan River, designated a National Wild and Scenic River, forms part of the boundary with the Fremont National Forest. This portion of the river flows through a rugged basalt canyon strewn with large water-carved boulders. The Sprague and Williamson Rivers flow through portions of the Forest. A few small seasonal streams here as well.

**Plants:** 95% of the area is forested. Three principal forest types, depending chiefly on elevation: ponderosa pine, mixed conifers, and lodgepole pine. Associated species include white fir, incense cedar, mountain hemlock, Douglas-fir. Understory species include bitter-brush, ceanothus, chinquapin, manzanita. Flowering species include arrow-leaved balsamroot, aster, bleeding heart, clarkia, penstemons, fireweed, foxglove, heartleaf arnica, phacelia, silvery lupine, twin-flower, woolly wyethia.

**Birds:** Checklist available. 239 species recorded. While the Forest includes only modest wetlands, it borders on some of the principal wetlands of the Pacific Flyway. Winter concentration of bald eagle. List includes all the grebes, white pelican, double-crested cormorant, great blue and green-backed herons, black-crowned night heron, great and snowy egrets, American and least bitterns, white-faced ibis, tundra swan, Canada, white-fronted, snow, and Ross's geese, 23 duck species, many hawks, sandhill crane, many shorebirds, 11 owl species, all the woodpeckers that occur in OR, plus a great variety of song-birds.

**Mammals:** Checklist. 80 species recorded. Prominent are mule deer, pronghorn, elk, black bear, coyote, bobcat, mountain lion. Also recorded: snowshoe hare, black-tailed jackrabbit, marmot, chickaree, beaver, porcupine, raccoon, marten, fisher, mink, wolverine, river otter.

**Reptiles and amphibians:** Checklist. 26 species recorded. Frogs, toads, fence lizard, western skink, rubber boa, gopher snake. Western rattlesnake present, seldom seen.

### Features

*Mountain Lakes Wilderness:* 23,071 acres. A large glacial basin surrounded by high peaks and hanging valleys. Highest point is Aspen Butte, 8,208 ft. Many mountain lakes with forested shores. Area is square, 6 by 6 mi., easy access. Hiking season July–Oct., warm days, cool nights.

*Sky Lakes Wilderness:* 113,590 acres, partly within the Rogue River National Forest. Undeveloped except for trails and campsites. High mountain plateau with many lakes and ponds. On Pacific Crest Trail.

*Mount Thielsen Wilderness:* 55,100 acres. Pristine high alpine forests and open meadows. "This is the real thing," the ranger told us. The Pacific Crest Trail winds through the wilderness for 26 mi. along the summit of the Cascade Range.

*Spring Creek,* on US 97, scenic area, noted for the large spring, 200 cu. ft. per second of water rising from lava formation. Many wildflowers in season.

*Lake of the Woods,* near the base of 9,500-ft. Mount McLoughlin, is heavily used, with resorts, homes, campgrounds, etc., on the shoreline. Easy access to wilderness and Pacific Crest Trail.

*Miller Lake,* near crest of the Cascades, is also a popular area for fishing, boating, camping. Access to Mount Thielsen Wilderness. Pacific Crest Trail is 3 mi. W of Miller Lake.

*Yamsay Mountain.* This peak also forms a crater rim at 8,196 ft. elevation. Sweeping views. Foot access into crater, then down Jackson Creek. An old jeep road, now closed to vehicles, serves as access to summit.

## Activities

*Camping:* 9 campgrounds, 295 sites. Mid-June to Oct.

*Hiking, backpacking:* Forest reports 154 mi. of trails, including 22 mi. of Pacific Crest Trail. Also many miles of unpaved, lightly used Forest roads. Open forest and moderate slopes make bushwhacking feasible in many areas.

*Hunting:* Chiefly deer, elk.

*Fishing:* Lakes and streams. Rainbow, cutthroat, German brown, eastern brook, kokanee. Spring runs of mullet in Williamson and Sprague Rivers.

*Swimming:* Lakes.

*Boating:* Upper Klamath Lake, Miller Lake, Lake of the Woods.

*Canoeing:* Williamson and Sprague Rivers; no white water. A fascinating 9.5-mi. canoe trail winds through a 15,000-acre marsh in the Forest and adjoining Upper Klamath National Wildlife Refuge. Excellent wildlife viewing. See leaflet listed under Publications.

*Horse riding:* Forest reports some use of horses. Outfitter at Rocky Point.

*Ski touring, snowmobiling:* Extensive marked trails and also on unplowed roads. 6 snow parks.

## Adjacent or Nearby

Deschutes National Forest (zone 3); Rogue River, Umpqua, and Fremont National Forests (zone 5); Klamath Forest and Upper Klamath National Wildlife Refuges (zone 5). (See entries.)

*Collier Memorial State Park:* 349 acres. 30 mi. N of Klamath Falls on both sides of US 97. At confluence of Spring Creek and Williamson River logging museum. Camping: 68 sites, season opening depending on end of winter weather.

*Jackson F. Kimball State Park:* 19 acres. 3 mi. N of Fort Klamath Junction on Hwy 232, at the edge of Sun Pass State Forest (see entry this zone). Camping: 10 primitive sites, season opening depending on end of winter weather.

## Publications

Maps: Forest, $3.25; Mountain Lakes Wilderness, $2.25; Mt. Thielsen Wilderness, $1.00; Sky Lakes Wilderness, $2.25; Jackson-Klamath winter trails.

*Forest Atlas,* $7.50.

*Climbing Mt. McLoughlin* (leaflet).

*Upper Klamath Canoe Trails* (leaflet).

## Headquarters

U.S. Forest Service, 2819 Dahlia, Klamath Falls, OR 97601; (541) 883-6714.

## Ranger Districts

Chemult R.D., P.O. Box 150, Chemult, OR 97731; (541) 365-7001. Chiloquin, R.D., 38500 Hwy 97 N, Chiloquin, OR 97624; (541) 783-4001. Klamath R.D., 1936 California Ave., Klamath Falls, OR 97601; (541) 885-3400.

## Zane Grey

U.S. Bureau of Land Management
18,460 acres.

From Grants Pass, about 16 mi. NW to Galice on county road, then 3 mi. N.

This irregularly shaped site includes 26 mi. of the Rogue Wild and Scenic River, upstream from the Medford County line. The W tip of the site adjoins the Wild Rogue Wilderness (see entries zone 1 for Siskiyou National Forest and Rogue Wild and Scenic River). Steep, mountainous terrain; elevations from 400 to 3,800 ft. Several smaller streams flow into the Rogue. Numerous small waterfalls, cascades, pools. Slopes of stream valleys commonly exceed 50%. Valley bottoms are narrow. Most of the surrounding land is forested and managed for timber production.

**Plants:** Dense vegetation. Mostly forested, mixed hardwoods and conifers. Some brush fields and open meadows.

**Birds:** Essentially the same species found in Siskiyou National Forest and along the Rogue Wild and Scenic River (see entries zone 1).

**Mammals:** Species essentially same as in the Siskiyou National Forest. Winter range for deer. Reported: mountain lion, black bear, Roosevelt elk.

### Activities

*Camping:* One BLM campground, Tucker Flat, near W end of site. Reached on local roads from Glendale. Local directions needed.

*Hiking, backpacking:* Rogue River Trail follows the river through the site.

*Fishing:* Chinook, coho, steelhead.

### Headquarters

Bureau of Land Management, Medford District, 3040 Biddle Rd., Medford, OR 97504; (541) 770-2200.

Z O N E

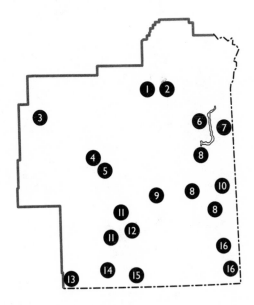

1. Castle Rock Area
2. Cottonwood Creek
3. Chickahominy Reservoir
4. Malheur National Wildlife Refuge
5. Diamond Craters
6. Lake Owyhee
7. Succor Creek State Recreation Area
8. Owyhee River
9. Sheepshead Mountains
10. Antelope Reservoir
11. Steens Mountain Recreation Lands
12. Alvord Basin
13. Hawks Valley
14. Pueblo Mountains
15. Trout Creek Mountains
16. Owyhee River, South Fork, and Louse Canyon

Z O N E

Includes these counties:

Harney          Malheur

The high desert of SE OR is the least-known part of the state, one of
the least-known regions of the nation. Only about 30,000 people live
in an area of 20,000 sq. mi., most of them in five towns, the largest
with a population of 8,000. Driving across it, one's impression is of an
endless expanse of sagebrush, a few brown hills on the horizon. But
highways follow the easiest routes; high ridges and deep canyons are
off the main tracks.

It is a dry region, for the most part receiving 10 in. or less of moisture per year, most of that in winter. The relatively few springs,
streams, and wetlands depend on the mountains high enough to
catch heavy snow. Summers are hot, winters cold. Hikers and backpackers prefer spring and fall. River runners have no choice; only in
late spring and early summer are a few streams high enough for rafting. Steens Mountain receives enough snow for ski touring and snowshoeing.

The highest point in the zone is just under 10,000 ft., but many
mountains, ranges, and buttes rise several thousand feet above the
flatlands. Most hikers prefer exploring the many canyons of the
region, some as much as 1,500 ft. deep. Here they may find alder, willow, and cottonwood, perhaps a spring, as well as shade and isolation.

Well over 95% of the zone is federal land, most of it public domain
administered by the Bureau of Land Management. The zone includes
a portion of the Ochoco National Forest and the Malheur National
Wildlife Refuge. The Refuge is famous, attracting birders from
throughout the U.S. and from overseas.

The Steens Mountain Recreation Lands is the only major BLM site
with formal boundaries. Its dramatic escarpment is one of the region's

chief scenic features. The Steens high country attracts campers, back-packers, hunters, and cross-country skiers, though it is rarely crowded. Lake Owyhee, 52 mi. long, is remarkably uncrowded, even in midsummer, both because it is far from any large city and because most of its shoreline is accessible only by boat.

We have necessarily been arbitrary in describing other portions of BLM lands. Usually we have selected a feature or cluster of features of special interest—such as a mountain, lake, or canyon—and as much of the surrounding country as seemed to be naturally related. The acreages need not be taken too seriously, because they do not measure sites with fixed boundaries. Usually the contiguous areas are also BLM lands.

An ordinary highway map is of little use in exploring the high desert. The roads described as "other all-weather" are usually good enough—at least in good weather. Those called "unimproved" are likely to be navigable by auto in dry weather. Thousands of miles of roads and ways are not shown on highway maps. Some have good surfaces; others are impassable. BLM offices have maps showing parts of their lands. It's advisable to talk with someone who knows the country before going far off the state and county roads. To explore this country, one needs a pickup truck or 4-wheel-drive vehicle.

The BLM district offices do have much information about the features of their districts, including lists of flora and fauna. We asked these offices if we should recommend that strangers to the area visit them and ask for information and advice in trip planning. Could they respond to such requests? Both replies were unqualified: Yes, we can and will help. But they also said they don't have much printed information to send in response to letters of inquiry. Don't write; come.

Burns District Office, BLM
HC74-12533, Hwy 20W
Hines, OR 97738
(541) 573-4400

Vale District Office, BLM
100 Oregon St.
P.O. Box 700
Vale, OR 97918
(541) 473-3144

## Alvord Basin

U.S. Bureau of Land Management
About 300,000 acres.

SW of Burns Junction. The official state highway map shows an unnumbered all-weather road running N from Denio, NV, through Fields and Andrews, meeting Hwy 78 about 26 mi. NW of Burns Junction. This marks the W boundary of the area. The map shows the area as roadless, but it has hundreds of miles of tracks and ways. Several routes begin at Whitehorse Ranch, 8 mi. S and 20 mi. E of Fields. All such routes should be used with caution, for the most part avoided in wet weather. Deep sand is a dry-weather hazard.

The basin, although spectacularly scenic, has been described in such terms as "harsh," "barren," "inaccessible," "fearsome," and "hazardous." Yet BLM specialists say this area and neighboring Steens Mountain are the principal attractions of the Burns District.

The center of interest is the Alvord Desert, a flat playa—dry lakebed—of alkali, almost totally lacking in vegetation. The playa is light-colored, dazzling in bright sunlight, often windswept. Unfortunately, this expanse—like many other desert sites—is much used by ORV enthusiasts for competitions. We were told their tracks on the lakebed are erased by spring rains, but the surrounding area is more fragile.

The basin is almost entirely ringed by mountains: Steens, Pueblo, Trout Creek, Sheepshead. Elevations begin at a bit over 4,000 ft., the highest butte rising to 6,170. Highest point on the periphery is Steens, 9,670 ft.

The desert lies close to the W boundary road, just E of Andrews. E of the desert are shifting and stabilized dunes, the latter vegetated with plants of interest to botanists. Beyond these to the E are cliffs rising 400–800 ft. above the desert floor, the W edge of a large, relatively flat plateau sloping gently E to the dry basin of Coyote Lake and its associated dunes.

Much of the basin to the N and E is flat to gently rolling. Terrain is somewhat more rugged to the S and E, rising to Lookout Butte, 6,170 ft. Whitehorse Creek drains from Steens Mountain into Alvord Lake, just S of Andrews, but for most of the year the lake is dry. The S end is marshy, attracting many birds in season.

A variety of shrubs grow on the dunes. Otherwise, except for the barren lakebeds, this is a region of sagebrush and sparse grasses. Cottonwood and willow border some of the intermittent streams.

The region has been called an extension of the Sonoran Desert, some plant and animal species here reaching the N limit of their range.

Most of this area is under wilderness study. Large sections of the basin are remote, far from any traveled road, seldom visited. They are fascinating to explore, by vehicle, by horse, or on foot, but one should be aware of the special hazards of desert country and be able to cope with them.

**Birds:** In the desert, any temporary pond attracts waterfowl and shorebirds. Here, at times, are numbers of avocet, black-necked stilt, willet, plover, lesser yellowlegs, as well as Wilson's phalarope, cinnamon teal, other waterfowl. Songbirds favor the trees and shrubs beside streams. Also: chukar, California quail, sage grouse, red-tailed hawk, killdeer.

**Mammals:** Feral horse, pronghorn, coyote often seen. Mule deer and bighorn sheep in winter. Black-tailed jackrabbit, ground squirrel. Small mammals, especially, seldom seen in full daylight. Habitat for kit fox.

### Activities

*Camping:* No designated campground. Informal camping is generally unrestricted. Visitors are reminded that this is a fragile environment, asked to leave no scars or trash behind.

*Hiking, backpacking:* Desert hiking is increasing in popularity. Adequate preparation is essential.

*For maps, information on current conditions, consult the BLM office at Burns.*

### Headquarters
Bureau of Land Management, Burns District, HC74-12533, Hwy 20W, Hines, OR 97738; (541) 573-4400.

## Antelope Reservoir

U.S. Bureau of Land Management
80 acres.

From Jordan Valley, about 12 mi. W on US 95, then 1 mi. S.

Camping on 4-mi.-long reservoir. Most of the surrounding area is BLM land, leased for grazing and other purposes, of no special interest. However, this is a good base for visits to the Owyhee River above Rome, Lava Beds, Leslie Gulch, The Honeycombs, etc. See BLM map, Central Vale District. No bird data here, but similar reservoirs in the area attract many waterfowl.

*Camping:* April–Nov. Primitive, no fixed sites.

### Headquarters

Bureau of Land Management, Vale District, 100 Oregon St., Vale, OR 97918; (541) 473-3144.

## Castle Rock Area

U.S. Bureau of Land Management
75,000 acres.

From Juntura on US 20, N on county road.

From Juntura, a good road follows the North Fork of the Malheur River, initially through farmland, then into a broad canyon, past a BLM riverside campground, and on to the Beulah Reservoir.

To the E is a 45,500-acre roadless area with great variety of terrain: mountains, buttes, ridges, canyons, foothills, flats. Numerous springs. Several creeks. Not a wilderness area, but excellent opportunities for primitive recreation. Vegetation is mostly juniper, sagebrush, native grasses.

4 mi. N of the reservoir is Castle Rock, 6,837 ft., an extinct volcano cone, a landmark visible for miles as one approaches Juntura from the

W. A good area for dayhikes. Horse Flat to the W, with Spring Creek flowing through. E section has steep slopes, rock outcrops, ponderosa pine stands.

5 mi. NE of Castle Rock is the Beaver Dam Creek area, under study for wilderness designation. Numerous canyons. Generally thick vegetative cover, sagebrush and mountain mahogany on slopes and ridges, aspen and riparian species in canyons. Heavy deer hunting pressure in season. Beaver in perennial streams.

*Camping:* The BLM's Chukar Park Campground, 19 sites. March–Dec. Primitive camping elsewhere. County primitive facilities on the reservoir.

### Headquarters

Bureau of Land Management, Vale District, 100 Oregon St., Vale, OR 97918; (541) 473-3144.

## Chickahominy Reservoir

U.S. Bureau of Land Management
200 acres.

From Riley, 5 mi. W on US 20.

Driving E from Bend, 106 mi. away, this was the first campground we saw. The reservoir is about 1 mi. long, shallow, surrounded—in summer—by hard-baked mudlfats much used by cattle. Surrounding country is sagebrush flats, hills of the Ochoco National Forest visible to the N. A nearby road leads into the Forest, toward Buck Spring and Delintment Lake.

**Birds:** Desert lakes attract waterfowl and shorebirds; many were here even in midsummer. Observed: blue-winged teal with clutch, pied-billed and western grebes, mallard, Wilson's phalarope, great blue heron, willet, killdeer, sage sparrow.

### Activities

*Camping:* Primitive. No fixed sites, but toilets, tables, fire rings, water. All year.

*Hiking:* Around the lake or toward the Forest.

*Fishing:* People we saw fishing said it's good. Ice fishing in winter.

*Boating:* Ramp.

## Headquarters

Bureau of Land Management, Burns District, HC 74-12533, Hwy 20W, Hines, OR 97738; (541) 573-4400.

---

## Cottonwood Creek

U.S. Bureau of Land Management
22,500 acres.

S and E of Jonesboro, 10 mi. E of Juntura, on US 20. Site extends about 15 mi. S, 7 mi. E. Access by local roads.

Cottonwood Creek flows NE, joining the Malheur River near Harper. In this area it flows through a steep, rugged canyon up to 1,200 ft. deep. Several steep, narrow side canyons entering from the N and W: Wildcat, Green, Long, Camp Creek. On E side, farther S, West Fork and Little Cottonwood Creek are rugged tributaries. Scenic area. Numerous rims, rock outcrops. Numerous springs. Cottonwood Creek has both perennial and intermittent sections.

Sagebrush, cheat grass, riparian plants, a few juniper. Above the canyon rim are sagebrush flats. The NW corner of the area, immediately SE of Jonesboro, has rough, broken terrain, rimrocked tables, 3 intermittent creeks in canyons 280–600 ft. deep. Wildlife said to be abundant: chukar, quail, raptors, coyote, jackrabbit, cottontail, mule deer, pronghorn, rattlesnake. General elevation about 4,000 ft. Accessibility of the area and availability of water make the area attractive for hiking or backpacking.

## Headquarters

Bureau of Land Management, Vale District, 100 Oregon St., Vale, OR 97918; (541) 473-3144.

## Diamond Craters

U.S. Bureau of Land Management
15,000 acres.

From Burns, 41 mi. S on Hwy 205, then E on Diamond Lane.

Recent lava flow, with an exceptional variety of relatively unweathered formations. The BLM has designated it an Outstanding Natural Area. Its features are comparable to those at Craters of the Moon National Monument (ID), but without visitor facilities and exhibits. Lava cones, ropy flows, cinder cones, spatter cones, and other products of volcanism cover several square miles. Vegetation includes a marsh community in the NW corner of the site; big sagebrush, greasewood, and juniper wherever they can sink roots; and low-growing pioneer plants adapted to the volcanic surface.

### Nearby

Malheur National Wildlife Refuge (see entry this zone).

### Headquarters

Bureau of Land Management, Burns District, HC74-12533, Hwy 20W, Hines, OR 97738; (541) 573-4400.

## Hawks Valley

U.S. Bureau of Land Management
340,000 acres.

On the NV border, W of Denio, NV. Area extends roughly 25 mi. W, 25 mi. N. Local and BLM roads from Hwy 140, at SW corner, and from Hwy 206 S of Frenchglen.

The area adjoins a large section of the Charles Sheldon Antelope Range in NV designated as wilderness. Just N of the border is a very large basin, ringed by hills on the W, N, and E, with an ephemeral lakebed known as "Hawksie Walksie." This S portion of the area includes Hawk Mountain, 7,000 ft., and Lone Juniper Mountain. To the E are rolling hills with minor rims.

A dominant feature on the NE is Catlow Rim, extending N–S about 15 mi., reaching elevations of nearly 6,000 ft. at Square Mountain in the N. Rugged rock cliffs face W. Several deep canyons cut the rim. Above the rim, plateau with some rolling hills. To the S, Lone Mountain, 6,520 ft., has interesting columns and pinnacles of volcanic rock. W of the rim is a flat, open valley. SE of Lone Mountain, about 1 mi. N of the border, is Oregon End Table, an irregularly shaped plateau about 3 by 5 mi., surrounded by rimrock.

Catlow Valley extends into the N portion of the area; flat, shallow, dry lakebeds; several rolling hills and buttes to the S. W of the valley are flat plateaus edged by rimrock. Far NW is Beaty's Butte (7,916 ft.), high point of the steep, hilly terrain rising from Ryegrass Valley.

The area has many intermittent streams, generally dry in summer. Vegetation is mostly sagebrush community, sparse junipers at higher altitudes, areas of salt desert shrub. This is important range for pronghorn, including herds moving from the Hart Mountain National Antelope Refuge (see entry zone 5) to the Sheldon for the winter.

Miles of ways penetrate and cross the area. Hiking and backpacking are most interesting in the hills and canyons.

### Headquarters

W portion: Bureau of Land Management, Lakeview District, 1000 S. 9th St., Lakeview, OR 97630; (541) 947-2177. E portion: BLM, Burns District, HC 74-12533, Hwy 20W, Hines, OR 97738; (541) 573-4400.

## Lake Owyhee

U.S. Bureau of Reclamation/U.S. Bureau of Land Management/Oregon Parks and Recreation Department
About 100,000 acres.

Principal access routes: (1) from Vale on US 20, S 41 mi. on well-marked county road to dam and State Park. (2) from Jordan Valley, N 18 mi. on US 95, then N and W on local roads to Leslie Gulch.

An isolated lake, narrow, 52 mi. long, desert hills rising steeply from the shoreline. One paved road leads to the dam and State Park at the

N end of the reservoir. The road to Leslie Gulch, near the S end, is well maintained. The BLM map shows 3 other access routes by primitive roads. Otherwise the lakeshore is roadless.

The lake is not heavily used. On a fine July weekend, only half the campsites at the small State Park were occupied, but we were told it is crowded on many holidays. A modest commercial resort nearby is the only other development. About 70,000 visitor-days per year, two-thirds for fishing. On the busiest day, 150 boats were on the lake, but most were within a few miles of launching sites. A boat camper can easily find solitude.

Landscape is dramatically scenic. On the W, steep rocky slopes cut by deep ravines, rising to tall, rimrocked buttes and tables. Prominent high points: Red Butte, 4,584 ft.; Dry Creek Buttes, 4,226 and 4,303 ft.; North and South Table Mountains, Black Butte, Nanny's Nipple. (Lake elevation is 2,670 ft.) Colors are mostly shades of brown, tan, and gray, with areas of red.

Extremely rough, broken terrain to the E, many rugged breaks draining to the lake. Major canyons include Iron Mountain, Painted, Carlton, Three Fingers, Craig. Area is best known for striking formations called The Honeycombs. Here erosion has carved the rock into a great variety of colors. Other prominent features: Steamboat Ridge, Shadscale Flat, Saddle Butte, Juniper Ridge, Sheepshead Basin.

**Plants:** Vegetation is sparse over most of the area, chiefly sagebrush community with scattered junipers. Willow, alder, cottonwood along watercourses. On foot one can see many wildflowers, depending on season, most of them not visible from passing automobiles.

**Birds:** No checklist. Observed: magpie, chukar, California quail, house finch, goldfinch, rough-legged hawk, northern harrier, crow, pied-billed grebe, mallard, Canada goose, meadowlark, tree swallow.

**Mammals:** No checklist. Species reported include pronghorn, mule deer, bighorn sheep, feral horse, black-tailed jackrabbit.

### Features

*Scenic drives:* Approach from the N through a 14-mi. long canyon below the dam. Canyon walls are steep, heavily eroded, colorful. Grass and trees along the river. Numerous places to pull off the road to picnic, wade, fish, camp. The road in Leslie Gulch offers a sample of The Honeycombs.

*The Honeycombs:* The term is applied to a large area within which characteristic bizarre formations occur and to the about 17 sq. mi. in which they are most concentrated. Easiest access is by boat, going ashore about 20 mi. above the dam. Primitive roads lead to the perimeter of the area, which is closed to vehicles. Consult the BLM Vale Office for route and current conditions.

## Activities

*Camping:* State Park, 40 sites; opening depends on winter weather. The BLM has primitive campgrounds at Leslie Gulch and at Twin Springs, the latter about 4 mi. from the lake, on the W side, reached by an unpaved road beginning on US 20, 4 mi. W of Vale. The Bureau of Reclamation has a primitive campground on the river below the dam.

*Hiking, backpacking:* Ample opportunities for those who enjoy desert hiking. Many seldom-traveled primitive roads, or go cross-country. Consult the BLM office for maps, best areas.

*Hunting:* Deer, pronghorn, chukar, quail, cottontail, ducks.

*Fishing:* Outstanding for black crappie. Largemouth bass in spring. Limited trout fishing.

*Boating:* Ramps at State Park and Leslie Gulch.

## Headquarters

Bureau of Land Management, Vale District, 100 Oregon St., Vale, OR 97918; (541) 473-3144.

## Malheur National Wildlife Refuge

U.S. Fish and Wildlife Service
185,543 acres.

From Burns on US 20, 2 mi. E on Hwy 78; 24 mi. S on Hwy 205; 6 mi. E on county road to HQ.

One of the largest and most important wetlands Refuges in the nation. A vital nesting, resting, and feeding area for Pacific Flyway birds. The area also supports a diverse population of mammals. Established by President Theodore Roosevelt in 1908. "A true gem of the National Wildlife Refuges system," was the way a U.S. Fish and Wildlife specialist characterized these wetlands to us.

Roughly T-shaped, the Refuge stretches 41 mi. S along Hwy 205 and 45 mi. across. Marshes, ponds, lakes, meadows, riparian zones, sagebrush uplands, and alkali flats support numerous bird species and a variety of other wildlife. Over 300 bird species have been recorded.

Semiarid high desert climate, with dry sunny summers and snowy winters. Temperatures seldom over 90 degrees or below zero. Droughts of several months' duration are not uncommon. Most of the year's precipitation is snow.

Winter snowmelt from Steens Mountain to the S and the Blue Mountains to the N provide vital water to the Refuge, via the Blitzen and Silvies Rivers. Malheur Lake and Harney Lake are the lowest points in the basin, Harney Lake being the final destination of the water supply. Three substations at P-Ranch, Double-0, and Buena Vista manage water and habitat for the benefit of wildlife.

Malheur Lake is a freshwater marsh with bulrush, bur-reed, and cattail as well as open water. It is both a feeding and breeding area for waterfowl. A current problem is controlling the population of carp, which interfere with the supply of sago pondweed, chief food supply for waterfowl.

Blitzen Valley, along Hwy 205, is flat and narrow, with many small ponds, willow-lined streams, irrigated meadows, bordered by sagebrush and juniper uplands. The valley is prime waterfowl nesting habitat.

Double-O Ranch was added to the Refuge in 1941. It has its own water supply, including a number of springs, developed in a series of ponds and meadows.

**Birds:** Checklist available at HQ visitor center. Notable species include trumpeter swan, sandhill crane, white-faced ibis, canvasback, bobolink, eastern kingbird. A great variety of songbirds, shorebirds, marshbirds, raptors, and waterfowl use the Refuge during migration and also for nesting and brooding. During the spring, tens of thousands of snow, Ross's and white-fronted geese, tundra swans, sandhill cranes, waterfowl, shorebirds, and songbirds may be seen from roadsides. In later spring, Refuge HQ is a "hot spot" for vagrant and rare warblers and other songbirds.

**Mammals:** Checklist available at HQ visitor center. Lists shrews, bats, pygmy rabbit, jackrabbit, marmot, squirrels, gophers, mice, wood rats, beaver, muskrat, porcupine, coyote, weasel, mink, badger, bobcat, mule deer, pronghorn.

**Feature**

*Blitzen Valley Center Patrol Rd.,* a 41-mi. self-guided auto tour through the heart of the Refuge from HQ to P-Ranch.

### Interpretation

Refuge HQ *visitor center* and *museum.*

*Buena Vista Overlook* and *information kiosks.*

*When to go:* Spring migration begins mid-Feb. with the arrival of tundra swans and snow geese. Waterfowl peak mid/late March to early April. Shorebirds arrive April/May, with songbirds peaking late May. *John Scharff Migratory Bird Festival* held first weekend of April. By end of June, marsh and meadow vegetation is high, making it difficult to see birds.

Fall migration peaks in Oct. Mule deer rut in late Oct.

### Activities

*Camping:* Prohibited on the Refuge, but the BLM's Page Springs Campground is near Frenchglen: 16 sites, April–Nov.

*Hiking:* Restricted to public roads March 1–Aug. 15. Unrestricted at other times except where posted.

*Hunting:* Designated areas. Special regulations. Inquire.

*Fishing:* Designated waters. Boats without motors permitted on Krumbo Reservoir in fishing season.

### Publications

Leaflet with map.

Checklists of birds, mammals.

Hunting and fishing leaflet.

### Headquarters

U.S. Fish and Wildlife Service, HC-72 Box 245, Princeton, OR 97721; (541) 493-2612.

........................................................................................................

### Owyhee River

U.S. Bureau of Land Management
About 100,000 acres.

Rome, on US 95, is midway in this section, which extends from Three Forks, SE of Rome, near ID border, to Lake Owyhee.

Tributaries forming the Owyhee River join at or near Three Forks. For 84 mi., to Lake Owyhee, the river flows in a deep canyon. Only at Rome, 32 mi. from the forks, does the terrain facilitate a road crossing. The section below Rome has been designated an Oregon Scenic Waterway, a legal bar to most streamside development. Although the section from Three Forks to Rome still lacks this protection, it is no less scenic and is unlikely to be much changed in the near future.

The river canyon is cut into a high plateau. From Three Forks to Rome, canyon depth is about 1,300 ft., walls of pinkish-brown rhyolite with tall pinnacles and chimneys. Walls are generally steep to sheer. Access is possible at only a few points. Canyon floor varies from wide, sandy bars to narrow rock-strewn rapids.

Rafting has become increasingly popular in recent years. Although the number of visitors is far less than in Hells Canyon, to the N, it is enough to arouse concern about damage to the fragile canyon vegetation, and the BLM is being urged to limit traffic.

It is not a river for the novice. At least 6 major rapids lie between Three Forks and Rome. Ratings differ according to water level and individual judgment, but we were told of one class VI rapid between Three Forks and Rome, two more between Rome and the lake. The season for river running is short, depending on snowmelt, about 6–8 weeks in late spring and early summer. Most rafters put in at Rome. Take-outs are possible at Black Rocks and Leslie Gulch. These are also access points for people visiting the canyon on foot.

Hiking or backpacking in the canyon is a memorable experience, but the BLM office should be consulted. Some sections are narrow, steep, rockstrewn, and virtually impassable. A section reported to be manageable extends from Rome N. Access roads should also be checked with the BLM. At the time of our visit, use of one was questionable for lack of an easement over some private land.

Several side canyons join the Owyhee above Rome. Antelope Creek is the largest. Others: Warm Springs, Long Canyon, Indian Canyon. Around Antelope Creek, land above the rim has rolling hills. Farther N are sagebrush flats.

Downstream from Rome the canyon has greater variety, though it is never less than 500 ft. deep. In places the walls are vertical, in others a stairstep complex of cliffs, alluvial fans, ravines, and slopes. Several creeks and side canyons join the Owyhee. Terrain above the rim also has somewhat more variety: several lava beds, hills, buttes, and ridges as well as sagebrush flats.

## Activities

*Camping:* No established campgrounds. Informal camping is generally permitted on BLM land except where posted.

*Hiking, backpacking:* Many opportunities in the canyon, along the rim, and in surrounding country. Spring and fall preferred, though access roads may be muddy in spring. Consult BLM office at Vale for maps and advice.

*Hunting:* Mule deer, pronghorn, chukar, quail.

## Publication

Map, Central Vale District (does not show area S of Rome). No U.S.G.S. topographic maps are available for the S portion of the district. The BLM has a planimetric map.

## Headquarters

Bureau of Land Management, Vale District, 100 Oregon St., Vale, OR 97918; (541) 473-3144.

---

## Owyhee River, South Fork, and Louse Canyon

U.S. Bureau of Land Management
About 200,000 acres.

SE corner of OR. Access by local and BLM roads from US 95. See BLM Vale Office for map and advice.

Some call this the best backpacking area in OR. It is certainly one of the wildest. A high plateau is cut by canyons up to 1,300 ft. deep, walls so steep or sheer as to allow only occasional access routes. From the ID border to Owyhee Reservoir, 150 mi. away, the Owyhee River canyon is crossed by only one way.

The 25 mi. of the South Fork from Idaho to Three Forks, where the main stem of the Owyhee is formed, has been designated an Oregon Scenic Waterway, an action that prohibits nearby commercial and other developments that would spoil the view. Most river running is farther downstream, but the South Fork can be run when the water is high enough in spring, usually a period of 6–8 weeks. Some prefer it.

Upstream from Three Forks, several streams converge, including Louse Canyon and Toppin Creeks, both in impressive canyons. Somewhat smaller canyons are Duke's Creek, Antelope, Twin Springs, Massie, Bald Mountain, Spring Creek, and Dry Canyons. In all, about 95 mi. of canyons. Canyon walls are mostly rhyolite in shades of red and yellow, with some sedimentary formations. Several caves are of interest to spelunkers.

Some sections of the canyon floors can be hiked. The going is uneven: ledges, boulders, sand, gravel, and streamside vegetation. At rapids it can be a difficult obstacle course, more rock climbing than hiking. Advice from the BLM could avoid a time-consuming descent into a forbidding section.

As recently as the 1940s, river runners reported that beaver, muskrat, deer, otter, and coyote had not yet learned fear of human beings. Wild animals are less wary of boats than of people on foot, so the change may not have been great. The cliffs are nesting sites for raptors. Ducks, geese, cormorants, and vultures are commonly seen.

*Louse Canyon,* shown on some maps as Larosa Canyon, is spectacular. The stream rises in high country near the NV border, flows N, and is joined by Toppin Creek. We found no evidence that rafting is ever feasible, but hiking the canyon, while certainly not easy, is said to offer fewer obstacles than the South Fork. Some experienced backpackers carry air mattresses for floating gear across deep pools. The BLM recreation guide map shows an unpaved road to the canyon, but advice from the Vale office should be obtained.

The plateau around the canyons is typical of OR high desert: sagebrush flats, playas, some gently sloping hills, a few buttes. Sacramento Hill, S of the confluence of Antelope Creek and the West Little Owyhee, is 5,395 ft. Horse Hill, about 20 mi. farther S, is 6,440 ft., highest point in the area.

Annual precipitation is under 10 in. Winter is the "wet" season, often with snow rather than rain. Temperatures can be extreme, from –30°F to 100°F.

Two roads penetrate the area, and it has many miles of ways. All precautions advised for desert travel should be observed.

### Adjacent
Owyhee River (see entry this zone).

**Headquarters**
Bureau of Land Management, Vale District, 100 Oregon St., Vale, OR 97918; (541) 473-3144.

·····························································································································

## Pueblo Mountains

U.S. Bureau of Land Management
77,400 acres (additional acreage in NV).

4 mi. SW of Fields. Mountains roughly parallel road from Fields to Denio, NV. Local and BLM roads into the area from Field-Denio Rd.

Rugged topography, including the high peaks of the Pueblo Mountains, basins between peaks, steep slopes, large drainages, canyons, and foothills. Two N–S ridges. E ridge includes Pueblo Mountain, 8,725 ft. Western ridge, generally over 7,000 ft., continues into NV near the Charles Sheldon Antelope Range wilderness area.

Vegetation includes sagebrush and grasses in the lower foothills, aspen and mountain mahogany higher. Aspen, willow, cottonwood by springs and streams. Some mountain meadows, grassy slopes. Snowfall rather heavy at high elevations, limiting access until early summer. Snowmelt supports springs and perennial streams.

Area is said to be rich in wildlife, as habitat conditions would indicate, but few details are available. Similarly, hikers have mentioned splendid late spring wildflower displays, but no species list is available.

*Hiking, backpacking:* A 22-mi. trail through the Pueblo Mountains from Denio Creek N to the Reoux Ranch. High desert hiking can be very hot in summer. In general, canyons are preferred travel routes. Consult the BLM Burns office for routes, current conditions.

**Headquarters**
Bureau of Land Management, Burns District, HC74-12533, Hwy 20W, Hines, OR 97738; (541) 573-4400.

## Sheepshead Mountains

U.S. Bureau of Land Management
190,000 acres.

W and NW of Burns Junction. W of Hwy 78. E of Steens Mountain and the Fields-Crowley Rd. Access by local and BLM roads from Hwy 78.

Nearby Steens Mountain attracts many more visitors. The roadless Sheepshead region is less dramatic but offers enough variety to interest hikers. E of the Steens Mountain escarpment are gently rolling hills and small ridges rising to a large N–S ridge. E of the ridge the land drops sharply to a valley with several dry lakebeds, small ridges and rimrocked buttes, scattered rock outcrops. Farther E is a major N–S ridge with a steep, though not high, W-facing escarpment, while S of this area are many steep ridgelines, small flat-topped buttes, a large dry lakebed. Numerous small canyons offer hiking routes, but much of the terrain has gentle to moderate slopes.

The area is arid, in the Steens Mountain rain shadow, and treeless except for a few junipers. Vegetation is mostly sagebrush and grasses. Water is unavailable except in spring runoff. Wildlife is said to be abundant, including pronghorn, wild horse, chukar.

### Publication
Burns District, South Half Recreation Lands map, (BLM), includes most of this area.

### Headquarters
Bureau of Land Management, Burns District, HC74-12533, Hwy 20W, Hines, OR 97738; (541) 573-4400.

## Steens Mountain Recreation Lands

U.S. Bureau of Land Management
147,773 acres.

60 mi. S of Burns on Hwy 205. Loop road begins at Frenchglen. Hiking routes from the E, N of Fields, are demanding.

In the high desert. Steens Mountain is a huge fault block, 30 mi. long. E face is a rugged escarpment rising 1 mi. above the desert floor to a high point at 9,773 ft. From the top of the escarpment, the land slopes gradually to the W, rolling hills cut by canyons. From the escarpment, one looks out over the Alvord Basin (see entry this zone). Seen to the W is the high plateau of Hart Mountain (see entry zone 5).

Climate is semiarid. Most precipitation falls as winter snow. Winters are cold, summers moderate. Because of snow, access to the high elevations is usually mid-July through late Oct. Summer thunderstorms are common, sometimes severe, sometimes with hail or snow.

An unusual feature is the presence of several U-shaped gorges, products of glaciation. Canyon of the Donner und Blitzen River runs generally N about 10 mi., up to 700 ft. deep, ¼–½ mi. wide, cut into the desert plateau. Kiger Gorge, also running N, is in the NE corner of the site. Most other drainages are canyons or gorges cut into the escarpment by W-flowing streams.

Chronic overgrazing altered the mountain's vegetation. Cattle are still grazed under permit, but domestic sheep have been removed.

Numerous streams, a few perennial, most intermittent. In the high country, a few small lakes formed by glacial action.

**Plants:** Below 5,500 ft., mostly sagebrush community. The juniper belt lies between 5,500 and 6,500 ft., aspen belt from there up to 8,000 ft., the alpine bunchgrass belt beyond. Variations depend on terrain, soils, and microclimates. Thickets of aspen, willow, alder along drainages. Mountain mahogany on some high slopes. An oddity is Fir Canyon, with several groves of white fir, remote from the general range of that species. We could find no wildflower list but were told that the displays are spectacular, moving up the slopes with the receding snow, reaching a climax in the upper alpine meadows where they appear as seas of yellow, sometimes purple.

**Birds:** No checklist. Game species include chukar, sage grouse, California quail, mourning dove. Others noted: golden eagle, red-tailed hawk, kestrel, prairie falcon, great horned owl, northern flicker, western kingbird, barn and cliff swallows, mountain bluebird, magpie, raven, rock wren, loggerhead shrike, yellow warbler, western meadowlark, sage sparrow, Cassin's finch.

**Mammals:** No checklist. Bighorn sheep reintroduced. Mule deer; pronghorn on lower slopes. Coyote, bobcat, mountain lion, marmot, beaver, black-tailed jackrabbit, ground squirrels, chipmunk, feral horse, elk.

## Feature

*Steens Mountain Rd.* begins at Frenchglen, ascends the slope to the ridge, turns S, and returns to Hwy 205 about 10 mi. S of the starting point. The highest section is usually closed Nov. 1–July 1, others Dec. 1–May 15, depending on weather. The road can be hazardous in summer storms.

## Activities

*Camping:* In designated sites only. 4 campgrounds, 86 sites. Limited facilities. Season linked to road opening.

*Hiking, backpacking:* Moderately popular backpacking area. BLM maps show primitive roads, not trails. Canyons and gorges are the natural routes, and most have visible trails, but conditions vary. Approaches from the E are steep, some with difficult sections, those from the W more gradual. Hiking along the ridge is impractical. Consult the BLM's Burns Office for current conditions. In the high country, be prepared for sudden changes in weather.

*Hunting:* State regulations.

*Fishing:* Fish and Wildlife Lakes stocked; also lower Donner und Blitzen River. Rainbow, redband, brook, and Lahontan trout. Special regulations established by OR Dept. of Fish and Wildlife.

*Snowmobiling:* By permit only, from the BLM.

*Alpine vegetation is fragile. Vehicles must stay on roads, and visitors are urged to walk only on well-defined paths.*

## Publications

BLM Burns District, South Half, Recreation Lands map.

High desert trail maps.

## Headquarters

Bureau of Land Management, Burns District, HC74-12533, Hwy 20W, Hines, OR 97738; (541) 573-4400.

## Succor Creek State Recreation Area

Oregon Parks and Recreation Department
1,910 acres.

From Nyssa on US 20/26, 30 mi. S on Hwy 201. Left turn into Park is
well marked.

Directly E of The Honeycombs (see entry this zone, Lake Owyhee) and
also an area of exceptionally colorful and scenic rock formations: pinnacles, towers, spires, buttresses, slides, balanced rocks. Good rockhounding, including thunder egg beds, and the usual State Park rules
have been modified to permit amateur collecting. Elevation about
2,650 ft., mountains over 5,000 ft. nearby. Succor Creek flows all year,
very heavily in spring.

**Plants:** Sagebrush and scrub brush. On hillsides, bitterbrush, choke-
cherry, broom snakeweed. Streamside: wheatgrass, alder, willow.

**Birds:** No checklist. Reported: California quail, chukar, rock dove,
red-tailed hawk, kestrel, golden eagle, swallows.

**Mammals:** No checklist. Reported: mule deer, raccoon, black-tailed
jackrabbit, cottontail, ground squirrels, coyote. Bighorn sheep reintroduced just W of site.

**Reptiles and amphibians:** No checklist. Reported: rattlesnake, gopher
snake, yellow-bellied racer, garter snake, tree frog, side-blotched, sagebrush, and collard lizard.

### Activities

*Camping:* 19 primitive sites. Late spring (May) through Sept. and early
Oct., depending on weather.

*Hiking:* A good base for exploring adjoining BLM lands. No marked
trails.

*Hunting:* Usual State Park rules modified to permit seasonal hunting of
upland game birds in portions of site. Inquire.

*Access road is impassable during and immediately after heavy rain.*

**Publication**
Special regulations.

**Headquarters**
OR Parks and Recreation Dept., c/o Farewell Bend State Park, Star Rt., Huntington, OR 97907; (541) 869-2365.

## Trout Creek Mountains
U.S. Bureau of Land Management
140,000 acres.

Just N of the NV border, E of Denio, NV. Within an area bounded by the border, a county road 13 mi. N from Denio, a road from there NE through Whitehorse Ranch to US 95, then along US 95 to the NV border at McDermitt. Access can be a problem because roads into the area cross private land and can be closed by landowners. Also, these roads require pickup trucks or 4-wheel-drive vehicles. Consult BLM office for current conditions.

A fault block range rising gradually from the N and W, much more sharply on the E side. Elevations to more than 7,000 ft. The high country receives heavy snow. Creeks have cut canyons, some over 1,000 ft. deep. Flowing generally NW and N: Trout, Willow, Whitehorse, Antelope, and Twelvemile Creeks.

Mountains have steep slopes, rugged terrain. On the W, rounded hillsides with intermittent streams. To the NW, flat-topped ridges deeply cut by streams. The N foothills have steep, rimrocked canyons, rounded ridges, plateaus. From the high places, tremendous views of distant mountains, Alvord Desert, Paradise Valley.

By contrast with the surrounding desert, the hills and ravines are refreshingly green. In addition to the usual sagebrush and bunchgrass, one sees scattered groves of aspen and mountain mahogany, clumps of snowberry and serviceberry, occasional junipers, alder and willow beside streams and springs. Wildflower displays are colorful as snow melts in late spring.

Wildlife is said to be abundant, as the habitat would indicate, but no details are available. Species mentioned include beaver, mule deer, pronghorn, coyote, black-tailed jackrabbit, ground squirrel, bobcat.

The area is well known to hunters, not yet discovered by many hikers and backpackers. Camping is at large, without facilities.

*Hiking, backpacking:* Late spring and early fall offer the best hiking weather. Spring is preferred, since by fall some streams are dry. Miles of ways, but hikers generally prefer the canyons.

## Headquarters

W portion of area: Bureau of Land Management, Burns District, HC74-12533, Hines, OR 97738; (541) 573-4400. E portion: BLM, Vale District, 100 Oregon St., Vale, OR 97918; (541) 473-3144.

# WASHINGTON

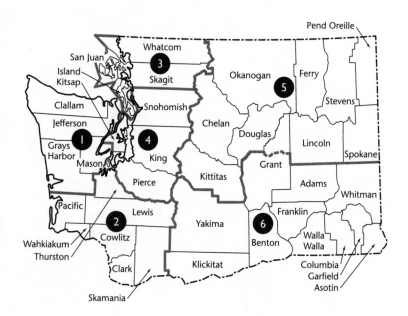

Whatcom

San Juan

Island

Kitsap

Clallam

Jefferson

Grays
Harbor

Mason

Pacific

Wahkiakum

Thurston

Cowlitz

Clark

Skamania

③ Skagit

Snohomish

④ King

Pierce

Lewis

Yakima

Klickitat

Chelan

Kittitas

Okanogan

Douglas

Grant

⑤

Ferry

Stevens

Lincoln

Spokane

Adams

Whitman

Franklin

⑥ Benton

Walla
Walla

Columbia

Garfield

Asotin

Pend Oreille

① ②

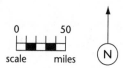

0        50

scale        miles

N

# WASHINGTON

Washington's best-known features are the Olympic Peninsula, Puget Sound and the associated straits, and the Cascade Range, a splendid array of high mountains extending from Canada to Oregon. And, since its dramatic eruption in 1980, Mount St. Helens volcano should be included by itself on the list. For those interested in natural areas, however, there is much more.

Travelers who have driven N along OR's scenic coastal highway will find no counterpart in WA. In the S, US 101 briefly skirts some interesting bays, but for only a dozen miles on the Olympic Peninsula does it run beside the sea. Those who take spur roads to the seacoast will find that little of it remains in public ownership. Several points and jetties offer good birding opportunities. Of the remaining natural areas on the S coast, Leadbetter Point is by far the most interesting. In the N, a long strip of seacoast is a disjunct part of Olympic National Park, a wilderness beach with few access points.

The Park and the Olympic National Forest occupy the heart of the Peninsula. Several roads penetrate the Park, but none cross it. On the W side of this mountainous region are rain forests receiving as much as 130 in. of precipitation yearly; on the E, in the rain shadow, precipitation is as little as 20–30 in. In the warmth of an area where snow rarely falls, one can look up to see snowfields in midsummer. Auto routes are wonderfully scenic, but this is chiefly country for the hiker and backpacker. One can stroll on an easy trail among giant trees or pack into the roadless high country where an ice axe is needed even in summer.

For sailors, NW WA is heaven. Under sail or power one could spend several lifetimes exploring the sounds, bays, straits, coves, and harbors of the region, as well as the hundreds of islands. Unfortunately for our purposes, little of the shoreline remains in public ownership. Of the fragments still owned by the state, most are state-owned only up to the high-water mark, with no access from any public road.

Those we saw offered little of interest except to clam diggers. We found a few sites to include as entries, chiefly on the San Juan Islands.

The Cascade Range is a formidable barrier both to the E flow of moist air and to human traffic. Until fairly recently, US 2 over Stevens Pass was the most northern transstate route, and only one other E–W crossing was kept open in winter. Now the heaviest traffic moves on I-90 from Seattle to Spokane. Hwy 20 across the North Cascades provides a northern route into the formerly isolated NE quarter of the state. One result has been a marked increase in visitors to the Pasayten Wilderness (see entry zone 5 for Okanogan National Forest).

National Parks and Forests form an almost solid block of public land along the Cascade Range, more than 10 million acres. Most of this region is heavily forested, and wildlife is abundant. The region has many lakes, more on the E side than the W, and many streams flow down from the high snowfields. Although few roads cross the range, many Forest roads enter it, usually following streams. Many Forest Service campgrounds and trailheads are along these roads, a number of which end near the boundaries of wilderness areas.

Much of the central part of the state is within the Columbia River basin. The once-free-flowing river is now a series of impoundments, and dams have also been built on a number of its tributaries. The climate of the basin is semiarid, annual precipitation averaging only 8–10 in. While the dams caused inundation of much wildlife habitat, they also created some; the basin has many seep lakes, potholes, marshes, and other wetlands that support large numbers of nesting and migrating waterfowl, wading birds, and shorebirds.

The NE corner of the state is mountainous, but these mountains are neither as high nor as rugged as the Cascades. Hiking trails in the Colville National Forest are open earlier in the season than those in the high Cascades. Even though Hwy 20 has made the Colville more accessible, many visitors from the W stop at the Cascades.

The E central portion of the state is agricultural land, mostly planted in wheat. The far SE corner includes a bit of the Blue Mountains, extending N from OR, and there is interesting country here and along the canyons of the Grande Ronde and Snake Rivers.

Unlike NV, CA, and OR, WA includes very little public domain land. These lands, managed by the federal Bureau of Land Management, make up 25% of the acreage of OR, but less than 1% of WA. WA has more Indian reservations; more public domain land went into railroad grants; more was suitable for homesteading; and the terms of statehood differed. Until 35 years ago, the policy was to sell off the public domain.

The first and most devastating eruption of Mount St. Helens occurred while we were gathering data for the first edition of this volume and just before a planned 2-month field trip in OR and WA. We learned that the most destructive effects were within the Gifford Pinchot National Forest, though a much larger area had received heavy ashfall. Substantial ashfall extended all the way to ID.

By early 1981, most of the Pinchot had been reopened. A year later, Mount St. Helens National Volcanic Monument was established within the Forest, and scientists were given an unparalleled opportunity to study the return of life to a volcanic landscape. In the succeeding 15 years, Mount St. Helens has been closely observed and monitored. It remains a quietly active volcano.

# Federal and State Agencies

## Federal Agencies

U.S. Forest Service
See Introduction for location, phone number, and publications.

U.S. National Park Service
See Introduction for location, phone number and publications.

Washington has three National Parks: Mount Rainier, North Cascades, and Olympic. The Ross Lake and Lake Chelan National Recreation Areas are not, technically, within North Cascades National Park. The NRA classification permits developments and activities excluded from National Parks. However, both are administered by the North Cascades National Park, and they adjoin it. We have written a combined entry.

Coulee Dam National Recreation Area is a strip of land along Franklin D. Roosevelt Lake, formed by Grand Coulee Dam.

U.S. Fish and Wildlife Service
See Introduction for location, phone number, and publications.

National Wildlife Refuges are scattered throughout the state. We have written 12 entries. The largest, Columbia, 23,200 acres, is in the Columbia basin. The smallest is a string of almost 900 tiny islands along the seacoast, none large enough to permit visitors ashore, many close enough that their seabird colonies can be observed from the mainland with binoculars. The islands are administered by the Willapa NWR and are described in that entry.

U.S. Bureau of Land Management
See Introduction for OR/WA State Office, phone number, and publications.

U.S. Bureau of Land Management
Spokane District
1103 N. Fancher
Spokane, WA 99212
(509) 536-1200

The BLM recommended 4 areas for entries. Two of the 4 are in the San Juan Islands, for which there is a collective entry.

U.S. Geological Survey
Earth Sciences Center
904 W. Riverside Ave.
Spokane, WA 99201
(509) 353-2524
(Direct order USGS topo maps)

## State Agencies

Washington State Parks and Recreation Commission
Parks Information
7150 Cleanwater Ln.
P.O. Box 42650
Olympia, WA 98504-2650
(360) 902-9500/8563

State Park camping reservations: (800) 451-5687
Snow park and winter recreation: (360) 586-0185, 902-8581

Information center: (800) 233-0321. For information about a particular State Park in WA, please use this number. At the Commission's request, we have included it in our State park entries.

Washington has 134 State Parks. We have entries for 33. A number of these are not, in themselves, natural areas. We included them because they adjoin natural areas. Of the State Parks, about 80 have campgrounds. Most are open all year. 35 are on a reservation system from April through Sept. (see number above).

### Publications

*Your Guide to Washington State Parks* (information, map, camping, fees).

State Park map (full-color, details activities), $3.00.

*Washington State Lodging and Travel Guide* (annual). (Privately published but distributed by the Commission. It is the "official Washington State Travel Planner.")

Brochures: *Reservation information, Camping and Day-Use Facilities, Using Group Facilities, Pass Programs, State Park Heritage Sites, Fishing in Washington State Parks, Trails in Washington State Parks, Cascadia Marine Trail, Iron Horse Trail, Winter Schedule, Marine Parks and Boat Moorage.*

Washington State Department of Natural Resources (DNR)
1111 Washington St. S.E.
P.O. Box 47000
Olympia, WA 98504-7000
(360) 902-1000
Photo and map sales: (360) 902-1234

In 1957, the State Legislature created the DNR to consolidate WA's land management agencies and protection activities into one agency. Today, the DNR manages more than 5 million acres of state-owned lands. About 2.1 million acres are forested (12% of the commercial forest land in WA), 2.1 million are aquatic (8,000 mi. of rivers, lakes, marine shore), and more than 1 million are range or agricultural lands, leased to ranchers and farmers.

Major functions of the agency are to protect 12 million acres of private and state-owned lands from wildfires and to regulate forest practices. The DNR also manages about 140 campgrounds and picnic, saltwater, and trailhead sites, where public use is compatible with management, and maintains 400 mi. of recreation trails. In recent years, Natural Resources Conservation Areas have been established to protect various native ecosystems, habitat for threatened species, and particularly scenic landscapes. These may offer opportunities for low-impact public use (about 44,000 acres on 23 sites). Finally, the DNR has created programs to identify and purchase Natural Area Preserves.

These provide protection for unique or typical natural features of the state (24,000 acres in 44 locations, including grasslands, wetlands, forests, and ocean cliffs).

DNR sites are often used by hunters and fishermen and -women. We could not visit them all. The ones we did see were wooded and attractive, with plenty of space available midsummer. Some did not have water. Most were near paved roads, with access roads functional. We did not consider these sites as entries, with a few exceptions, because we could not assess surrounding areas. It was hard to tell where state lands ended and private land began.

### Publications

*Washington State Major Public Lands* (describes DNR operations, with map).

*Recreation Guide* (lists recreation sites, facilities, map, annual).

DNR Public Lands Quadrangle maps (by area).

(DNR on-site employees highly recommended *The Washington Gazeteer,* privately published, as a good source of information about DNR lands.)

Washington State Department of Fish and Wildlife
600 Capitol Way N.
Olympia, WA 98501-1091
(360) 902-2200

Hunting and fishing regulations: (360) 753-5700
Saltwater fishing/shellfish: (360) 902-2200
Freshwater fishing: (360) 902-2737
Shellfish beach closures: (800) 562-5632

The agency will also provide information on wildlife viewing opportunities in the state. Area leaflets with maps and checklists are available. The department manages about 800,000 acres of land for wildlife-oriented recreation. The largest Wildlife Area is about 150,000 acres; several have less than 1,000. All are busy in hunting season. At other times, especially in spring and early summer, they are delightful places for camping, hiking, birding, and—in some cases—canoeing.

Like wildlife departments in many states, WA's Fish and Wildlife Dept. is giving increasing attention to nonhunted wildlife species and to "nonconsumptive users," visitors who don't hunt or fish.

Camping is permitted in most Wildlife Areas. Campsites are usually simple and may not have water. We saw a number of campgrounds beside small lakes. Overnight RV parking is generally permitted at the Department's many boat-access points. Dept. of Fish and Wildlife campgrounds may not be listed in popular national directories. In midsummer, we were the only campers at several of them; we saw none crowded.

Many of the Wildlife Areas, chiefly the larger ones, have on-site headquarters. However, we were advised to list the regional offices rather than local HQs in our entries. Local managers are more likely to be out in the field than in their offices, and they aren't equipped to handle mail inquiries.

Washington State Department of Transportation
Public Affairs Office
P.O. Box 47322
Olympia, WA 98504-7322
(360) 705-7075

### Publication

Washington Official State Highway map.

Marine Division
Washington State Ferry information: (800) 84-FERRY, (206) 464-6400

### Publications

*Passenger and Vehicle Fares* (leaflet).

*Sailing Schedule* (leaflet).

Bicycle program: (360) 705-7277
Map and information on bicycling in the northwest.

Mountain pass report, Oct. 1–April 15: (900) 407-7277 (35 cents per min.)

# Private Organizations

Washington Trails Association
1305 4th Ave. #512
Seattle, WA 98101-2401
(206) 392-1367

### Publication

*Whom to Ask?* (a directory of state and federal agencies that offer information on trail and road conditions, campsites, hiking and other recreational activities).

Washington State Outfitters and Guides Association
704 228th Ave. N.E. #331
Redmond, WA 98053
(206) 392-6107

List of outfitters, guides, and river outfitting members.

Washington Scuba Alliance
120 State Ave. N.E. #18
Olympia, WA 98501-8212

Information on underwater preserves, parks, wreck sites, geological formations, and natural habitats.

Z O N E

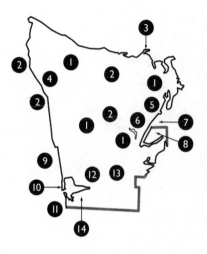

# ZONE 1

Includes these counties:

Jefferson    Mason

The Olympic Peninsula is bounded on three sides by the Pacific Ocean, the Strait of Juan de Fuca, and the Hood Canal. The central portion, more than half the total area, is within the Olympic National Forest and Olympic National Park. This central portion is mountainous, heavily forested, and largely wilderness.

US 101 encircles the Peninsula. N of Aberdeen, the traveler enters the National Forest. Even a short detour to Quinault Lake offers a look at splendid old-growth rain forest. US 101 then turns seaward. A side road follows the Queets River into the S part of the National Park, another through state-owned forests to the Hoh River. US 101 enters the Pacific Coast area of the National Park, then turns inland, following the Hoh. In about 10 mi. it turns NW, while a side road continues E into the Hoh Rain Forest.

Just beyond Forks is the road to La Push, a seaside fishing community within the Pacific Coast Area of the Park. Beyond here, the only access to the Park beach is on foot. Soon US 101 turns E, passes through a part of the Forest, and—for the only time—passes through a bit of the main Park, following the S shore of Lake Crescent.

Now 101 becomes a somewhat busier road for a while, entering the city of Port Angeles, gateway to the principal Park entrance. One can turn back to the W on Hwy 112, following the Strait of Juan de Fuca, coming eventually to Cape Flattery, westernmost point of the conterminous U.S. A path leads to a viewpoint on a rocky cliff, looking down at caves and arches worn into the rock by breaking waves.

US 101 stays on private land, passing through or near several communities, until it turns S, passes Quilcene, and enters the National Forest again. At Dosewallips a road leads W through the Forest and into the Park. Then, for some miles, 101 is beside or near the Hood

Canal. Here and on the shore of the Canal after it turns NE are a number of small State Parks. We have not included them as entries because they are recreation sites rather than natural areas, but most have boat-launching ramps.

Along this route are various sites described in the following entries, such as the Dungeness National Wildlife Refuge to the E of Port Angeles. One can also find many opportunities to wander and explore. For example, a large block of state-owned Forest lies N of the Hoh River, between the main body of the Park and its Pacific Coast area. This is managed by the WA Dept. of Natural Resources for timber production, but it's open to visitors. Ten small primitive campgrounds are within the area, none mentioned in any of the campground directories we have at hand.

But by far the greatest opportunities for exploration are within the more than 1.5 million acres of National Park and Forest. Most of the Park is roadless. The surrounding Forest is not. You need the Forest map, which shows hundreds of miles of Forest roads, few carrying any traffic.

Forest maps as well as free brochures on the National Forests and National Parks are available from the U.S. Forest Service and National Park Service's Northwest Interpretive Association (see Introduction).

## Bogachiel State Park

Washington Parks and Recreation Commission
123 acres.

On both sides of US 101, 6 mi. S of Forks.

Small Park with 2,800-ft. frontage on Bogachiel River. Sample of rain forest with interpretive trail. Nearby trail along the Bogachiel River into Olympic National Park.

### Activities

*Camping:* 42 sites. All year.

*Fishing:* Salmon, steelhead, trout.

### Headquarters

WA Parks and Recreation Comm., 185983 Hwy 101, Forks, WA 98331; (360) 314-6356/(800) 233-0321.

## Dosewallips State Park

Washington Parks and Recreation Commission
425 acres.

On US 101, 1 mi. S of Brinnon, exit 104.

5,000 ft. of saltwater shoreline on the Hood Canal and 5,400 ft. of freshwater frontage on both sides of the Dosewallips River. From here a road goes W along the river, through a section of Olympic National Forest, and in the W entrance of Olympic NP, about 14 mi. from the State Park.

The flat meadows were old homesteads before acquisition as a Park. Some wooded upland. The Park is a wintering ground for a herd of elk.

### Activities

*Camping:* 129 sites. All year. Reservations (800) 452-5687.

### Headquarters

WA Parks and Recreation Comm., P.O. Drawer K, Brinnon, WA 98320; (360) 796-4415/(800) 233-0321.

## Dungeness National Wildlife Refuge

U.S. Fish and Wildlife Service
631 acres.

From 4 mi. W of Sequim on US 101, turn N on Kitchen-Dick Rd., 3 mi. to Refuge, following signs.

When most of the Olympic Peninsula is wet and chilly, this site is likely to be dry and sunny; Sequim is in the mountains' rain shadow and receives less than 18 in. of rain per year. A favorite spot for birders, partly because of large numbers of species. The calm waters make this an outstanding shorebird area.

The Refuge is a natural sand spit projecting 5½ mi. into the Strait of Juan de Fuca. Parking is at the entrance. Only foot travel beyond that point. The sand spit curves to the NE. About 2 mi. before the tip, Graveyard Spit projects due S into New Dungeness Bay.

Sand beaches, tidelands, protected bay waters, open saltwater beds of eelgrass, a small forested area near the base of the spit.

**Birds:** Checklist available. A key wintering and spring gathering area for brant and other waterfowl. The checklist includes 28 "accidentals," among them yellow-billed loon, Buller's shearwater, mute swan, gyrfalcon, skua, parakeet auklet, and skylark.

Not including these, 246 species recorded. Winter populations include up to 1,500 brant as well as arctic and red-throated loons, grebes, double-crested and Brandt's cormorants, Canada goose, mallard, pintail, green-winged teal, canvasback, greater scaup, common and Barrow's goldeneye, bufflehead, oldsquaw, harlequin duck, common, white-winged, and surf scoters, common and red-breasted mergansers. Also killdeer, surfbird, dunlin, black turnstone, sanderling. Many more species are seen in spring and fall migrations, while species such as rhinoceros auklet and tufted puffin are most often seen in summer.

**Mammals:** Occasional marine mammals, including killer whales. Pupping and hauling-out area for harbor seals.

### Adjacent
*Dungeness Recreation Area,* 216 acres. On the Strait of Juan de Fuca, at the National Wildlife Refuge entrance. Camping, hunting.

### Publications
Leaflet with map.

Bird checklist.

### Headquarters
U.S. Fish and Wildlife Service, c/o WA Coastal Refuges, 33 S. Barr Rd., Port Angeles, WA 98362; (360) 457-8451.

---

## Hood Canal Beaches
Washington Department of Natural Resources

The DNR has responsibility for the remaining fragments of WA's public beaches. In the great majority of cases, state ownership goes only to the mean high-water line. The adjoining beaches and area above high water are privately owned, and the state has no right-of-way.

Most of the beaches are inaccessible except by boat. Frontages range from 514 to 12,050 ft. One beach just N of Hoodsport is accessible by land; the state owns the strip from the water's edge to the highway. This beach, of cobbles, is 2,951 ft. long.

### Headquarters
WA Dept. of Natural Resources, S. Puget Sound Region, 28329 S.E. 448th St., P.O. Box 68, Enumclaw, WA 98504; (360) 825-1631.

---

### Johns River Wildlife Area
Washington Department of Fish and Wildlife
1,450 acres.

From Aberdeen, 12 mi. SW on Hwy 105. Just beyond bridge, turn SE, then N to access.

From near Hwy 105 and the river's mouth on Grays Harbor, the site extends upstream about 4 mi. on both sides of the Johns River. A dike extends upstream for about 1 mi. on the S side, with a footpath on the dike. The opposite shore is also diked. Tidewater, with tides fluctuating as much as 14 ft. The floodplain is grassy, often wet, cut by channels. Higher ground is woodland, young alder and fir.

Fishermen use the ramp at the HQ area, as do hunters in season. Hunters also hike along the S dike to reach upstream hunting grounds. Otherwise, public use is light. We met no one in a visit of several hours.

**Birds:** Partial checklist in leaflet. Upland game species include blue and ruffed grouse, band-tailed pigeon, Chinese pheasant. Waterfowl in migration: dusky Canada goose, mallard, wigeon, green-winged teal, pintail, scaup. Also noted: red-tailed and Cooper's hawks, northern harrier, merlin, kestrel, osprey, bufflehead, wood duck, goldeneye, killdeer, great blue heron, rufous hummingbird, red-winged and Brewer's blackbirds, downy woodpecker, dark-eyed junco, evening and black-headed grosbeaks, violet-green, cliff, barn, and tree swallows, varied thrush, marsh wren, golden-crowned kinglet, 5 species of warblers.

**Mammals:** Big game species include mule deer, Roosevelt elk, black bear. Other mammals include muskrat, mink, coyote, weasel, raccoon, river otter.

## Activities

*Camping:* Not prohibited, but no campground and few suitable sites.

*Hiking:* Easy hiking on dikes, both sides. Leaflet mentions an access road on the N side of the river.

*Hunting:* Designated areas, including an island N of the river's mouth.

*Fishing:* Cutthroat, steelhead, silver salmon.

*Boating:* Ramp at HQ.

*Horse riding:* On dikes and established roads only.

## Publication

*Wildlife Recreation Areas 4 and 24* (leaflet with map).

## Headquarters

WA Dept. of Fish and Wildlife, Montesano Regional Office, 48 Devonshire Rd., Montesano, WA 98563; (360) 249-4628.

...........................................................................................................................

## Lake Cushman State Park

Washington Parks and Recreation Commission
603 acres.

From Hoodsport on US 101, 7 mi. NE on Lake Cushman Rd.

Lake Cushman was formed by damming the North Fork of the Skokomish River, which flows from Olympic National Park. The NW tip of the 10-mi.-long lake is about ½ mi. from the SE corner of the National Park. The lakeshore road ends inside the National Park's Staircase entrance, a major trailhead. National Forest land is on both sides of the lake's upper third, but with little actual waterfront. The Park has 41,500 ft. of freshwater shoreline.

**Plants:** Most of the State Park is forested: Douglas-fir with hemlock, western red cedar, white pine. Deciduous trees include alder, bigleaf maple, wild cherry. Understory includes Oregon grape, huckleberry, salal, vine maple, sword fern. Much bear grass, usually seen only at higher elevations. Lake elevation is 750 ft.

**Birds:** Essentially the species noted in the Olympic National Park and National Forest entries this zone.

**Mammals:** Seen at or near the lake, include Olympic elk, mule deer, raccoon, rabbit, coyote, squirrel, chipmunk, river otter.

### Interpretation

Saturday *campfire programs.*

Staff-led *nature hikes,* Saturday mornings.

### Activities

*Camping:* 83 sites. All year. Reservations accepted.

*Fishing:* Rainbow, cutthroat, Dolly Varden, kokanee.

*Swimming:* Lake, unsupervised. Waterskiing allowed.

*Boating:* 3 ramps.

### Headquarters

WA Parks and Recreation Comm., N. 7211 Lake Cushman Rd., Hoodsport, WA 98548; (360) 877-5491/(800) 233-0321.

## Olympic Beaches

Coast of lower Olympic Peninsula, along Hwy 109.

This section of the coast is more scenic than most of the coastline farther S. In the N section, land rises rather steeply from the beach. Hills are mostly forested, and some sections of forest are quite handsome. Viewpoints are limited, however, and the land is almost all privately owned. However, in the N section, development outside the resort communities is, as yet, relatively light.

*Ocean City State Park:* 168 acres. The largest public site and heavily used.

*Damon Point State Park and Natural Area:* 61 acres. Protected snowy plover nesting area. Interpretive station explaining layout and points of interest of Damon Point and brief narrative on snowy plover.

*Pacific Beach State Park:* 10-acre in-town campground. Congested and unattractive. The state has also provided a number of beach-access points.

The most interesting area is the S tip. See entry this zone for Oyhut Wildlife Area.

*Camping:* Ocean City State Park, 179 sites. Pacific Beach, 138 sites. Both require reservations. Ocean City HQ: 148 Hwy 115, Hoquiam, WA 98550; (800) 233-0321.

## Olympic National Forest

U.S. Forest Service
632,324 acres.

Olympic Peninsula. All access roads from US 101, which circles the peninsula.

The Forest surrounds Olympic National Park (see entry this zone). Together they occupy the mountainous heart of the Olympic Peninsula. Although parks and forests are governed by different policies (e.g., no logging or hunting in National Parks), for the hiker these two are an entity, many trails from the Forest leading into and crossing the Park.

Highest point in the complex is 7,965-ft. Mount Olympus at the center of the Park. The range of high, craggy peaks extends into the Forest. Mount Fricaba, 7,134 ft., is the highest of many high peaks in the E part of the Forest. Terrain is rugged, mountains and ridges radiating in all directions, a pattern carved by ice and water. On the W, some of the land is somewhat less steep, more rolling. The backcountry has alpine meadows, high lakes, rushing streams with falls and cataracts.

The Olympic Peninsula is known for sharp contrasts of climate: Mount Olympus has 200 in. of precipitation per year, while an area 40 mi. away has only 17. Contrasts in the National Forest are not quite so great: about 140 in. a year on the W side, 60 in. on the E. Winters are wet, midsummers dry. The climate is generally wild. At lower elevations winter temperatures are seldom below freezing, and summer days are seldom as hot as 80°F. Heavy snow falls on the high elevations, but most trails are open by June, almost all snow-free in July. Snow rarely accumulates below 1,500 ft.

US 101 is the only highway within the Forest boundaries. It cuts across the SW corner near Quinault Lake, across the NW corner, and for a mile or two on the E side. Otherwise, wheeled travel is on Forest roads, built for logging, their pattern on a map resembling a mass of worms. The wilderness inventory identified 10 roadless areas of 5,000 or more acres.

A moderate climate and 12 ft. of rainfall per year produce a lush rain forest, one of the major timber production areas of the nation. Countless streams carry the runoff, combining in a number of rivers: the Dungeness, Big Quilcene, Dosewallips, Duckabush, Hamma Hamma, South Fork Skokomish, Wynoochee, Humptulips, Quinault, Sitkum, and Soleduck. The Forest borders on 3,730-acre Lake Quinault (controlled by the Quinault Tribal Council) and 1,600-acre Lake Cushman. Wynoochee Lake, 1,120 acres, is within the Forest, although a few inholdings are on its shores. The Forest has about ½ mi. of tideland on the Hood Canal.

A few resorts have been developed in the Forest, notably on the S shore of Quinault Lake, and the popular campgrounds are often full in July and Aug. However, only limited areas of the Forest are accessible by road. The backcountry is open to hikers, hunters, people who fish, and others who travel on foot.

**Plants:** Heavily forested below 4,000 ft. except for areas recently logged. Principal tree species: Douglas-fir, western hemlock, western red cedar, Sitka spruce. Groves of bigleaf maple. Vegetation is lush and dense in the rain forest, the ground thickly carpeted with mosses, ferns, wood sorrel, oxalis, and decaying vegetation, tree branches draped with moss, giant trees forming a dark canopy overhead. More than 1,000 plant species have been identified on the peninsula, the variety attributable to the wide range of elevations and climate conditions.

Common understory species include coastal rhododendron, salal, swordfern, red and blue huckleberry. Other rain forest species include western coolwort, Dewey sedge, nodding trisetum, false lily-of-the-valley, western spring beauty ferns. Alpine wildflower meadows with avalanche lily, phlox, glacier lily, cinquefoil, paintbrush, white valerian.

**Birds:** Much of the Forest is now protected for populations of spotted owl and marbled murrelet. 136 species recorded. Partial checklist available. Includes great blue heron, tundra and trumpeter swans, Canada goose, brant, white-fronted and snow geese, green-winged teal, many duck species, goshawk, Cooper's, Swainson's, and red-tailed hawks, bald eagle, blue and ruffed grouse, California and mountain quail, 6 woodpeckers, 5 swallows, 3 chickadees, red-breasted nuthatch, dipper, 4 wrens, water pipit, Bohemian and cedar waxwings, Hutton's and warbling vireos, 7 warblers, and 7 sparrows.

**Mammals:** The Olympics have the nation's largest herd of Roosevelt elk. Mountain goat, introduced to the area, have multiplied. The mountain lion population is exceptionally large, although seldom seen. Mule deer are abundant. A curiosity of the area is that, for reasons going back to the Ice Age, a number of mammals common to the Cascades are not found here, among them red fox, lynx, golden-mantled ground squirrel, pika, and wolverine.

A partial checklist of the species found here includes black bear, coyote, raccoon, marten, fisher, short-tailed and long-tailed weasels, mink, spotted and striped skunks, river otter, mountain beaver, chipmunks, chickaree, beaver, porcupine, snowshoe hare, mountain cottontail, brush rabbit; opossum.

**Reptiles and amphibians:** Partial checklist includes 7 salamanders, tailed frog, northwestern toad, Pacific tree frog, Washington frog, bullfrog, Pacific green turtle, Pacific blue-bellied lizard, northwestern rubber snake, dusky and northwestern garter snakes.

## Features

The Washington State Wilderness Act of 1984 created five wildernesses in the Olympic Forest.

*The Brothers Wilderness:* 16,682 acres. Mountainous, rugged terrain including Mount Jupiter, 5,701 ft., and The Brothers, 6,866 ft. Adjoins the E boundary of the National Park. Trail along the Duckabush River links with backcountry Park trails. Forest of western hemlock and Douglas-fir up to timberline. Includes Jupiter Lake and several small ponds.

*Buckhorn Wilderness:* 43,258 acres. On the E boundary of the National Park, N of The Brothers Wilderness, separated from it by the Forest road leading to the National Park's Dosewallips entrance. Heavily forested lowland valleys lead into this high-peak mountain meadow country from the N and E. Includes Mount Fricaba, 7,134 ft., highest in the Forest, several others over 5,000 ft. Several lakes and ponds. Many streams.

*Colonel Bob Wilderness:* 12,961 acres. Just E of Quinault Lake. Rain forest. Colonel Bob Mountain, 4,492 ft., is one of a cluster of peaks between the Quinault and Humptulips Rivers. Features include the Fletcher Canyon fault escarpment, Gibson slide. Small, open, marshy area E of Colonel Bob Mountain. Dense coniferous forest.

*Mount Skokomish Wilderness:* 13,015 acres. At the SE corner of the National Forest, a large roadless area, bounded by the National Park on the N and W. High mountains, notably Skokomish, 6,434 ft., Stone, 6,612 ft., Pershing, 6,154 ft., Cruiser, 6,104 ft., Washington, 6,255 ft. Headwaters of the Hamma Hamma River. Includes the 3 Mildred Lakes totaling 55 acres, several smaller ponds. S boundary is close to Lake Cushman. Valley bottoms have dense stands of western hemlock, Douglas-fir, western red cedar. At higher elevations: subalpine fir, western white pine; dwarf juniper near timberline. Upper slopes are rocky, barren, except for many wildflowers in the few mountain meadows.

*Wonder Mountain Wilderness:* 2,349 acres. One of the smallest wildernesses in the W. Borders the National Park and is located W of Lake Cushman. Terrain is rugged and ranges from 1,740 ft. at McKay Creek to the summit of Wonder Mountain at 4,758 ft.

*Quinault Lake area.* Just off US 101. National Forest borders the S shore, National Park the N, Quinault Indian Reservation on the W; the Tribal Council controls the lake. On the S shore, resorts, campground, marina. Nearby: *Big Tree Grove,* prime example of old-growth rain forest, with ¼-mi. nature trail, other trails. Also nearby: *Quinault Research Natural Area:* 1,468 acres. Old-growth western hemlock, Sitka spruce, western red cedar, Douglas-fir with luxuriant understory. Quinault area is wintering ground for Roosevelt elk. Forest road continues beyond the lake, along the river, ending a few miles inside the National Park at Graves Creek Campground.

*Mount Walker viewpoint.* From US 101 near Quilcene, a 5-mi. drive to the 2,800-ft. summit. Views of the Olympic Mountains, Puget Sound, Cascades. Rhododendron display June–July. 2-mi. moderately steep trail to summit begins at start of Forest Rd. 2730.

*Wynoochee Lake.* Popular area for camping, boating, fishing, swimming. Nature trail. Trails into the National Park. A National Recreation Trail makes a 10-mi. circuit of the lake.

## Activities

*Camping:* 20 campgrounds, 457 sites. 6 campgrounds open all year, others closed mid-Sept.–May.

*Hiking, backpacking:* 239 mi. of trails, many links to trails in the National Park. Backcountry permits not required in the Forest, required in the Park; access to some backcountry Park areas limited.

*Hunting:* Elk, deer, mountain goat.

*Fishing:* Good fishing in many streams and lakes. Rainbow, cutthroat, brook trout.

*Swimming:* Wynoochee and Quinault Lakes, Hood Canal, a few other lakes.

*Boating:* Some power boating on Wynoochee Lake. Ramps at Lake Quinault; rules fixed by Tribal Council.

*Canoeing:* Lakes. Humptulips River, from Fish Trap Rd., about 21 mi. upstream from Humptulips. Some class II rapids.

*Horse riding:* Forest HQ report some trail riding; no livery within the site.

*Ski touring:* Some, on unplowed roads.

## Publications

Forest map (includes Olympic National Park), $3.25.

Campground information.

Trail information.

## Headquarters

U.S. Forest Service, 1835 Black Lake Blvd. S.W., Olympia, WA 98512-5623; (360) 956-2400.

## Ranger Districts

Hood Canal R.D., 150 N. Lake Cushman Rd., Hoodsport, WA 95848; (360) 877-5254. Quilcene R.D., 20482 Hwy 101S, Quilcene, WA 98376; (360) 765-2200. Quinault R.D., 353 S. Shore Rd., Quinault, WA 98575; (360) 288-2525. Soleduck R.D., 12628 Hwy 101, Forks, WA 98331; (360) 374-6522.

## Olympic National Park

U.S. National Park Service
892,578 acres.

Center of the Olympic Peninsula; circled by US 101. Several entrances on the perimeter.

Established by President Theodore Roosevelt as an elk refuge in 1909; National Park status was achieved in 1938 after a planning period. The natural terrain and planning combined to make the Park less vulnerable to overuse than many others. Several roads penetrate, but none cross the Park. Most of the area, including the central portion, is roadless. Those who travel by car enjoy splendid vistas and close-up looks at many Park features, but most of the area can be visited only on foot or horseback.

Near the Park's center is 7,965-ft. Mount Olympus, the highest point, snowcapped for much of the year, with 6 major glaciers visible in midsummer. Several other peaks exceed 7,000 ft., with many ridges and crests between 5,000 and 6,000 ft. The Park has at least 60 glaciers. Peaks are jagged, a sign of geological youthfulness. There are U-shaped valleys on the W side, while many river-cut valleys are steeply V-shaped.

Below the glaciers are alpine meadows, bright with wildflowers when the snowfields melt. Lower elevations are forested. Many streams flow from the mountains, join in a number of rivers, notably the Sol Duc, Elwha, Dosewallips, Duckabush, Dungeness, Quinault, Queets, Hoh, and Bogachiel. Lake Crescent is the largest body of water, about 10 mi. long, at the N edge of the Park. US 101 passes along its S shore. 2 resorts are on the lake. Numerous small lakes are found in the high country, in basins formed by glaciers.

The Park is surrounded by the Olympic National Forest (see entry) and is linked to it by numerous trails.

Most visitors enter the Park by driving S from Port Angeles and up a good mountain road to Hurricane Ridge, one of the Park's most scenic points. In summer, cars can drive about 8 mi. more on a steep gravel road to Obstruction Point, 6,100 ft., with a fine view of Mount Olympus. Another paved road enters the Park along the Elwha River, a few miles to the W.

Another popular entrance, on the W side, leads to the Hoh Rain Forest, which receives about 140 in. of rainfall yearly. On the SW, roads penetrate the Park at the Queets River and near the N shore of Lake Quinault. On the E and SE, several roads lead to campgrounds a short distance inside Park boundaries.

The separate Pacific Coast area of the Park is described in Features.

**Plants:** The life zones and plant species of the Park are much the same as those described for the adjoining National Forest. Park roads do reach higher elevations, giving motorists views of the subalpine and arctic-alpine life zones.

Treeline is about 6,000 ft. In the upper part of the subalpine zone, as at Hurricane Ridge, are prairielike meadows. In early summer, some slopes are carpeted with white avalanche lilies; some have great patches of yellow glacier lilies. Other wildflowers of the zone are lupines, larkspur, buttercup, cinquefoil, paintbrush, arnica, tiger lily, and mountain buckwheat. The arctic-alpine zone has mostly perennials adapted to its harsh conditions: rocks, shallow soil, long winters, high winds. Plant life includes mosses, lichens, and a variety of touch, ground-hugging flowering species. The Olympic Mountains have a number of species of mountain plants found nowhere else.

Rain forests are characteristic of the W side of the Park, especially in the Hoh, Queets, and Quinault Valleys. The Hoh is most accessible, by road to a visitor center and by easy, well-maintained trails beyond. Some trees in the rain forest valleys are gigantic: a western red cedar 630 ft. in circumference, a Sitka spruce 58 ft. in circumference, a Douglas-fir 44 ft. in circumference. The ground, including the trunks of fallen trees, is thickly carpeted with mosses, club mosses, oxalis, bead-ruby, and other plants. Many trees have sprouted from the downed trunks and attained considerable size. Bigleaf maples are covered with fantasy draperies of club moss.

**Birds:** Checklist available. About 300 resident and migrating species identified, generally the same species as reported in the National Forest, cited in that entry. Principal difference is for the Pacific Coast area; species noted there include common, arctic, and red-throated loons, sooty and pink-footed shearwaters, Leach's petrel, double-crested, Brandt's, and pelagic cormorants, white-winged and surf scoters, black oystercatcher, surfbird, black turnstone, knot, dunlin, short-billed and long-billed dowitchers, 6 gulls, pigeon guillemot, common murre, marbled and ancient murrelets, Cassin's and rhinoceros auklets, tufted puffin.

**Mammals:** Checklist available. Essentially the same species as those in National Forest entry. Because hunting is not permitted in the Park, some species are seen more often and show little fear of humans. Roosevelt elk, black-tailed deer, and black bear are often seen. The Olympic marmot, similar to hoary and yellow-bellied marmots, occurs only in the Olympic Mountains.

### Features

*Pacific Coast area.* A narrow strip of Pacific coastline, over 60 mi. long. US 101 runs near the southern 12 mi. of the strip. A road leads to the coast at Rialto Beach. Otherwise the area is roadless, reached and traveled only on foot. The coastline is a succession of sandy beaches separated by rocky points and headlands. Numerous needle rocks and small islands are offshore.

*Olympic Coast National Marine Sanctuary:* 3,300 sq. mi. offshore. This is the nation's 14th established marine sanctuary, containing some of the richest fishing and shellfish grounds "on the planet." 29 species of marine mammals, including harbor seals, gray whales, dolphins, and porpoises, visit the area, and many raise their young here. The Sanctuary is also home to one of the largest colonies of seabirds and bald eagles on the West Coast. During nesting season, thousands of gulls, murres, rhinoceros auklets, tufted puffins, and pigeon guillemots make the islands their home. The purpose of the Sanctuary is to protect the marine resources through education and research.

About 870 islands off the Washington coast, from Cape Flattery to Copalis Beach, are included in the Sanctuary. All are small, some only a few yards across. All are also closed to visitors, but many can be observed from the coast with binoculars or spotting scope.

In many places along the coast, tide pools are exposed at low tide, showing a rich assortment of marine flora and fauna. Coastal forest is just above the beach. Raccoon, skunk, deer, bear, and elk are sometimes seen on the beaches.

One of the most popular trails to the beach begins at the N end of Lake Ozette. Indeed, so many people hiked the trail that a single-plank boardwalk was installed to minimize damage to the environment.

Beach hiking and backpacking are popular, especially in winter when the high country is snowbound. Most campers don't travel far from the access trails. Walk a few miles more and you'll have little company.

Before hiking far, study the leaflet *A Strip of Wilderness* and tide tables. Some points can't be rounded except at low tide, some not at all; trails lead over them. Fatalities have occurred when hikers were trapped by incoming tides.

Backcountry permits are required, and reservations are required in some areas.

## Interpretation

*Visitor centers:* Only the main Olympic National Park visitor center (formerly the Pioneer Memorial Museum) is open and staffed year-round. Storm King (at Lake Crescent) and Kalaloch information stations and the Hurricane Ridge visitor center are open and staffed seasonally. All have audio-visual programs, talks, exhibits, literature, information.

*Nature trails* are at numerous places, among them Lake Crescent, Hurricane Ridge, Heart O' the Hills, Staircase, Hoh.

*Campfire programs* and *guided walks* in summer. *Winter snowshoe walks* at Hurricane Ridge. *Education programs* for school groups spring and fall. Schedules posted.

## Activities

*Camping:* 16 campgrounds, 914 sites. Some campgrounds at lower elevations open all year. Those at high elevations usually closed by snow from early Nov. to late June or early July.

*Hiking, backpacking:* About 600 mi. of trails. Many short day trips. Longer, more difficult routes may take a week or more. Backcountry permits required for all overnight trips. Daily entry quotas limit access to Lake Constance, Flapjack Lakes, Grand Valley area, and the Cape Alava/Sandpoint area. There are a limited number of designated sites in the Seven Lakes Basin area, in effect limiting use there at busy times. Check trail conditions and necessary equipment before backpacking into the high country. Information available through the wilderness information center, located behind the visitor center in Port Angeles.

*Caution:* When hiking beaches along the coast, beware of high tides and sudden high waves. The waves can pick up logs, turning them into weapons.

*Fishing:* Cutthroat, rainbow, brook, and steelhead in streams. Rainbow and brook trout in some mountain lakes. Special regulations.

*Swimming:* Crescent Lake, Lake Ozette.

*Boating:* Ramps on Crescent Lake, Lake Ozette. Boat-in campsite on Lake Ozette.

*Canoeing, kayaking:* Hoh River, from the road's end at the rain forest visitor center to the sea. Upstream portion in the Park. Class II and III rapids. Quinault River from bridge on road to Graves Creek Campground to Lake Quinault, about 10 mi. Some class II rapids. Best in summer. River below lake is controlled by Quinault Tribal Council.

*Horse riding:* HQ will provide current list of packers. Several backcountry trail routes are suitable for pack trips. Hitchracks and loading ramps at several locations. Special regulations.

*Mountain climbing:* For the experienced and well-prepared climber. Register at the ranger station nearest your route. Never climb alone.

*Ski touring, snowshoeing:* Late fall to spring. Trails suitable for short day trips or overnight.

## Publications

Leaflet with map.

*A Strip of Wilderness* (leaflet with map of Pacific Coast area).

Combined checklist of Olympic wildlife (birds, mammals, amphibians and reptiles), $0.95.

Mimeo information pages: Park history, suggested day hikes, rain forests, glaciers, Park features by car, fishing regulations, climbing Mount Olympus, winter activities at Hurricane Ridge, pack and saddle stock use.

*For further information contact:*

> Northwest Interpretive Association, 3002 Mt. Angeles Rd., Port Angeles, WA 98362; (360) 452-4501, ext. 230.

> Olympic Coast National Marine Sanctuary, 138 W. First St., Port Angeles, WA 98362; (360) 457-6622.

## Headquarters

National Park Service, 600 E. Park Ave., Port Angeles, WA 98362; (360) 452-0330. Wilderness information/backcountry reservations: (360) 452-0300.

## Olympic Wildlife Area

Washington Department of Fish and Wildlife
962 acres.

15 mi. N of Aberdeen on Wishkah Rd.

Mostly open fields and brushfields surrounded by tree farms. Managed to promote winter use by elk, deer, and bear. Crossed by the Wishkah River and its West Fork. The area is well away from traveled routes and likely to be people-free outside hunting season. The road passes field HQ just beyond Greenwood, and a stop is worthwhile when it's open.

### Headquarters

WA Dept. of Fish and Wildlife, 48 B Devonshire Rd., Montesano, WA 98563; (360) 249-6522/753-2600.

## Oyhut Wildlife Area; Ocean Shores

Washington Department of Fish and Wildlife
682 acres.

From Hoquiam, W 16 mi. on Hwy 109, then S on Hwy 115 2 mi. to end. Left through Ocean Shores gates and 4.6 mi. on S. Point Brown Ave. Right on S. Tonquin, over bridge, to end.

Ocean Shores, a burgeoning resort, is on a peninsula, the northernmost of two enclosing Grays Harbor. At the S end are several areas of interest: the ocean beaches ending at Point Brown, North Jetty, the Oyhut Wildlife Area, and Damon Point.

No trails, but easy walking over brushy salt meadow. Walk SW. On the left is a salt marsh and Armstrong Bay.

An alternative approach is to turn seaward at Ocean Shores and take Ocean Shores Blvd. S to the North Jetty, turn left, drive along the seawall, and park near the sewage treatment plant. The Wildlife Area boundary is behind the plant. Keep to the right and out along the sand spit enclosing Armstrong Bay.

To reach Damon Point, drive N from the sewage plant, turn right on Marine View Drive, pass the first entrance just mentioned and turn right over a jetty onto Protection Island. Park and explore the beach. From the end of March through Aug., the W end of Damon Point and the E end of Oyhut are managed for snowy plover, currently listed as endangered. These areas are signed and are off limits to people. All dogs must be leashed during snowy plover closures.

We don't know the ownership of the dunes and ocean beach near Pt. Brown. We saw people swimming, sunbathing, beachcombing, surf fishing; several had apparently camped or parked RVs overnight in the dunes. Fishing and picnicking seemed to be popular at North Jetty. We saw no one within the Wildlife Area.

**Birds:** The area is well known to local birders. Geese, mallard, pintail, wigeon, and green-winged teal are the chief game species. Species noted along the shores, dunes, marsh, and meadow include black turnstone, surfbird, rock sandpiper, wandering tattler, snowy, semi-palmated, and golden plovers, whimbrel, willet, knot, dunlin, short-billed dowitcher, marbled godwit, Virginia rail, sanderling, northern harrier, horned lark. The jetty is said to be excellent for seabirds, including species such as shearwaters, kittiwake, murre. Rafts of ducks are often seen near the jetty. Like many coastal peninsulas, this one is a funnel for migratory species.

### Nearby
*Ocean City State Park:* 112 acres. 1 mi. N of Ocean Shores. Also said to be a good birding area. Camping, 177 sites, all year. Seacoast.

### Headquarters
WA Dept. of Fish and Wildlife, 48 B Devonshire Rd., Montesano, WA 98563; (360) 249-6522/753-2600.

...........................................................................................................................................

## Schafer State Park
Washington Parks and Recreation Commission
119 acres.

From Elma on US 12, 12 mi. N on E. Satsop Rd.

Heavily wooded site, including large old-growth firs. On the East Fork of the Satsop River, with 4,200 ft. of freshwater shoreline on river. Canoeing and kayaking on the Middle and West Forks, nearby. Some class II and III rapids.

### Activities

*Camping:* 55 sites. All year.

*Fishing:* Trout, salmon, steelhead.

### Headquarters

WA Parks and Recreation Comm., W. 1365 Schafer Park Rd., Elma, WA 98541; (360) 482-3852/(800) 233-0321.

---

## Tahuya State Forest

Washington Department of Natural Resources
23,000 acres.

On the Tahuya Peninsula, SW corner of Kitsap Peninsula, SW of Bremerton, within the Big Bend of the Hood Canal. By local roads from Belfair.

Early in the 19th century, the area was logged off and abandoned. County governments deeded it to the State Forest Board in return for 75% of future income. As noted in the WA introduction, much of the land managed by the DNR consists of widely scattered small tracts. Here and in several other cases, blocks are large enough to be managed for broader purposes. The DNR emphasizes, however, that these are trust lands managed primarily for timber production and other revenue-generating activities.

Most of the acreage is in one large, irregularly shaped block. Another, smaller block lies in the SW. Green Mountain State Forest lies to the NE. And although close to the Hood Canal, the Forest has little actual frontage on it. Most of the peninsula is between 200 and 500 ft. elevation. The Green and Gold Mountains in the NE reach about 1,700 ft.

Tidelands, brushy swamps, bogs—wetlands make up about 2% of the Forest. About 95% of the site is forested. 68 small lakes on the peninsula. Annual precipitation is about 60 in., half of which falls between Nov. and Feb.

This Forest is not shown on the state's official highway maps and its campgrounds are not listed in popular campground directories. Mountain biking, motorized vehicles, and equestrians are the heaviest users of the Forest.

**Plants:** 95% forested: Douglas-fir with western red cedar, hemlock, and western white pine, with red alder, cottonwood, quaking aspen along streams and beside swamps. Understory of rhododendron, Oregon grape, salal, evergreen huckleberry, sword fern. Many wildflowers, including tiger lily, daisy, twinflower, princes pine, avalanche lily.

**Birds:** No checklist. More than 180 species recorded. Game species include waterfowl, ring-necked pheasant, mountain and California quail, ruffed and blue grouse, band-tailed pigeon. Also, northern flicker, goldfinch, osprey, great blue heron, kingfisher, marsh wren, Steller's jay.

**Mammals:** Species reported include black bear, coyote, bobcat, mule deer, river otter, beaver, red fox, rabbits.

### Feature
*Viewpoint* on Green Mountain NE of Forest.

### Activities
*Camping:* 11 campgrounds, 61 sites. Most open all year.

*Hiking:* Trail system also used by hikers, horses, mountain bikes, and ORVs.

*Hunting:* Deer, bear, game birds.

*Fishing:* Many of the lakes are stocked. Fish and Wildlife Dept. has provided 10 public accesses. Chinook, coho, chum salmon, rainbow trout, cutthroat, and steelhead.

*Swimming:* Lake, unsupervised.

*Boating:* Ramps at Aldrich, Howell, Robbins, and Twin Lakes. Nearby access to Hood Canal.

### Nearby
*Belfair State Park:* 62 acres. 3 mi. W of Belfair on Hwy 300, exit 132W. On the Hood Canal. 184 campsites. Popular swimming site.

### Publications
Tahuya State Forest map.

Tahuya trail map.

Green Mountain State Forest trail map.

Public lands: Shelton quadrangle, $5.40.

Public lands: Tacoma quadrangle, $5.40.

## Headquarters

WA Dept. of Natural Resources, S. Puget Sound Region, P.O. Box 68, Enumclaw, WA 98022-0068; (360) 825-1631.

## Twin Harbors Beaches

Washington Parks and Recreation Commission

Coast, between Grays Harbor and Willapa Bay, along Hwy 105.

Generally a wide sand beach sloping gently to shallow water. Backed by low dunes. Behind the dunes, in undisturbed locations, are shrubs and wildflowers; few trees. Most of the coastal land is privately owned. Largest public sites are *Grayland Beach State Park*: 411 acres, and *Twin Harbors State Park:* 172 acres, both heavily used. The state has also provided a number of beach-access points. Motorized vehicles use the beach.

## Activities

*Camping:* Grayland Beach, 60 sites. Twin Harbors, 303 sites. Both require reservations: (800) 233-0321.

*Hiking:* ¾ mi. nature trail.

*Fishing:* Salmon, perch, flounder, sole; also digging for razor clams.

*Horse riding:* Twin Harbors only.

## Headquarters

WA Parks and Recreation Comm., Twin Harbors State Park, Westport, WA 98595; (800) 233-0321.

ZONE

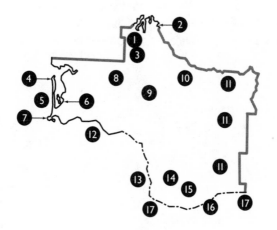

Z O N E

Includes these counties:

| | | |
|---|---|---|
| Thurston | Wahkiakum | Clark |
| Pacific | Cowlitz | |
| Lewis | Skamania | |

This zone extends from the Olympic Peninsula to the Columbia River, from the ocean to the Cascades. By far the largest block of public land is in the Gifford Pinchot National Forest. Mount St. Helens National Volcanic Monument was established within the Forest 15 years ago.

Tourists who have followed the OR coast N are likely to find WA's S coast a disappointment. Grays Harbor and Willapa Bay divide it into 3 sections. Except for a few miles of Hwy 109 in the N section, there is no scenic drive. The coastal roads are behind low dunes. Most of the land is privately owned. Only a few small State Parks and state rights-of-way provide access to the beaches. Most of the beaches are wide and sandy, sloping gently to shallow water. Motor vehicles are allowed to drive on them.

Coastal peninsulas tend to concentrate the flow of migrating birds, and this coastline has a number of birding hot spots. S of Ocean Shores, on Grays Harbor, are the Oyhut Wildlife Area and North Jetty. At the extreme S, Fort Canby State Park on Cape Disappointment attracts many birders in season. The most outstanding natural area on this section of coast is Leadbetter Point, its tip a federal Wildlife Refuge, the adjacent land an undeveloped State Park.

Near the coast and along the Columbia River are a number of fine state and federal Wildlife Refuges. Some offer good wildlife viewing from your automobile, others pleasant hiking, while several can be visited only by private boat. The state areas are likely to be almost deserted except in hunting season.

The two largest state-owned sites are the Capitol State Forest a few miles SW of Olympia and the Yacolt Burn State Forest a few miles NW of Vancouver.

Other public recreation sites are small, scattered, and with limited natural features. We have included a few as entries despite their smallness because no larger natural areas are nearby.

## Battle Ground Lake State Park

Washington Parks and Recreation Commission
280 acres.

21 mi. NE of Vancouver; 8 mi. N on I-5, 8 mi. E on Hwy 502, 3 mi. on local road to Park.

Rolling terrain, elevations 500 to 690 ft. 28-acre lake. Site is about 65% forested, balance brush and grassy meadows. Douglas-fir dominant, with some old growth. Precipitation about 80 in. annually. Most development is on the SE side of the lake. Heavily used in season.

No data on flora and fauna available. Park manager says about 150 flowering plant species are present, good dogwood display in spring.

**Birds:** Steller's jay, crow, sapsucker, northern flicker, robin, wrens, snow bunting. Some ducks at lake.

**Mammals:** Include raccoon, opossum, coyote, fox.

### Interpretation
*Nature trail,* ½ mi., self-guiding.

### Activities
*Camping:* 50 sites. All year, weather permitting. Reservations May 23–Sept. 1.

*Hiking:* About 9 mi. of trails and fire roads. 1 mi. hike to outlook.

*Fishing:* Rainbow trout, bass.

*Swimming:* Lake, supervised. Scuba diving.

*Boating, canoeing:* Motorboats must only use electric motors.

*Horse riding:* 5 mi. of trails. Horse camp. No rentals.

**Headquarters**
WA Parks and Recreation Comm., 18002 N.E. 249th St., Battleground,
WA 98604; (360) 687-4621/(800) 452-5687.

## Beacon Rock State Park

Washington Parks and Recreation Commission
4,482 acres.

On the Columbia River Hwy, Hwy 14, 4 mi. W of Bonneville Dam.

Hilly to steep terrain. Highest point about 2,800 ft. elevation. 2,700 ft.
of shoreline. Beacon Rock, a huge monolith, is between the highway
and the river, rising 848 ft. Nearly 1 mi. trail, 15% grade, to top; spectacular views of Columbia Gorge. Most of the Park is across the highway, including all of Hamilton Mountain, most of Little Hamilton,
part of Table Mountain. Two high, rocky ridgelines. A popular Park,
close to Vancouver and Portland, campground often full on summer
weekends. However, most of the site is undeveloped except for trails,
and it's usually possible to enjoy a hike without too much company.

**Plants:** About 60% forested, most of the remainder in tall, heavy
brush. Douglas-fir predominates, including some old-growth specimens, over 300 years old, mixed with hardwoods. Other tree species
include western hemlock, bigleaf maple, red alder. Heavy understory
of vine maple, Pacific dogwood, willow, serviceberry, snowberry, Oregon grape, poison oak, mock orange, ocean spray, salmonberry, hazel,
blackberry. The high ridges resemble subalpine areas, open with many
wildflowers. Over 100 flowering species occur in the Park, among
them trillium, vanilla leaf, bleeding heart, violets, penstemons, monkeyflowers, phlox, buttercup, cinquefoil, wallflower, paintbrush.

**Birds:** No checklist. Park ranger reports many hawks, ducks, woodpeckers, thrushes, sparrows, jays, finches, and swallows; turkey vulture, red-tailed hawk, northern flicker, pileated woodpecker, varied
thrush, dark-eyed junco, violet-green swallow, ruffed grouse, Canada
goose, mallard, great blue heron, rufous hummingbird, Steller's jay,
western tanager.

**Mammals:** No checklist. Reported: mule deer, chickaree, skunk, opossum, porcupine, ground squirrel, cottontail, muskrat, raccoon, coyote, with occasional sightings of elk, otter, beaver, black bear, mountain lion. We saw pika, usually found only at much higher elevations.

### Interpretation
*Nature trail.* 1¼ mi.

### Activities
*Camping:* 35 sites. All year.

*Hiking:* About 10 mi. of trails to such destinations as Rodney Falls, Hardy Falls, crest of Hamilton Mountain. Also 15 mi. of fire road in the back area of the Park, open to ORVs and hiking.

*Fishing:* River, stream. Salmon, sturgeon, shad, trout, bass, crappie.

*Boating:* Ramp on river. Dock with limited moorage.

*Mountain Biking:* Trails, fire road.

*Horse riding:* 13-mi. equestrian trail.

### Publication
Site map.

### Headquarters
WA Parks and Recreation Comm., 34841 Hwy 14, Skamania, WA 98648; (509) 427-8265/(800) 233-0321.

---

## Capitol State Forest
Washington Department of Natural Resources
90,000 acres (including adjacent Lower Chehalis State Forest).

SW of Olympia. Coming from the S on I-5, take Maytown Exit W to Little Rock and follow signs. Or take Black Lake Blvd. Exit off US 101, S on Black Lake to Delphi Rd. Left on Delphi roughly 2 mi. to Waddell Creek Rd. Y. Then right for 1 mi. to Waddell Creek entrance.

Logging and fires devastated this area by the early 1900s. State land acquisition began in the 1930s, much bought for 50¢ an acre. Intensive tree planting and forest management began, with 7 million seedlings being planted by 1942. The area was opened to public use in 1955.

Located in the Black Hills, the Forest is bounded roughly by Hwy 8 on the N, US 12 on the W, the Black River on the E. Highest point is Capitol Peak, 2,658 ft., lowest, 120 ft. Several cold, fast-flowing creeks flow to the Chehalis River, which runs between Capitol State Forest and Lower Chehalis State Forest lands. No lakes, but beaver dams have formed some large, shallow ponds.

Annual precipitation is 50–65 in. Summers have warm days, cool nights, with some rain.

This is a working forest, managed for timber production. Facilities for recreation are primitive. The 360 mi. of roads are mostly single-lane and gravel. Ever-present logging trucks have the right of way. The DNR's State Forests aren't shown on the official state highway map, and its campgrounds aren't listed in major campground directories.

The N half of the trail system has been designated for ORV use. The DNR reports that trail biking is the most popular recreation in the Forest.

**Plants:** Lower ridges and midslopes have a mix of Douglas-fir, western hemlock, western red cedar, red alder, bigleaf maple, with scattered grand fir and Sitka spruce. Subordinate species include cascara, dogwood, vine maple, Pacific yew; willow, black cottonwood, alder, and maple along creeks. Abundant groundcover of salal and sword fern. Some higher peaks have silver fir/Douglas-fir forest with grand and noble firs, vine maple, big huckleberry. Meadow flowers include camas, violets, wild daisy, buttercup.

**Birds:** Checklist available. Species reported include goshawk, red-tailed hawk, northern harrier, kestrel, blue and ruffed grouse, rock dove, screech, great horned, pygmy, and spotted owls, Vaux's swift, northern flicker, 3 woodpeckers, western flycatcher, wood pewee, violet-green swallow, Steller's jay, raven, crow, Clark's nutcracker, chestnut-backed chickadee, red-breasted nuthatch, brown creeper, 3 wrens, 4 warblers, 3 thrushes, Hutton's and solitary vireos, western tanager, Cassin's finch, American goldfinch, 4 sparrows.

**Mammals:** Checklist. Forest management has yielded larger, more diverse mammal population. The numbers of deer and black bear have increased; beaver have returned, especially in Upper Sherman Valley. Other species reported include brush rabbit, cottontail, mountain beaver, chipmunk, chickaree, coyote, weasel, bobcat, muskrat, river otter, red fox.

### Features

*Mima Mounds Natural Area Preserve:* Grass-covered hummocks, 5–10 ft. high, 15–25 ft. in diameter, scattered over a natural meadow.

*Old Fuzzy Top:* Hill with young forest on its slopes, a patch of 200-year-old Douglas-fir and hemlock near the crest.

*E. Line Rd.* provides vistas of the Chehalis Valley.

## Interpretation

*McLane Creek Nature Trail, self-guiding.*

McLane Creek Centennial Demonstration Forest. *Interpretive signs* at many campgrounds and along main visitor routes.

## Activities

*Camping:* 9 campgrounds, 90 primitive sites.

*Hiking:* 12 mi. of trails for hikers only. Site map shows 100 mi. of trails in the S half, where use is limited to hikers and horses. Some forest roads offer good hiking, and bushwhacking is feasible in some areas.

*Hunting:* Deer, grouse, pigeon, bear, elk. Lower Chehalis State Forest (nearby) is known for elk, deer, blue and ruffed grouse, and wild turkey.

*Fishing:* Beaver ponds stocked.

*Horse riding:* Designated trails. Horse tie rails.

## Publications

Forest map.

Checklists of birds, mammals.

McLane Creek nature trail guide.

## Headquarters

WA Dept. of Natural Resources, Central Region, 1405 Rush Rd., Chehalis, WA 98532; (360) 748-2383.

## Columbia River Gorge National Scenic Area

U.S. Forest Service
292,000 acres in WA and OR

From Vancouver, follow Hwy 14 E parallel to the Columbia River for 75 mi. (See also entries in OR zones 2 and 3).

The Columbia River Gorge National Scenic Area is a spectacular river canyon cutting through the volcanic rock of the Cascade Mountain Range. Following the river's course (and the S boundary of WA), it cuts across both zones 2 and 6. We have somewhat arbitrarily placed the WA entry here. 3 bridges from Hwy 14, at Stevenson, Bingen, and Dallesport, take the visitor over to I-84 and the OR side of the area.

Evidence of the age of volcanism in the area can be viewed at Beacon Rock, an 848-ft. volcanic plug named by Lewis and Clark. The mountain eroded around the plug, leaving the volcanic remnant.

Ancestors of today's Yakama, Warm Springs, Umatilla, and Nez Perce tribal nations lived and fished along the river's banks, trading their dried, smoked salmon. It is still possible to see them fishing from platforms with dip nets in the E section of the gorge, in the tradition of long ago.

Experiencing some of the WA side of the gorge on foot is strongly recommended. There are 200 mi. of maintained trails, at all levels of hiking. Try the wildflower-abundant Dog Mountain Trail 13 mi. E of Stevenson (well marked from Hwy 14).

### Headquarters

U.S. Forest Service, Pacific NW Region, 902 Wasco Ave., Suite 200, Hood River, OR; (541) 386-2333.

## Fort Canby State Park

Washington Parks and Recreation Commission
1,882 acres.

From US 101 at Ilwaco, 2½ mi. SW, Exit 39.

A developed, heavily used Park on Cape Disappointment, on the Columbia River and Pacific Ocean. More than 8 mi. of ocean shoreline (Benson Beach) as well as frontage on the river and Baker Bay. Includes 40-acre Lake O'Neil. Historic site.

Natural features of interest include the beach, a patch of virgin Sitka spruce–western hemlock forest with trees up to 500 years old, and North Jetty, well known to local birders as a hot spot for sea- and shorebirds.

### Interpretation
*Nature hikes* and *campfire programs* about various historic, geological, and natural features of the Park, June 15–Labor Day.

### Activities
*Camping:* 250 sites. All year. Reservations.

*Hiking:* On beach and in forest.

*Swimming:* Ocean, unsupervised.

*Boating:* Two ramps. Float moorage surfing.

### Publications
Leaflet.

Forest trail guide.

### Headquarters
WA Parks and Recreation Comm., P.O. Box 488, Ilwaco, WA 98624; (360) 642-3078/(800) 233-0321.

---

## Gifford Pinchot National Forest; Mount St. Helens National Volcanic Monument
U.S. Forest Service

1,372,000 acres; including 110,000 acres in the Monument.

From Mount Rainier National Park to the Columbia River. Crossed by US 12. E access via Hwy 141 through Trout Lake; W access via I-5, exit at Hwy 503 at Woodland or Hwy 504 at Castle Rock.

In Feb. 1980, Forest HQ returned our original data sheets with a fine stack of maps, trail guides, and other information. We knew this Forest fairly well from previous visits and planned no extensive field work here. In the file was this note on geologic history: "Although Mount St. Helens has been dormant since 1857, its active and violent history leads many geologists to predict that the mountain will erupt again, perhaps before the end of the century."

The mountain erupted violently on May 18. In the National Forest, 20,000 acres were devastated, another 200,000 heavily damaged. The destruction included 1.6 billion board ft. of timber, 100 mi. of streams, 27 recreation sites, 63 mi. of roads, 12 bridges, 97 mi. of trails, 15 Forest Service buildings.

For all practical purposes, the Forest was closed to the public. Outside the area of destruction, much of the Forest had a layer of volcanic ash. No one knew what the mountain would do next.

One reason for keeping people out was concern about what would happen in another eruption. We heard stories in Aug. 1980 of hikers who had been on Mount Adams at the time of the March eruption. The dense cloud of ash had caused a blackout, blinding them, and they had to grope their way down on hands and knees. While we were in WA two more eruptions occurred, both minor, but enough to dust ash on our campground 100 mi. from the mountain.

By Jan. 1981, most of the Forest was open again to public use.

15 years later, homes, roads, and bridges have been rebuilt. Timberlands have been salvaged and replanted. More than 110,000 acres have been set aside by Congress as a National Monument. Color and life have returned to the blast zone, as the few hardy survivors were joined by ever-increasing numbers of colonizing plants and animals.

The Gifford Pinchot is one of the oldest National Forests, parts of it having been set aside in 1897. It is named after an active conservationist and the first chief of the U.S. Forest Service. The Forest lies along the W slope of the Cascade Mountains. Average height of the mountain ridges is between 3,000 and 4,000 ft. Mount St. Helens *was* 9,677 ft. Mount Adams is 12,326 ft. Several peaks in the Goat Rocks area approach 8,000 ft.

Average precipitation is 60 in. on the W side of the range, up to 100 in. at the summit. It is far less on the E side, about 25 in. per year in the lower valleys. June through Aug. are dry on both sides. Temperatures seldom reach 0°F on the W side, often drop to −10° on the E. Summers are hot.

Many streams flow from the peaks, over 1,300 mi. in all. The Cispus and Lewis Rivers as well as the Clear Fork and the Muddy Fork of the Cowlitz River have been recommended as additions to the Wild and Scenic Rivers System. The Forest has nearly 100 alpine lakes, where salmon and trout are found.

There are over 1,110 mi. of trails in the Pinchot, most in upper-elevation forest and alpine areas, at many hiking levels, and over 300 mi. of trails in the 7 wildernesses, which cover 180,600 acres. The Pacific Crest Trail traverses the Forest.

Within the Forest are many signs of past volcanic activity, including vast lava beds and numerous lava caves. Most are located in the Mount St. Helens National Volcanic Monument, but some are in the Mount Adams Ranger District.

Forest roads are usually open from late May through Nov. Travelers should check road conditions carefully, however, before setting out. Heavy, widespread flooding in the winter of 1995 caused over $15 million worth of damage to roads and bridges, and also destroyed camping areas in the Forest. "It's the most significant natural disaster in the state since Mount St. Helens," one Forest Service employee told us. A number of roads and campsites will not be usable for some time. If you know where you're heading, inquire about specific conditions within that Ranger District. If not, be sure to check with HQ ahead of time for a general update on roads and campgrounds in the Forest.

**Plants:** Difference in precipitation between W and E is reflected in vegetation. The moist W slopes have heavy stands of timber, impressive Douglas-fir, western hemlock, western red cedar, red alder, and Pacific yew. At higher elevations: Pacific silver fir, Alaska yellow cedar, noble fir, western white pine. On the E fringe of the Forest: grand fir, white ponderosa, and lodgepole pines. This part of the Forest contributes a significant volume of timber to the nation's economy each year.

The wide range of elevations, exposures, precipitation, and soils produces many different plant communities, from ferns and thick mosses in the moist and shaded ravines of the W side to the short-lived, summer-blooming heathers on the high slopes of the Goat Rocks. Shrubs of the W slopes include vine maple, rhododendron, chinquapin, hazel, western yew, Pacific dogwood, red huckleberry, Oregon grape, salal, trailing blackberry. Wildflowers include deerfoot vanilla leaf, evergreen violet, trillium, twinflower, white inside-out flower, starflower, bear grass, princes pine, orchids.

On the high slopes: avalanche fawn lily, elkslip marsh marigold, subalpine lupine, paintbrush, red mountain heath, spreading phlox, mountain daisy, alpine cat's-ear, penstemons.

**Birds:** No checklist. Species differ markedly from habitat to habitat. White-tailed ptarmigan, for example, occur on Mount Adams, not on the W slopes. Hermit warblers have been observed near US 12 W of White Pass, not on the E side. Species noted in various parts of the Forest include western and pied-billed grebes, great blue heron, American bittern, mallard, gadwall, pintail, all three teals, wood duck, turkey vulture, sharp-shinned, Cooper's, red-tailed, Swainson's, and rough-legged hawks, golden and bald eagles, blue, spruce, and ruffed grouse, ring-necked pheasant, band-tailed pigeon, mourning doves, screech, great horned, snowy, pygmy, and long-eared owls, nighthawk, Vaux's swift, rufous hummingbird, belted kingfisher, northern flicker, hairy, downy, and white-headed woodpeckers, Say's phoebe, Hammond's flycatcher, wood pewee, horned lark, 5 swallows, gray and Steller's jays, yellow-headed and red-winged blackbirds, raven, crow, Clark's nutcracker, 4 chickadees, red-breasted and pygmy nuthatches, dipper, house and Bewick's wrens, robin, varied, hermit, and Swainson's thrushes, mountain bluebird, golden-crowned and ruby-crowned kinglets, water pipit, cedar waxwing, solitary and warbling vireos, 11 warblers, northern oriole, western tanager, black-headed and evening grosbeaks, pine siskin, red crossbill, rufous-sided towhee, 9 sparrows.

**Mammals:** Species reported include opossum, several species of shrew, deer mouse, various voles, many species of bat, pika, snowshoe hare, white-tailed jackrabbit, mountain beaver, several chipmunks, yellow-bellied and hoary marmots, California and Cascade golden-mantled ground squirrels, western gray and Douglas squirrels, pocket gophers, beaver, coyote, red fox, raccoon, marten, weasel, badger, skunks, river otter, mountain lion, bobcat, Roosevelt elk, mule deer, black-tailed deer, mountain goat, black bear.

### Features

*Goat Rocks Wilderness:* 105,600 acres. Between Mounts Rainier and Adams. US 12 passes near the N boundary. Several Forest roads lead to trailheads near the W and E boundaries. Rugged, beautiful, mountainous terrain; elevations from 3,000 ft. to 8,201-ft. Gilbert Peak. The wilderness derives its name from the mountain goats that inhabit its peaks. Much of the central portion of the wilderness is above timberline. Pinnacles rise from snowfields. Glaciers are surrounded by colorful mountain meadows. Streams meander through meadows, cascade down rocky slopes. Many small alpine lakes. Most of the area is under heavy snow in winter and spring. Cross-country skiing and snowshoeing are popular. Avalanches may be a hazard following winter storms.

Trails are usually open to foot travel by about July 15, but some snow persists into Aug. The trail system allows both day hikes and long loop trips. Permits are required. Sudden, violent storms can occur in any season. Some trails are open to horse travel; feed must be carried in. The wilderness map has trail information.

*Glacier View Wilderness:* 3,000 acres. On the W boundary of Mount Rainier National Park (see entry zone 4). The topography allows considerable solitude, and the scenic views are outstanding. Permits required.

*Mount Adams Wilderness:* 47,270 acres. Bounded on the E by the Yakima Indian Reservation. Mount Adams, 12,276 ft., is second only to Mount Rainier in elevation among WA mountains. Average elevation in the wilderness is 5,500 ft.; timberline is about 6,000 ft. The summit is a mile-long ridge. Heavy snow here feeds a number of glaciers. Adams Glacier, 3 mi. long, fan-shaped, dominates the NW face.

The lower slopes have an exceptionally diverse flora; species native to the moist W slopes and the drier E side sometimes intermix. Many alpine meadows, flowers usually at their peak in late July, early Aug.

The wilderness has heavy use in the hiking season, and it shows, in groundcover damage and erosion. Permits are required. Hikers are asked to camp at forest edges, not in fragile meadows, and to leave no traces behind. The wilderness map shows access routes.

The usual hiking season is July–Nov., but early and late snowstorms occur.

*Indian Heaven Wilderness:* 20,400 acres. About 13 mi. directly W of Trout Lake. The area has been culturally important to native Americans. Broad rolling country, with elevations from 3,900 to 5,927 ft. Large and small meadows, sparse forest of firs and hemlock at higher elevations, denser stands of firs, hemlock, lodgepole and white pines at lower elevations. Seasonal wildlflowers and huckleberries. The area includes 175 lakes and ponds, the largest about 20 acres, most less than 5 acres. Marshy areas. Snow melts about mid-July, patches remaining on N slopes. Best season is Sept., when mosquitoes are gone. The Pacific Crest Trail crosses the area. Permit necessary.

*Tatoosh Wilderness:* 15,800 acres. On the S boundary of Mount Rainier NP. Elevations from 1,400 to 5,900 ft., from river bottoms to subalpine ridgetops. Upper elevations almost entirely open or semiopen meadows; rocky outcrops on steeper slopes. Several lakes, waterfalls. Permit necessary.

*Trapper Creek Wilderness:* 6,000 acres. Includes a number of ecological and geological zones. Old-growth Douglas-fir at lower elevations. Also, rocky peaks, huckleberry fields, high meadows. No permit required at this time.

*William O. Douglas Wilderness:* 166,600 acres shared with Wenatchee National Forest. Contains scattered peaks, sharp ridges, steep slopes, and hundreds of small lakes. Fish and wildlife are abundant. Permit necessary.

*Big Lava Bed:* 12,500 acres. 14 mi. SW of Trout Lake. Oddly shaped lava formations originated from a deep crater at the N end of the area.

*Dark Divide Roadless Area.* Rock outcroppings and alpine vegetation. Panoramic views of snowcapped mountains in all directions. Includes Badger Lake, Craggy Peak, Shark Rock, Hat Rock, and Badger Peak. The Boundary Trail travels the Forest E–W for 50 mi. along high ridges. Wonderful view of Mount St. Helens and its crater.

*Midway High Lakes:* 5 high-elevation lakes within 7-mi. radius. Excellent fishing, with access to Mount Adams Wilderness trails. The area offers outstanding views of Mount Adams. Can be reached by car in the summer.

*Lone Butte Wildlife Emphasis Area:* 12,500 acres of distinctive habitat. Lone Butte, Cayuse, and Skookum Meadows are rich communities offering many opportunities to view elk, deer, beaver, common snipe, warblers, turtles, orchids. Roads are closed to motorized vehicles; bicycles and horse riding allowed. Snowmobiles permitted Dec. 1–April 16.

These are by no means all of the areas of interest in the Forest. Indeed, some of the less well known areas, also accessible by trail, are no less attractive and have fewer visitors. Inquire at HQ and ranger stations.

### Mount St. Helens National Volcanic Monument

On May 18, 1980, Mount St. Helens was shaken by an earthquake measuring 5.1 on the Richter scale. The N face of the mountain subsequently collapsed into a massive avalanche of rock and ice that slammed into Spirit Lake, crossed a ridge, then moved 14 mi. down the Toutle River. At the same time, the avalanche released highly pressurized gases within the volcano. The eruption released a turbulent, debris-filled wind that wreaked havoc over nearly 150 sq. mi. of Forest and sent a column of ash thousands of feet high that turned day into night in the E portions of WA and beyond. Massive flows of rock, mud, and searing pumice spilled out and down the sides of the mountain. It was over in about 9 hours, but the eruption left a vast, still, gray landscape where the glaciers and lovely forested slopes of Mount St. Helens had stood the day before. The volcano continued to erupt, less dramatically, for 6 years, gradually forming a lava dome.

Mount St. Helens's symmetrical 9,677-ft. peak was transformed by the blast into a truncated cone, 1,300 ft. lower. A crater over 2,700 ft. deep now opens to the N. At 8,365 ft., the rim of the volcano offers climbers spectacular views of the crater, the lava dome, and the blast area as a whole. Entry into the crater is strictly prohibited. All climbing above 4,800 ft. requires a permit. For more information, call the Climbing Hotline: (360) 750-3961.

Numerous viewpoints and miles of trails have been created for visitors to explore on foot. Interpretive programs are available to help hikers better understand this unusual area. When winter conditions permit, the Monument may also be enjoyed on cross-country ski and snowmobile trails.

### Interpretation

*Visitor centers:* Mount St. Helens visitor center is located 5 mi. E of I-5 on Hwy 504, on the shores of Silver Lake. It provides theater presentations, interpretive exhibits, an information desk, and books.

Coldwater Ridge *visitor center* is on the North Fork of the Toutle River at Coldwater Lake, E of Mount St. Helens visitor center on Hwy 504. (The highway here becomes *Spirit Lake Memorial Hwy.* This part is particularly scenic, and offers views of Mount St. Helens's crater and the NW lava dome.) This visitor center's interpretive focus is the reappearance of life throughout the blast zone. It provides broad views of the volcano, the newly formed lakes, and the debris-filled Toutle River valley. Coldwater Lake itself was formed by the blast. The Lakes Trail and the Elk Bench Trail provide extended hiking opportunities from the visitor center. The upper section of Elk Bench Trail offers fine views of the crater and the lava dome.

*Lava tubes, caves,* and *casts* have formed on the S flank of Mount St. Helens over centuries of volcanic eruptions. *Ape Cave,* 12,810 ft., is the longest lava tube in the continental U.S. and has been developed for self-guided exploration at several levels of difficulty. Be prepared with warm clothing, heavy shoes, and two light sources. Lanterns may be rented at the cave HQ. Nearby is the Trail of Two Forests, an 0.25-mi. barrier-free interpretive trail through a lava tree–cast area.

*Coldwater Lake Recreation Area* offers beautiful lake and mountain views, birdwatching, a boat launch, and fishing.

*June Lake Trail,* off Forest Rd. 83, is a gentle, forested climb to the crystal blue waters of its namesake. A large, ancient lava flow formed the lake. This is a popular 3-mi. roundtrip well suited to families and less-experienced hikers. It also provides access to the more extensive Loowit Trail. This 27-mi. loop encircles the volcano between 3,500 and 4,500 ft., traversing some of the most dramatic and dynamic landscape in the Monument. The Loowit is rated a difficult trail.

*Mount St. Helens State Wildlife Area:* 2,500 acres. Acquired in 1990 to protect elk habitat on the Toutle River debris area W of Mount St. Helens. The elk are easily viewed from Spirit Lake Memorial Hwy throughout the year. Peak use by over 500 animals occurs during the winter months.

Hoffstadt Bluffs *visitor center,* located 27 mi. E of I-5 on Hwy 504, is run by the Cowlitz County Department of Tourism in Kelso. Open daily all year. (360) 577-3137. 6 mi. E of the visitor center is its *Forest Learning Center,* donated by Weyerhaeuser Lumber. Open daily, 10–7, May–Oct. (360) 414-3439.

## Activities

*Camping:* As of summer 1996, 36 campgrounds, 907 sites, 4 group camps. Seasons vary. Most open late May or June, some July, and close Sept. or Oct. Heavy flooding recently damaged roads and camping areas. Call ahead!

*Hiking, backpacking:* Extensive trail system, all levels of difficulty. See Forest brochure and map, as well as trail guides for the area.

*Hunting:* Black-tailed deer, Roosevelt elk, black bear, mountain goat, blue and ruffed grouse.

*Fishing:* Lakes, streams. Chinook and coho salmon, steelhead trout. Several resident salmonoid species include rainbow, brown, and cutthroat trout, kokanee salmon, 2 species of char (eastern brook trout, bull trout). High mountain lakes not accessible until June.

*Swimming:* Lakes, ponds, unsupervised. May be chilly!

*Boating:* Boat launches at Walupt, Takhlakh, Ollalie, Oklahoma, Goose Lakes, Coldwater Lake Recreation Area, and Trout Creek. Packwood Lake, near the W boundary of Goat Rocks Wilderness, is larger than these, but one must hike in 3 mi.; boat rentals available. Call HQ ahead of time for motor, speed, and other craft limitations.

*Canoeing, kayaking:* Cispus and Upper Lewis Rivers.

*Horse riding:* Many good trails. Several designated horse camps.

*Cross-country skiing, snowshoeing, snowmobiling:* Many opportunities, both developed and undeveloped. Use undeveloped areas above

2,200 ft. to avoid wildlife wintering areas. Be aware of snow avalanche hazard, especially following winter storms. Year-round U.S. Forest Service avalanche information in Seattle, winter (206) 526-4666, summer (503) 326-2400.

*Llama pack trips:* May–Oct. in the N portions of the Forest. Reservations: Llama Tree Ranch, (360) 491-5262.

*Fire hazard closures are possible in Aug. Expect delays for road repair throughout the Forest.*

## Publications

Gifford Pinchot National Forest (map, camping information, roads, trails, points of interest), $3.25.

Additional Forest Service visitor maps available, as follows, each $3.25.

Maps: Mount Adams Wilderness; Goat Rocks Wilderness; Indian Heaven and Trapper Creek Wilderness; Mount St. Helens National Volcanic Monument; Pacific Crest National Scenic Trail; Tatoosh and Glacier View Wilderness.

Mount St. Helens National Volcanic Monument Trail Guide (includes descriptions, difficulty, elevations, interconnecting trails, facilities, maps), $7.95.

Volcano Review (newspaper with yearly update on Mount St. Helens National Volcanic Monument, including scientific developments, the latest on roads and trails, upcoming interpretive programs, events).

## Headquarters

U.S. Forest Service, 6926 E. 4th Plain Rd., P.O. Box 8944, Vancouver, WA 98668-8944; (360) 750-5000 (information)/5009 (24 hours).

## Ranger Districts

Mt. Adams R.D., 2455 Hwy 141, Trout Lake, WA 98650; (509) 395-3400. Mt. Saint Helens National Volcanic Monument, 42218 N.E. Yale Bridge Rd., Amboy, WA 98601; (360) 750-3900 (information)/3903 (24 hours). Packwood R.D., 13068 US 12, Packwood, WA 98361; (360) 494-0600. Randle R.D., P.O. Box 670, Randle, WA 98377; (360) 497-1100. Wind River R.D., 1262 Hemlock Rd., Carson, WA 98610; (509) 427-3200.

## Visitor Centers

Mount St. Helens, 3029 Spirit Lake Hwy, Castle Rock, WA 98611; (360) 274-2100 (information)/2103 (24 hours). Coldwater Ridge, 3029 Spirit Lake Hwy, Castle Rock, WA 98611; (360) 274-2131.

## Julia Butler Hansen Refuge for the Columbian White-Tailed Deer

U.S. Fish and Wildlife Service
5,383 acres, including 2,606 acres in OR.

SW WA, on Columbia River. From Skamokawa on Hwy 4, SE on Steamboat Slough Rd.

A small Refuge established to maintain this endangered deer sub-species. River bottomland: moist floodplain, pastures separated by blocks of trees. Numerous sloughs and channels. Several islands are included within the Refuge. Wintering area for waterfowl. Many shorebirds.

The mainland portion of the Refuge is not open to visitors, but it is readily observed from a county road on the perimeter. One can hike along the road, but automobiles are effective blinds. Tenasillahe Island, accessible only by boat, about 2½ mi. by 1½ mi., offers good hiking and birding.

**Birds:** Checklist. Large wintering populations most years of tundra swan, dusky Canada goose, wigeon, mallard, pintail, loon. Other resident or migratory species often seen include bald eagle, great blue heron, common snipe, western grebe, red-tailed hawk, varied thrush, goldfinch, Steller's jay, Bewick's wren, many gulls.

**Mammals:** Deer often seen from county road, morning and evening. Also present: mink, beaver, river otter, raccoon, Roosevelt elk.

### Activities

*Hunting:* Waterfowl. Designated area. Special regulations.

*Fishing:* Prohibited within Refuge boundaries but permitted in sloughs on the perimeter.

*Boating:* Launching sites on Hwy 4, 4 mi. W of Cathlamet and at Cath-lamet Moorage Basin. Boats prohibited on the interior waters of the Refuge.

*NOTE: This HQ also manages the Lewis and Clark National Wildlife Refuge, a large area of islands, bars, and mudflats on the OR side of the Columbia River main channel.*

## Publications

Leaflet.

Bird checklist.

Hunting regulations.

## Headquarters

U.S. Fish and Wildlife Service, 46 Steamboat Slough Rd., Cathlamet, WA 98612; (360) 795-3915.

----

## Leadbetter Point

U.S. Fish and Wildlife Service/Washington Parks and Recreation Commission
Refuge: 1,700 acres/Park: 947 acres.

From US 101 at Seaview, N on Hwy 103 to its end at Oysterville, then N on Stackpole Road to end.

Called "one of the most outstanding natural areas of the Pacific NW." The Refuge occupies the tip of the Long Beach peninsula, between the ocean and Willapa Bay. Only foot travel is permitted within the Refuge. The adjacent State Park, which also extends from sea to bay, is largely undeveloped. Conservationists urge that it be kept that way, as part of a unique seacoast natural area. Although the dune ecosystem is fragile, often greatly altered by storms, recovery is rapid. This area was logged and grazed until the 1940s, but few signs remain.

The ocean beach is sandy, flat, about 300 ft. wide. Back of the beach and at the tip of the peninsula are young, unstable dunes. Older dunes stabilized by vegetation occupy the central portion. Between the two sets of dunes are troughs that become ponds in winter, the wet season. Between the sand and Willapa Bay are an extensive salt marsh and mudflats. In the bay just E of the point is a small island, surrounded by marsh and mudflats.

The sea-to-bay width is greater in the State Park. Here there is a back dune forest with a dense understory. At the forest margin, trees are beginning to invade the Refuge dunes.

Dunes are up to 45 ft. high, and one can easily become lost wandering among them if the sun is obscured. One can hear the sound of surf, but it seems to come from all directions.

The bay and salt marsh are an important feeding and resting area for waterfowl, the mudflats for shorebirds. One source calls Willapa Bay "the last major undeveloped estuary on the West Coast of the U.S."

A snowy plover nesting area, from mean high-tide mark up to the dunes, is closed to all entry April through Aug.

**Plants:** Species establishing vegetative cover on dunes include beachgrass, American dunegrass, sea rocket, coastal strawberry, beach pea, pearly everlasting, seashore lupine, smooth and hairy cat's-ear, dune goldenrod, western tansy, sand verbena, kinnikinnick. In the winter pond zone, sedge, mints, rushes, owlclover, buttercup, yellow-eyed grass. Tree species include lodgepole pine, spruce, western hemlock, red alder, with dense understory including California wax myrtle, thimbleberry, salal, evergreen huckleberry, salmonberry, sword and bracken ferns, nootka rose. In salt marsh, chiefly salicornia and arrowgrass.

**Birds:** Checklist available for Willapa National Wildlife Refuge (see entry this zone), which includes Leadbetter Point. 180 species identified at the Point. Offshore: fulmar, parasitic jaeger, Brandt's cormorant, common murre, tufted puffin, rhinoceros and Cassin's auklets; large numbers of sooty shearwater pass each August. Waterfowl include many brant, as well as common and arctic loons, 4 grebes, Canada and white-fronted geese, mallard, gadwall, pintail, wigeon, greater scaup, goldeneye, bufflehead, white-winged and surf scoters, common merganser. Shorebirds include dunlin, black turnstone, black-bellied plover, long-billed dowitcher, western sandpiper, sanderling. Also black-legged kittiwake, 7 gulls. Upland species include sharp-shinned, red-tailed, Swainson's, and rough-legged hawks, northern harrier, merlin, bald eagle, ruffed grouse, ring-necked pheasant, killdeer, kingfisher, flicker, Traill's and western flycatchers, cedar waxwing, red crossbill, 4 sparrows.

Birding is generally most productive along the bayshore, fall and spring.

**Mammals:** Include voles, shrews, deer mouse, raccoon, muskrat, beaver, snowshoe hare, chickaree, black-tailed deer.

**Reptiles and amphibians:** Include five salamander species, rough-shinned newt, red-legged and tailed frogs, western toad, painted turtle, northern alligator lizard, garter snake.

## Activities

*Hiking:* Trails through dunes and woods in State Park.

*Hunting:* In National Wildlife Refuge only, subject to special regulations.

*Fishing:* In State Park only.

## Publications

Leaflet.

Bird checklist (Willapa National Wildlife Refuge).

Hunting regulations (Willapa National Wildlife Refuge).

## Headquarters

U.S. Fish and Wildlife Service, Willapa National Wildlife Refuge, Ilwaco, WA 98624; (360) 484-3482. WA Parks and Recreation Comm., 7150 Cleanwater Lane, Olympia, WA 98504; (800) 233-0321.

## Lewis and Clark State Park

Washington Parks and Recreation Commission
620 acres.

12 mi. SE of Chehalis on Jackson Hwy 99, Exit 68.

Washington's second State Park included the largest easily reached stand of virgin timber in this part of the state. A storm in 1962 downed two-thirds of it, but many impressive specimens remain. Douglas-fir was planted in the blowdown area. A nature trail passes through old-growth and recovering areas. Rolling terrain.

**Plants:** 99% forested: Douglas-fir, western red cedar, hemlock; understory includes vine maple, sword fern, salal. Flowering species include bleeding heart, lady's slipper, trillium, dogwood, gooseberry, rhododendron.

## Interpretation

1.25-mi. *nature trail.*

*Slide programs* of area history and old-growth forest in *interpretive center.*

## Activities

*Camping:* 25 sites. All year.

*Hiking:* Trails.

*Horse riding:* 5 mi. of trails.

*Fishing:* Cutthroat trout.

**Publication**

Leaflet.

**Headquarters**

WA Parks and Recreation Comm., 4583 Jackson Hwy, Winlock, WA 98596; (360) 864-2643, (800) 233-0321.

---

## Long Beach

Public and private lands.

SW WA, along Hwy 103.

28 mi. of sand beach, from Cape Disappointment on the S to Leadbetter Point on the N end of the peninsula. Most of the land area is privately owned, and there are several small resort communities. The beach is wide, backed by small dunes. The sea is shallow close to shore; distance between high- and low-tide marks is exceptionally great.

The largest developed public site is Fort Canby State Park at the S end (see entry). The state maintains 6 beach-access points at intervals along the ocean shore. At the N end is Leadbetter Point, a fine natural area (see entry).

Motor vehicles are allowed on the beach.

---

## Mount Baker–Snoqualmie National Forest

About 70,000 acres of this Forest are in zone 2. The entry appears in zone 4, which has over a million acres of the Forest. The zone 2 portion is isolated from the main body of the Forest and is administered by the Gifford Pinchot National Forest. On the state highway map, this portion appears as a solid block N of Morton and W of Hwy 7. It is actually a checkerboard of 1-mi. squares, alternating with private land. The highest point is about 4,300 ft. No Forest campgrounds are within the area. Principal visitor activities are hunting and fishing.

## Mount St. Helens National Volcanic Monument
See Gifford Pinchot National Forest this zone.

## Nisqually National Wildlife Refuge
U.S. Fish and Wildlife Service
2,817 acres.

From Tacoma, SW on I-5 to Exit 114. Turn N (right, under the freeway), then right again on Brown Farm Rd. to entrance.

Open daylight hours 7 days a week.

This areas lies between I-5 and Puget Sound. It includes the delta of the Nisqually River, McAllister Creek, and tidal flats. A large part of the land between the two streams is diked, creating freshwater ponds and marshes. The land extends from I-5 out to the extreme low-tide line. Within the boundaries are several large blocks of state and private land.

The Nisqually Delta is one of the largest remaining undisturbed estuaries in W WA. Access to the Refuge is by foot trail only, beyond the HQ area. There are two short walks, one of them a nature trail and the other a loop to an education center and observation deck at "Twin Barns." A 5-mi. circuit of the dike offers a longer walk past most of the major habitat types.

In addition to the freshwater impoundment, the tidal flats, and salt marsh, the area includes open grassland, mixed coniferous woods along McAllister Creek, and a patch of deciduous forest near I-5. The entrance road crosses a meadow edged with second-growth red alder, maple, and willow.

**Birds:** Some 10,000 waterfowl winter here, and up to 20,000 pass through in migration. Birds commonly observed include wigeon, mallard, pintail, green-winged teal, goldeneye, bufflehead, scaup, scoters, western grebe, Canada goose, great blue heron, greater yellowlegs, western sandpiper, northern harrier, red-tailed hawk, kestrel. A few eagle, white-fronted goose, and brant. Also many gulls, shorebirds, and passerines.

**Mammals:** Include shrew, vole, cottontail, squirrel, mountain beaver, river otter, coyote, raccoon, muskrat, mink, mule deer, seals.

8 mi. of walking trails, birdwatching platform, interpretive center, and fishing facilities are available.

*Pets and bicycles prohibited. No hunting.*

### Publications
Leaflet.

### Headquarters
U.S. Fish and Wildlife Service, Nisqually National Wildlife Refuge, 100 Brown Farm Rd., Olympia, WA 98516;(360) 753-9467.

---

## Rainbow Falls State Park
Washington Parks and Recreation Commission
125 acres.

From Chehalis, W 18 mi. on Hwy 6, Exit 77.

A small Park, with some old-growth timber and 3,400 ft. of frontage on the Chehalis River, including Rainbow Falls and a basalt gorge. Level to rolling terrain. 45 acres N of the river are developed; 80 acres S of the river, reached by bridge, are hilly, forested, undeveloped except for trails. Self-guiding nature trail. The falls above the bridge create a rainbow, giving the Park its name.

### Activities
*Camping:* 50 sites. All year.

*Fishing:* Trout.

*Swimming:* Pool at foot of falls.

*Canoeing, kayaking:* River.

### Headquarters
WA Parks and Recreation Comm., 4008 State Hwy 6, Chehalis, WA 98532; (360) 291-3767, (800) 233-0321.

## Ridgefield National Wildlife Refuge

U.S. Fish and Wildlife Service
5,250 acres.

From Vancouver, 15 mi. N on I-5 to Ridgefield Exit, W 3 mi. to Ridgefield. HQ is in town at 301 N. Main St. Refuge adjoins town.

The Refuge's wetlands, grasslands, and woodlands are characterized by two types of management—natural and agricultural. Preservation of the natural Columbia River floodplain is the management objective on the Carty and Roth Units. Spring snowmelt from the mountains and heavy winter rains result in periodic flooding of portions of these units. The Bachelor Island Unit is protected from flooding by dikes and is actively managed to grow crops and provide winter food for waterfowl. The River "S" Unit is also protected by dikes and used to grow crops for winter wildlife. The flooded wetlands and pastures provide winter food for Canada geese. The Ridgeport Dairy Unit is also managed to provide wetlands and pastures for wintering wildlife.

Winter is the major viewing season, with up to 40,000 geese and 20,000 ducks, although birders will find many interesting birds in all seasons. Four units are open for wildlife observation and other wildlife related activities. Contact HQ for seasonal closures. The Carty, River "S," and Roth Units are accessible from Ridgefield.

The Carty Unit, located N of town, has outcroppings of basalt that form knolls above the high-water level. These are wooded with ash, oak, and Douglas-fir. In the spring the knolls are bright with wildflowers; in summer they become dry, in contrast to the surrounding marsh. The Carty Unit has a 2-mi. Oaks to Wetland interpretive trail, but the rest of the unit is also open to foot traffic.

The River "S" Unit, has a 2-mi. road that takes visitors near wetlands and crop fields, allowing close-up views of wintering waterfowl. An observation blind and outhouse are accessible to the disabled.

The Roth Unit is more primitive and accessible only by foot.

The Ridgefield Dairy Unit can be reached from Vancouver on the Lower River Rd. The unit is closed to foot traffic but has numerous roadside wildlife viewing opportunities.

**Birds:** Checklist available. 206 species reported. Numerous or common species include Canada goose, tundra swan, mallard, pintail, cinnamon and green-winged teals, shoveler, gadwall, sandhill crane, great blue heron, red-tailed hawk, and a wide diversity of migratory and resident songbirds.

**Mammals:** Species most frequently seen include black-tailed deer, coyote, beaver, river otter, nutria, and cottontail.

### Activities

*Hunting:* Waterfowl, in designated blinds on River "S" Unit. Special regulations; call HQ.

*Fishing:* Follow state and Refuge regulations.

### Publications

Leaflet with map.

Bird checklist.

Hunting leaflet.

Oaks to Wetlands Trail leaflet.

Wildlife leaflet.

### Headquarters

U.S. Fish and Wildlife Services, 301 N. 3rd St., P. O. Box 457, Ridgefield, WA 98642; (360) 887-4106.

## Scatter Creek Wildlife Area

Washington Department of Fish and Wildlife
1,161 acres.

18 mi. S of Olympia, just W of I-5. Turn W at Maytown Exit, then immediately S on Case Rd. to Case Segment of Wildlife Area. For Township Segment, continue to Lincoln Rd., then W.

The two segments are about half a mile apart, but they adjoin other state land and a large timber company holding. Flat prairie: grassfields, Scotch broom, oak and evergreen woodlands. This is the state's most heavily hunted pheasant release site. Case Segment is used year-round for dog training and field trials. Township Segment is closed to this activity April–July. For those with interests other than hunting and dogs, Township Segment in spring and summer is the choice. Vehicles are banned; foot travel only.

Scatter Creek, crossing the Township Segment, is dammed, due to beaver activity. The beaver ponds attract waterfowl and are open for fishing after June. Both segments, but especially Case, have a number of Mima mounds, gravel hummocks of uncertain origin.

**Birds:** Checklist of 64 species. A few waterfowl in season, plus hawks, great blue heron, California quail, band-tailed pigeon, many song-birds.

## Publications
*Wildlife Recreation Areas, 26, Scatter Creek WRA.*

Leaflet with map.

Bird checklist.

## Headquarters
WA Dept. of Fish and Wildlife, 48 Devonshire Rd., Montesano, WA 98563; (360) 249-6522.

## Willapa National Wildlife Refuge
U.S. Fish and Wildlife Service
11,000 acres (plus 21,000 acres, mostly water, closed to waterfowl hunting).

HQ at Milepost 24.5 on US 101, NE of Seaview. Long Island, largest section of Refuge, is directly across a narrow channel. A second section is at the S end of the bay. For the third section, see entry for Leadbetter Point.

Willapa Bay has been called the largest undisturbed estuary in the western U.S. About 20 mi. long, the bay is shallow, almost empty at extreme low tides, with vast areas of mudflats exposed. The waters, flats, salt marshes, and higher ground are richly productive, providing excellent wildlife habitat.

Long Island is reached by boat from a ramp in the HQ area. Much of the 5,000 acres is forested, including a virgin stand of western red cedar. The island is surrounded by salt marshes and mudflats. Camping is permitted on the island at designated areas, and there are miles of trails and roads.

About 5½ mi. SW on US 101, just beyond a small bridge, Jeldness Rd., to the right, leads 1.2 mi. to a parking area and locked gate, entrance to the Lewis Unit. The Riekkola Unit can be reached by Yeaton Rd. from Long Beach. This area has pastures and freshwater marshes protected by dikes and tidegates. Roads open to foot travel provide excellent opportunities to see waterfowl.

Some areas are closed to nonhunters in hunting season.

**Birds:** Checklist available. Over 256 species recorded, 118 of these common in one or more seasons, 86 known to nest on the Refuge. Common species include common and arctic loons, red-necked, horned, eared, western, and pied-billed grebes, double-crested, Brandt's, and pelagic cormorants, great blue heron, tundra and trumpeter swans, Canada goose, brant, mallard, gadwall, pintail, green-winged teal, wigeon, shoveler, wood duck, ring-necked duck, canvasback, greater scaup, common goldeneye, bufflehead, oldsquaw, white-winged and surf scoters, hooded, common, and red-breasted mergansers. Also blue and ruffed grouse, ring-necked pheasant, snipe, spotted sandpiper, greater and lesser yellowlegs, dunlin, semipalmated, least, western sandpipers, sanderling. Also many birds of prey, gulls, owls, songbirds.

**Mammals:** Notably on Long Island. Good populations of black bear, Roosevelt elk, mule deer, coyote, beaver, otter, muskrat.

## Activities

*Camping:* Designated sites at 5 locations on Long Island. Primitive.

*Hiking:* Miles of roads, trails, dikes.

*Hunting:* Designated areas. Special rules. Inquire.

*Boating:* Although the crossing to Long Island seems easy, those unfamiliar with the bay should inquire. Low tide can leave a beached boat far from the water, and wind can kick up rough water quickly.

## Publications

Leaflet.

Long Island leaflet.

Bird checklist.

Hunting regulations.

## Headquarters

U.S. Fish and Wildlife Service, HC01, Box 910, Ilwaco, WA 98624; (360) 484-3482.

## Yacolt Burn State Forest

Washington Department of Natural Resources
168,000 acres.

From Vancouver, NE about 20 mi. to Hockinson, then E on NE 139th St. into the Forest. This is one of several access routes. Signing is good, but Forest map is desirable.

Much of this area was swept by repeated forest fires, 9 major burns in the first half of this century. Forest rehabilitation has made great progress: felling snags, planting, fertilizing, thinning, and improving fire protection. With recovery well along and wildlife populations restored, the area has been opened for recreation. However, these state trust lands are managed to provide for specific beneficiaries. Timber harvest is still the primary activity in the Yacolt. Logging trucks are present and have the right of way.

Elevations from about 500 to 3,500 ft. Terrain above 1,500 ft. is steep and rugged, considered part of the Cascade Range. Below 600 ft. are bottomlands and alluvial terraces. Climate is affected by proximity to the Columbia Gorge and is highly variable. Summer temperatures are generally in the upper 70s by day, 50s at night, but readings of over 100°F are not unknown. Occasional rain. Winter temperatures tend to be moderate, but ice storms can occur. East winds up to 70 mph may occur in Jan.–Feb. and late July to early Nov.

Numerous small creeks, several of them tributaries to the Washougal River and the East Fork of the Lewis River.

Good blacktop roads lead into the Yacolt. Unpaved roads differ in design and maintenance. Some are unsuitable for ordinary automobiles. All should be approached with caution in bad weather. Some are closed and gated to vehicles for land management purposes.

The Yacolt isn't shown on the official highway map, nor are its campgrounds listed in popular directories.

**Plants:** Douglas-fir is the dominant tree species, with western hemlock and firs. A variety of soil types occur, influencing vegetation. Western red cedar, western hemlock, vine maple, red alder, willow, hazel, cherry, bigleaf maple, black cottonwood, dogwood, and cascara are found on poorly drained soils and along streams. Brush and groundcover species include salal, bear grass, salmonberry, huckleberry, blackberry, snowberry, thimbleberry, with mosses and ferns.

**Birds:** No checklist available. Species mentioned include grouse, red-tailed hawk, bald eagle, nighthawk. One would expect to find most of the species common to the Douglas-fir–western hemlock forests of the western Cascades.

**Mammals:** Include black bear, black-tailed deer, coyote, chipmunk, squirrel, badger, marmot. Several elk herds.

### Interpretation
*Interpretive signs* at Tarbell Trail Camp, Larch Mountain Picnic Area, Rock Creek, and Grouse Creek camp and picnic areas.

### Activities
*Camping:* 3 campgrounds: Cold Creek, Dougan Falls, and Rock Creek horse camp, 21 sites in all.

*Hiking:* Trails and unimproved roads. Trails are multiuse.

*Hunting:* Deer, bear, game birds. State regulations apply.

*Fishing:* Rainbow and cutthroat trout. Runs of silver, chinook, and jack salmon. State regulations apply.

*Horse riding:* Multiuse trails: 25-mi. Rock Creek with horse camp, also Tarbell, Larch Mountain, Cold Creek. Stanchions, manure boxes, loading ramp.

*Mountain biking:* 10-mi. 3 Corner Rocks Trail. Multiuse trails.

*ORV, motorcycle:* 13 mi. of trails, trailhead at Jones Creek.

### Adjacent or Nearby
Battle Ground Lake State Park, Beacon Rock State Park, Gifford Pinchot National Forest (see entries this zone).

### Publication
Forest map.

### Headquarters
WA Dept. of Natural Resources, SW Region, Box 280, 601 Bond Rd., Castle Rock, WA 98611; (360) 577-2025, (800) 562-6010 (in WA).

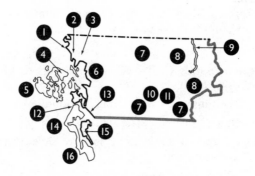

# 3

Z O N E

Includes these counties:

San Juan          Skagit
Whatcom           Island

This is the smallest of the six zones we delineated, but it offers a great variety of fine natural areas.

The San Juan Islands and surrounding waters are a special case. The land area of all the islands combined is not large, and the four ferry-served islands, largest of the group, are, for the most part, privately owned and developed as resorts. Federal and state sites, including Parks and Refuges, are scattered through many of the islands. Most of these holdings are small. Most of the islands in the federal Refuge system are off limits; one can look but not go ashore. Getting to any of these publicly owned sites, except those on the four main islands, requires a private boat.

If one has a suitable craft, and is an experienced boater with knowledge of tides, currents, rocks, etc., however, this is a fascinating area to explore. Even the ferry trip is scenic, and one is likely to spot seabirds not often seen from the mainland.

Without a boat, and without boarding the ferry, one can join those who consider Fidalgo and Whidbey Islands part of the San Juans. Both are linked to the mainland. Hwy 20 is a well-traveled highway. But they are islands, with complex and interesting coastlines and a number of interesting natural areas, as well as splendid scenery.

No road clings to the mainland coast. I-5 is generally a few miles inland. Spur roads lead to such coastal points of interest as Birch Bay and Larrabee State Parks. Largest of the coastal natural areas is the Skagit Wildlife Area, a major station on the Pacific Flyway.

Well over half of the land area in zone 3 is to the E, a large block made up of portions of the Mount Baker–Snoqualmie National Forest,

North Cascades National Park, and Okanogan National Forest. This is a region of mountains, glaciers, high lakes, dense forests, and rushing streams. A single road, Hwy 20, crosses it. Large portions are roadless wilderness, accessible only on foot or horseback.

## Birch Bay State Park
Washington Parks and Recreation Commission
193 acres.

From I-5, Exit 270. W on Grandview Rd.; N on Jackson Rd.; W on Helwig Rd. About 8 mi. from I-5.

About 1 mi. of frontage on Birch Bay, off the Strait of Georgia, N of the San Juan Islands, near the Canadian border. Slightly rolling terrain sloping gently from the bayshore. Birch Bay Dr. is between the bay and the major Park area. Terrell Creek flows through a freshwater marsh at the S of the Park, then turns and flows N beside the drive. Most of the upland area is forested: fir, cedar, birch, alder, maple. Highest point is about 150 ft. Winter and spring are "wet" seasons, but annual rainfall is only about 20 in.

**Birds:** The shallow bay is a good feeding, resting, and wintering area for waterfowl, and the Park is one of the best observation sites. No checklist. Species mentioned include brant, green-winged teal, mallard, coot, harlequin duck, wood duck, common loon, black surf, and white-winged scoters. Many shorebirds. Also noted: kingfisher, cormorant, robin, starling, red-winged blackbird.

**Mammals:** Mule deer, raccoon, skunk, opossum, muskrat, beaver.

### Interpretation
*Guided trail and beach walks,* weekends, July–Aug. Habitat and life cycle panels about shellfish and crabs.

### Activities
*Camping:* 166 sites. All year. Reservations required.

*Swimming:* Bay. Unsupervised. Scuba and snorkeling popular. Also windsailing.

*Boating:* Ramp nearby.

## Publication
Leaflet.

## Headquarters
WA Parks and Recreation Comm., 5105 Helwig Rd., Blaine, WA 98230; (360) 371-2800, (800) 233-0321.

---

## Camano Island State Park
Washington Parks and Recreation Commission
134 acres.

14 mi. SW of Stanwood, I-5 Exit 212.

On Saratoga Strait between Whidbey Island and the mainland. 6,700 ft. of beach. Rolling hills. Highest point 312 ft. Cliffs along the shore. About 85% forested, chiefly Douglas-fir and white fir. Some old growth; specimens 300–500 years old along the nature trail. Cliff Trail has scenic overlooks. Climate is moderate and relatively dry, 15–20 in. of rain annually, most of this in winter and spring. Park is popular, likely to be at capacity on major holidays and—according to the manager—at low clamming tides.

**Birds:** Good birding area. No checklist. Bald eagles winter here. Many waterfowl, shorebirds.

**Mammals:** Manager reports mule deer, raccoon, opossum, rabbit, squirrel, weasel, fox, muskrat.

## Interpretation
*Interpretive* and *nature programs* for groups, upon request (about 4 per year).
½-mi. self-guided *nature trail*.

## Activities
*Camping:* 87 sites. All year.
*Hiking:* 3 mi. of marsh/beach/forest trails.

*Fishing:* Salmon, perch, flounder, sole, rockfish. Also clamming. State regulations apply.

*Boating:* Ramps.

### Publications

Leaflet.

Nature trail guide.

### Headquarters

WA Parks and Recreation Comm., 2269 S. Park Rd., Stanwood, WA 98292; (360) 387-3031, (800) 233-0321.

........................................................................................................................

## Deception Pass State Park

Washington Parks and Recreation Commission
4,128 acres.

On Hwy 20, 8 mi. N of Oak Harbor.

At Deception Pass, Hwy 20 crosses a high bridge linking Whidbey and Fidalgo Islands. Many motorists stop at the parking area next to the bridge to enjoy the view. The channel between the islands looks like a deep gorge with rocky cliffs, forested slopes. Tidewater flows swiftly, forming whirlpools and boils, dangerous for a small craft.

The Park is on both islands, with 19 mi. of saltwater shoreline on Rosario Strait, Deception Pass, Cornet Bay, Bowman Bay, and Canoe Island. It includes Cranberry Lake, on Whidbey Island, and Pass Lake, on Fidalgo Island, with a combined shoreline of over 4 mi.

Hilly. Moderate to steep slopes. The Park has great variety: sandy and stony beaches, tide pools, rocky headlands, coves, bays, cliffs, wetlands, coastal brush, forested hills.

**Plants:** Forest of Douglas-fir, western hemlock, western red cedar, shore pine, grand fir. Some old growth. Understory and forest openings have salal, Oregon grape, ocean spray, red huckleberry, rhododendron, ferns. Also wetland plant communities.

**Birds:** Checklist available. Species include great blue heron, cormorants, puffin, bald eagle, glaucous-winged gull, terns, great horned owl, winter wren, dark-eyed junco. Local birders recommend the site because of its diverse habitats.

**Mammals:** Species include bats, raccoons, cottontail, chipmunk, red fox, beaver, muskrat, river otter, weasel, black-tailed deer. Orca (killer whale) and other whales sometimes seen. Also sea lion, seal.

### Includes

*Hope Island:* 166 acres. In Skagit Bay. Boat access. 5 primitive campsites and a small picnic area. Bluffs, beach, forest.

*Canoe Island* lies between Whidbey and Fidalgo, serving—in effect—as the bridge's center span. Parking area. Trails along the cliffs to the E tip. Stunted trees, brush, grasses, wildflowers. Exercise caution on trails.

*Fort Casey State Park,* 3 mi. S of Coupeville on Hwy 20. 35 campsites. 1-mi. beach walk. Surf fishing, underwater reserve. Historic fort and Admiralty Head Lighthouse.

*Fort Ebey State Park* S of Oak Harbor, off Hwy 20. Take Libbey Rd. Fantastic views of the Strait of Juan de Fuca. 7,000 ft. of freshwater frontage, 10,810 ft. of saltwater shoreline on Admiralty Inlet. Salmon, rockfish, halibut, steelhead. Scuba diving. 1.5-mi. beach trail, 3-mi. bluff trail, and 2-mi. nature trail. Mountain bike area. 50 campsites. Bass fishing in Lake Pondilla. Fishing also for salmon, steelhead, rockfish, halibut. Park closed Nov.–Feb.

*Cranberry Lake,* about 0.8 mi. long, on NW tip of Whidbey. Campground; fishing; swimming; boating (no motors). Nature trail in forest. Hilly, forested area. Nearby: West Beach, West Point, North Beach. Rocky headlands, stony and sandy beaches, dunes, bog.

*Bowman Bay,* on Fidalgo, W of Hwy 20. On the S is Reservation Head, almost an island, rocky shore, hilly, forested, trails. Rosario Head, on the N, is smaller. Seabirds on offshore rocks. Campground; hiking; boat launching.

*Rosario Bay,* NW of Bowman, is noted for marine life, tide pools. A marine research site. Seabirds on offshore rocks. Reservations required for tide pooling.

*Cornet Bay,* on Whidbey E of the highway, is more sheltered. Launching and other marine facilities. Nearby salt- and freshwater marshes. Side road continues to Hoypus Point. Trail circles Hoypus Hill.

*Pass Lake,* 100 acres, on Fidalgo, can be seen from the highway. Only boats without motors are allowed. A quiet area; wildlife often seen at dawn and dusk. Fly fishing. License required.

*Goose Rock,* 450 ft., is the highest point on Whidbey Island. Trail. Vista. 0.7 mi.

*Deception Pass Discovery Nature Trail.*

### Activities

*Camping:* 2 campgrounds. 251 sites. All year.

*Hiking:* 43.5 mi. of trails. Keep children on trail. Watch out for steep cliffs.

*Fishing:* Fresh and salt water. Lakes stocked with trout.

*Swimming:* Lakes.

*Boating:* Launch and other facilities on salt and fresh water.

*Canoeing:* Lakes. Rentals, summer, on Cranberry Lake.

### Publications

Leaflet with trail maps.

Nature trail guide.

Cornet Bay Environmental Learning Center leaflet.

### Headquarters

WA Parks and Recreation Comm., 5175 N. State Hwy 20, Oak Harbor, WA 98277; (360) 675-2417, (800) 233-0321.

## Lake Terrell Wildlife Area

Washington Department of Fish and Wildlife
1,041 acres.

From Ferndale on I-5 (N of Bellingham), W about 5 mi. on Mountain View Rd.; N on Lake Terrell Rd.

Managed for waterfowl and pheasant. All duck species found in western WA are seen here as winter residents or migrants. Used by duck and pheasant hunters in the fall season. Few visitors at other times. Largemouth bass fishing in spring and summer.

Lake Terrell has 3 satellite units: The Tennant Lake Wildlife Area has a boardwalk, trails through marsh (good birding), *interpretive center,* scent garden for the blind, upland trails. The Intalco Unit is mostly used for waterfowl and pheasant hunting and bass fishing. It has an archery range. The ARCO Unit is also primarily for waterfowl and upland game hunting.

Contact HQ for more information on hunting and fishing seasons and permits.

### Headquarters
WA Dept. of Fish and Wildlife, 5975 Lake Terrell Rd., Ferndale, WA 98248; (360) 384-4723.

## Larrabee State Park
Washington Parks and Recreation Commission
2,685 acres.

From Bellingham, 7 mi. S on Hwy 11, Exit 250.

WA's first State Park attracts almost half a million visitors per year. However, the manager says that while summer weekends are "quite busy," the Park is never uncomfortably crowded. About 1,800 acres are undeveloped forest, with 2 lakes that can be reached only on foot.

8,100 ft. of saltwater shoreline on Samish Bay. Steep, rolling terrain back of the bayfront. Sandstone headlands worn into bizarre shapes by wind and sea. Highest point is 1,940 ft. The bay is cold and shallow close to shore; people wade rather than swim.

**Plants:** About 96% forested. Typical NW coastal forest, logged 40–60 years ago. Douglas-fir, western red cedar, grand fir, western hemlock, red alder, bigleaf maple. Scattered old-growth specimens. Lush understory of willow, elderberry, salmonberry, sword fern, salal, so dense that off-trail hiking is difficult. The many wildflowers include bleeding heart, trillium, paintbrush, currant, dogwood, columbine, wild rose, calypso orchid, skunk cabbage. Peak season: March–June.

**Birds:** No checklist. Said to be a reasonably good birding site: seabirds offshore, shorebirds at low tide, upland species.

## Features

*Fragrance Lake* (7 acres) and *Lost Lake* (12 acres) are reached by 2-mi. forest trail from developed area.

*Cyrus Gates overlook,* reached by Cleator Rd., 1,900 ft., looks out toward San Juan Islands. Short trail to E-facing overlook, with views of Mount Baker, North Cascades.

## Activities

*Camping:* 90 sites. All year.

*Fishing:* Lakes stocked.

*Boating:* Ramp on bay. Also waterskiing.

## Publications

Site map.

2 pamphlets.

## Headquarters

WA Parks and Recreation Comm., 245 Chuckanut Dr., Bellingham, WA 98225; (360) 676-2093, (800) 233-0321.

## Moran State Park

See San Juan Islands this zone.

## Mount Baker–Snoqualmie National Forest

819,082 acres of this Forest are in zone 3. The entry appears in zone 4, which includes a larger acreage. Most of the portion in zone 3 is along the W boundary of North Cascades National Park. The zone 3 portion includes Mount Baker, highest point in the Forest, the approach road to the Mount Baker ski area, and Heather Meadows, along the Nooksack River. This part of the Forest is crossed by Hwy 20, the highway leading to the National Park. A part of the Glacier Peaks Wilderness is in the SE corner of the zone.

The Forest land on the E side of the National Park, including part of the Pasayten Wilderness, is technically part of Mount Baker–Snoqualmie National Forest but is administered by the Okanogan National Forest and is described in zone 5.

## North Cascades National Park Service Complex, including Ross Lake and Lake Chelan National Recreation Areas

U.S. National Park Service
684,000 acres.

Both sides of Hwy 20, between Burlington and Twisp. Access to the Lake Chelan National Recreation Area is by boat, float plane, or trail from Chelan on US 97.

One of the newest National Parks and unusual in many ways. Until 1968, almost all of the area was National Forest land. Some developments were in place: Ross Dam, forming Ross Lake; Gorge and Diablo Dams, the powerhouses and associated structures, including residences; tourist facilities at Newhalem, Diablo, and Stehekin. Hwy 20, which had ended at the lake, was pushed E to link with the road from Twisp shortly after the Park was inaugurated. A broad band of land on both sides of Hwy 20 and on both sides of Ross Lake was designated the Ross Lake National Recreation Area. The Stehekin Valley area became the Lake Chelan National Recreation Area. Limited recreation development is permitted within these NRAs. Hunting, forbidden in National Parks, is also allowed. The National Park itself is in two huge blocks, N and S of Hwy 20, nearly roadless, accessible only by foot or on horseback. The Park and NRAs are under common management. In this entry, "the Park" includes the entire complex. In the rugged Cascade Range, the Park extends from the Canadian border to the upper 4 mi. of Lake Chelan. It is surrounded by National Forests: Mount Baker–Snoqualmie, Okanogan, and Wenatchee. The Pasayten Wilderness is to the E, the Glacier Peak Wilderness to the S.

The region has so many peaks it would be misleading to mention one or two. Numerous peaks are between 7,000 and 9,000 ft., still more over 6,000, steep, jagged, carved into spires, horns, and ridges. On the slopes are 318 glaciers, countless snowfields. Slopes on the W side receive as much as 516 in. of snow per year. More than 127 alpine lakes are in cirque basins. Valleys are U-shaped, narrow, deep, the valley floors up to 2,000 ft. elevation. One description compares the North Cascades with the European Alps—"but with better weather, more diverse forests, and richer wildlife."

Annual precipitation on the upper W slopes is as much as 110 in., on the E slopes 34 in. Snowfall on the E side, which includes the Stehekin Valley, is thus much less than on the W. Snow is off all but the higher trails by July, but summer storms are common, so hikers should be prepared for rain and wind. Lower elevations and the big lakes are generally snow-free from early April to mid-Oct.

Hwy 20 is a fine scenic route, and development is limited to a few short stretches. Trailheads along the way offer opportunities for short and easy day hikes or strenuous wilderness treks. Campgrounds on Ross Lake can be reached by boat or trail. From Chelan, a privately operated boat makes the 55-mi. trip to Stehekin daily in summer, several days weekly in winter.

Ross Lake, formed by a power company dam, is 24 mi. long, 2 mi. wide. Conservationists have long resisted a proposal to build the dam higher, widening the lake and extending it farther into Canada. Diablo and Gorge Lakes, also formed by dams, are smaller, and both are near Hwy 20.

Only the upper end of Lake Chelan is within the Park. About 35 mi., the center portion, is within the Wenatchee National Forest (see entry zone 5). The lower end is in private ownerships; Chelan is a busy resort.

Principal rivers are the Chilliwack and Baker in the North Unit, the Skagit in the Ross Lake National Recreation Area, and the Stehekin in the South Unit and Lake Chelan National Recreation Area. Many creeks.

An unpaved road leads from Marblemount, on Hwy 20 W of the Park, through the National Forest, and into the South Unit, ending below Cascade Pass. A trail leads over the pass and down to the Stehekin Valley road.

Hwy 20 is normally kept open in winter from the W entrance to Ross Dam trailhead. The only other road penetrating the area crosses the Canadian border at the upper end of Ross Lake.

**Plants:** Great differences in moisture between E and W slopes, as well as variation in altitude, have produced a wide variety of plant communities: rain forest, subalpine coniferous forest, high meadows, alpine tundra, pine forest, dry shrub lands.

At low elevations, W side, western hemlock with grand fir, lodgepole and western white pines, Douglas-fir, western yew, black cottonwood, Pacific willow, red alder, black birch, California hazel, vine maple, bigleaf maple, Pacific dogwood, bitter cherry, cascara. This is the plant community most visitors see. Trails pass through lush vegetation under the high canopy: ferns, mosses, herbs, shrubs. Moving upward, there is a shift toward species such as subalpine fir, Pacific silver fir, whitebark pine, mountain hemlock, Alaska cedar, with red mountain heather, huckleberry, Cascades azalea, showy sedge, pine-mat manzanita.

**Birds:** Checklist available and includes habitats where birds occur, such as mountain streams, lakes and ponds, and marsh areas as well as vegetation types. Areas said to offer good birding: Skagit River, the head of Lake Chelan, Big Beaver Valley. The wetland areas attract a great variety of swans, geese, ducks, herons, shorebirds. In the alpine tundra zone, horned lark, mountain bluebird, water pipit, northern shrike, gray-crowned and Hepburn's rosy finches. Lowland areas are generally more populated. Species here include blue and ruffed grouse, California quail, bald and golden eagles, numerous hawks and owls, woodpeckers, flycatchers, swallows. Species found in a number of the habitats include black-capped chickadee, Swainson's thrush, northern shrike, orange-crowned and MacGillivray's warblers, western tanager, various sparrows.

**Mammals:** Checklist available. Known to be present: various shrews, moles, bats, chipmunks, voles, snowshoe hare, pika, mountain beaver, yellow-bellied and hoary marmots, golden-mantled ground squirrel, chickaree, red squirrel, northern flying squirrel, beaver, muskrat, porcupine, red fox, coyote, raccoon, marten, long-tailed and short-tailed weasels, mink, striped and spotted skunks, otter, wolverine, lynx, bobcat, mountain lion, mule deer, mountain goat, gray wolf, black bear, grizzly bear.

### Features

*Ross Lake National Recreation Area:* 117,000 acres. Skagit River drainage, ringed by mountains, separating the Park's North and South Units. Roughly L-shaped, the bottom is the route of Hwy 20. Resorts and other developments are along Hwy 20, chiefly at Newhalem, Diablo, and Ross Dam. Also on the route are 3 drive-in campgrounds: Goodell Creek, Newhalem Creek, and Colonial Creek. The vertical stroke of the L is a broad N–S corridor on either side of Ross Lake, extending to the Canadian border. The only road access is from Canada by a 40-mi. unpaved road branching S from Canadian Rt. 1 to the Mount Hozomeen area on the upper end of the lake. Mount Hozomeen has a campground, launching ramp, nature trail.

Diablo Lake, on Hwy 20, is a center of visitor activity, site of the Colonial Creek Campground, launching ramp, and head of Thunder

Creek Trail. Many people make short day hikes, enjoying an impressive forest and the deep stream canyon, with falls and rapids. The trail can be followed all the way to Stehekin, and several loop routes are possible. Evening programs are offered in an amphitheater just beyond the parking area; check bulletin boards for schedule. Just upstream from the amphitheater is the 0.8-mi. Thunder Woods Nature Trail.

Except at the Mount Hozomeen area, Ross Lake is accessible only by trail and boat, the latter over Diablo Lake. Small craft are launched at Colonial Creek; at the upper end they must be portaged over a 1-mi. jeep road. Ross Lake Resort portages small boats and canoes by truck, rents boats, and operates a water taxi service. A boat makes twice-daily runs from Diablo Dam to Ross Dam carrying only people and personal gear.

17 boat-in camping areas are on the lakeshore. Most of them can also be reached by trail. Seven major trails lead from the lake into the backcountry.

*Lake Chelan National Recreation Area:* 62,000 acres. On both sides of the upper 5 mi. of Lake Chelan, extending along the Stehekin Valley and N toward Twisp Pass. No road access. Most visitors take the cruise boats from Chelan, which make the 55-mi. run to Stehekin daily in summer, several times weekly in winter. This small community has a lodge, shops, and marina. A shuttle bus operates on a road along the valley to within a few miles of Cascade Pass in the South Unit. (Autos can reach Stehekin only by weekly barge.) A boat-in campground is on the lakeshore. Several campgrounds are spaced along the Stehekin Valley. Trails lead into the adjacent National Forests and the South Unit.

Stehekin has information and visitor centers. Nature trails at Rainbow Falls, 3½ mi. upstream, and at Stehekin Landing.

### Interpretation

*Visitor centers:* Golden West visitor center at Stehekin, open 8–4:30 daily mid-March–mid-Oct.; (360) 856-5703. North Cascades visitor center, near Newhalem, (360) 386-4495. Wilderness information station, at Marblemount, on Hwy 20 about 14 mi. W of Park boundary, open 7–6 summer; (360) 873-4500.

### Activities

*Camping:* 24 sites at Goodell Creek; 165 sites at Colonial Creek; 122 at Hozomeen. Goodell is open all year, others April 15 through Nov.

Newhalem Creek has 129 sites. All other campgrounds are boat-in or hike-in.

*Hiking, backpacking:* A Park leaflet warns: "There are no other mountains like the North Cascades in the U.S., and for this reason people who are familiar with mountains in other parts of the country sometimes encounter difficulties traveling here." Hazards include steep, rugged terrain, treacherous glaciers and snowfields, swift and cold streams. The region has no monopoly on insects, but bring repellent.

Over 300 mi. of trails in wilderness. The Pacific Crest Trail crosses the South Unit. Most trails follow streams, leaving dense timber at 4,000–5,000 ft. Backcountry permits are required for overnight use. Overuse has damaged some sites, and access to these may be limited.

*Hunting:* Prohibited in North and South Units. Permitted in designated portions of National Recreation Areas, subject to special regulations.

*Fishing:* A major activity. Lakes, streams. Rainbow, brook, cutthroat, Dolly Varden trout. State regulations apply.

*Boating:* Ross, Diablo, and Chelan Lakes. Commercial rentals.

*Horse riding:* One outfitter, at Stehekin, offers pack trips. Not all trails are suitable for horses, and horse parties are restricted to use of designated campgrounds. Inquire.

*Ski touring:* No developed ski areas. Rangers report increased winter use by skiers and snowshoers.

*Dogs and other pets are prohibited in the North and South Units except on the Pacific Crest Trail, where they must be leashed. Pets must be leashed in the National Recreation Areas.*

### Publications

Park leaflet with map.

*North Cascades Challenger* (newspaper).

Checklists of birds, mammals.

A variety of free information sheets are available, may change from year to year.

### Headquarters
National Park Service, 2105 Hwy 20, Sedro Woolley, WA 98284; (360) 856-5700.

## North Puget Sound Beaches

Washington Department of Natural Resources

Beaches of Skagit, Whatcom, and Island Counties have frontages ranging from 800 to 9,000 ft., average about 3,500 ft. Most of the beaches can be reached only by boat. State ownership extends only to the mean high-water line. Adjacent beaches and the upland are privately owned.

*South Dugulla Bay* can be reached by car or on foot across state-owned land. It has 4,800 ft. of frontage. It is of interest chiefly to clam diggers.

*Point Partridge Recreation Site* can be reached by car and has been developed with parking, campsites, and beach trail. It is on the W side of Whidbey Island, W of Coupeville on Hwy 20. Reached by taking Libby Rd. W from Hwy 20 toward West Beach, turning S on the marked access road.

### Publications

*Puget Sound Public Shellfish Sites.*

Public Land quadrangle map for Port Townsend and Bellingham.

### Headquarters

WA Dept. of Natural Resources, NW Region, 919 N. Township St., Sedro Woolley, WA 98284-9395; (360) 856-3500.

## Rockport State Park

Washington Parks and Recreation Commission
457 acres.

1 mi. W of Rockport on Hwy 20.

On the lower slope of Sauk Mountain, close to (though not on) the Skagit River. Includes a fine stand of old-growth Douglas-fir. Close to the Mount Baker–Snoqualmie National Forest. Sauk Mountain Rd., beginning on the Park's W boundary, leads 7½ mi. to a parking area and trailhead for a 1½-mi. trail to an observation tower at the summit.

Several short trails in and around the Park. 5 mi. of foot trails through ancient forest.

The Skagit River Bald Eagle Natural Area (see entry this zone) is across the river. Eagles can often be seen from the Park and nearby in winter.

Rockport is about 12 mi. W of the entrance to North Cascades National Park. *Camping:* 48 sites plus 12 walk-in sites. All year.

### Publication
Leaflet.

### Headquarters
WA Parks and Recreation Comm., 5051 Hwy 20, Concrete, WA 98237; (360) 853-8461, (800) 233-0321.

## Ross Lake National Recreation Area
See North Cascades National Park this zone.

## San Juan Islands
Multiple private, federal, state, and local ownerships. (Entry does not include sites on Fidalgo and Whidbey Islands, which are linked to the mainland by highways and bridges. See Deception Pass State Park entry this zone.)
About 170,000 acres.

By ferry from Anacortes or by private boat.

The islands are the tips of submerged mountains, projecting above the water in the Straits of Georgia and Rosario, where they meet the Strait of Juan de Fuca and Puget Sound. Three large islands—Orcas, Lopez, and San Juan—comprise four-fifths of the total area. 169 other islands are large enough to have names. The total depends on how small a rock is counted and the height of the tide, but the accepted number is about 700.

Ferries from Anacortes serve the four largest islands (those just mentioned, plus Shaw). These are popular resorts, and motorists are warned of long delays at times. Indeed, the State Ferries leaflet urges motorists to leave their cars behind and walk aboard to avoid delay. The ferry-served islands are, of course, the most developed. The largest single public site, Moran State Park, is on Orcas Island. The smaller islands can be reached only by private boat.

Cruising the islands is, for the naturalist, the way to enjoy them. Developments and the many No Trespassing signs are less visible from afloat. Some public areas can be approached only by boat because they are hemmed in by private holdings. About 80 of the islands in the *San Juan National Wildlife Refuge* can be seen only from a boat; going ashore is forbidden. Visitors must stay at least 200 yds. off-shore to protect colonies of nesting seabirds, harbor seals, and their young. This hardly matters; these islands are so small one can see quite well from offshore. All of these federal islands together have only 454 acres.

Two islands—Matia and Turn—within the federal Refuge are open to visitors. Each has a small State Park with a campground.

Moran, 5,176 acres, is by far the largest of 14 State Parks on the islands (see following information). The others total only 1,555 acres; 7 have less than 100. The state also lists 7 Natural Area Parks, ranging in size from ½ to 5 acres. All but one of the Parks have campgrounds.

Here as elsewhere the DNR has the difficult task of managing what's left of WA's beaches. Scattered among the islands are beaches the state owns—up to the mean high-water line, with private beaches on either side. Most such beaches can't be reached by land without trespassing. The DNR's attempts to install markers visible from the water have been at least partially frustrated by vandalism.

The DNR has 7 small, primitive campgrounds, 2 on Orcas Island, 2 on Cypress, 1 on Lummi, 1 on San Juan, 1 on Strawberry. All except Obstruction Pass Campground on Orcas are accessible by boat only. These campgrounds aren't listed in popular campground directories; check the DNR's *Recreation Guide* (see WA introduction) or ask State Park rangers.

A few bits of public domain still remain, managed by the Bureau of Land Management. The 200 acres on Lopez Island, including Point Colville, Watmough Bay, and Chadwick Hill area, are little-disturbed coastal natural areas with shoreline, bogs, some old-growth Sitka spruce and Douglas-fir, brush, meadows, and bluffs. Iceberg Point, 80 acres, also on Lopez Island, is a long, narrow point, 2 mi. of irregular shoreline, half forested, half open grassland with rock outcrops. Public access to Iceberg Point is by water only.

Highest point on the islands is Mount Constitution, 2,408 ft., on the edge of Moran State Park, reached by road or trail. Climate is moderate, with less than 30 in. of rain per year. Temperatures rarely exceed 80°F or drop below 32°.

**Birds:** More bald eagles than in any other region in the U.S. Glaucous-winged gull, tufted puffin, guillemot, auklet, pelagic cormorant.

**Mammals:** Harbor seal, porpoise, whales.

### Features

*Moran State Park* (Washington Parks and Recreation Comm.): 5,176 acres. On Orcas Island near Rosario. Occupies the interior portion of the E lobe of Orcas Island. Rolling to mountainous terrain. Includes Mount Constitution, Mount Pickett, and Little Summit. Mountain Lake is about 1½ mi. long, Cascade Lake a bit under 1 mi., Twin Lakes much smaller. 26 mi. of trails, including trails to mountain peaks, around the lakes, and beside the falls of Cascade Creek. Considerable forest, with some virgin cedar and hemlock, salal and Oregon grape in understory. Plant list. Bird and mammal lists available at office. *Camping:* 4 campgrounds, one open in winter. 151 sites. Reservations. *Fishing:* Brook, rainbow, cutthroat, silver trout. *Swimming:* Lake. *Boating:* Two large lakes. No motors. Rowboat rentals. Leaflet available. *Headquarters:* WA Parks and Recreation Comm., Star Rt. Box 22, Eastsound, WA 98245; (360) 376-2326/(800) 233-0321.

*Stuart Island Marine State Park* (Washington Parks and Recreation Comm.): 148 acres. 10 mi. NW of Friday Harbor. Boat access. Irregular coastline; long narrow bays; forested. *Camping:* 19 sites. *Boating:* Mooring, floats and buoys in sheltered harbor.

*Jones Island Marine State Park* (Washington Parks and Recreation Comm.): 188 acres. SW tip of Orcas Island. Boat access. Valley between two hills links North Cove and South Cove. Rocky ground, heavily wooded. Open bluffs above the sea. One large meadow. Woodland is cool, damp, with mosses, ferns, mushrooms, wildflowers. Mapboard and interpretive panels. *Camping:* 2 campgrounds, 20 sites. *Boating:* Dock, mooring float and buoys.

*Clark Island Marine State Park* (Washington Parks and Recreation Comm.): 55 acres. 9 mi. NE of Orcas Island. Boat access. Narrow island about 1 mi. long. Largest of a cluster of rocky islands, it has a bit of forest, brush. Low tide exposes sandflats, tide pools. *Camping:* 8 sites. *Boating:* Mooring buoys but no sheltered harbor.

*Spencer Spit State Park* (Washington Parks and Recreation Comm.): 130 acres. E side of Lopez Island. Heavily used because of location on a ferry-served island. Sand spit with shallow lagoon, sandy slopes, forested hillside. *Camping:* 28 sites plus primitive hiker-biker camp. *Boating:* Mooring buoys. *Hiking and biking trails.*

*Sucia Island Marine State Park* (Washington Parks and Recreation Comm.): 562 acres. 2½ mi. N of Orcas Island. Boat access. One of the most popular marine parks and often crowded. A cluster of islands arranged in a horseshoe, with numerous bays and coves. The state has made several land purchases but some private holdings remain. Rocky and sandy beaches; eroded cliffs; upland forest. One of the few boat-access islands with opportunities for hiking. Some trails are steep, slippery when wet. Many seabirds. *Camping:* 55 sites at several locations. *Boating:* Docks and buoys, often fully utilized. Check weather and tides.

*Turn Island Marine State Park* (Washington Parks and Recreation Comm.): 35 acres. E of San Juan Island. So close to ferry-served San Juan Island that a canoe or rowboat crossing is feasible in good weather. Thus the campsites are often crowded in summer. The island is part of the National Wildlife Refuge. Partially wooded; tideflats on the W; steep banks back of the beach on the N and E. *Camping:* 12 sites. *Boating:* Mooring buoys.

*Matia Island Marine State Park* (Washington Parks and Recreation Comm.): 145 acres. N of Orcas Island. Boat access. Part of the federal Wildlife Refuge and wilderness system. About ¾ mi. long. Most of the shoreline is rocky, some steep banks sculptured by wave action. Forested, trees coming close to shoreline. *Trails.* A sandy cove at the E end looks out on Puffin Island, one of those off limits to visitors. Public use is presently restricted to 5 acres at the NW end of the island. *Camping:* 6 sites. *Boating:* Pier, hinged dock, float, buoys.

## Activities

*Camping:* State Parks accept reservations. Several county Parks have campsites, and there are a few commercial facilities. The total is small by comparison with demand.

*Hiking:* Moran State Park has 30 mi. of multiuse trails, including various interpretive trails.

*Fishing:* Fresh and salt water.

*Swimming:* Many beaches and a few interior lakes and ponds.

*Boating:* These are popular boating waters, but one needs a sound craft, navigation charts, and ability to handle both. *These waters can be very dangerous* and are not for the inexperienced boater. *Always Be Aware.* Stay away from pupping areas for seals.

*Bicycling:* Seasonally. Rentals and tours available on Lopez, Orcas, and San Juan Islands.

## Publications

*Your Guide to the San Juan Islands,* 1995 (San Juan Islands Visitor Information Service).

*San Juan Islands National Wildlife Refuge and Wilderness Areas* (U.S. Fish and Wildlife Service).

*Your Guide to Marine Parks and Boat Moorage* (WA Parks and Recreation Comm.).

*Your Public Beaches, San Juan Islands,* 1985 (WA Dept. of Natural Resources), $3.00.

## Headquarters

WA Parks and Recreation Comm., 7150 Cleanwater Lane, Olympia, WA 98504; (800) 233-0321. San Juan Islands National Wildlife Refuge Headquarters, c/o Nisqually National Wildlife Refuge Complex, 100 Brown Farm Rd., Olympia, WA 98518; (360) 753-9467. San Juan Islands Visitor Information Service, P.O. Box 65, Lopez Island, WA 98261; (360) 468-3663.

## Skagit River Bald Eagle Natural Area

Washington Department of Fish and Wildlife/The Nature Conservancy
1,500 acres.

Along the Skagit River, beside Hwy 20, between Rockport and Marblemount.

Each winter at least 300 bald eagles gather at the Skagit River to feed on spawned-out salmon. The first of them arrive in late Oct. By mid-Feb., the eagles begin migrating to their northern nesting grounds.

For survival, the eagles require a relatively undisturbed habitat with large hardwood trees for perching near the sand and gravel bars where they feed. To provide this protected habitat, The Nature Conservancy originally purchased over 870 acres of land along the river. Most of this was sold to the Dept. of Fish and Wildlife, added to lands already in state ownership. TNC organized a national fund-raising drive to complete the project. TNC has made recent purchases and retained ownership. It also employs a full-time steward.

Eagles can be seen from various points along Hwy 20.

### Publication
Leaflet.

### Headquarters
WA Dept. of Fish and Wildlife, 16018 Mill Creek Blvd., Mill Creek, WA 98012-1296; (206) 775-1311. The Nature Conservancy, 217 Pine St., Suite 1100, Seattle, WA 98101; (206) 343-4344.

## Skagit Wildlife Area
Washington Department of Fish and Wildlife
10,160 acres.

From I-5, Conway/LaConner Exit. W through Conway on Fir Island Rd. Left on Mann Rd. and S 1 mi. to HQ.

The most important waterfowl area in western WA. About 5 mi. of frontage on Skagit Bay between the mouths of the N and S Forks of the Skagit River. Extensive tideflats, sloughs, cattail salt marsh, sedge-bulrush areas, wooded stream banks, cultivated fields, lowland brush, and upland forest.

The Wildlife Area has two large pieces and a number of smaller ones, with different access points, so it's advisable to stop at HQ for a map and advice. Fall and spring are the peak seasons, but thousands of waterfowl winter here, and broods of nesting species can be seen in spring and early summer.

Near HQ is a 2-mi. walk on the dike. Fir Island Rd. leads into Maupin Rd. and the Jensen Access, strategic point for overlooking tideflats. Turning N, then left on Rawlins Rd., leads to a parking area near the Skagit's North Fork. Other access points to areas of interest are reached by turning S from Conway on Old Hwy 99.

**Birds:** Checklist available. Nearly 200 species recorded, including all waterfowl species common to the region. 20,000 to 35,000 snow geese winter here. Also many tundra swan, brant. Mallard, wood duck, cinnamon and blue-winged teals, Virginia and sora rails, and marsh wren are among the nesting species. Many gulls, terns, shorebirds. Eagles and hawks most numerous in winter.

**Mammals:** Black-tailed deer, coyote, fox, raccoon, weasel, mink, beaver, otter, muskrat.

### Activities

*Hunting:* Designated areas. Special regulations in some areas. Check regulations pamphlet.

*Fishing:* Spring through fall best seasons. Dolly Varden, cutthroat trout, steelhead, salmon. State regulations apply.

*Boating, canoeing:* Ramp near HQ. Boaters are advised to check tide tables, watch out for tidal and river currents—and not get lost in the twisting tidal channels.

### Publication
Leaflet.

### Headquarters
WA Dept. of Fish and Wildlife, Skagit Wildlife Area, 2214 Wylie Rd., Mt. Vernon, WA 98273; (360) 445-4441.

## South Whidbey State Park
Washington Parks and Recreation Commission
347 acres.

On Whidbey Island, 4½ mi. SW of Greenbank by county road.

A small park with 4,500 ft. of shoreline on Admiralty Inlet. Old-growth forest with Douglas-fir, western red cedar, Sitka spruce. Weekend interpretive campfire programs, during heavy use season. Guided group walks and talks, upon request.

*Camping:* 54 sites.
*Hiking:* 3½ mi. of hiking trails, 2-mi. shoreline trail.
*Fishing:* Salmon, perch. State regulations apply.

**Headquarters**
WA Parks and Recreation Comm., 4128 S. Smugglers Cove Rd., Free-
land, WA 98249; (360) 331-4559, (800) 233-0321.

## Tennant Lake Natural History Interpretive Center

Washington Department of Fish and Wildlife/Whatcom County Parks
700 acres.

From Ferndale on I-5 (N of Bellingham), S ¼ mi. on Hovander Rd., then
SW 1½ mi. on Nielson Rd.

*Open:* 10 A.M. to dusk.

The site borders the Nooksack River, includes Tennant Lake and surrounding wetlands. An observation tower overlooks the lake. Boardwalk, ½ mi. long, through the swamp. Upland nature trail.

**Birds:** Checklist available. Great blue heron seen regularly. Green-
backed heron, uncommon in the NW, is seen almost daily in summer.
Summer ducks include blue-winged and cinnamon teals, mallard,
wood duck. Common winter species include wigeon, shoveler, ring-
necked duck, scaup, bufflehead, pintail, Barrow's and common goldeneyes, ruddy duck. Red-tailed hawk and northern harrier seen all year.
Barn, screech, and great horned owls nest. Marsh birds include marsh
wren, common yellowthroat, red-winged blackbird. Many others.

**Interpretation**
*Interpretive center* is open Wed.–Sun. Exhibits, special programs, tours.

**Publications**
Leaflet.
Bird checklist.

**Headquarters**
WA Dept. of Fish and Wildlife, 5236 Nielson Rd., Ferndale, WA 98248;
(306) 384-4723.

Z O  N E

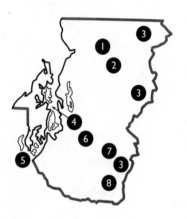

1 Mount Pilchuck Recreation Area

2 Wallace Falls State Park

3 Mount Baker–Snoqualmie National Forest

4 Blake Island State Park

5 South Puget Sound Beaches

6 Green River Gorge Conservation Area/Flaming Geyser Recreation Area/Nolte State Park/Kanaskat-Palmer State Park

7 Federation Forest State Park

8 Mount Rainier National Park

Z O N E

ncludes these counties:

| | |
|---|---|
| Snohomish | King |
| Kitsap | Pierce |

The E portion of this zone is occupied by the Mount Baker–Snoqualmie National Forest and Mount Rainier National Park, on the slopes of the Cascade Range. Puget Sound is on the W.

We reviewed all of the State Parks in the zone and visited most of them, finally omitting all but a few. Those we visited are attractive but small, generally surrounded by developed areas, and heavily used.

The entry on "Puget Sound Beaches" does not signify that these beaches are more significant natural areas than the omitted Parks. We though it important to report on the status of public beaches.

..................................................................................................................................

## Blake Island State Park
Washington Parks and Recreation Commission
476 acres.

In Puget Sound near Seattle. Boat access only. Twice-daily ferry service from Pier 56, Seattle, June 3–Oct. 15.

Once an elaborate private estate with fine gardens, abandoned after 1929, structures later burned. Now densely wooded. Mostly native plants, but some exotics remain. The developed area includes Tillicum Village, offering Indian dancing and barbecued salmon. 4 mi. of beaches. Wildlife includes a few deer, plus small mammals; no data on birds.

## Activities

*Camping:* 48 sites. All year.

*Hiking:* Trail circles island.

*Boating:* Many visitors come by private boat. Dock and mooring buoys.

*Bicycling:* Trail around island.

## Publication
Leaflet.

## Headquarters
WA Parks and Recreation Comm., Box 287, Manchester, WA 98353; (360) 731-0770/(800) 233-0321.

## Federation Forest State Park

Washington Parks and Recreation Commission
619 acres.

From Enumclaw, 18 mi. SE on Hwy 410.

Traveling to or from Mount Rainier National Park on Hwy 410, this is a mandatory stop. The site, with much virgin timber, was acquired through efforts of the Washington State Federation of Women's Clubs. Funds willed to the Federation were used to build the Catherine Montgomery Interpretive Center, one of the best anywhere, unique in the WA State Parks system. Exhibits inside the structure describe the flora and fauna of WA's principal life zones. Through large windows, one looks out on small gardens with living specimens of many of the plants mentioned in the exhibits. Various nature trails.

19,800 ft. of freshwater shoreline on White River. Fishing for Dolly Varden and rainbow trout.

## Publication
Leaflet.

## Headquarters

WA Parks and Recreation Comm., 49201 Hwy 410, Enumclaw, WA 98022; (360) 663-2207/(800) 233-0321.

## Flaming Geyser Recreation Area/Nolte State Park/Kanaskat-Palmer State Park

See Green River Gorge entry below.

## Green River Gorge Conservation Area

Washington Parks and Recreation Commission
2,008 acres.
About 6 mi. N of Enumclaw off Hwy 169 on Green Valley Rd.

The Green River attracts whitewater enthusiasts in winter and early spring. The gorge is scenic. One viewpoint is the highway bridge near the Park entrance. Others are nearby; inquire locally.

The *Flaming Geyser Recreation Area* has well-manicured day-use facilities beside the river: extensive lawns, playground, picnic tables. About 60% of the site is forested: second-growth Douglas-fir, western hemlock, western red cedar, bigleaf and vine maples, black cotton-wood, red alder, willow, Sitka spruce, cascara, with salmonberry, thimbleberry, Oregon grape, sword fern, red elderberry, devil's club, twinflower. A small swamp has cattails, reeds, bamboo. A 1-mi. River Trail follows the river upstream into the gorge, where there are native American petroglyphs. A 1½-mi. Hill Trail ascends the wooded hillside above the day-use area.

The "flaming geyser" is an old drill hole that spouts methane. The gas, when ignited, creates a small flame in a rock pit.

Nearby *Nolte State Park* has a small lake, self-guiding nature trail.

*Kanaskat-Palmer State Park* has interpretive display boards and several river safety signs along the Green River.

## Activities

*Camping:* Kanaskat-Palmer State Park, 50 sites.

*Hiking:* Trails at Flaming Geyser through lowland forest are pleasant. 3-mi. trail along the river at Kanaskat-Palmer.

*Fishing:* Deep Lake at Nolte State Park. The Green River is one of the most popular steelhead rivers in WA. Steelhead, rainbow trout, silvers, panfish, catfish, bass, kokanee, yellow perch. State regulations apply.

*Swimming:* Unsupervised. The area at Flaming Geyser seemed better for wading than swimming. Beach at Nolte State Park. River swimming at Kanaskat-Palmer.

*Canoeing, rafting, kayaking:* Class II, III, and IV rapids in and around the area. Water is controlled at Howard Hansen Dam and can change from day to day. Flaming Geyser is a popular inner-tube float site during the summer.

### Publications

Flaming Geyser leaflet.

Nolte nature trail guide.

### Headquarters

WA Parks and Recreation Comm., Flaming Geyser Recreation Area, 23700 S.E. Flaming Geyser Rd., Auburn, WA 98092; (360) 931-3939, (800) 931-3930.

## Mount Baker–Snoqualmie National Forest

U.S. Forest Service
2,100,000 acres within boundaries; 1,700,000 acres of Forest land.

On the W slopes of the Cascade Range, from the Canadian border to Mount Rainier. Crossed by Hwy 20, US 2, I-90, Hwy 410.

Mount Baker and Snoqualmie were combined as one National Forest in 1974. They are elements of a huge block of National Forest and National Park land extending along the Cascades from Canada to Oregon. The Forest is on the W side of the range, from Canada to

Mount Rainier. Rugged, mountainous terrain: peaks, ridges, deep glacier-carved valleys. More than 100 of the glaciers are still here. Several hundred alpine lakes, many in cirque basins below glaciers. Elevations range from 400 to 10,778 ft. Annual precipitation ranges from 40 to 180 in., depending on elevation and location. Most of this falls as snow at high elevations.

The Forest is not a solid block of federal land. S of the Canadian border it adjoins North Cascades National Park (see entry zone 3). This entry is concerned only with the area W of the Park; that to the E, including part of the Pasayten Wilderness, is administered by the Okanogan National Forest and is described in that entry.

On the W, the continuity of Forest land is broken by a wide band of private holdings along Hwy 20. Another wide band extends from the W boundary along Hwy 530 to Darrington. These are linked by a N–S band of private land along the Sauk River.

Next to the S is a large block of Forest land adjoining the South Unit of the North Cascades National Park and the Wenatchee National Forest (see entry zone 5). Irregular in shape, this block includes some inholdings, especially in the S portion. It ends just N of I-90. For the next 22 mi. S, the Forest land is a checkerboard of 1-mi. squares, alternating with private holdings. Then comes another solid block on the N boundary of Mount Rainier National Park (see entry this zone).

To the S and SE of the Park is a large block of Forest land technically within Mount Baker–Snoqualmie but administered by Wenatchee, and it is described in that entry.

The Forest includes some of the wildest country in the NW. Half of it is still covered by virgin timber, preserved thus far by the difficult terrain. Large areas are roadless wilderness. The first phase of a permit system to limit the number of day and overnight visitors in designated areas begins in 1997.

Several roads are the principal corridors for Forest visitors. Generally these are scenic routes with campgrounds and trailheads along the way.

- Hwy 542, E from Bellingham, along the Nooksack River, deadending at the Mount Baker ski area, within the Heather Meadows area.
- Hwy 20, E from Sedro Woolley, access to Baker Lake, continuing into North Cascades National Park.
- Hwy 530, from I-5 to Darrington, beyond which are several Forest roads.
- Hwy 92 to Granite falls, continuing E beyond Verlot to Forest roads along the Stillaguamish River.

- US 2 along the Skykomish River. About 8 mi. beyond Gold Bar, a Forest road follows the North Fork to the NE. US 2 continues along the South Fork and over Stevens Pass.
- Hwy 410, E from Enumclaw and SE to Mount Rainier National Park.

These are the primary routes for the motorist-sightseer and RV camper. The Forest has hundreds of miles of Forest roads, shown only on the National Forest map. The Forest has a trail system of 1,446 mi. 583 of those mi. are on its 718,000 acres of designated wilderness.

Weather and snow cover depend on altitude and location. Trails over the high passes may be closed by snow until late July or even early Aug., then remain open through Oct. Main highways are usually kept open. Many Forest roads are left unplowed unless in use for logging. At lower altitudes the camping season is April–Oct., a few campgrounds remaining open all year.

**Plants:** 85% forest. Most of the remainder is above timberline. About half the forest is virgin; some old growth. Dense stands of Douglas-fir, Pacific silver fir, western hemlock on W slopes up to about 3,000 ft. elevation. Associated species include western red cedar, bigleaf and vine maples, red alder. Understory is luxuriant, including raspberry, rhododendron, salal, salmonberry, vanilla leaf, wild ginger, dogwood, cascara, evergreen huckleberry, devil's club, western yew. The many ferns include sword, bracken, lady, spinywood and maidenhair. Between 3,000 and 5,000 ft., Douglas-fir with western white pine, grand fir, lodgepole pine. In the subalpine zone, open stands of mountain hemlock and subalpine fir.

Still higher are open heather-covered meadows with stunted subalpine fir and mountain hemlock, many brightly colored flowers in season.

More than 200 flowering species recorded, including paintbrush, glacier lily, mountain valerian, shooting star, queen's cup, orange honeysuckle, bleeding heart, columbine, mountain spirea, Jacobs ladder. Wildflower checklist available on request.

**Birds:** No checklist available. Forest reports over 150 species. Species include grebes, great blue heron, tundra and trumpeter swans, Canada, white-fronted and snow geese, various ducks, goshawk, sharp-shinned, Cooper's, red-tailed, and Swainson's hawks, golden and bald eagles, osprey, merlin, kestrel, blue, spruce, ruffed, and sharp-tailed grouse, California and mountain quails, screech, flammulated, great horned, pygmy, snowy, spotted, great horned, long-eared, and short-eared owls, black and Vaux's swifts, northern flicker, 4 woodpeckers, yellow-bellied, red-breasted, and Williamson's sapsuckers, 5 flycatchers, 5 swallows, gray and Steller's jays, magpie, raven, crow, Clark's nutcracker, 5 chickadees, 3 nuthatches, 3 thrushes, golden-crowned and ruby-crowned kinglets, 3 vireos, dipper, and 8 warblers.

**Mammals:** No checklist. Species reported include opossum, various shrews, moles, voles, mice, and bats, pika, cottontail, snowshoe hare, mountain beaver, chipmunks, yellow-bellied and hoary marmots, ground squirrels, red squirrel, chickaree, northern flying squirrel, beaver, porcupine, coyote, red fox, raccoon, marten, fisher, mink, wolverine, otter, lynx, bobcat, mountain lion, Roosevelt elk, mule deer, mountain goat, wolf, black bear, grizzly bear.

## Features

*Glacier Peak Wilderness:* 576,600 acres, slightly more than half of this in the Wenatchee National Forest. This huge wilderness area, roadless and undeveloped, stretches from Lake Chelan to the Suiattle River. Glacier Peak is 10,528 ft., and the area has more than 30 other peaks, 3 of them over 9,000 ft., and over 90 glaciers. Glaciers and snowfields are the sources of hundreds of streams with many cascades, falls, and pools, as well as many high lakes. Vegetation ranges from lush rain forests along several of the lower valleys, notably the Suiattle, to high meadows and rocky peaks supporting little more than lichens.

Fish and game are plentiful, and the wilderness attracts many hunters and fishermen, on foot and horseback. Climbers are challenged by several of the peaks. The principal visitor activity is backpacking. The Pacific Crest Trail crosses the area. Connecting trails enter from the E and W, generally follow the drainages. Several large areas have no maintained trails, and the terrain is unsuitable for horses; these are areas for experienced hikers. Trails that have much horse traffic during the hunting season may be in bad condition for summer hikers. Inquire at a ranger station. Wilderness permits are required.

*Goat Rocks Wilderness.* Although a portion of this wilderness is in the Mount Baker–Snoqualmie National Forest, that portion is administered by the Wenatchee National Forest (see entry in zone 5. The other portion is in the Gifford Pinchot National Forest, entry in zone 2).

*Skagit Wild and Scenic River.* In 1978 Congress so designated the Skagit and its tributaries. This includes the river and a strip of land ¼ to ½ mi. wide along the main stem of the Skagit and along these tributaries:

Cascade River, Suiattle River, Sauk River, North and South Forks of the Sauk. 50% of the river system is located outside the forest on nonfederal lands. River floating is popular, as is trout and salmon fishing.

*Alpine Lakes Wilderness:* 393,000 acres, 61% in the Wenatchee National Forest. The Mount Baker–Snoqualmie portion is generally to the N of I-90 at Snoqualmie Pass. This is also rugged country, but less so than the Glacier Peaks area. Here the highest peak is 6,800 ft. More than a dozen others are over 1 mi. high. The most striking feature of the area is the lakes, more than 700 of them if you include those as small as an acre. The map is dotted with them, the largest about 1½ mi. long, three others close to a mile, perhaps a dozen in the ¼-mi. range. Lake elevations from 2,100 to 6,000 ft. Trails generally follow the drainages, and a number of them are easy going, the destination lakes being only a couple of miles from the trailhead.

In season, both day and overnight permits are required, and overnight access may be rationed in some areas. Camping is not permitted within 200 ft. of the shoreline, and fires may be prohibited over 4,000 ft. elevation. Alpine Lakes information hotline (recorded) (800) 627-0062.

*Boulder River Wilderness:* 49,000 acres. Elevations from 1,000 to 7,000 ft. Dense, mossy forest and steep ridges rise to snowcapped Three Fingers and Whitehorse Mountains. The low elevation of the Boulder River Valley offers year-round snow-free hiking.

*Clearwater Wilderness:* 14,300 acres. On the N border of Mount Rainier National Park. Ancient forest with sites sacred to native Americans. 8 small lakes. Bear grass common, often in the foreground of one's view of Mount Rainier.

*Henry M. Jackson Wilderness:* 103,100 acres, some in Wenatchee National Forest. Adjacent to Glacier Peak Wilderness. Flower-covered ridges of the Cascades meet the rugged Monte Cristo Range and Sloan Peak. 30 lakes for the angler.

*Mount Baker Wilderness:* 117,600 acres. 10,778-ft. Mount Baker, a dormant volcano that occasionally emits steam and sulfurous fumes, is the prominent feature. Over 10,000 climbers attempt to scale the mountain each year. The wilderness seems to wrap around high, meadow-covered ridges framing peaks like Tomhoi, American Border, and the Twin Sisters Range.

*Noisy-Diobsud Wilderness:* 14,100 acres. Adjacent to North Cascades National Park, which protects the trailless valleys of Noisy and Diobsud Creeks. Huge trees cover the areas that have not been cleared by repeated winter avalanches. Watson Lakes are 2 subalpine "jewels," though they are considered inaccessible.

*Norse Peak Wilderness:* 51,300 acres. In the "rain shadow" of Mount Rainier. High ridges, mountain lakes, parklike basins, and the long, forested valley of the Greenwater River. The Pacific Crest Trail traverses its heart.

*Darrington Ranger Station:*
- *Mountain Loop Hwy.* From Granite Falls E through Verlot. From Barlow Pass NW to Darrington, a usually good gravel road follows the Sauk River. However, this section may be closed by flood damage after heavy winter rains. Inquire.
- *Ice Caves.* Trail No. 723, a National Recreation Trail, begins at the site of an old inn, crosses the river on a footbridge, then moves through timber to a snowfield. Caves form as snow melts here in late July and early Aug. It is dangerous to enter the caves.

*Mount Baker Ranger Station:*
- *Picture Lake.* An easy ½-mi. scenic walk from Mount Baker Hwy 20 mi. E of the ranger station. Circles Picture Lake in the Heather Meadows area.
- *Mount Baker Viewpoint.* Because of intervening ridges, Mount Baker can't be seen from most areas. An exception is at the end of Glacier Creek Rd. (No. 3904). Parking area overlooks Coleman Glacier.
- *Nooksack Falls.* Turn at sign on Mount Baker Hwy 7 mi. E of the ranger station. Follow Wells Creek Rd. ½ mi. to parking. Falls, 170 ft. high.
- *Rainbow Falls.* Turn off Baker Lake Rd. just beyond Boulder Creek bridge; follow Rd. 385, 4½ mi. High falls.
- *Baker Lake,* 5,000 acres, is largest in the Forest. About 9 mi. long. Numerous campgrounds and launch points. Fishing, boating, swimming. Speed limits on motorboats.

*Skykomish Ranger Station:*
- *Deception Falls Nature Trail,* 6 mi. E of Skykomish on US 2. ½-mi. loop.
- *Iron Goat Trail,* 6 mi. E of Skykomish off US 2. To Forest Rd. 67, 2.3 mi. to Forest Rd. 6710. Almost 7 mi. of trails along Old Burlington Northern Railway grade.

*North Bend Ranger Station:*
- *Franklin Falls,* about 150 ft., on the South Fork, Snoqualmie River, W of Snoqualmie Pass. Exit 52 from I-90E, then Forest Rd. 2219 about 1 mi. W. Short trail.

- *Asahel Curtis Nature Trail* through old-growth Douglas-fir and western hemlock, 600-year-old trees, 250 ft. tall, 5 ft. diameter. Off I-90 W of Snoqualmie Pass.

*White River Ranger Station:*
- *Suntop Lookout.* Spectacular view of Mount Rainier. Forest Rds. 186 and 188, 8 mi. from Hwy 410.
- *Crystal Mountain Area.* Alpine ski area in winter. Chairlifts operate on weekends in summer. Hwy 410 and Forest Rd. 1802.
- *White River Elk Herd View Site.* Over 1,000 elk may winter here. Smaller numbers in summer. Along Forest Rd. 72, off Hwy 410.

### Interpretation
*Campfire programs* in summer at Horseshoe Cove and Gold Basin Campgrounds.

### Activities
*Camping:* 44 campgrounds including 12 that serve groups of 25–100, 1,318 sites. Most open Memorial Day–Labor Day. Some free campgrounds.

*Hiking, backpacking:* Over 1,400 mi. of trails. Numbered trails are shown on the Forest map. Each Ranger District has good information on trails and can suggest routes. Topo maps advisable for backcountry travel.

*Hunting:* Deer, elk, bear, mountain goat.

*Fishing:* Many lakes, streams. 5 species of salmon, 3 species of sea-run trout, 5 native resident trout across the Forest.

*Boating:* Baker Lake. Boat rentals.

*Canoeing, kayaking:* Whitewater streams include sections of the South Fork of the Stillaguamish River, Upper Skykomish River, Upper Sauk River. Other whitewater streams are just outside the Forest. Water levels are generally best late spring to fall.

*Bicycling:* Miles of logging roads. Bikes not permitted in wilderness areas.

*Horse riding:* About half the trail system is usable by horses. Much of that use occurs in the 2-week early deer hunt in Sept. Riding is more popular in the Wenatchee, Okanogan, Colville, and Umatilla National Forests.

*Skiing:* Downhill: 7 ski areas, commercially operated. Usual season: Thanksgiving to end of April.

*Ski touring:* 2 commercial areas in the Forest. Also, wherever snow conditions permit. Weather is often rainy, snow wet. Better ski conditions are usually found E of the Cascades crest.

*Snowmobiling:* Prohibited in wilderness areas. Elsewhere as conditions permit, generally on unplowed Forest roads.

*Note: Many areas have high avalanche hazard in winter. Visitors should inquire about current snow conditions in areas they plan to enter.*

## Publications

Maps: Alpine Lakes Wilderness, $7.95; Darrington Ranger District, $3.25; Glacier Peak Wilderness, $3.25; Goat Rocks Wilderness, $2.25; Henry M. Jackson Wilderness, $2.25; Mount Baker–Snoqualmie National Forest, $3.25; North Bend Ranger District, $3.25; Skykomish Ranger District, $3.25; White River Ranger District, $3.25.

Leaflets: *Campgrounds and Picnic Sites; Forest Facts;* others on hikes by ranger station.

*Alpine Lakes Trip Planner.*

*Celebrating Wildflowers, 1996.*

*North Cascades Challenger* (newspaper).

## Headquarters

U.S. Forest Service, 21905 64th Ave. W., Mountlake Terrace, WA 98043; (206) 775-9702.

## Ranger Stations

Darrington R.S., 1405 Emmens St., Darrington, WA 98241; (360) 436-1155. Mount Baker R.S., 2105 State Rt. 20, Sedro Woolley, WA 98284; (360) 856-5700. North Bend R.S., 42404 S.E. North Bend Way, North Bend, WA 98045; (206) 888-1421. Skykomish R.S., P.O. Box 305, Skykomish, WA 98288; (360) 677-2414. White River R.S., 857 Roosevelt Ave. E., Enumclaw, WA 98022; (360) 825-6585.

## Information Centers

E. King County I.C., 520 112th Ave. N.E., Suite 101, Bellevue, WA 98004; (206) 450-5641. Glacier Public Service Center, Star Rt. 542, Glacier, WA 98244; (360) 599-2714. Outdoor Recreation I.C., 915 Second Ave., Room 442, Seattle, WA 98174; (206) 220-7450. Snohomish County I.C., 101 128th St. S.E., Suite 5000, Everett, WA 98208; (206) 745-4133. Snoqualmie Pass Visitor Center, P.O. Box 17, Snoqualmie Pass, WA 98022; (206) 434-6111. Verlot Public Service Center, Mountain Loop Hwy, Granite Falls, WA 98252; (360) 691-7791.

## Mount Pilchuck Recreation Area

Washington Parks and Recreation Commission/U.S. Forest Service
1,893 acres.

From Granite Falls, 7 mi. E on Mount Loop Hwy, following signs to
Mount Pilchuck.

5,324-ft. Mount Pilchuck is wooded, with some impressive stands. At
the top is a large parking area. And an impressive view. This was a
state-managed ski area, but state management ended in 1981 and the
ski lifts and buildings were removed. The site is now jointly administered by the WA Parks and Recreation Comm. and the Mount
Baker–Snoqualmie National Forest.

Principal visitor activities are hiking, snowshoeing, and mountain
climbing. Several trailheads are marked along the mountain road. A
strenuous 3-mi. trail near the parking lot rises from 3,000 to 5,324 ft.

The National Forest has a roadside campground at Verlot. Beyond
the Mount Pilchuck Rd., the route enters the Forest along the Stillaguamish River, a popular area with many campgrounds.

### Headquarters

WA Parks and Recreation Comm., P.O. Box 230, Gold Bar, WA 98251;
(800) 233-0321. Darrington Ranger Station, 1405 Emmens St., Darrington, WA 98241; (360) 436-1155.

## Mount Rainier National Park

U.S. National Park Service
235,612 acres.

65 mi. SE of Tacoma on Hwys 7 and 700. Other approaches via US 12
and Hwys 123, 410, and 165.

Part of the huge block of National Forest and National Park land
extending from Canada to OR along the Cascades. Mount Rainier,
14,411 ft., is the most prominent peak of the Cascades, a composite
volcano surrounded by 34 sq. mi. of glaciers on its upper slopes.

Many visitors come to climb the mountain, many more to hike on its extensive trails, most simply to look. This is one of the National Parks threatened by overuse. On a recent visit, backpacking above timberline, we were shocked to see how much damage had occurred since our visit a few years before. To limit damage, backcountry travel is rationed now. Revegetation of many of the trampled meadows was begun in 1986, and resource education programs are having a beneficial effect. In 1988, almost 97% of the Park was designated wilderness, thus protecting and preserving areas even more. Management is encouraging additional public transportation, has moved some support facilities outside the Park, and is adopting other changes designed to protect the environment without curtailing public enjoyment.

It is one of the snowiest places on earth. At Paradise in the winter of 1971–72 snowfall totaled 94 ft., a world record; the average here is 48 ft. Snowfall is heaviest from Paradise, at 5,500 ft. elevation, up to 9,500 ft. Annual precipitation ranges from 60 to 110 in. per year in different locations.

Moisture, soil conditions, and topography—from 1,560 to 14,411 ft.—combine to produce rich plant growth. Four major life zones are represented: Transition, Canadian, Hudsonian, and Arctic Alpine. Deep forests, including extensive virgin stands, are on the lower slopes. Between 5,000 and 6,500 ft. are spectacular subalpine meadows and fields of bright flowers.

Heaviest visitor traffic is from the Nisqually entrance at the SW corner to Paradise, site of the Paradise Inn and other facilities. Along the way are trailheads and such features as Longmire Meadow, Christine Falls, and Narada Falls. Beyond Paradise are several lakes, Martha Falls, Box Canyon, Grove of the Patriarchs, and Silver Falls. Near the SE corner of the Park, one can turn N to Cayuse Pass and the White River entrance, then W to Sunrise, said by some to offer the most splendid view of the mountain. The entire route is scenic, and all along are places to stop to enjoy a vista, waterfall, cascade, lake, canyon, or meadow. Turning S on Hwy 123 leads near Silver Falls and the tall trees and hot springs of Ohanapecosh.

Much less traveled are two other Park routes. One turns N about 1 mi. beyond the Nisqually entrance. The other enters the Park at its NW corner, following the Carbon River to Ipsut Creek with a branch route to Mowich Lake.

The Park is open in winter. The road from the Nisqually entrance to Paradise is plowed; snow may close it temporarily, and chains may be required. The Jackson visitor center at Paradise is closed Mon–Fri.,

Nov.–April. Other Park roads are usually closed from late Nov. to June or July. About 70% of the 2 million visitors per year come June–Sept., less than 10% Dec.–March. More than half come on weekends. 90% come only for the day.

**Plants:** Over 700 plant species have been identified. In the Transition zone, dense stands of Douglas-fir and western hemlock with western red cedar, bigleaf maple, red alder. Dense understory includes lichens, mosses, sword, bracken, and lady ferns, rhododendron, salal, vanilla leaf. From 3,000 to 5,000 ft., Douglas-fir and Pacific silver fir with western white pine, grand fir, Engelmann spruce. In the understory and forest openings: vine maple, bleeding heart, fireweed, queen cup, coltsfoot. The subalpine meadows are dominated by herbaceous flowering species. A long list of wildflowers recorded at Paradise includes bear grass, bog orchid, white heather, avalanche lily, pearly everlasting, spring beauty, pasqueflower, cinquefoil, broadleaf arnica, elephants head, glacier lily, columbine, rosy spirea, scarlet paintbrush, moss campion, alpine aster, mountain daisy.

**Birds:** Checklist of 163 species, 40 considered accidental or very rare. Abundant or common species include rough-legged and red-tailed hawks, kestrel, blue grouse, band-tailed pigeon, Vaux's swift, rufous hummingbird, northern flicker, yellow-bellied sapsucker, western flycatcher, western wood pewee, barn and violet-green swallows, Steller's and gray jays, Clark's nutcracker, raven, mountain chickadee, brown creeper, hermit thrush, golden-crowned kinglet, water pipit, Dark-eyed junco.

**Mammals:** Checklist available. Common species include elk, mountain goat, mule deer, black bear, mountain lion, coyote, raccoon, pine marten, porcupine, beaver, snowshoe hare, hoary marmot, pika, golden-mantled ground squirrel, yellow pine chipmunk.

## Interpretation

*Visitor centers* at Longmire and Jackson are open all year, except Jackson closes weekdays Nov.–April. Those at Sunrise and Ohanapecosh are summer only.

*Nature walks* and *evening slide programs,* late June–Labor Day. Notices posted.

*Nature trails* at Kautz Creek Mudflow, Longmire Meadows, Sourdough Ridge, Nisqually Vista, Emmons Vista, Ohanapecosh, Hot Springs, Grove of the Patriarchs, and Carbon River.

## Activities

*Camping:* 5 campgrounds, over 600 sites (about 280 of these are for backpackers). Also 4 horse sites. Only Sunshine Point, near the Nisqually entrance, is open all year. No reservations.

*Hiking, backpacking:* Rainier is a hiker's park with more than 300 mi. of trails leading into the backcountry. Many trails offer day hikes to points of interest. Hiking season in the high country is usually mid-July–mid-Oct.

The Wonderland Trail, 93 mi. long, encircles the mountain crossing alpine meadows, glacial streams, mountain passes, valley forests, reaching a maximum elevation of 6,500 ft. 10 days is the minimum recommended time for a complete circuit. Many trails from below meet the Wonderland Trail, so there are many opportunities for loop hikes of fewer than 10 days. Backcountry permits are required year-round, and camping in some areas is limited. Permits specify the campsites to be used. Off-trail camping is available but specific rules apply.

The Pacific Crest Trail skirts the Park's E boundary.

*Mountain Climbing:* The climbing zone begins at the glacier line, about 7,000 ft. About 8,000 people climb the mountain each year. Climbers generally spend the first night at Camp Muir or Camp Schurman. Climbers must register and a fee is charged.

*Fishing:* Stocking of lakes was discontinued in 1972. Fishing is not a major activity.

*Horse riding:* Terrain is not favorable for horse travel. Horses are limited to 90 mi. of designated trails. No livery or grazing is available in the Park.

*Ski touring:* Ski touring has become increasingly popular. Usual season: Dec.–May.

*Pets permitted only in developed areas, on leash. No pets in backcountry.*

## Adjacent

Gifford Pinchot (zone 2), Mount Baker–Snoqualmie (zone 4), and Wenatchee (zone 5) National Forests.

## Publications

*Mount Rainier* (official map and guide).

*Evolution of Mount Rainier's Landscape.*

Checklists of birds, mammals, amphibians and reptiles, fish, and trees.

*Wildflowers of Paradise.*

*Hiking in Mount Rainier National Park.*

*Backcountry trail mileages.*

*Climbing Mount Rainier* (leaflet).

**Headquarters**
National Park Service, Ashford, WA 98304; (360) 569-2211.

........................................................................................................................................

## South Puget Sound Beaches
Washington Department of Natural Resources

There are over 30 DNR-managed, state-owned beaches in Snohomish, King, Pierce, and Kitsap Counties. The DNR manages 2.1 million acres of state aquatic lands, including the remaining fragments of WA's public beaches. In the great majority of cases, state ownership goes only to the mean high-water line. The adjoining beaches and area above mean high water are privately owned, and the state has no right of way. Throughout Puget Sound, DNR beaches are interspersed with State Park beaches.

Many are accessible only by boat. Frontages range from 627 to 5,872 ft. These beaches seem to be of interest chiefly to clam diggers.

*Joemma Beach* is 2 mi. W of Longbranch, N of Whitman Cove. It has 8 tent sites and a launching ramp on a partially wooded site. Road access. Joemma Beach is now under WA Parks and Recreation Comm. ownership.

**Publications**
*Puget Sound Public Shellfish Sites,* 1989.

*Your Guide to Marine Parks and Boat Moorage* (WA Parks and Recreation Comm.).

Public Lands quadrangle maps (Seattle, Tacoma, Port Townsend).

**Headquarters**
WA Dept. of Natural Resources, S. Puget Sound Region, 28329 S.E. 448th St., Enumclaw, WA 98022; (360) 825-1631.

## Wallace Falls State Park

Washington Parks and Recreation Commission
1,422 acres.

From I-5 at Everett, E about 30 mi. on US 2 to Gold Bar, then N on marked county road.

A Park for hikers, featuring the 5½-mi. trail to the falls. In the Cascade foothills near the boundary of Mount Baker–Snoqualmie National Forest (see entry this zone). The trail enters a mixed second-growth forest, winds along the Wallace River, then moves higher on a bench above the river. Viewpoints of smaller falls at the 2-mi. rest stop. Viewpoints farther up the switchbacking trail look out at 250-ft. Wallace Falls and the Skykomish River Valley.

**Plants:** Forest of Douglas-fir, western red cedar, western hemlock, red alder, bigleaf maple, black cottonwood. In the understory: vine maple, red elderberry, sword fern, salal, Oregon grape, salmonberry, red huckleberry, wild blackberry, strawberry.

Returning from the falls one can take the Old Railroad Grade Trail—1 mi. longer, gentle grade.

### Activities

*Camping:* 6 sites. Tents only.

*Mountain biking:* Allowed on trail to falls.

### Publication

Leaflet with map.

### Headquarters

WA Parks and Recreation Comm., P.O. Box 230, Gold Bar, WA 98251; (360) 793-0420/(800) 233-0321.

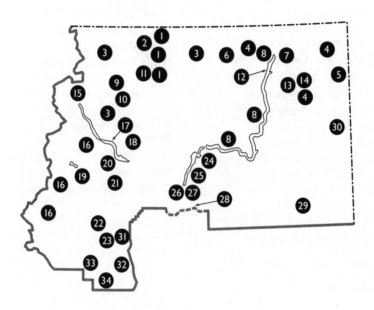

1 Loomis State Forest;
   Sinlahekin Wildlife Area

2 Chopaka Mountain

3 Okanogan National Forest

4 Colville National Forest

5 Idaho Panhandle National
   Forest (Kaniksu National
   Forest)

6 Curlew Lake State Park

7 Williams Lake

8 Coulee Dam National
   Recreation Area

9 Pearrygin Lake State Park

10 Methow Wildlife Area

11 Conconully State Park

12 Sherman Creek Wildlife Area

13 Rocky Lake Natural
   Recreation Area

14 Little Pend Oreille National
   Wildlife Refuge

15 Lake Chelan National
   Recreation Area

16 Wenatchee National Forest

17 Twenty-Five-Mile Creek
   State Park

18 Alta Lake State Park

19 Lake Wenatchee State Park

20 Lake Chelan State Park

21 Colockum Wildlife Area:
   Chelan Butte, Entiat,
   Swakane Units

22 Squilchuck State Park

23 Colockum Wildlife Area

24 Steamboat Rock State Park

25 Banks Lake Wildlife Area

26 Sun Lakes State Park/Sun
   Lakes Wildlife Area

27 Billy Clapp Lake Wildlife
   Area

28 Columbia Basin Recreation
   Areas

29 Turnbull National Wildlife
   Refuge

30 Mount Spokane State Park

31 Quilomene Wildlife Area

32 Ginkgo Petrified Forest State
   Park/Wanapum State Park

33 L. T. Murray Wildlife Area

34 Yakima Canyon Scenic
   Highway

Z O N E

Includes these counties:

| | | |
|---|---|---|
| Okanogan | Chelan | Spokane |
| Ferry | Douglas | Kittitas |
| Stevens | Grant (N tip only) | |
| Pend Oreille | Lincoln | |

The W boundary of this zone generally follows the crest of the North Cascade Mountains. The W and N portions of the zone are mountainous. The Selkirk Mountains are in the NE corner, on the Canada and ID boundaries. Most of the public lands are in these mountainous regions: several National Forests and a part of North Cascades National Park.

The SE part of the zone, roughly half of its total acreage, lies in the Columbia Basin. Most of this area is agricultural, chiefly great fields of wheat. Here there are many State Parks, Wildlife Areas, and Department of Natural Resources sites, much smaller than the National Forests but offering much of interest.

For those seeking escape from crowds, this is a good place to look. Spokane is the only large city in the zone. Most of WA's residents live on the other side of the Cascades. With so many delightful places closer to them, why should they drive the additional hours to—say—the Colville National Forest?

Hunters are attracted by a kind of big game hunting more typical of Canada than the U.S. Backpackers rate the Pasayten Wilderness high on their lists, but the zone also offers much backcountry at lower elevations, to be enjoyed in April and May while waiting for the deep snow to melt in the high country. Canoeists have a choice of many lakes, several quiet streams, and a few whitewater courses.

Climate of the zone is much affected by the Cascade Range. At high elevations, annual precipitation is high and winter snow is deep.

Lower elevations are in the rain shadow. Parts of the Columbia Basin are semiarid.

Exploring the zone in midsummer, we found the heaviest clusterings of people around the larger and most accessible lakes, including the Columbia River impoundments. We had no difficulty finding natural areas with few if any visitors. When we stopped for the night at Dept. of Fish and Wildlife or DNR campsites, we were usually alone; in National Forests we had only to avoid the few large campgrounds.

## Alta Lake State Park

Washington Parks and Recreation Commission
182 acres.

4 mi. SW of Pateros on Hwy 153, then SW on marked road.

A small Park at the edge of Okanogan National Forest, on a route to Twisp and Hwy 20 across the North Cascades. More than half a mile of shoreline on an attractive lake. In pine forest. In 1996, there were signs explaining beetle damage.

### Activities

*Camping:* 198 sites.

*Hiking:* Trails, including 1-mi. trail to lookout.

*Fishing:* Rainbow trout. State regulations apply.

*Boating:* Lake. No ramps.

### Headquarters

WA Parks and Recreation Comm., 191 A Alta Lake Rd., Pateros, WA 98846; (509) 923-2473/(800) 233-0321.

## Banks Lake Wildlife Area

Washington Department of Fish and Wildlife
44,662 acres, including 27,000 acres of water.

Between Grand Coulee Dam and Coulee City, on Hwy 155.

The lake is a narrow irrigation reservoir, 27 mi. long, between high cliffs of basalt. Hwy 155, on the E shore, is an exceptionally scenic drive. The Wildlife Area land extends from the water's edge to the cliffs, width averaging about ¼ mi. A similar strip on the W shore is also within the Wildlife Area; this seems accessible only by boat. Sections of the shore are tule marshes. Sagebrush and grasses are on the slightly higher ground near the cliffs. The valley is 2–4 mi. wide, between clifftops.

Public access is limited. Along the lower two-thirds of the lake we saw no parking areas, and few places on the road shoulders offered adequate parking. About 13 mi. from Coulee City is a public-access point with parking and an unpaved boat ramp. Farther to the N is a larger access area with enough level parking for RV camping. Most camping is informal, or at Coulee City Park campground.

April–June is said to be the best time for a visit. To fully enjoy the scenery, drive N in the morning, when sunlight is on the W cliffs; return in the afternoon, with the sunlight on your side.

**Birds:** No checklist. The Dept. of Fish and Wildlife says the lake is "noted for its waterfowl," without giving details. We visited in summer, when populations were small. Geese are attracted by the lake and nearby wheatfields. Upland species include raven, chukar, pheasant, golden eagle.

**Mammals:** A few mule deer. Also coyote, marmot, porcupine, raccoon, bobcat.

### Activities

*Camping:* Informal, in access area.

*Fishing:* Said to be good. Rainbow, kokanee, largemouth bass, perch, pike.

### Adjacent

Steamboat Rock State Park (see entry this zone).

*Municipal parks* at Coulee City and Electric City have boat ramps, swimming; Coulee City includes a campground.

### Nearby

Sun Lakes State Park (see entry this zone).

### Headquarters

WA Dept. of Fish and Wildlife, Regional Office, Ephrata, WA 98823; (509) 754-4624.

## Billy Clapp Lake Wildlife Area

Washington Department of Fish and Wildlife
6,000 acres.

From Coulee City, S on Pinto Ridge Rd. Access to Billy Clapp Lake at
Summer Falls State Park. Or continue S past Main Canal to Hwy 28, left
to dam.

The larger of two lakes is shown on some maps as Long Lake Reservoir, on others as Billy Clapp Lake. The smaller is sometimes Stratford Lake, sometimes Brook Lake. Desert terrain. Basalt cliffs and terraces. The lakes attract many waterfowl in migrations; geese winter and nest here.

*Summer Falls State Park,* 260 acres, is at the head of Billy Clapp Lake. The entrance road passes through a ravine, and the falls appear with dramatic suddenness, a wide rush of water dropping 30–40 ft. into the lake, sending up great clouds of spray. The falls are active only in summer when irrigation water is being released. The Park is a day-use area.

### Activities

*Hunting:* Most of the public land area is posted as a game reserve.

*Boating:* Ramps at the S end, near the dam.

### Headquarters

WA Dept. of Fish and Wildlife, Regional Office, Ephrata, WA 98823;
(509) 754-4624.

## Chopaka Mountain

U.S. Bureau of Land Management
5,520 acres.

From US 97 N of Tonasket, W on local road to Loomis. N about 2 mi.
on local road, left on Toats Coulee Rd. about 2 mi., right on gravel road
about 6 mi. to Chopaka Lake.

Elevations 1,200 to 5,600 ft. Most of the unit lies on the steep, rugged E slopes of the Chopaka Mountain Range. The S third of the unit contains Bowers Lake, the N half of Chopaka Lake, and steep grassland. Unit adjoins Loomis State Forest (see entry this zone). Pasayten Wilderness in Okanogan National Forest (see entry this zone) is 6 mi. W.

Slopes are partially forested, with pockets of subalpine fir, whitebark pine, lodgepole pine, Engelmann spruce, Douglas-fir, ponderosa pine, with associated shrubs and grasses. Mountain goats sometimes seen.

Steep terrain limits recreation opportunities, generally to the 2 lakes. A site at the N end of Chopaka Lake is often used for informal camping. A DNR campground is just S of the BLM land, on Chopaka Lake.

*Fishing:* Fly fishing, barbless hooks only.

### Headquarters

Bureau of Land Management, Spokane District Office, Wenatchee Resource Area Office, 915 N. Walla Walla Ave., Wenatchee, WA 98801; (509) 655-2100.

## Colockum Wildlife Area

Washington Department of Fish and Wildlife
119,167 acres.

From Kittitas, on I-90 E of Ellensburg, the highway map shows a local road running N and NE over Colockum Pass to Malaga. Colockum Pass is within the Wildlife Area. Unimproved roads lead from it. The Pass road may require 4-wheel drive.

Largest single holding by the Dept. of Fish and Wildlife. E boundary is the Columbia River. Rolling, open sagebrush hills drop off to steep cliffs along the river. At higher elevations, timbered draws merge with stands of ponderosa pine. Cottonwood and brush along streams.

Roads within the Wildlife Area are primitive and may require 4-wheel drive, but hiking is a fine way to see the area, outside of hunting season. The diversity of habitats is reflected in the many species of wildlife.

A smaller, separate portion of the Wildlife Area, also on the Columbia River, lies N and W of Vantage. The S boundary is the Old Vantage Hwy, paralleling I-90 between Ellensburg and Vantage.

**Birds:** No checklist. Grainfields, flats, and protected bays along the Columbia River attract waterfowl. Game species include chukar, quail, Merriam turkey, ruffed grouse, sage hen, pheasant, mourning dove. Upland species include western tanager, Bullock's oriole, lazuli bunting, western meadowlark, lark sparrow, red-winged blackbird, rock wren, Lewis's woodpecker, yellow-bellied sapsucker, western kingbird, violet-green and cliff swallows, magpie, mountain bluebird.

**Mammals:** Species reported include Rocky Mountain elk, mule deer, pronghorn, bighorn sheep, coyote, bobcat, marmot, ground squirrel, chipmunk.

### Headquarters

WA Dept. of Fish and Wildlife, Region 3 office, 1701 S. 24th Ave., Yakima, WA 98902-5720; (509) 575-2740.

## Colockum Wildlife Area: Chelan Butte, Entiat, and Swakane Units

Washington Department of Fish and Wildlife
28,488 acres.

W of Columbia River and US 97, between Wenatchee and Chelan.

These 3 units border the Wenatchee National Forest (see entry this zone). Dept. of Fish and Wildlife publications describe them briefly but don't say how to find them. Even with maps we could not find the Entiat and Swakane Units, and the road that apparently leads into the Chelan Butte Unit was unsuitable for our vehicle. We suggest inquiring at HQ, on US 97 about 2 mi. beyond where it turns N along the Columbia River. Chances are you'll need a 4-wheel-drive vehicle.

The *Chelan Butte Unit*, 8,614 acres, is reached by a road leading off US 97 just E of Chelan marked "Chelan Butte Lookout." For a mile or two the road is paved, steep, narrow, passing private homes, offering fine view of Lake Chelan. Then it becomes a gravel road. This unit is characterized by flat ridges, deep canyons, steep grassy slopes. It has frontage on the Columbia River. High chukar and quail populations.

The *Entiat Unit,* 9,675 acres, is just W of US 97, N and W of Entiat. Ponderosa pine forests on steep hillsides; grasslands; basalt benches. Abundant quail and chukar.

The *Swakane Unit,* 11,199 acres, is also just W of US 97, along Swakane Creek, N of Wenatchee. Ponderosa forest on steep slopes, grassy areas, basalt cliffs near the Columbia River. Bear, mountain lion, blue grouse, mule deer, chukar, quail. California bighorn sheep were introduced in Swakane Canyon in 1969. The herd increased and is now stable.

In hunting season, these units are best left to hunters. At other times, they offer opportunities for hiking, birding, and primitive camping in solitude, near a main highway.

### Headquarters
Local HQ is on US 97 near the S boundary of the Swakane Unit. Region 3 Office: Dept. of Fish and Wildlife, 1701 S. 24th Ave., Yakima, WA 98902-5720; (509) 575-2740.

### Columbia Basin Recreation Areas
See entry zone 6.

### Colville National Forest
U.S. Forest Service
1,095,368 acres.

NE WA. In several blocks, crossed by or reached from Hwys 20, 21, US 395, Hwys 25 and 31.

The mountains of NE WA are neither as high nor as rugged as those to the W. The highest peak is Gypsy Peak, 7,309 ft., near the NE corner. About a dozen peaks are above 6,000 ft., many more between 4,000 and 6,000 ft.

The Colville Forest is a collection of many parts, large and small. The largest solid block extends from the Canadian border S across Hwy 20 to the Colville Indian Reservation, a block about 20 mi. wide, between Republic and the Columbia River. To the W is a somewhat narrower block with the same N and S boundaries, broken into several parts by inholdings. Across the Columbia River, the E half is even more fragmented. The largest solid block, in the NE corner, adjoins the Kaniksu National Forest, which extends into ID. Just W of the Pend Oreille River the Forest land is irregular in shape, broken by many inholdings, with areas of checkerboard farther S. Some of the inholdings are state land. The Forest has no frontage on the Columbia River, only a few miles on the Pend Oreille.

Because of the more gentle terrain and the drier climate, the hiking season is longer here than in the Cascades. The Forest has one downhill ski area, 49 Degrees North, Chewelah, WA, and cross-country, or ski touring, is growing in popularity. The snow season generally ends in early May. The main hiking season begins at the end of May, but many trails are open earlier.

This is a region of mixed forest types and winding valleys, offering good hiking, fishing, hunting, and camping. The Forest has 59 lakes, from 1 acre to 1,291 acres in size. Despite these attractions, visitation is relatively light. The only large city nearby is Spokane. Residents of the more populous W counties are likely to stop at the Cascade Mountains rather than drive another hundred miles or so.

**Plants:** Large Douglas-fir and western hemlock forest; local plant communities vary according to elevation, history of fire and logging, and moisture. In general, medium dense to open forest, fairly open ground cover of grasses and scattered shrubs. Other tree species include western larch, western white, lodgepole, and ponderosa pines, grand and subalpine firs, Engelmann spruce, and whitebark pine. Understory of the western hemlock forest includes oak fern, rusty menziesia, bear grass, wild sarsaparilla, and queen cup. Understory associated with Douglas-fir forests includes ninebark, pine grass, twinflower, huckleberry, serviceberry. Plants of high open ridges may include bear grass, huckleberry, white rhododendron.

**Birds:** Checklist available. Lakes, streams, and marshes attract some waterfowl, gulls, shorebirds: western and pied-billed grebes, tundra swan, Canada goose, mallard, pintail, green-winged, blue-winged, and cinnamon teals, wigeon, shoveler, redhead, ring-necked duck, lesser scaup, common and Barrow's goldeneyes, common merganser, ruddy duck, great blue heron, Virginia rail, common snipe, lesser yellowlegs, ring-billed gull. Birds of prey include sharp-shinned, Cooper's, goshawk, and red-tailed hawks, northern harrier, osprey, kestrel, 4 owls. Also Franklin's, blue, and ruffed grouse, mourning dove, nighthawk, Vaux's swift, 3 hummingbirds, northern flicker, 5 woodpeckers, yellow-bellied sapsucker, eastern and western kingbirds, 6 swallows, gray and Steller's jays, black-capped and mountain chickadees, brown creeper, dipper, 3 thrushes, mountain bluebird, water pipit, solitary and red-eyed vireos, 8 warblers, western tanager, evening grosbeak, lazuli bunting, pine siskin, red crossbill, rufous-sided towhee, savannah and vesper sparrows.

**Mammals:** Checklist available. Includes shrews, various bats, deer mouse, voles, pika, snowshoe hare, red squirrel, marmot, Columbian ground squirrel, yellow pine and red-tailed chipmunks, northern flying squirrel, beaver, porcupine, coyote, raccoon, short-tailed and long-tailed weasels, mink, marten, striped skunk, black bear, mountain lion, bobcat, elk, white-tailed and mule deer. Caribou frequently cross the Canadian border into the Salmo Priest Wilderness and adjacent areas.

**Reptiles and amphibians:** Checklist available. Includes 2 salamanders, northwestern boreal toad, Pacific tree frog, western spotted frog, western painted turtle, northern alligator lizard, western skink, Rocky Mountain rubber boa, valley garter snake, western yellow-bellied racer, Great Basin gopher snake, northern Pacific rattlesnake.

## Features

*Salmo Priest Wilderness:* 41,000 acres, including acres in the Kaniksu National Forest. In the far NE corner. Includes Gypsy Peak, highest in eastern WA, 7,309 ft. Lowest elevation: 2,720 ft. Mountainous, slopes averaging 50% or greater. Except for high peaks and ridges, heavily forested. Includes the *Salmo Research Natural Area* 1,390 acres, established in part because of its exceptional wildlife. Caribou, grizzly bear, lynx, and gray wolf have been seen here, although not regularly. Several species are here at their range limits; these include boreal chickadee, pine grosbeak, crossbills.

*Kettle Range Limited Access Area:* 80,000 acres. In the W half of the Forest, N and S of Sherman Peak. This area was proposed for wilderness status by conservationists, but opposed by Forest Service. There are 990 mi. of Forest roads and trails for hiking, mountain biking, horse riding. Four roadless areas: rolling peaks, ridges, meadows, grassy open forest. Most of the area is over a mile high.

*Sullivan Lake,* SE of Metaline Falls. Largest lake in the Forest, about 3½ mi. long. Elevation 2,583 ft. Road along the W shore, trail along the E. Campgrounds at N and S ends. From the N end of the lake, Forest Rd. 654 leads NE to Salmo Mountain, near the Canadian border, skirting the wilderness area. Good area for birding; pine forests, large stands of cottonwood, birch, and aspen, open meadows, streams. Bighorn sheep are also seen on 6,222-ft. Hall Mountain, E of the lake, reached by trail from the S end.

*Crawford Cave State Park:* 48.5 acres. Within the Forest, NW of Metaline Falls, off Hwy 31. Feature is Gardner Cave, second-largest limestone cavern in WA. 1,500-ft. underground trail, half of it illuminated. Bring flashlight and sweater. Tours. 12 campsites. Nearby: Boundary Dam on the Pend Oreille River; Crescent Lake. About 1 mi. S of the dam, on the W side, misnamed Peewee Falls drops into the reservoir.

*East Portal Interpretive Area* on Hwy 20, 6 mi. W of Kettle Falls. On Sherman Creek. Steep slopes forested with Douglas-fir, western red cedar, larch, ponderosa pine. Nearby is Sherman Creek Wildlife Area (see entry this zone).

*Crystal Falls,* just off Hwy 20 about 16 mi. E of Colville. Water drops 30 ft. over large boulders.

*Lake Thomas* is among the Little Pend Oreille Lakes. Campground.

## Activities

*Camping:* 30 campgrounds, 404 sites. Campgrounds are at elevations from 2,000–5,400 ft. Most are on lakes or streams. Camping season: May 31–Sept. 15. These dates vary according to weather conditions. No electrical hookups. No generators allowed.

*Hiking, backpacking:* 305 mi. of trails, most maintained yearly. The Forest has available simple but valuable trail guides. Each has a trail map and text giving mileage, trail conditions, other features. Obtain from HQ.

*Hunting:* Selkirk Mountains are known for outstanding mule deer hunting. Also white-tailed deer, bear, quail, chukar, dove, pheasant, Canada goose, brant.

*Fishing:* Lakes, streams. Cutthroat, rainbow, brown, brook trout.

*Swimming:* Several lakes, including Sullivan, Leo, Trout.

*Boating:* Power boats on Sullivan.

*Horse riding:* Mostly in the Salmo Priest area, the Abercrombie-Hooknose area NW of Metaline Falls, and the Kettle Crest. No outfitters presently operating.

*Skiing:* One downhill ski area, 10 mi. E of Chewelah.

*Ski touring:* Ski touring wherever conditions are suitable. For information on groomed trails: (509) 935-6649 (Spokane).

## Nearby

Coulee Dam National Recreation Area, Little Pend Oreille National Wildlife Refuge, and Sherman Creek Wildlife Area (see entries this zone).

*Curlew Lake State Park:* 130 acres. 10 mi. NE of Republic on Hwy 21. 4,600 ft. of freshwater shoreline; camping (70 sites), hiking, fishing, boating.

## Adjacent

Kaniksu National Forest, mostly in ID.

## Publications

Forest map, $3.25.

Campground list.

Checklists of birds, mammals, reptiles and amphibians.

Trail guides available at Ranger Districts.

## Headquarters

U.S. Forest Service, Forest Supervision Office, Federal Building, 765 S. Main, Colville, WA 99114; (509) 684-7000.

## Spokane Information Office

Spokane Post Office, W. 904 Riverside, Spokane, WA 99202; (509) 456-2574.

## Ranger Districts

Colville R.D., Colville, WA 99114; (509) 684-7000. Kettle Falls R.D., Kettle Falls, WA 99141; (509) 738-7200. Newport, R.D., Newport, WA 99156; (509) 447-7000. Republic R.D., Republic, WA 99166; (509) 775-3305. Sullivan Lake R.D., Metaline Falls, WA 99153; (509) 446-7500.

---

## Conconully State Park

Washington Parks and Recreation Commission
87 acres.

16 mi. NE of Omak, off Hwy 97.

The Park is on a small irrigation reservoir. The site is developed, not a natural area, but it's a pleasant base for exploring nearby areas. A bit over a mile beyond the Park, the road enters the Colville National Forest (see entry this zone), a part of the Forest with numerous trails and campgrounds. A road to the NE—which first looks likely to become impassable but then greatly improves—passes several small lakes and enters the Sinlahekin Wildlife Area, a delightful, broad valley.

## Activities

*Camping:* 83 sites.

*Hiking:* ½-mi. nature trail.

*Swimming:* Artificial pond.

*Fishing:* Rainbow trout, bass.

## Nearby

Loomis State Forest/Sinlahekin, Wildlife Area (see entry this zone).

## Headquarters

WA Parks and Recreation Comm., Box 95, Conconully, WA 98819; (509) 826-7408, (800) 233-0321.

---

## Coulee Dam National Recreation Area

U.S. National Park Service
80,000 acres of water, 20,000 acres of land.

From Coulee Dam on Hwy 174 almost to the Canadian border. Hwy 25 parallels for some miles. Hwy 20 crosses at Kettle Falls.

Franklin D. Roosevelt Lake, formed by damming the Columbia River, is 130 mi. long, has 660 mi. of shoreline within the National Recreation Area. Although 20,000 acres of land seems large, extended along so much shoreline it makes a narrow band, too narrow to be shown on the site map.

The basin is generally drier to the S of Fort Spokane than to the N. About a fourth of the surrounding land is rolling dry land, grass and sagebrush; another fourth is rolling hills and bluffs with scattered ponderosa pine; about half, mostly in the N, is mixed conifer forest.

Winter is the drawdown period for the reservoir. The lake is raised to its maximum level in late June or early July and remains full during the warm season. Summer daytime temperatures range from 75°F to 100°, nights from 50° to 60°.

S of Kettle Falls, the developed areas are on the S and E sides of the lake, except for several areas administered by native American tribes on the W side. In all, there are 23 campgrounds, several large and developed, others primitive, a few accessible only by boat. All can be reached by boat, and most have launching facilities.

The lake is on a secondary flyway, attracting considerable numbers of migratory waterfowl. Bald eagles in fall and winter. Bird and mammal species are essentially the same as those of the nearby Colville National Forest (see entry this zone).

Roads parallel the lakeshore from Fort Spokane N, with many scenic sections. Hwy 21 crosses the lake by a free ferry. On the N side of the lake, Hwy 21 follows the Sanpoil River through the Colville Indian Reservation. The lake is a water route into Canada; boaters should ask about border inspection procedures before crossing.

### Interpretation

*Campfire programs* in summer. Occasional *guided hikes*. Schedules posted.

*Nature trails* at the major campgrounds.

### Activities

*Camping:* 23 campgrounds. Some open all year. Fee charged. Largest campgrounds are those near Coulee Dam, Keller Ferry, Fort Spokane, Porcupine Bay, Kettle Falls, and Evans. Campgrounds often at capacity on holidays and summer weekends.

*Hiking:* Few opportunities when Lake Roosevelt is full, in summer. In winter and spring, when the water level is down, one can hike for miles on sandy shores.

*Hunting:* Chiefly deer, game birds.

*Fishing:* Trout, walleye, kokanee.

*Swimming:* Gravel and sand beaches. Most are unsupervised.

*Boating:* Many launching points. Several marinas with services. Launch fee charged.

### Publications

Leaflet with map.

*Walleye Fishing on Lake Roosevelt.*

*Grand Coulee Dam.*

*Birds of the Grand Coulee.*

Checklists of birds, mammals, reptiles and amphibians, trees.

Mimeo information pages: Fort Spokane, Kettle Falls, St. Paul's Mission, Ft. Colville.

### Headquarters
National Park Service, 1008 Crest Dr., Coulee Dam, WA 99116; (509) 633-9441.

### Ranger Districts
Coulee Dam, R.D., 1008 Crest Dr., Coulee Dam, WA 99116; (509) 633-9441. Fort Spokane, R.D., HCR 11, Box 51, Davenport, WA 99122; (509) 725-2715. Kettle Falls, R.D., Rt. 1, Box 537, Kettle Falls, WA 99141; (509) 738-6266.

--------

## Curlew Lake State Park
Washington Parks and Recreation Commission
123 acres.

From Republic, 10 mi. NE on Hwy 21.

A pleasant, out-of-the-way campground in a valley between two sections of the Colville National Forest. The lake is narrow, about 5 mi. long. The first state fly-in park; airplane tie-downs.

### Activities
*Camping:* 75 sites, including walk-in sites.

*Hiking:* 2-mi. nature trail.

*Fishing:* Largemouth bass, trout in lake.

*Swimming:* Lake. Unsupervised.

*Boating:* No ramps. Waterskiing at lake.

### Headquarters
WA Parks and Recreation Comm., 974 Curlew Lake State Park Rd., Republic, WA 99166; (509) 775-3592.

## Ginkgo Petrified Forest State Park; includes Wanapum State Park

Washington Parks and Recreation Commission
7,469 acres.

E of Ellensburg, where I-90 crosses the Columbia River. On W side of bridge, look for marked right turn.

A visit should begin at the interpretive center, about 1 mi. N of the bridge, high above the impounded river, with a splendid view. Some millions of years ago, climate, terrain, and soil were quite different, and a great variety of trees grew here: redwood, magnolia, cypress, mahogany, hickory, elm, Douglas-fir, sassafras, banded gordonia, maple, myrtle, coffee tree, box elder, Spanish cedar, and many more. Mature trees fell, were carried by streams into a swamp, eventually were engulfed by lava. Six other sites in the U.S. are noted for petrified wood, but none has so many tree species.

Petrified ginkgo is found nowhere else. The ginkgo is known today only as a tree grown in cultivation; no wild specimens remain. Petrified wood cannot be collected within the Park. A map inside the center shows the site. 2½ mi. up the road are trails.

The Columbia River is impounded by Wanapum Dam, below the I-90 bridge. The Park has 5 mi. of shoreline. The Wanapum area, sometimes listed separately as Wanapum State Park, has campground, beach, and boating facilities.

Birds reported in the area include bald eagle, white-throated swift, prairie falcon, raven, sage thrasher, sage sparrow, meadowlark. Deer, elk, and coyote are common. Reptiles are common, including Pacific rattlesnake.

### Interpretation
Ginkgo interpretive center, open Thurs.–Mon., May–Sept., 10–6. Open for groups by advance appointment.

### Activities
*Camping:* 50 sites. All year.

*Hiking:* ¾-mi. interpretive trail, with number of petrified logs shown as found. 3-mi. hiking trail. Other routes possible, between the hwy and river. Hiking most pleasant in early morning. Permits needed for backcountry travel.

*Fishing:* Trout, steelhead, salmon, walleye.

*Swimming:* 3,500 ft. of beach, unsupervised.

*Boating:* Launching ramps. 13 mi. between dams. High winds are common. Waterskiing.

### Nearby
Quilomene Wildlife Area (see entry this zone).

### Publication
Leaflet.

### Headquarters
WA Parks and Recreation Comm., Vantage, WA 98950; (509) 856-2700, (800) 233-0321.

## Idaho Panhandle National Forest, also known as Kaniksu National Forest.
U.S. Forest Service
298,113 acres, 267,191 acres in WA.

Along ID border, from Canada to just N of Newport. No paved road access in WA. Access by Forest roads from Colville National Forest or from a paved secondary road W of Priest Lake, ID.

Most of this National Forest is in ID. The acreage in WA adjoins the Colville National Forest (see entry this zone) and includes a portion of the Salmo Priest Wilderness and, from the visitor's viewpoint, can be considered an extension of the Colville. Highest peaks in this WA section, over 6,000 ft., are on the ridge that is the boundary between the two Forests. Several Forest roads and trails lead in from the Colville. This portion of the Kaniksu has only one small campground.

### Headquarters
U.S. Forest Service, 3815 Schreiber Way, Coeur d'Alene, ID 83814-8363; (208) 765-7223.

# Lake Chelan National Recreation Area

See North Cascades National Park zone 3.

# Lake Chelan State Park

Washington Parks and Recreation Commission
127 acres.

9 mi. W of Chelan, off US 97, on South Shore Dr.

Most of the shoreline at the lower end of this long, narrow lake is privately owned, much of it developed. At the Park, the boundary of Wenatchee National Forest is about 2 mi. W of the lake. Beyond the Park, the strip of privately owned land is narrower; it ends near Twenty-Five-Mile Creek State Park (see entry this zone), as does the road.

The upper end of the lake, reached only by boat, by float plane, or on foot, is within the Lake Chelan National Recreation Area of North Cascades National Park (see entry zone 3).

The Park has 6,454 ft. of waterfront. A forested, hillside site. Nearby an unpaved road leads into the Forest a short distance. Interpretive bulletin board.

## Activities

*Camping:* 144 sites.

*Fishing:* Rainbow trout, salmon, Mackinaw trout, burbot, smallmouth bass.

*Swimming:* Lake. Supervised in season.

*Boating:* Ramp, dock.

## Headquarters

WA Parks and Recreation Comm., Rt. 1, Box 90, Chelan, WA 98816; (509) 687-3710, (800) 233-0321.

## Lake Wenatchee State Park

Washington Parks and Recreation Commission
488 acres.

From US 2 at Coles Corner, 3 mi. N on Hwy 207.

The Park is deep within the Wenatchee National Forest, though in an area with many inholdings, including about half of the lakeshore. Three National Forest campgrounds are also on the lake. Beyond the lake the road divides, branches going W and N, both leading to Forest campgrounds and trails into the Glacier Peak Wilderness (see Wenatchee National Forest entry this zone).

The Park has 12,623 ft. of frontage on Lake Wenatchee, 7,000 ft. on both sides of the Wenatchee River. The lake is about 6 mi. long, a bit less than 1 mi. wide, surrounded by ponderosa pine forest. Elevation is about 1,870 ft. The Park is popular, often near capacity in season. Most visitor activity is water-based.

### Interpretation

Some *evening programs, nature hikes* May–Sept.

### Activities

*Camping:* 197 sites. Some kept open in winter.

*Hiking:* Trails into the National Forest. 7-mi. hike to Alpine Lookout, 6,237 ft. 11 mi. of multiuse trails.

*Fishing:* Trout, sockeye salmon.

*Swimming:* Beach.

*Boating, canoeing:* Ramps. Local canoe outfitters offer day and overnight trips, May–Oct.

*Ski touring:* Chiefly on trails and unplowed Forest roads.

*Horse riding:* Rentals in summer.

*Snowmobiling:* Dec.–March. Parks Comm. and Forest Service cooperate in trail grooming.

**Publication**
Leaflet.

**Headquarters**
WA Parks and Recreation Comm., Star Rt., Leavenworth, WA 98826; (509) 763-3101, (800) 233-0321.

## Little Pend Oreille National Wildlife Refuge

U.S. Fish and Wildlife Service
39,999 acres.

From Colville, 6 mi. E on Hwy 20. S on Rocky Lake Rd. and look for marked left turn. Then follow signs. Entrance is 13 mi. from Colville. HQ is on this road.

One of the largest Refuges in WA. The area was homesteaded, logged, and grazed. Most of it was acquired by the Resettlement Administration in the 1930s. It then became a federal Wildlife Refuge. When Fish and Wildlife suffered severe budget cuts, the site was placed under state management, but in 1994 U.S. Fish and Wildlife resumed on-site management. The site now has a managed forest and supports a vigorous population of wildlife.

Near the entrance one enjoys a splendid view across a valley to the N-facing slopes. Elevations range from 1,800 ft. in the SW to 5,610 ft. on the E drainage divide. Terrain is gently rolling in the SW, steep in the E. The Little Pend Oreille River forms part of the N boundary. The Kaniksu National Forest adjoins on the E, the Colville National Forest on the S.

Temperatures are moderate in summer, usually cold Dec.–Feb. Annual precipitation is 18–24 in. Snowfall is fairly heavy and accumulations of several feet persist through late spring on N-facing slopes. However, the area is popular with backpackers in spring, because it is snow-free weeks earlier than the higher country in the National Forests.

Bear Creek, tributary of the Little Pend Oreille, and Bear Canyon Creek are the principal streams. Bayley Lake (70 acres) and McDowell Lake (about 60 acres) are within the site, Long Lake, on the E boundary.

More than 100 mi. of roads cross the area. The principal roads are all-weather and maintained.

Hunters and fishermen make up more than half of the visitors, but nonconsumptive use is increasing. Don't be surprised if you encounter bands of military men; the Air Force uses the site for survival training.

**Plants:** Three principal forest types: pine, pine-fir, and mixed woodlands. Pine woodland, at lower elevations, is important winter range for white-tailed deer. Here ponderosa pine predominates with understory of wheatgrass, Idaho fescue, bearberry, bitterbrush. Somewhat higher are stands of ponderosa and Douglas-fir, denser on N-facing slopes; understory species include ceanothus, serviceberry, huckleberry, snowberry, bearberry, spirea. Other tree species occurring include tamarack, lodgepole, western hemlock, western white pine, western red cedar, Engelmann spruce, alpine fir, cottonwood, quaking aspen, western yew. Many even-aged stands reflect past history of logging and fires. Forest openings occur throughout the site, but they are larger and more numerous on the W side and along major drainages.

**Birds:** Checklist available. Site is a transition zone between eastern and western species. Some waterfowl. Nesting mallard, green-winged teal, ring-necked duck, hooded merganser. Tundra swan, great blue heron, grebes, and shorebirds make some use of water areas. Golden and bald eagles, osprey, great horned, barred, and flammulated owls, peregrine falcon, ruffed, spruce, and blue grouse, pheasant, American redstart, common yellowthroat, catbird, Vaux's swift, common snipe, northern waterthrush, pileated and northern three-toed woodpeckers.

**Mammals:** Refuge was established for western race of Columbian white-tailed deer; latest population estimate, 2,000. Mule deer present in limited numbers. Elk have been seen but are not considered resident. Black bear common. Also resident: mountain lion, lynx, bobcat, coyote, beaver, mink, muskrat, badger, weasel, skunk, raccoon, red squirrel, Columbian ground squirrel, northern flying squirrel.

## Activities

*Camping:* Several informal campgrounds in attractive places. Latrines. Not listed in popular campground directories. Information at HQ. Some are crowded on fine weekends, but you can find a spot.

*Hiking, backpacking:* No trail map available. Many good places to hike, and in much of the site bushwhacking is pleasant. Some old logging roads are now closed to vehicles.

*Hunting:* Deer, bear, upland birds.

**Publication**
Site map.

**Headquarters**
U.S. Fish and Wildlife Service, 1310 Bear Creek Rd., Colville, WA 99114; (509) 684-8384.

## Loomis State Forest; Sinlahekin Wildlife Area
Washington Department of Natural Resources/Washington Department of Fish and Wildlife
177,000 acres/14,035 acres.

W of US 97, N of Okanogan. For the *Sinlahekin Wildlife* Area, W from US 97 at Tonasket to Loomis, then S. The larger portion of the Loomis State Forest lies between the W side of Sinlahekin Valley and the Okanogan National Forest and extends N to the Canadian border. A smaller portion lies S of Conconully, adjoining the Okanogan National Forest; it is crossed by Hwy 20.

Much of the land in this region is publicly owned but boundaries are not always conspicuous. Within a 10-mi. drive from the town of Loomis, one can be within a State Park, a National Forest, State Forest lands, and the Wildlife Area.

We turned N at Conconully on Sinlahekin Rd., along Lake Conconully (not to be confused with the reservoir). The lake is long, narrow, with steep slopes on either side, forested with talus and rock outcrops. The narrow road, surfaced but rough, is on a ledge. Part way along the lake the road deteriorates, passing through a narrow canyon with impressive talus slopes. 2 mi. later we joined a far better road, unpaved but broad and well kept. It is important to bear in mind that the ever-present logging trucks *have the right of way.*

We were now within the Wildlife Area, a strip of land a mile or more wide on the floor of a broad, scenic valley. The area was acquired as a winter range for mule deer. Along the valley are several small lakes. The Dept. of Fish and Wildlife maintains a number of primitive campgrounds, most of them beside lakes: level sites, modern latrines, but no water. We judged them unusually attractive, with light use in midsummer. A few people were fishing, swimming, and boating. Traffic along the valley road seemed to be about 5–10 cars per hour.

Terrain in the much larger Loomis State Forest is more geographically dramatic: massive stone mountains deeply scored by canyons, coulees, and ravines; great slides of black talus; rolling Aeneas and Douglas Mountains. Highest point in the N is 8,251-ft. Tiffany Mountain, in the Okanogan National Forest. Average elevation in Loomis is 4,900 ft.

Roads into and through the multipublic-ownership areas are best shown on the Okanogan National Forest map, not highway maps. Some are paved, some unpaved but maintained. The primary purpose of these roads is to support timber harvest and forest protection. We repeat, logging trucks have the right of way. Most roads are passable but primitive.

**Plants:** The ecosystem contains the following zones: shrub steppe valley, ponderosa pine and Douglas-fir, lodgepole pine and true conifers, Engelmann spruce in subalpine, and mosses and flowers above treeline. A S-facing slope may have few if any trees on its upper portion. The N-facing slope may have a dense stand of Douglas-fir, larch, and spruce. In many valleys, beaver dams have formed ponds and marshes with wetland vegetation. Juniper occurs on the ridges, with thick stands of lodgepole and true fir just below. Wildflowers are typical of the North Cascades.

**Birds:** Species are much the same as those occurring in the adjacent Pasayten Wilderness (see Okanogan National Forest entry this zone).

**Mammals:** Include mule deer, black bear, mountain lion, lynx, coyote, porcupine, raccoon, weasel, and other species found in the adjoining National Forest. Moose have been seen infrequently in the North Fork of the Toats Coulee drainage, near the Canadian border. Mountain goats on Chopaka. Bighorn sheep were reintroduced in the Sinlahekin Wildlife Area.

### Activities

*Camping:* Ample supply of campsites in the multipublic-owned areas. Facilities are primitive. Check with specific agency for more details.

*Hiking:* There are no signed hiking trails. Trails exist, used by hunters, fishermen, cattle owners, but you have to find them. Logging roads currently closed to vehicles are open to hikers. (They will be gated.)

*Hunting:* For mule deer, attracts large numbers of hunters.

*Fishing:* In Aeneas, Chopaka, Leader, and other lakes. State regulations apply.

*Swimming:* Fish Lake, Blue Lake, perhaps elsewhere. No beaches. Unsupervised.

*Boating:* Chopaka, Leader, and Conconully Lakes. Lakes are small, best suited to canoes and car-toppers.

*Snowmobiling:* On historic trails, ungroomed. Contact Okanogan County Snowmobile Assoc., P.O. Box 1098, Okanogan, WA 98840.

ORVs are permitted on most roads, unless posted. State and County roads may have use restrictions.

## Publications
Okanogan National Forest map (shows roads), $3.25.

Public Lands Oroville guadrangle, $4.95.

## Headquarters
WA Dept. of Natural Resources, NE Regional Office, P.O. Box 190, Colville, WA 99114; (509) 684-7474. WA Dept. of Fish and Wildlife, Regional Office, 1550 Alder St. N.W., Ephrata, WA 98823; (509) 754-4624.

## L. T. Murray Wildlife Area
Washington Department of Fish and Wildlife
103,000 acres.

On foot, from Yakima Canyon Scenic Hwy (see entry this zone), into S Unit. By road, W from Ellensburg on I-90 to Exit 106. S over bridge; left on Brown Rd. to end; right on Damman Rd., which becomes Umtanum Rd. 4 mi. from end of Brown Rd. go S on Durr; Wildlife Area boundary is then about 2 mi. ahead. N Unit is W of I-90, NW of Ellensburg. Several roads lead in: Robinson Canyon, Watt Canyon, Taneum Creek. Local advice on road conditions is desirable.

Typical E slope timberland, grass rangeland. Pine forests, bald hilltops, canyons cut through lava, attractive streams. Roads range from fairly good to difficult, not for cars or RVs; muddy spring conditions may last until May. Considerable traffic in hunting season, otherwise very little. Spring and early fall are the best times to visit.

The backpacker can park at the Umtanum Creek Recreation Site on Hwy 821, in the Yakima River Canyon S of Ellensburg, walk over a footbridge, and be in a roadless part of the Wildlife Area, with a choice of trails.

Elevations range from about 1,500 to 2,500 ft., with a high point of about 4,900 ft. in the S Unit. Climate is semiarid. Vegetation is fairly sparse: some open stands of ponderosa on N-facing slopes, scattered trees on other hillsides. Grassy slopes, some with sagebrush. Willow, cottonwood, and aspen along streams.

Flora and fauna lists can be seen at the Regional Office. Species are much the same as in the E portion of the Tieton and Naches Ranger Districts, Wenatchee National Forest. Good chukar population. Birds reported include Swainson's hawk, prairie falcon, sage grouse, white-headed woodpecker, pine grosbeak, flammulated and spotted owls, sage and Brewer's sparrows, pine siskin, Williamson's sapsucker. Game mammals include elk, bighorn sheep, mule deer.

Dept. of Fish and Wildlife maps show no local headquarters, no designated campgrounds, no facilities other than roads. Camp where you wish.

For such a large area, the information we could gather was scanty. Our motor home could not negotiate several of the roads, including a narrow track that dropped steeply into a canyon with several tight switchbacks. Hiking, we found the area delightful even in midsummer. Managers told us that area now attracts hikers and campers year-round.

### Nearby
Oak Creek Wildlife Area (see entry zone 6).

### Publications
North and South Unit maps.

### Headquarters
WA Dept. of Fish and Wildlife, Regional Office, 1701 S. 24th Ave., Yakima, WA 98902-5720; (509) 575-2740.

## Methow Wildlife Area

Washington Department of Fish and Wildlife
14,500 acres (25,516 total acres with satellite units).

About 2 to 4 mi. E of Hwy 20 between Winthrop and Twisp. Take local road on E side of Methow River; turn E on road to Davis Lake; follow signs to HQ.

A 17-mi. strip, 1–3 mi. wide. Area lies between lowland river valley and high mountains. Rolling to rugged terrain. Open sage and bitter-brush at lower elevations, semiopen ponderosa pine forest above. Several small lakes.

Key winter range for mule deer. The Wildlife Area is also home to hundreds of species of birds, mammals, amphibians and reptiles, in addition to fish and invertebrate species. Checklist available with map.

Late March into April is the best time to see deer. May and June offer good birding and wildflower displays.

The Wildlife Area contains the following satellites, managed primarily as mule deer winter and spring ranges and migratory corridors: Big Buck Wildlife Area: 5,600 acres; Big Valley Wildlife Area: 847 acres; Golden Doe Wildlife Area: 1,389 acres; and Rendezvous Wildlife Area: 3,180 acres.

### Activities

*Camping:* Informal.

*Hiking, horse riding, ski touring:* No developed trails, but no problem finding areas to use. Beware of rattlesnakes.

*Hunting:* Upland birds, grouse, bear, mule deer, white-tailed deer, mountain lion. In designated seasons, throughout area except in posted safety zones.

*Fishing:* Seasonal. State regulations apply.

### Adjacent

Pearrygin Lake State Park and Okanogan National Forest (see entries this zone).

### Publication

*Methow Valley Wildlife Area* (leaflet with map and checklists).

**Headquarters**
WA Dept. of Fish and Wildlife, Regional Office, 1540 Alder St., N.W., Ephrata, WA 98823; (509) 754-4624.

## Mount Spokane State Park

Washington Parks and Recreation Commission
16,040 acres.

From Spokane, N 6 mi. on US 2, then NE 15 mi. on Hwy 206.

Mount Spokane, 5,881 ft., dominates the landscape. A paved road goes 7½ mi. to the top with fine views along the way. From the top one can see the Selkirks and the Rockies, look into three states and Canada. The Park includes most of the mountain and adjoining ridges. Most of the slopes are forested.

This was the first WA State Park E of the Cascades, and it is one of the largest in the state. We were surprised to find it lightly used. The small campground, we were told, is almost never full. In 2 hours at the top, we saw one other party.

On the way up, the road passes a ski area: tows, runs, ski lodge. Nearby, on the mountain but just outside the Park, are 7 condominium buildings with restaurant, pool, tennis court, and other facilities. Judging from the size of the parking area, the ski slopes are popular.

The on-site Park office offers the visitor Park information, trail guides, and ski brochures. 70 mi. of marked multiuse trails are available to the hiker, mountain biker, horseback rider, and cross-country skier, plus, according to the park ranger, "umpteen" miles of unmarked trails. Trails are marked No Motor Vehicles.

**Plants:** Almost entirely forested except for tundralike vegetation near the crest and a few high mountain meadows with shrubs and bear grass. Marked contrast between vegetation of N-facing and S-facing slopes. Trees are mostly conifers: alpine fir, grand fir, lodgepole pine, western larch, Douglas-fir, western hemlock, western red cedar, western white pine. Also cottonwood, quaking aspen, alder, Rocky Mountain maple. Understory includes willow, huckleberry, ocean spray, serviceberry. Many ferns in lower, moister areas. Many wildflowers, including paintbrush, aster, lupines, golden aster.

**Birds:** No checklist. Species noted by ranger include black-capped chickadee, red-breasted nuthatch, dipper, raven, Steller's jay, hairy woodpecker, dark-eyed junco, fox sparrow, varied thrush, red-tailed hawk, cedar waxwing, pine grosbeak.

**Mammals:** Noted by ranger: black bear, moose, elk, mountain lion, mule and white-tailed deer, coyote, bobcat, porcupine, badger, skunk, ground squirrels, pika.

## Activities

*Camping:* 12 sites. June 1–Oct. 15.

*Hiking:* 70 mi. of trails. Shown on map in Park leaflet.

*Horse riding:* All trails open to horses. Tie-up racks.

*Skiing:* 5 chairlifts, 2 rope tows, 31 runs, 2 day lodges. Usual season Dec.–April.

*Ski touring:* 15½ mi. of cross-country trails.

*Snowmobiling:* Groomed trails, about 50 mi.

*Mountain biking:* Multiuse trails.

## Publications

Park leaflet.

Ski information.

## Headquarters

WA Parks and Recreation Comm., N. 26107 Mt. Spokane Park Rd., Mead, WA 99021; (509) 456-4169, (800) 233-0321.

## Okanogan National Forest

U.S. Forest Service
1,745,054 acres.

N and S of Hwy 20, adjoining North Cascades National Park on the W and SW. Several disconnected blocks are E of US 97, adjoining Colville National Forest.

The Okanogan bridges the gap between the high, rugged North Cascades and the gentler mountains of E WA. Until the late 1960s no road crossed these mountains because of the difficult terrain. Hwy 20, the North Cascades Hwy, finally made it, but snow closes the route for about half of the year. Half a million acres are in the Pasayten Wilderness, an area on the Canadian border. The Forest has 1,200 mi. of roads, including primitive tracks requiring 4-wheel drive. Even so, there is plenty of wilderness, in the Pasayten and other areas, for backcountry adventuring.

The highest peaks, over 8,000 ft., are in the W and N, but peaks over 1 mi. high can be found in almost every part of the Forest, including the detached blocks in the E. The rain shadow effect is conspicuous on the E slope of the Cascades. Precipitation there decreases sharply with decreasing elevation. Annual precipitation near a ridgetop may be more than 90 in., but little more than 20 in. in the valley below. Much of this precipitation falls as snow in winter, about 400 in. at the summits, about 75 in. at 2,000 ft.

The North Cascades Hwy, Hwy 20, eastbound, enters the Forest about a mile S of the end of Ross Lake. In 2 mi. it turns SE, its closest point to the wilderness. For the next 17 mi. it parallels the North Cascades National Park boundary, then crosses the Pacific Crest Trail and turns NE, soon crossing over Washington Pass. At Early Winters it meets the Methow River and turns SE in a long corridor. The all-weather road along this corridor is one of the principal approach routes to wilderness area. On and near it are a number of Forest campgrounds.

Other all-weather roads, routes to campgrounds, to wilderness, and other areas, lead N from Winthrop on Hwy 20 and NW from Omak. These and other roads are shown on the Forest map, not on highway maps. Studying the Forest map for a few minutes will enable you to identify the areas that are popular and thus likely to be crowded at times, and areas offering more solitude. The disconnected pieces of the Forest to the E should not be ignored. One of them contains over 55,000 acres and a number of attractive lakes.

These and several other lakes at lower elevations can be reached by auto, and one can camp near the shores. Many high mountain lakes can be reached only by trail. The Forest map shows hundreds of small streams that gather in rivers flowing to the Columbia.

A few of the campgrounds are accessible as early as April 15. Most are open by June 1, but a few at higher elevations not until July 1. Most are snowed in by Nov. 15. One can camp in the Forest at any season.

**Plants:** 85% of the area is forested. The remainder consists chiefly of meadows and rocky slopes above timberline. Principal tree species are Douglas-fir, ponderosa pine, Engelmann spruce, subalpine fir. Much of the Forest is open, parklike, brush-free, with grassy floor. Old growth remains at all elevations, occurs extensively in the wildernesses. Many wildflowers, over 500 species recorded, various seasons and habitats. These include paintbrush, lavender penstemon, wood trillium, false Solomon's seal, wild lily-of-the-valley, vanilla leaf, little flower collinsia, narrow-leaved montia, vernal draba, shining chickweed, western yarrow, yellow salsify, arrowleaf balsamroot, sagebrush buttercup, pussytoes, slender fringecup. Blooming season at high altitudes peaks in mid-July.

**Birds:** Checklist available. Common species (resident or seasonal) include western, eared, and pied-billed grebes, great blue heron, Canada goose, mallard, pintail, wigeon, shoveler, blue-winged, green-winged, and cinnamon teals, redhead, bufflehead, Cooper's, sharp-shinned, rough-legged, red-tailed, and Swainson's hawks, northern harrier, golden eagle, kestrel, blue, spruce, and ruffed grouse, white-tailed ptarmigan, California quail, screech, great horned, long-eared, saw-whet, and pygmy owls, calliope and rufous hummingbirds, northern flicker, hairy and downy woodpeckers, eastern and western kingbirds, 4 flycatchers, 6 swallows. Also 3 chickadees, dipper, 3 nuthatches, 4 wrens, Bohemian and cedar waxwings, 6 warblers.

**Mammals:** Checklist available. Common species include several shrews, 4 bats, deer mouse, voles, pika, snowshoe hare, yellow-bellied and hoary marmots, 2 ground squirrels, chipmunk, red squirrel, northern flying squirrel, beaver, porcupine, raccoon, short-tailed and long-tailed weasels, mink, badger, striped skunk, coyote, mountain lion, bobcat, mule and white-tailed deer, black bear. Elk are uncommon, moose occasional.

## Features

*Pasayten Wilderness:* 529,607 acres. Partly in Mount Baker–Snoqualmie National Forest but administered by Okanogan. About 40 mi. W–E, 20 mi. N–S. Roadless, old-growth forest unbroken except by peaks and high meadows. Wide range of topography, elevations, forest types, 94 mountain lakes, most stocked. Many streams; largest is the Pasayten River flowing to Canada and E to the Okanogan River.

Much of the area is rugged, difficult going for the hiker. Part of it has been kept free of trails, and this is for the experienced. However, several auto routes lead close to the wilderness boundaries, and several trails, following watercourses, have easy grades and are well maintained. The popularity of the Pasayten and the fragility of the alpine and subalpine environments have made some restrictions essential. Permits to enter are required and group size is limited. Some areas are closed to horses. Camping at several popular sites is rationed; reservations should be made well in advance, especially for Sept., when a special deer hunt occurs. The Pasayten Wilderness map shows the locations of trailheads and the routes of numbered trails. We suggest you visit a Ranger District to get advice on routes.

*Lake Chelan–Sawtooth Wilderness:* 151,564 acres. This area is described in our entry for Wenatchee National Forest (this zone). It is jointly administered by Okanogan and Wenatchee. Extending S from the North Cascades Scenic Hwy (20), it curves like the head of a question mark around both sides of the N Twisp River, then proceeds SE as a wide funnel that abuts Lake Chelan National Recreation Area on the W, and eventually descends almost half the length of the lake. Its lower portions meet the Wenatchee National Forest.

The Lake Chelan–Sawtooth Wilderness is part of the Sawtooth Area described below. We found a slight difference of opinion about the name of the wilderness. A Lake Chelan NRA recreation director assured us it was officially the Chelan–Sawtooth Wilderness, whereas the Forest Service printed matter we received, including maps, kept Lake intact, as did the person we spoke with.

*Tiffany Area:* 25,200 acres. By Forest Rds. 364 and 370 from Conconully. Two Forest campgrounds are on the roads. Tiffany Lake, one of 3 lakes in the area, is reached by a short trail. Seven peaks in the area exceed 7,000 ft. All the high peaks have alpine characteristics, supporting only grass and heather. At slightly lower elevations, whitebark pine, lodgepole pine; Engelmann spruce in moister areas. N-facing slopes have dense timber stands; S-facing slopes are more open. Tiffany Lake, elevation 6,500 ft., has excellent fishing.

*Long Draw Area:* 8,600 acres. A mile-wide strip extending S from the Canadian border between the Pasayten Wilderness and the Forest boundary. Elevations 4,400 to 7,408 ft. Separated from Long Swamp Area by Iron Gate Rd. S exposures have grass, shrubs; N slopes have shrubs and timber. Marshy bottoms in NE portion have abundant wildlife, including some waterfowl.

*Long Swamp Area:* 10,200 acres. N of Toats Coulee Rd. E portion (about three-quarters of the area) has broad, high ridges. W portion plunges down to steep-walled Chewack River Canyon. Elevations from 3,600 ft. on the Chewack to 7,800 ft. atop Windy Peak. Pasayten Wilderness borders the area on the N and W. Most of the area is in the subalpine zone. Extensive lodgepole forests. Douglas-fir, larch, ponderosa pine, and aspen are more common at lower elevations. Between the Middle Fork of Toats Coulee Creek and Hodges Horse Pasture, hardwoods with many small openings, fine wildlife habitat. Excellent summer mule deer range.

*Liberty Bell Area:* 112,430 acres. On the S boundary of the Pasayten Wilderness, just W of Harts Pass. Steep, rugged mountains, sharp or knife-edged ridges. Glaciated valleys. Elevations from 1,800 ft. on Ruby Creek to 8,806 ft. on Golden Horn's Peak. Pacific Crest Trail passes through the area. Most of the area is in the alpine or subalpine zone. Stunted, widely scattered trees, grass, huckleberry, heather. Some old-growth Douglas-fir stands on Ruby Creek. Diverse wildlife habitats. Fishing in Ruby, Granite, and Canyon Creeks.

*Sawtooth Area:* 230,900 acres. Along the S boundary of the Forest, from North Cascades Highway near Ruby Creek to the Gold Creek Road. Includes large portions of the Wolf Creek and Cedar Creek drainages. Elevations from 2,400 ft. to the nearly 9,000-ft. summit of Gardner Mountain. Rugged terrain. Deep valleys. The S ridge has more lakes, meadows, gentler slopes. Trails travel through most of the S drainages; few cross the rugged N part. Open meadows and rocky slopes at high elevations. Mountain Forest Zone is lower, but with great differences in vegetation. Avalanche paths into valleys become a tangle of alder, shrubs, broken trees. Large areas of lodgepole pine in the S cover both Mountain Forest and Subalpine Zones. A number of cirque lakes in the high country, many with trout.

*Bonaparte Lake, Lost Lake, Beaver Lake* are in one of the detached blocks of Forest land E of US 97. From Tonasket, 20 mi. E on Hwy 20, then N on Forest Rd. 396. Several other small lakes are in this block. It's a resort area with some roadside commercial development and some lakefront residences. However, a substantial part of the block is road-less, with good cross-country hiking opportunities. The *Big Tree Botanical Area* is between Bonaparte and Lost Lakes; ⅔-mi. trail passing exceptionally large trees, the largest of them larches.

*Buttermilk Butte,* 5,474 ft., SW of Twisp, reached by a Forest road, offers a limited view of the Methow Valley and the Sawtooth Ridge. Blackpine Lake and campground are nearby.

*Cedar Falls,* one of the Forest's more spectacular falls. From the North Cascades Hwy (20) about 3 mi. W of Early Winters Campground, turn S on Sandy Butte/Cedar Creek Rd. Look for trailhead in ½ mi. Easy 45-minute hike to the falls. The hiking trail continues beyond.

*Goat Wall,* rising 2,000 ft. above the Methow Valley, is often likened to the rock walls of Yosemite Valley.

*Harts Pass,* about 14 mi. beyond Goat Wall, is on an all-weather road, steep and narrow, closed to all trailers. Three campgrounds are clustered in this area. The Pacific Crest Trail passes through. A spur road leads to Slate Peak, 7,500 ft., offering a breathtaking view of the North Cascades, a seemingly unlimited array of snowy peaks. This road is not for large RVs, requires extreme caution.

*Lost River Canyon,* near the S boundary of the Pasayten Wilderness, is an outstanding geological area. Called a "challenging hike," it is approached from a trailhead in the Methow Valley near the Lost River Airstrip, but there is no trail in most of the gorge itself. Not suitable for rafting or kayaking. Look out for rattlesnakes.

*Lyman Lake* and *Crawfish Lake* are in a detached block on the N border of the Colville Indian Reservation. Take Hwy 20 E for 13 mi., then SE on Aeneas Valley Rd. to Lyman Lake. The Forest map shows a loop route into the Reservation, then NW on Haden Creek Rd. Three Forest campgrounds on the route.

*Rainy Pass,* on Hwy 20. 0.8-mi. paved wheelchair trail to Rainy Lake. Accessible by July 15 until early Nov.

*Sweetgrass Butte,* 6,109 ft., is the high spot of a 27-mi. scenic loop route that begins at Winthrop. Stop at the Winthrop Ranger District for a leaflet describing the route and check the route numbers: those on the leaflet don't entirely agree with those on the Forest map. Splendid view of peaks to the N in the Pasayten Wilderness, W to Sawtooth River.

*Washington Pass Overlook,* on the North Cascades Hwy (20), is another scenic point, looking out to Liberty Bell Mountain and Early Winters Spires. Interpretive exhibit. 400-ft. wheelchair trail.

### Interpretation

Methow Valley *visitor center,* W of Winthrop, Hwy 20. Open all year.

*Evening programs* at Lost Lake Campground, in summer. Notices posted.

## Activities

*Camping:* 59 campgrounds, 490 sites. A few are accessible as early as April 15, most by May 15 or June 1, a few not until July.

*Hiking, backpacking:* 1,200 mi. of trails (about 1,000 in the Pasayten Wilderness), plus opportunities for cross-country hiking and hiking on little-used logging roads. Trail information is available at HQ and each Ranger District.

*Hunting:* Deer, black bear, mountain goat.

*Fishing:* Lakes and streams. Said to be excellent. Rainbow, cutthroat, Dolly Varden, brook trout.

*Swimming:* Chiefly in Bonaparte and Lost Lakes, and in other lakes in E portions of the Forest.

*Boating:* Mostly on Bonaparte, Lost, other lakes in E portions of the Forest.

*Horse riding:* 7 improved campgrounds have pack and saddle stock facilities. 6 of these are just outside the Pasayten Wilderness. Outfitter-Guide information sheet lists outfitters for pack trips, horse rentals. Inquire at Ranger Districts for trails suitable for horse travel, regulations. In some areas all feed must be carried in.

*Skiing:* Loup Loup Ski Area on Hwy 20 E of Twisp.

*Ski touring:* *Recreation Reports* include seasonal information on best locations, snow conditions.

*Snowmobiling:* Some trails are groomed. *Recreation Reports* include seasonal information on best locations, snow conditions. Special WA state parking permits are required at some trailheads to cover plowing costs.

## Adjacent or Nearby

Loomis State Forest/Sinlahekin Wildlife Area, Conconully State Park, Chopaka Mountain, Pearrygin Lake State Park, Methow Wildlife Area, Alta Lake State Park (see entries this zone).

## Publications

Forest map, $3.50.

Pasayten Wilderness map, $2.15.

Checklists of birds, wildlife.

*Recreation Reports* (issued at intervals).

*Fishing Directory.*

Mimeo information pages: Methow in winter, winter sports, Outfitter-Guide sheet.

## Headquarters
U.S. Forest Service, 1240 S. Second Ave., Okanogan, WA 98840; (509) 826-3275.

## Ranger Districts
Methow Valley R.D., Twisp, WA 98856; (509) 977-2131. Tonasket R.D., Tonasket, WA 98855; (509) 486-2186. Winthrop R.D., Winthrop, WA 98862; (509) 996-4000.

## Pearrygin Lake State Park
Washington Parks and Recreation Commission
578 acres.
5 mi. N of Winthrop, off Hwy 20.

In the Methow Valley, at the gateway to the North Cascades Hwy (20), Okanogan National Forest, and Forest roads to the edge of the Pasayten Wilderness. 8,200 ft. of shoreline on a pleasant lake.

## Activities
*Camping:* A popular campground. 83 sites. Reservations required.

*Hiking:* Trails along lake.

*Fishing:* Rainbow trout, crawfish.

## Adjacent
Methow Wildlife Area (see entry this zone).

## Nearby
Okanogan National Forest (see entry this zone).

## Headquarters
WA Parks and Recreation Comm., Rt. 1, Box 300, Winthrop, WA 98862; (509) 996-2370, (800) 233-0321.

## Quilomene Wildlife Area

Washington Department of Fish and Wildlife
45,143 acres.

NW of Vantage on I-90. Access from Old Vantage Hwy and from the road leading N from Vantage past the Ginkgo State Park.

Above the Columbia River Canyon, including most of the Whiskey Dick and Quilomene Creek drainages, N of the State Park. The Wildlife Area has several miles of frontage on the river. Its two sections are separated by an E–W strip about 2 mi. wide.

Desert country. Hills, rolling to steep, with sparse cover of sagebrush, bunchgrass, other desert vegetation. Hunting is for elk, deer, and upland birds, with some waterfowl on the river.

For the visitor who is not hunting, spring and early summer are the best times to visit. Proper conditions produce a fine wildflower display. As the weather warms, early morning hiking is enjoyable. Most of the roads into the backcountry require a pickup or 4-wheel drive.

Petrified wood of many tree species can be found.

No designated campgrounds. Camp where you please, but no fires are permitted, April 15–Oct. 15.

### Publication
Map.

### Headquarters
WA Dept. of Fish and Wildlife, Regional Office, 1701 S. 24th Ave., Yakima, WA 98902; (509) 575-2740.

## Rocky Lake Natural Recreation Area

Washington Department of Natural Resources
About 800 acres.

From Colville, take Hwy 20E 5.9 mi. Turn right on Artman Gibson Rd., go 3.2 mi. Turn right on gravel road for ½ mi. Stay to left, go 2 mi. on paved road, 2 on gravel.

A small, shallow, weedy pond with rocky, forested shores. Forest is mostly ponderosa pine, larch, Douglas-fir, some trees of considerable size. Wildflowers: sticky cinquefoil, goldenrod, golden aster, woolly mullein, Klamath weed, Oregon grape, bull thistle. A mechanical aerator keeps the lake surface from freezing in winter. Hand boat launch.

*Camping:* 7 sites. Primitive.

### Nearby
Little Pend Oreille National Wildlife Refuge (see entry this zone).

### Headquarters
WA Dept. of Natural Resources, NE Area Office, P.O. Box 190, Colville, WA 99114; (509) 684-7474.

## Sherman Creek Wildlife Area
Washington Department of Fish and Wildlife
8,068 acres.
On Hwy 20 at Franklin D. Roosevelt Lake (Columbia River), W side. 5 mi. W of Kettle Falls.

The main portion of the site is about 6 mi. square, Hwy 20 crossing its lower third. Most roads once open to vehicles are now closed. Several parking areas along the road. Rather steep, ascending to the ponderosa pine forest of the Okanogan highlands. Slopes face E and S. Elevations from 1,289 ft. at the lake to 4,208 ft. Annual precipitation is 16–19 in. at low elevations, to more than 30 in. at highest level. Site is bordered on the S by the lower drainage of Sherman Creek. Winter range for mule and white-tailed deer.

**Plants:** Ponderosa pine, widely scattered in bunchgrass areas, relatively heavy stands with Douglas-fir at 3,500 ft. Also lodgepole pine, western larch, Engelmann spruce, aspen, bitter cherry, black cottonwood. Shrubs include alder-leaved buckthorn, ceanothus, blue and white clematis, sticky currant, dogwood, blue elderberry, mountain gooseberry, kinnikinnick, thimbleberry. May and June are best wildflower season, species including aster, heartleaf arnica, balsamroot, bluebell, camas, columbine, delphinium, lupines, mariposa lily, mullein, penstemon, pussytoes, phlox, western trillium, yarrow.

**Birds:** No checklist. List for Colville National Forest is applicable. Species noted include Canada goose, tundra swan, osprey, golden and bald eagles, kestrel, Cooper's hawk, Lewis's and northern three-toed woodpeckers, blue, ruffed, and spruce grouse, violet-green swallow, mountain chickadee, cedar waxwing, crossbills, Steller's jay.

**Mammals:** Shrews, bats, cottontail, snowshoe hare, chipmunk, marmot, ground squirrels, red squirrel, northern flying squirrel, pocket gopher, deer mouse, beaver, porcupine, coyote, red fox, raccoon, marten, weasel, mink, badger, striped skunk, wolverine, cougar, lynx, bobcat, mule and white-tailed deer, black bear. Occasional elk.

**Reptiles and amphibians:** 2 salamanders, northwest toad, Pacific tree frog, 2 frogs, western painted turtle, wandering garter snake, western yellow-bellied racer, gopher snake, Pacific rattlesnake.

### Adjacent

Colville National Forest, Coulee Dam National Recreation Area (see entries this zone).

### Headquarters

WA Dept. of Fish and Wildlife, Regional Office, N. 8702 Division St., Spokane, WA 99218; (509) 456-4082.

## Squilchuck State Park

Washington Parks and Recreation Commission
286 acres.

12 mi. SW of Wenatchee. From Appleyard, just S of Wenatchee, local road along Squilchuck Creek.

In a steep-walled canyon at the edge of Wenatchee National Forest (see entry this zone). Forested site, mostly ponderosa pine with cottonwood, quaking aspen, sumac, sagebrush.

### Activities

*Camping:* 20 sites.

*Hiking:* Trails into the National Forest.

*Skiing:* 2 ski tows.

*Other winter sports:* Sledding, tobogganing.

## Headquarters

WA Parks and Recreation Comm., 2805 Mission Ridge Rd., Wenatchee, WA 98801; (509) 664-7377, (800) 233-0321.

## Steamboat Rock State Park

Washington Parks and Recreation Commission
3,523 acres.

From Grand Coulee, 12 mi. SW on Hwy 155.

On Banks Lake, a narrow reservoir 27 mi. long, between high basalt cliffs. Steamboat Rock is a flat-topped butte rising 1,000 ft. above the lake surface, at the tip of a peninsula of rolling land. Adjacent land is the Banks Lake Wildlife Area (see entry this zone). The Park has over 5 mi. of shorefront.

The developed portion of the Park is a popular, neatly barbered recreation area. Hiking trail to the top of the butte, which is a nature area and wildflower preserve. Some tule marshes on the lakeshore. Upland areas mostly grasses and sagebrush with scattered conifers.

No published bird or mammal lists. See entry for Banks Lake Wildlife Area. A sign warns Rattlesnake Area.

## Activities

*Camping:* 138 sites. All year. Reservations required Memorial Day–Labor Day.

*Hiking:* 12 mi. of trails within Park.

*Fishing:* Lake fishing said to be good. Trout, bass, crappie, catfish.

*Swimming:* Lake.

*Boating:* Ramp on lake.

*Winter sports:* Ice skating, ice fishing.

## Headquarters
WA Parks and Recreation Comm., P.O. Box 370, Electric City, WA 99123; (509) 633-1304, (800) 233-0321.

..................................................................................................................................

## Sun Lakes State Park; Sun Lakes Wildlife Area
Washington Parks and Recreation Commission/Washington Department of Fish and Wildlife
4,024 acres/8,941 acres.

From Coulee City, SW along Hwy 17.

Hwy 17 is at least as scenic as Hwy 155 NE of Coulee City (see entry for Banks Lake Wildlife Area, this zone). Both run through valleys framed by towering basalt cliffs, but this 27-mi.-long valley has a chain of lakes and marshes on the desert floor. Near Coulee City, the road is high, providing fine views of the meandering stream below. Then it drops to the valley floor, skirting pothole lakes that are populated by waterfowl in season.

This is the Grand Coulee, a unique geological area called "channeled scablands"—huge, dry, deeply cut channels in basalt. One of the most conspicuous features is Dry Falls (see description below). Typical vegetation on the desert floor: big sagebrush, wheatgrass, Idaho fescue, western yarrow, with a variety of flowering annuals. Cattail marshes.

**Birds:** The Wildlife Area is managed for waterfowl. It is an important link in the migration route of the lesser Canada goose. Ring-billed and California gulls nest. Reported species include Forster's tern, long-billed dowitcher, avocet, blue-winged and cinnamon teals, Barrow's goldeneye, eared grebe, Wilson's phalarope. Many ducks. Also red-winged and yellow-headed blackbirds, cliff swallow, white-throated swift, Say's phoebe, magpie, rock wren, lazuli bunting, western tanager, lark sparrow, northern oriole, various warblers.

## Features

*Sun Lakes State Park* includes Dry Falls and Lake Lenore Caves. The major Park development is on Park Lake: campground, marina, gas station, other facilities. Park Lake is heavily used by water skiers, other boaters.

*Dry Falls* is a 3-mi.-wide, 400-ft.-high ancient waterfall, long dry. A National Natural Landmark. A handsome interpretive center overlooks the falls, houses exhibits, information counter; open May 15–Sept. 30.

*Lake Lenore Caves* are high on the cliff wall, carved by glacial meltwater, later used as shelters by native Americans. A trail at the N end of the lake leads to several of the caves. Day use only.

*Sun Lakes Wildlife Area* is an irregularly shaped strip of land extending from N of Park Lake to the S end of Lenore, generally adjoining State Park lands. Wildlife Area boundary signs are posted along the highway. At Lenore, several dirt tracks lead to parking at the lakeshore. This area is closed after 10 P.M., and camping is banned.

## Activities

*Camping:* At Park Lake. 224 sites. All year.

*Hiking:* Mostly on informal trails, on the valley floor, skirting lakes and stream.

*Hunting:* In the Wildlife Area. Chukar, some waterfowl.

*Swimming:* Supervised, at Park Lake, June 20–Labor Day.

*Boating, canoeing:* Most boating activity is on Park Lake. One can canoe the length of the chain, 12 mi., with 3 portages, one of them over ½ mi. No motors on Lake Lenore.

*Fishing:* Lake Lenore is stocked with alkaline-resistant Lahontan cutthroat trout. Special regulations. Also catfish and panfish.

## Publications

State Park leaflet.

Dry Falls leaflet.

## Headquarters

Sun Lakes State Park, Star Rt. 1, Box 136, Coulee City, WA 99115; (509) 632-5583, (800) 233-0321. WA Dept. of Fish and Wildlife, 1550 Alder St. N.W., Ephrata, WA 98823; (509) 754-4624.

## Turnbull National Wildlife Refuge

U.S. Fish and Wildlife Service
15,565 acres.

From Spokane, about 9 mi. SW on I-90. Left on Hwy 904 6 mi. to
Cheney, then left on Cheney Plaza Rd. 4 mi. to entrance.

Managed for waterfowl on the Pacific Flyway. The original lakes and
marshes of this area were almost entirely drained by the 1920s. Farming was not successful, and land for the Refuge was acquired in 1937.
Lakes and marshes were then restored.

Gently rolling to flat terrain. Ponds, cattail marshes, meadows,
groves of ponderosa pine. 2,200 acres are open to public use. The
entrance road leads to HQ and is the beginning of a 5-mi. auto-tour
route. Leaflet and bird checklist are available at the beginning of the
route. The tour passes several wetlands. Visitors can park and walk to
or around the wetlands, or, if they wish, can walk the entire route.

**Birds:** Over 200 species recorded. Checklist available. Species nesting
include horned, eared, and pied-billed grebes, great blue heron, American bittern, Canada goose, mallard, gadwall, pintail, green-winged,
blue-winged, and cinnamon teals, wigeon, shoveler, wood duck, redhead, ring-necked duck, canvasback, lesser scaup, bufflehead, ruddy
duck, hooded merganser. Seasonally common species include red-
tailed hawk, northern harrier, kestrel, California quail, killdeer, Wilson's phalarope, black tern, great horned owl, northern flicker, downy
woodpecker, eastern kingbird, willow flycatcher, western wood
pewee, 4 swallows, magpie, black-capped and mountain chickadees,
white-breasted and pygmy nuthatches, marsh wren, robin, western
and mountain bluebirds, water pipit, northern shrike, 3 warblers,
western meadowlark, yellow-headed, red-winged, and Brewer's blackbirds, American goldfinch, 5 sparrows.

**Mammals:** Include Rocky Mountain elk, white-tailed deer, coyote,
beaver, raccoon, badger, muskrat, mink, porcupine, chipmunk, red
squirrel, ground squirrel.

## Publications

Leaflet with map.

Bird checklist.

Environmental education curriculum.

## Headquarters

U.S. Fish and Wildlife Service, 26010 S. Smith Rd., Cheney, WA 99004; (509) 235-4723.

---

## Twenty-Five-Mile Creek State Park

Washington Parks and Recreation Commission
235 acres.

From Chelan, 20 mi. N along the lakeshore, off US 97.

Most of the lakeshore from Chelan to this Park is privately owned. The shore road ends here. Beyond is the Wenatchee National Forest and, at the head of the lake, the Lake Chelan National Recreation Area of North Cascades National Park (see entry zone 3), reached only by boat, by float plane, or on foot.

The Park has 1,500 ft. of waterfront. A forest road leads inland, past a number of forest campgrounds, eventually connecting with a paved forest road along the Entiat River.

## Activities

*Camping:* 66 sites.

*Fishing:* Burbot, salmon, trout.

*Swimming:* Unsupervised.

*Boating:* Ramp and marina. Also waterskiing.

## Nearby

Lake Chelan State Park (see entry this zone).

## Headquarters

WA Parks and Recreation Comm., c/o Lake Chelan State Park, Rt. 1, Box 142A, Chelan, WA 98816; (509) 687-3710, (800) 233-0321.

## Wenatchee National Forest

U.S. Forest Service
2.2 million acres.

Central WA, encompassing lands within Chelan, Kittitas, and Yakima
Counties. Major travel corridors are US 2, US 97, and I-90.

The Forest extends from the crest of the Cascades E to the Columbia
River, and lengthwise from scenic Lake Chelan in the N to its border
with the Yakima Reservation in the S. It is part of a huge block of federal land occupying the mountains from Canada to OR and beyond.
The highest country is in the W portion. Here annual precipitation
and snowfall are heavy. Snow remains until early July, and early season snow often falls before the end of Aug. Much of the Forest is in
the rain shadow of the Cascades, however, and precipitation declines
with decreasing altitude to semiarid conditions at the Columbia River.

The Forest includes portions of 7 wilderness areas (Glacier Peak,
Henry M. Jackson, Alpine Lakes, Lake Chelan–Sawtooth, Norse Peak,
William O. Douglas, and Goat Rocks) that comprise 40% of the land
area and are open only to foot and horse travel. However, nearly
5,000 mi. of Forest roads wind through a boundless variety of scenery
and topography and lead to trailheads providing over 2,500 mi. of
recreation trails crisscrossing the Forest. Nearly 1,000 mi. of this trail
system are open to motorized trail bikes and mountain bikes as well as
to hikers and equestrians. Most trails are snow-free by late July or Aug.
But many variables can affect accessibility, such as heavy winter
snowpack, flood damage, trail elevation. Current information should
be obtained from Ranger District offices.

Because of its scenic and geographic diversity, its location in the
"sun belt" of North Central WA, and the variety and abundance of
recreation opportunities, the Wenatchee National Forest is one of the
most heavily visited National Forests in the country.

A striking feature of the Forest is the extraordinary number of
lakes, 237 named and listed, 156 of them 10 acres or more in area.

Largest is Lake Chelan, 55 mi. long, the third-deepest lake in North America, at nearly 1,500 ft. It is still clean and clear enough to be classified as pristine. Many of the smaller lakes are in high country, including roadless areas and classified wildernesses.

Elevations in the Forest range from 700 to 9,511 ft. Conditions differ so much from place to place and season to season that visits require some planning. Recreation reports are issued frequently describing road and trail conditions, which campgrounds are open, and snow cover. Developed campgrounds in the Forest are generally open by Memorial Day weekend, depending on the severity of the previous winter's snowpack and any resulting flood damage. In 1996, some campgrounds were not accessible until June, due to heavy snowpack and damage to roads and facilities from flooding in Nov. Usually, trail and road travel becomes possible in stages between late April and late June. The snow level in early July ranges from 4,500 ft. on the N-facing slopes to 6,000 ft. on S-facing slopes. Some of the higher elevations may not be accessible until July or Aug. Always check with Ranger Districts for current snow information and road conditions.

**Plants:** Mostly forested, chiefly ponderosa pine with Douglas-fir, Engelmann spruce, subalpine fir. Alpine meadows at higher elevations. Much of the forest is open, parklike. Willow, aspen, and alder along streams. Little old-growth timber remains. Many wildflowers. Blooming season begins in the low country in April, prominent species including balsamroot, trillium, spring beauty, yellow bells, glacier lily. Blooming follows the receding snow line. June display includes wild garlic, avalanche lily, phlox, currant. In the high country, July is the peak blooming time. Among the species visitors are likely to see around campgrounds: American brooklime, dwarf waterleaf, blue penstemon, forget-me-not, lupines, blue vetch, wood anemone, meadow rue, pipsissewa, snowberry, twinbells, columbine, Oregon grape, ocean spray, ox eye daisy, ceanothus, thimbleberry.

**Birds:** Checklist available. Species recorded include pintail, northern shoveler, blue-winged, green-winged, and cinnamon teals, mallard, gadwall, lesser scaup, redhead, canvasback, common and Barrow's goldeneyes, bufflehead, Canada and white-fronted geese, great horned and spotted owls, golden eagle, Cooper's, Swainson's, and sharp-shinned hawks, goshawk, great blue heron, American bittern, osprey, cedar and Bohemian waxwings, chukar, spruce and sage grouse, blue and Steller's jays, dipper, 3 finches, hermit and Swainson's thrushes, northern flicker, 5 woodpeckers, 3 chickadees, magpie, pine grosbeak, red- and white-winged crossbills, mountain and western bluebirds, red-breasted, white-breasted, and pygmy nuthatches, warbling, red-eyed, and solitary vireos, 4 sparrows.

**Mammals:** Checklist available. Species listed include 2 bats, 3 chipmunks, porcupine, mountain beaver, beaver, northern flying squirrel, hoary and yellow-bellied marmots, marten, fisher, striped skunk, muskrat, raccoon, badger, red fox, coyote, lynx, bobcat, mountain lion, wolverine, black bear, moose, elk, mule and white-tailed deer, mountain goat, bighorn sheep.

## Features

*Alpine Lakes Wilderness:* 364,226 acres. Jointly managed by the Wenatchee National Forest, 246,330 acres, and the Mount Baker–Snoqualmie National Forest, 117,889 acres. I-90 is close to the wilderness boundary where it enters the Forest at Snoqualmie Pass. The wilderness lies to the N and E of the Pass, N of Lakes Keechelus, Kachess, and Cle Elum. The terrain is rugged, but less so than in the Glacier Peak Wilderness. Many peaks are over 4,000 ft., a few over 7,000. The area is best known for its lakes, more than 700 of them including those as small as an acre. The largest is about 1½ mi. long, 3 others close to a mile.

The Enchantments Area is about 3,500 acres in the heart of the wilderness, a unique and fragile ecosystem. High elevations, rugged granite relief, snow remaining until midsummer. Glaciers. Several small lakes. Special rules protect this delicate area. Reservation permits are required June 15–Oct. 15 for overnight trips to the Enchantments, Lake Stuart, Snow Lakes, Eightmile Lake, Caroline Lake, and Mount Cashmere areas of the Alpine Lakes Wilderness. Dogs are not allowed within any of these permit areas. Permits for day hiking within the reservation area as well as day use and overnight trips in other areas of the Alpine Lakes Wilderness are available on a self-issued basis at ranger stations and trailheads. For detailed information, inquire at the Leavenworth Ranger District office. Foot travel only.

Trails in the wilderness generally follow drainages. Some are easy-going; many destination lakes are only 2–3 mi. from trailheads.

*Glacier Peak Wilderness:* 572,738 acres. Jointly managed by Wenatchee National Forest, 289,234 acres, and Mount Baker–Snoqualmie National Forest, 283,504 acres. The wilderness lies in the North Cascade Mountain Range and features heavily forested stream courses, steep-sided valleys, and peaks with more active glaciers than any other range in the Lower 48. Climate is moist on the W side of the range, producing verdant forests and deep snows. Vegetation is more open on the drier E side.

Glacier Peak is the dominant feature, at 10,542 ft. Early native people called the mountain Da Kobad—Great White Mother Mountain. More than 30 major peaks, 3 of them over 9,000 ft., also highlight the landscape. The snowfields and glaciers are the source of hundreds of streams with many cascades, falls, and pools. There are many high mountain lakes. The wilderness boundary comes close to the upper end of Lake Chelan, where the Forest adjoins the Lake Chelan National Recreation Area. Its general course is then SW, irregularly, because the boundary line was drawn to exclude existing roads. The ends of several of these roads are wilderness trailheads. Trailheads along Lake Chelan are only accessible by boat, by float plane, or by hiking from the W side of the mountains. A shuttle bus service operates between Lucerne and Holden Village.

The area has 450 mi. of trails as well as large areas where off-trail hiking is possible for the experienced. Fish and game are plentiful, attracting many hunters and fishermen, on foot and horseback. A portion of the Pacific Crest Trail crosses the wilderness. Glacier Peak Wilderness lies adjacent to the Henry M. Jackson Wilderness (see below) to the SW.

Commercial outfitters are located on the principal approaches. Ask Forest HQ for addresses. Not all trails are suitable for horses. The maximum group size is 12 (any combination of people and stock). Smaller groups are recommended.

In winter, visitors can enter the area by the White Pass chairlift and ski to Hogback Mountain. Wilderness permit is required.

*Goat Rocks Wilderness:* 108,439 acres. Located between Mount Rainier and Mount Adams in a portion of the volcanic Cascades in SW WA. The wilderness is jointly managed by the Naches Ranger District of Wenatchee National Forest, 37,236 acres, and the Packwood Ranger District of Gifford Pinchot National Forest, 71,203 acres. The Wenatchee Forest portion is S of US 12, SW of Rimrock Lake in the Naches Ranger District.

The Goat Rocks are remnants of a large volcano, extinct for some 2 million years. This ancient volcano once towered over the landscape at more than 12,000 ft. but has since eroded into several peaks averaging around 8,000 ft. The cluster of rocks and peaks are known as Goat Rocks because of the bands of mountain goats that live here. The area features mountainous terrain with elevations from 3,000 to 8,201 ft.

on Gilbert Peak. Other flinty peaks include Tieton Peak, Ives Peak, and Old Snowy Mountain. Much of the wilderness lies above timberline, providing outstanding alpine scenery. Cross-country travelers are challenged by a wide variety of landforms, from vertical rock walls to glaciated, domelike peaks. Streams meander through meadows and cascade down hillsides. The Tieton and Klickitat River systems drain the E side of the wilderness.

The N portion of Goat Rocks Wilderness offers good loop trips and some views of Mount Rainier. However, many high-elevation trails remain impassable, due to snow, until July, and snow can return as early as Sept. In July, the snow covering the meadows is rapidly replaced by the white blossoms of avalanche lilies. Lupines, paintbrush, scarlet and magenta painted cup, red mountain heather, and spreading phlox are notable wildflowers found in the high meadows scattered among the rugged rocks and glaciers. Self-issued wilderness permits, available at all wilderness trailheads, are required for entry to the wilderness.

The Pacific Crest Trail passes through the Goat Rocks. The Yakima Indian Reservation, bordering the wilderness on the SE side, is closed to the general public except for the PCT route.

*Henry M. Jackson Wilderness:* 100,867 acres. Jointly managed by the Wenatchee National Forest, 25,416 acres, and the Mount Baker–Snoqualmie National Forest, 75,451 acres. This wilderness was created by the 1984 Wilderness Act. It lies between Glacier Peak Wilderness and Alpine Lake Wilderness and contains a portion of the Pacific Crest Trail, from Stevens Pass off US 2 to Kodak Peak, where it enters the Glacier Peak Wilderness. The terrain is steep and forested, with a scattering of scenic high mountain lakes. Heavy winter snows melt out slowly. Mountain meadows abound with wildflowers that follow the snowline into the fall months.

*Lake Chelan–Sawtooth Wilderness:* 151,564 acres. Jointly managed by the Wenatchee National Forest, 56,456 acres, and the Okanogan National Forest, 95,108 acres. Approximately 194 mi. of trails traverse the wilderness with major trailheads located along the North Cascades Hwy (Hwy 20), the Twisp River on the NE, Cooper Mountain and Grade Creek Rds. to the S, and Lake Chelan on the SW. Designated a wilderness in 1984, it contains a diverse mixture of dense forest, lush meadows, and alpine slopes. Climate is dry and the rocky soils are thin and sandy. Trailheads along Lake Chelan can be reached by boat or float plane. The *Lady of the Lake* offers daily boat service on

Lake Chelan during the summer months. The boat can be "flagged down" from the Prince Creek or Moore Point access points.

*Norse Peak Wilderness:* 52,180 acres. Jointly managed by the Wenatchee National Forest and the Mount Baker–Snoqualmie National Forest. Created in 1984, this wilderness is located along the Pacific Crest Trail, N of Chinook Pass and E of Mount Rainier National Park. Forested slopes and exposed volcanic peaks highlight the terrain. Along the PCT, the topography is characterized by broad open basins.

*William O. Douglas Wilderness:* 168,157 acres. Designated in 1984, the area is jointly managed by the Wenatchee National Forest, 152,688 acres, and the Gifford Pinchot National Forest, 15,469 acres. The wilderness is located between the White Pass and Chinook Pass Hwys. It shares a boundary with Mount Rainier National Park on the W. Approximately 25 mi. of the Pacific Crest Trail travel along the Cascade crest between its boundaries. The Cougar Lakes portion is characterized by high alpine lakes, and the Tumac Plateau is dotted with numerous lakes in a forested setting. The *Meeks Table Natural Research Area,* located on a basalt mountain, is at the E boundary.

The area is named for the late U.S. Supreme Court Justice who was noted for his concern for civil rights and environmental protection issues during his career. Justice Douglas himself spent many summers at his cabin in Goose Prairie, a small mountain community surrounded by the present wilderness.

*Lake Chelan,* 55 mi. long, ½ to 2 mi. wide, lies between steep-sided mountains with peaks to 8,000 ft. on both sides. About 15 mi. at the S end are within privately owned land. At the N, about 5 mi. are within the Lake Chelan National Recreation Area. All the shoreline between, except for a few small inholdings, is National Forest. Beyond Twenty-Five-Mile Creek, the lakeshore is inaccessible for cars. Campgrounds on the shore are patronized chiefly by boaters, although a few visitors hike in.

The National Recreation Area also has no road access. Most visitors come by the daily boat from Chelan. The N end of the lake also provides a close approach to the Glacier Peak Wilderness. For about 10 mi. S of the NRA boundary, a trail follows the lakeshore. Otherwise, the map shows no shoreline trails, and only a few follow drainages back from the shore.

*Lake Wenatchee,* N of Leavenworth, about 5 mi. long, is a popular resort, much of the shoreline privately owned. Two Forest campgrounds and a State Park are on the shore. Forest roads beyond the lake lead to camps and trailheads near the Glacier Peak Wilderness boundary.

*Keechelus, Kachess,* and *Cle Elum Lakes,* 5 to 7 mi. long, roughly parallel, are in a part of the Forest checkerboarded with inholdings. I-90 is near the E shore of Keechelus. Lake elevations are between 2,200 and 2,500 ft. All 3 are busy resort areas. From Cle Elum Lake, a Forest road follows the Cle Elum River to several Forest campgrounds and the Pacific Crest Trail.

*Rimrock Lake,* along US 12, SW of Tieton, is about 7 mi. long and heavily used, featuring several developed campgrounds, resorts, and nearby trailheads.

*Bumping Lake,* accessed from Hwy 18, is about 4 mi. long with nearby developed campgrounds and trailheads.

## Activities

*Camping:* 120 campgrounds, 18,000 sites, including campgrounds accessible by boat only, not including those reached only by foot or horse. Earliest opening April 15, latest about July 15. Earliest closing Oct. 1, latest Nov. 15.

*Hiking, backpacking:* 2,500 mi. of trails. Detailed trail guides (some for sale) at Ranger District offices.

*Hunting:* Deer, bear, elk, bighorn sheep, grouse. Some hunters use guides and pack animals for backcountry hunting.

*Fishing:* Said to be excellent. Many out-of-the-way lakes and streams. Rainbow, cutthroat, brook, and Dolly Varden trout; steelhead. Bass and perch in Fish Lake.

*Swimming:* Chiefly in the lakes at low elevations.

*Boating:* On the larger lakes.

*Canoeing, kayaking:* Wenatchee River from Lake Wenatchee to Tumwater Campground; 19 mi., some class II rapids. There's a 4-mi. run from Fish Lake to Cle Elum Lake on the Cle Elum River with class II rapids, including a slalom course.

*Horse riding:* Many hunters and summer travelers use pack and saddle stock for wilderness visits. Commercial packers operate on several approach routes. Names and addresses from Forest HQ. Unless you are using a guide, check with a Ranger District for trail conditions and restrictions, need to carry feed, etc.

*Skiing:* Ski areas at Echo Valley, Hyak, Leavenworth, Mission Ridge, Ski Acres, Snoqualmie Summit, Stevens Pass, and White Pass. Consult Ranger District for details and current snow conditions.

*Ski touring, snowshoeing, snowmobiling:* Groomed cross-country ski and snowmobile routes within Forest during the winter months. Some cross-country ski routes are designated with "level of difficulty" signing. Details and current conditions at Ranger District offices.

## Adjacent or Nearby

Mount Baker–Snoqualmie National Forest (see entry zone 4).

Okanogan National Forest (see entry this zone).

Gifford Pinchot National Forest (see entry zone 2).

North Cascades National Park (see entry zone 3).

Mount Rainier National Park (see entry zone 4).

State Parks: Alta Lake, Lake Chelan, Twenty-Five-Mile Creek, Lake Wenatchee, Squilchuck. See entries this zone.

## Publications

*Lady of the Lake* (Chelan boat schedule).

Forest, Ranger District, and Wilderness area maps, (maps include campgrounds, roads, trails, and points of interest), $2.25–$3.25.

## Headquarters

U.S. Forest Service, 215 Melody Lane, Wenatchee, WA 98801; (509) 662-4335.

## Ranger Districts

Chelan R.D., Rt. 2, Box 680, Chelan, WA 98816; (509) 682-2576. Cle Elum R.D., 803 W. 2nd St., Cle Elum, WA 98922; (509) 674-4411. Entiat R.D., 2108 Entiat Way, Entiat, WA 98822; (509) 784-1511. Lake Wenatchee R.D., 22976 State Hwy 207, Leavenworth, WA 98826; (509) 763-3103. Leavenworth R.D., 600 Sherbourne, Leavenworth, WA 98826; (509) 548-6977. Naches R.D., 10061 Hwy 12, Naches, WA 98937; (509) 653-2205.

## Williams Lake

Washington Department of Natural Resources
About 600 acres.

From US 395 about 1 mi. NW of Colville, about 13 mi. N on Echo County Rd. (also known as Williams Lake Rd.).

A small, shallow lake in an attractive, forested setting. The road from Colville offers a quiet drive through a farming valley. Part of the shoreline is marshy. A meadow near the campsite has many wildflowers. Mechanical aerator keeps the lake ice-free in winter. Hiking and mountain biking trails. Interpretive site.

*Camping:* 8 sites. Hand water pump.

### Headquarters

WA Dept. of Natural Resources, P.O. Box 190, Colville, WA 99114; (509) 684-7474.

## Yakima Canyon Scenic Highway

Washington State Department of Transportation/U.S. Bureau of Land Management

Hwy 821 between Ellensburg and Yakima.

The canyon, about 20 mi. long, is a scenic recreation area. The highway, broad and well paved, is sometimes close to the river, sometimes 100 ft. above. Dry hills on either side, sparsely covered with sagebrush and bunchgrass. Along the stream, some large ponderosa, as well as cottonwood, alder, shrubs. The river is about 50 ft. wide, swift-moving, popular with rafters and canoeists.

Many turnouts are along the route. Camping is limited to the 3 Bureau of Land Management Recreation Sites (Roza, Squaw Creek, and Umtanum Creek) and to the privately owned campground located midway through the canyon. Other facilities at the Recreation Sites include picnic tables, vaulted toilets, and boat launches. Full service hookups are available at the private campground. There is one foot bridge that provides access to the *L. T. Murray Wildlife Area* (see entry this zone), a quick entry into good backpacking country. This bridge is located at the Umtanum Creek Recreation Site.

The Roza Recreation Site, located at the N end of the Roza Dam Pool, draws the largest crowds. This is because the pool is large enough for boats with motors, pleasant for swimming, and is the final take-out point for those floating down the river.

## Headquarters

Bureau of Land Management, Spokane District, Wenatchee Resource Area Office, 915 N. Walla Walla Ave., Wenatchee, WA 98801; (509) 655-2100.

Z O N E

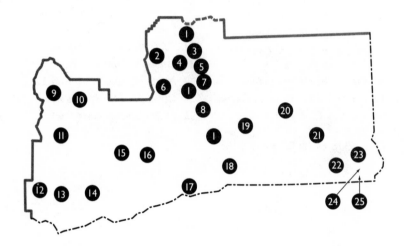

Z O N E 6

Includes these counties:

| | | |
|---|---|---|
| Grant (except N tip) | Klickitat | Columbia |
| Adams | Benton | Garfield |
| Whitman | Franklin | Asotin |
| Yakima | Walla Walla | |

The NW corner of this zone is mountainous, a part of the Cascade Range just E of Mount Rainier National Park. A bit to the S, a part of Goat Rocks Wilderness extends into the zone. Still farther S, Mount Adams likes on the zone boundary. In the far SE, the Blue Mountains and Umatilla National Forest project into the zone from OR.

Except for these areas, the zone is predominantly semiarid to arid. However, it includes much of the basins of the Columbia, Yakima, Snake, and lesser rivers. Almost all these rives have been dammed, and the zone has many irrigation reservoirs. These and associated works have produced many interesting wetlands, waterways, and seep lakes. The contrasts between wetlands and surrounding desert are often dramatic. For example, driving through a dry canyon, one turns a corner and is confronted by a fine waterfall. The many wetland areas attract large numbers of waterfowl, shorebirds, and other fauna.

Many of the larger reservoirs have heavy water-based recreational use: boating, waterskiing, sailing. We include such sites only if they are in natural settings. Usually this means that a significant portion of shoreline is within a Wildlife Area or undeveloped Park.

The Columbia Basin has a remarkable array of these wetland areas, extending from Grand Coulee in zone 5 to the OR border. See the Columbia Basin Recreation Areas entry for a list of sites.

One of the least-known parts of WA is the extreme SE corner, along the canyons of the Snake and Grande Ronde Rivers and in the Wenaha-Tucannon Wilderness of Umatilla National Forest.

## Ahtanum Multiple Use Area

Washington Department of Natural Resources
39,000 acres.

From Yakima, S on I-82 and US 12 about 2 mi. to Union Gap, Exit 36.
Then W 1 mi. to First St. Take a left on First St., then right on Ahtanum
Rd. 20 mi. to Tampico. There take North Fork Rd. 10 mi. into the
Multiple Use Area. Total from Yakima, 30 mi.

About 10 mi. beyond Tampico on North Fork Rd., one enters the Multiple Use Area. The road divides again at the Ahtanum Campground. Turn left or right to travel a 27-mi. loop, including Darland Mountain, back to the fork. The MUA map shows HQ at this point; what one actually sees is a gate marked Private Residences. In fact, it's a DNR work center in addition to residences.

Justice Douglas said Darland Mountain has "the most commanding view in the Cascades." 6,981 ft. high, it's the second-highest point in WA to which one can drive. The road is quite satisfactory as far as Eagle Nest vista. Beyond that we consider it unsuitable for large RVs.

The Multiple Use Area's N and W boundaries adjoin the Tieton Ranger District, administered by Wenatchee National Forest (see entry zone 5). The Goat Rocks Wilderness is 6 mi. W of Darland Mountain. Trails from the MUA lead to the wilderness and to the Rimrock Lake area of the Ranger District. The Oak Creek Wildlife Area (see entry) is on the NE. To the S is the Yakima Reservation. The DNR manages these trust lands to provide revenue for specific beneficiaries, in this case for public school construction. Timber harvest is the major activity. Logging trucks are present and have the right of way.

**Plants:** Ponderosa pine forest in the valleys. On forested slopes, pine with Douglas-fir, spruce, larch, and hemlock. Much of the forest is relatively open, the understory including some low shrubs. Transition to subalpine vegetation on Darland Mountain. The area is noted for its wildflower displays May–Aug. In Aug. many hillsides are carpeted with yellow aster. Also seen then: scarlet gilia, purple monkeyflower, devil's club, larkspur, sunflower, Queen Anne's lace, fireweed.

**Birds:** No checklist available. Species should be much the same as in Okanogan National Forest (see entry zone 5). A few mallard and teal nest along Ahtanum Creek. Chukar, ruffed and blue grouse, pheasant, and California quail are the principal game birds.

**Mammals:** No checklist. Area is noted for a large herd of elk that migrate through. Few mule deer. Also beaver, skunk, muskrat, marmot, chickaree, golden-mantled ground squirrel, chipmunk.

### Features

*Darland Mountain Viewpoint.* The mountain is on the National Forest boundary, and on a clear day you can see Mounts Rainier, St. Helens, Adams, Hood, and Jefferson, and the Goat Rocks.

*Eagle Nest Viewpoint* is on a cliff, less dramatic but offers a good view of a valley within the Multiple Use Area.

*Diamond* and *Cirque Lakes* are on the SW boundary at 5,600 ft. elevation. *Blue* and *Green Lakes* are higher, smaller. Only Green Lake is accessible by 4-wheel-drive vehicle; it has a campground. Blue Lake can be reached with a 4-wheel-drive or all-terrain vehicle.

### Activities

*Camping:* 6 campgrounds, 70 sites. Primitive. Only 2 campgrounds have drinking water. DNR campgrounds are not listed in popular directories. Use is heavy in hunting season. In main campgrounds sites are full most weekends.

*Hiking:* The Ahtanum Trail is used by horses and motorcycles as well as hikers. The 13-mi. Gray Rock Trail lies on the North Fork of Ahtanum Trail and is also multiple use. We saw abandoned logging roads that can be hiked, and the forest is sufficiently open to make bushwhacking feasible.

*Hunting:* Game birds. Elk, deer, coyote.

*Fishing:* Ahtanum Creek and some lakes stocked. Rainbow, cutthroat, whitefish.

*Horse riding:* Some camps have stanchions, other facilities.

*Snowmobiling:* On unplowed roads and trails.

### Publication
Map.

### Headquarters
WA Dept. of Natural Resources, SE Region Office, 713 E. Bowers Rd., Ellensburg, WA 98926; (509) 925-8510.

## Asotin Creek Wildlife Area

Washington Department of Fish and Wildlife
8,725 acres.

From Clarkston on US 95, on the ID border, 6 mi. S on Hwy 129 to
Asotin, then 13 mi. SW along Asotin Creek.

Here is an opportunity for a quiet, pleasant adventure in an out-of-
the-way corner of WA. The road passes through a scenic canyon, dry
slopes with rock outcrops, talus, rimrock, sparse vegetation. Scattered
trees along the valley floor, mostly ponderosa pine with cottonwood,
willow. Spring is the best time to visit, for the fine wildflower display.
Summers are dry, and the area is best left to hunters in the fall.

The road continues into the NE corner of the Umatilla National Forest, in OR (see OR entry zone 4), higher country with many streams,
campgrounds, and trails into the Wenaha-Tucannon Wilderness.

### Activities

*Camping:* Informal; no designated sites.

*Hunting:* Chukar, elk.

*Fishing:* Creek. Best in early summer.

### Headquarters

WA Dept. of Fish and Wildlife, Regional Office, N. 8702 Division St.,
Spokane, WA 99218; (509) 456-4082.

## Brooks Memorial State Park

Washington Parks and Recreation Commission
701 acres.

On US 97, 12 mi. N of Goldendale.

Traveling S on US 97, one leaves dry sagebrush country on the climb to Satus Pass, 3,149 ft., in the Simcoe Mountains; scenic, forested. The road passes through a native American reservation, closed to public use.

The Park is forested: ponderosa, Douglas-fir, spruce. Some Oregon white oak. Cottonwood, willow, and aspen in the draws.

### Activities
*Camping:* 45 sites.

*Hiking:* 9 mi. of trails, 1½-mi. nature trail.

*Fishing:* Trout.

*Snowmobiling:* 3-mi. trail.

### Nearby
Toppenish National Wildlife Refuge (see entry this zone).

### Headquarters
WA Parks and Recreation Comm., 2465 Hwy 97, Goldendale, WA 98620; (509) 773-4611/(800) 233-0321.

## Chief Joseph Wildlife Area
Washington Department of Fish and Wildlife
9,176 acres.

From Clarkston on US 95 at the ID border, S 6 mi. to Asotin, then S about 25 mi. on local road following the Snake River Canyon. Beyond Rogersburg and the Grande Ronde River, the Wildlife Area is on both sides of the road.

In the far SE corner of WA, a lightly traveled area. The Wildlife Area is known to hunters for big game and upland birds. Out of hunting season, and especially in spring and early summer, it's a quiet, scenic area for undisturbed camping, hiking, and fishing. Between Rogersburg and Hwy 129 no road follows the twisting canyon of the Grande Ronde River. From Hwy 129, County Rd. 100 follows the canyon into OR, and this drive is well worthwhile, although it requires a bit of backtracking from the Wildlife Area. NW of Clarkston the Snake River Canyon is 2,000 ft. deep and is accessible by road.

Except for a dirt road to HQ, the Wildlife Area is practically road-less. However, the terrain is dry and open, making for easy cross-country hikes, pleasant rather than challenging for the backpacker.

### Activities

*Camping:* Informal. No designated sites.

*Fishing:* Smallmouth bass, trout, steelhead.

### Headquarters

WA Dept. of Fish and Wildlife, Regional Office, N. 8702 Division St., Spokane, WA 99218; (509) 456-4082.

## Columbia Basin Recreation Areas

Washington Department of Fish and Wildlife/Washington Parks and Recreation Commission/U.S. Fish and Wildlife Service/U.S. Forest Service

From Grand Coulee Dam to the OR border, along and E of the Columbia River. W of US 395 and Hwy 21. Crossed by US 22, I-90, several state highways.

The region is predominantly arid: mountains, canyons, bluffs, mesas, channeled scablands, rolling hills, low dunes, sagebrush flats, as well as irrigated cropland. Almost all the recreation sites are based on water: reservoirs, streams, marshes, seep lakes, waterways. Thus, they attract much wildlife. Department of Fish and Wildlife areas were known as Habitat Management Areas. Most were renamed in 1988. The former title may still appear on some maps and in other references.

Following are sites for which we have entries:

*In zone 5:* Banks Lake Wildlife Area, Billy Clapp Lake Wildlife Area, Steamboat Rock State Park, Sun Lakes State Park/Sun Lakes Wildlife Area.

*In zone 6:* Columbia National Wildlife Refuge, Lower Crab Creek Wildlife Area, Desert Wildlife Area, Gloyd Seeps Wildlife Area, McNary National Wildlife Refuge, Potholes State Park, Quincy Lakes Wildlife Area, Two Rivers and Peninsula Habitat Management Units, Wahluke Wildlife Area.

## Columbia National Wildlife Refuge

U.S. Fish and Wildlife Service
23,200 acres.

From I-90 at Moses Lake, SE about 2½ mi. on Hwy 17, then S 5 mi. on M-SE Rd. Across bridge, turn right and look for Refuge sign on left.

*Open:* Daylight hours.

A visit here should include the Potholes Wildlife Area (see entry this zone), adjacent, the Gloyd Seeps Wildlife Area to the N (see entry this zone), and perhaps the Sun Lakes area farther N on Hwy 17 (see entry zone 5).

This is an area of the Columbia Basin called "channeled scablands." A great lava field was slightly tilted, then scoured by torrents released by the melting of gigantic Ice Age dams. Until recently this was desert, waterless except for a few alkali ponds. Building O'Sullivan Dam, creating an irrigation reservoir, made a great change. Seepage crated many marshes, sloughs, and lakes, as well as numerous water-filled potholes.

The Refuge is a scenic mixture of lakes, canyons, rugged cliffs, and arid sagebrush grasslands providing nesting, feeding, and wintering grounds for over 100,000 ducks and geese. Irrigated croplands produce browse and grain. Fishing is popular in the several lakes.

The Drumheller Channels at the north end of the Refuge is a spectacular complex of buttes, basins, and abandoned cataracts.

Elevations range from 600 to 1,200 ft. Annual precipitation is a mere 8 to 9 in.

Almost the entire Refuge area is open during the spring and summer months. Closed fall and winter to provide undisturbed sanctuary for the birds. Good viewing of the ducks and geese at Royal Lake is available from the overlook at the S end of Byers Rd.

**Plants:** Several plant communities, depending on moisture conditions: cattail-bulrush marsh, sedge meadow, saltgrass meadow, greasewood, sagebrush, and grassland. Wildflowers include aster, phlox, lupines, balsamroot.

**Birds:** Checklist available. Common species include red-tailed hawk, kestrel, great-horned and barn owls, raven, cliff swallow, great blue heron, black-crowned night heron, sandhill crane, northern harrier, magpie, pheasant, California quail. Long-billed curlew and American avocet are less common. Common waterfowl include mallard, gadwall, cinnamon teal, redhead, and ruddy duck. Coots are abundant nesters.

**Mammals:** Beaver, muskrat, marmot, coyote. Towsend ground squirrel, small number of mule deer, occasional badger.

**Reptiles and amphibians:** Pacific tree frog, western spadefoot, sagebrush lizard, common garter snake, Pacific gopher snake, western yellow-bellied racer, bull snake, western rattlesnake.

## Activities

*Camping:* One campground, primitive, no fixed sites. Camping is also available at several nearby Dept. of Fish and Wildlife sites and Potholes State Park.

*Hiking:* 3 interpretive trails highlighting 3 different habitats.

*Hunting:* Waterfowl and upland birds. Check regulations.

*Fishing:* 50 seep lakes, sloughs, 15 mi. of streams and canals. Rainbow and German brown trout, largemouth bass, bluegill, black crappie, yellow perch, walleye. Special regulations.

*Boating and canoeing:* Not allowed on impoundments on and along Crab Creek in Marsh Units I and II. Canoe route from Hutchinson Lake to Shiner Lake.

## Publications

Leaflet with map. (Maps in the hunting and fishing leaflets are much better.)

Bird checklist.

Hunting information.

Fishing information.

## Headquarters

U.S. Fish and Wildlife Service, P.O. Drawer F, Othello, WA 99344; (509) 488-2668.

## Conboy Lake National Wildlife Refuge

U.S. Fish and Wildlife Service
5,884 acres.

From Trout Lake on Hwy 141, take Rd. E toward Glenwood about 8 mi. Entrance on right.

This is a Refuge in the making. Authorized in 1965, only two-thirds of the planned acreage has been acquired. Nor have water needs been met. Conboy Lake was drained in 1910 by digging a canal. Blocking the canal today would flood privately owned land within the old lakebed. Aquatic habitat now depends on runoff exceeding the canal's capacity and on limited restoration sites on Refuge canals. Between Dec. and May there are usually 1,000–5,000 acres of wetland, enough to attract up to 10,000 waterfowl. When we visited in summer most of the lakebed was dry. Several streams, canals, and ditches provide summer habitat for limited numbers of wood duck, mallard, other summer residents.

The Refuge is in a small, quiet, attractive valley not far from Mount Adams and the Gifford Pinchot National Forest (see entry zone 2). Elevations from 1,800 to 2,000 ft. About 2,500 acres of seasonal wetlands, 2,200 of forest and uplands. Most of the forest has been logged at least once, but a few old-growth ponderosas remain.

March and April have large migratory waterfowl concentrations, including tundra swans. Scenically the Refuge is at its best in the fall, usually mid-Oct. when the aspens turn color with Mount Adams as a backdrop.

It's a pleasant place for a 2-hour hike if you happen to be driving this way. The Klickitat Wildlife Area (see entry this zone) is nearby, as well as the National Forest, and the route from Goldendale to Trout Lake is scenic. Except in hunting season, you may be the only visitors.

**Birds:** Checklist available. 150 species recorded. Manager reports that virtually the entire WA population of sandhill cranes, about 20, are found on the Refuge. Seasonally common species include great blue heron, Canada goose, mallard, pintail, green-winged and cinnamon teals, wood duck, red-tailed hawk, northern harrier, kestrel, ruffed grouse, common snipe, Wilson's phalarope, mourning dove, great horned owl, rufous and calliope hummingbirds, northern flicker, hairy woodpecker, eastern and western kingbirds, Say's phoebe, 3 fly-catchers, western wood pewee, 6 swallows, raven, crow, western and mountain bluebirds, pine siskin, American goldfinch. 1 to 10 bald eagles usually present when waterfowl are abundant.

**Mammals:** Beaver, chipmunk, flying squirrel, golden-mantled ground squirrel, gopher, porcupine, black-tailed deer, coyote, skunk. Present but seldom seen: river otter, elk, bobcat, badger, weasel, raccoon, pine marten, black bear.

## Interpretation

*Willard Springs Trail* 2 mi., near headquarters, passes through a variety of habitats. Beavers active. *All other areas of the Refuge are closed to public entry except as noted below.*

## Activites

*Hunting:* Waterfowl, upland game birds, deer. Special rules; see Refuge manager.

*Fishing:* Limited. Rainbow and brook trout, catfish, bullhead.

## Publications

Leaflet.

Bird checklist.

## Headquarters

U.S. Fish and Wildlife Service, Box 5, Glenwood, WA 98619; (509) 364-3410.

## Desert Wildlife Area, The

Washington Department of Fish and Wildlife
27,719 acres.

From I-90 W of Moses Lake, S on Dodson Rd. about 3 mi., then either right or left.

The Frenchman Hills and Winchester Wasteways cut through this previously dry sandy area, developing a striking contrast of extensive wetlands amidst dry sand dunes and sagebrush. Desert, Harris, and Beda Lakes are managed for trout; walk-in access only. The wasteway systems have trout and warm-water species. Many waterfowl, shorebirds. Wildlife is much the same as in the adjoining Potholes Wildlife Area (see entry this zone).

Good canoeing on quiet waters in spring and early summer. Two small waterfalls require portaging.

*Camping:* Informal, at boat-access points.

### Headquarters
WA Dept. of Fish and Wildlife, Regional Office, 1550 Alder St., N.W., Ephrata, WA 98823; (509) 754-4624.

## Fields Spring State Park
Washington Parks and Recreation Commission
793 acres.

Extreme SE WA, 30 mi. S of Clarkston, off Hwy 129.

Near the ID and OR borders, in the Blue Mountains. On the edge of the breaks of the Grande Ronde River Canyon, deep, winding, spectacular. Park elevations from 3,980 to 4,450 ft. Site is partly forested: ponderosa pine, grand fir, western larch, Douglas-fir. Wild rose and berry species in understory. Fine wildflower display in spring and early summer. A plant list was being prepared in 1996.

The Park is often crowded in hunting season since several public hunting areas are nearby. Otherwise, it's a quiet, scenic camping spot in an out-of-the-way region with many day-trip possibilities.

Hwy 129 to the S descends into the gorge, crosses the river, ascends into OR. There are side roads along the river. Other roads enter the Umatilla National Forest. A canyon overlook is a 1-mi. hike from the campground.

**Birds:** Checklist available. Seasonally common or abundant species include sharp-shinned, red-tailed, and rough-legged hawks, kestrel, great-horned owl, rufous and calliope hummingbirds, ruffed grouse, northern flicker, pileated and hairy woodpeckers, yellow-bellied and

Williamson's sapsuckers, Hammond's and dusky flycatchers, western wood pewee, Steller's jay, crow, 3 chickadees, red-breasted nuthatch, mountain bluebird, ruby-crowned kinglet, solitary and warbling vireos, 6 warblers, Cassin's finch, red crossbill, dark-eyed junco, house wren.

**Mammals:** Include black bear, mule and white-tailed deer, elk, coyote, marmot, porcupine, raccoon, squirrels, chipmunk.

### Activities

*Camping:* 20 sites.

*Hiking:* 7 mi. of trails, including fire roads. 1-mi. trail to Puffer Butte overlook. The Umatilla National Forest map shows unpaved roads leading from the Park to Anatone Butte at the Forest boundary and Forest Rd. 4304.

*Ski touring:* Excellent area for ski touring and snowshoeing. Warming huts, covered shelters. Entry from Anatone, Asotin, or in OR.

### Nearby

Asotin Creek Wildlife Area (see entry this zone).
Umatilla National Forest (see OR entry, zone 4, and entry this zone).

### Headquarters

WA Parks and Recreation Comm., P.O. Box 37, Anatone, WA 99401; (509) 256-3332/(800) 233-0321.

---

### Gloyd Seeps Wildlife Area

Washington Department of Fish and Wildlife
10,111 acres.

From Moses Lake on I-90, N on Stratford Rd. Public-access areas on left at Rds. 9, 12, 14, 16.

One might not plan a special trip just to Gloyd Seeps, but it can be part of an exploration of the channeled scablands. The Wildlife Area is about 11 mi. long, NW–SE, on Crab Creek, which has several small impoundments. Average width: a bit over 1 mi. Swampy region of saltgrass flats, marsh, extensive cattail patches surrounded by sage-brush desert. Waterfowl habitat also supports populations of pheasant, quail, cottontail. A good birding area in spring. Popular hunting area. Homestead and Magpie Lakes are managed for trout; walk-in access.

**Birds:** No checklist. Species generally the same as at Columbia National Wildlife Refuge (see entry this zone). Those noted here include white pelican (in spring), blue and green-backed herons, common snipe, green-winged teal, shoveler, Wilson's phalarope, yellow-headed blackbird, magpie, western kingbird, kingfisher.

*Camping:* Informal.

## Nearby
See Columbia Basin Recreation Areas (entries zone 5 and this zone).

## Headquarters
WA Dept. of Fish and Wildlife, Regional Office, 1550 Alder St. N.W., Ephrata, WA 98823; (509) 754-4624.

## Juniper Dunes Wilderness
U.S. Bureau of Land Management
7,140 acres.

18 mi. NE of Pasco. There is no legal access to the wilderness. Visitors should always contact the BLM's Spokane District's Border Resource Area office for information regarding access before attempting to enter the area.

The largest area of active sand dunes in WA and the largest concentration of western juniper. Site consists of mostly sand dunes up to 150 ft. high in various stages of stabilization. Active dunes in the central and NE portions. There are 6 major groves of western juniper within the wilderness.

**Plants:** Aside from juniper there are scattered pockets of sagebrush, bitterbrush, wheatgrass, needlegrass, cheat grass.

**Birds:** Noted here or nearby, ferruginous, Swainson's, and red-tailed hawks, great horned, barn, short-eared, and burrowing owls, long-billed curlew, sage thrasher, sage sparrow.

**Mammals:** Kangaroo rat, mule deer.

## Headquarters

Bureau of Land Management, Spokane District, Border Resource Area, 1103 N. Fancher Ave., Spokane, WA 99121; (509) 536-1200.

## Klickitat Wildlife Area

Washington Department of Fish and Wildlife
14,000 acres.

From Goldendale on US 97, W on Hwy 142 about 10 mi. to Glenwood Rd. NW toward Glenwood about 5 mi. Look for dirt roads on the left, then HQ. The more accessible public areas are beyond HQ, after the road drops down into the canyon.

The road to Glenwood and Trout Lake is scenic, lightly traveled. For some miles it passes through unbroken forest. Between the Wildlife Area and Glenwood, look for Outlet Falls, an overlook well worth a brief stop.

The Wildlife Area is on the meandering Klickitat River, a swift stream. The river seemed popular with boaters. We saw rafts, kayaks, and drift boats taking out at Stinson Flat. Almost all, we were told, are steelhead anglers. Here the river is about 50 ft. wide, apparently shallow.

Some of the roads into the Wildlife Area may require 4-wheel drive, at least in wet weather. Beyond HQ, however, the highway drops down into the river canyon, with some fine views along the way. The area within the river canyon rises from 800 ft. along the river to the ridges 2,000 ft. above. At the bottom, the road into Stinson Flat is adequate for any vehicle.

Slopes are partially forested, varying from grassy areas to moderately dense stands. Mostly ponderosa and other conifers on the slopes, deciduous trees and shrubs in the draws. Stinson Flat has a handsome grove of OR oaks and several large ponderosa pines.

The Wildlife Area was established as a wintering area for black-tailed deer coming down from nearby high country, and this is still its chief purpose.

**Birds:** Checklist available. Species noted include Merriam's turkey, chukar, mountain quail, band-tailed pigeon, golden eagle, prairie falcon, mountain bluebird, northern pigmy owl, Say's phoebe, savannah sparrow.

**Mammals:** Checklist available. Species include black bear, mule deer, marmot, mink, muskrat, porcupine, Rocky Mountain elk. Also many bats.

**Reptiles and amphibians:** Checklist available. Includes gopher, several garter snakes, northern Pacific rattlesnake, Rocky Mountain boa, fence lizard, 2 alligator lizards, western skink, western toad, bullfrog, long-toed salamander.

## Activities

*Camping:* Map available at HQ shows 3 campgrounds, other camping areas. Primitive. Area is usually snow-free by March. Open forest offers numerous sites for informal camping.

*Hiking, backpacking:* No marked trails, but they're not really needed in such open country.

*Hunting:* Excellent deer hunting. Upland birds.

*Fishing:* Steelhead. Good summer-run stream. Rainbow trout, whitefish, Chinook, coho salmon.

## Nearby

Conboy Lake National Wildlife Refuge (see entry this zone).

## Publications

Leaflet with map.

Checklists of birds, mammals, reptiles and amphibians.

## Headquarters

WA Dept. of Fish and Wildlife, Regional Office, 5405 N.E. Hazel Dell, Vancouver, WA 98666; (360) 696-6211.

## Lower Crab Creek Wildlife Area

Washington Department of Fish and Wildlife
25,243 acres.

From Beverly on Hwy 243, beside the Columbia River, E about 1 mi.
toward Smyrna and Corfu. The Wildlife Area is mostly between Beverly
and Smyrna. On both sides of the road, but most of the acreage is on N
side.

The Priest Rapids Wildlife Area is a 3,642-acre satellite, on the Columbia River just W of Mattawa. We thought the road between Beverly
and Smyrna unsuitable for large RVs but we were told it is usually well
maintained by the county.

The Lower Crab Creek Wildlife Area is about 13 mi. E–W, 3 mi.
N–S, lying along Crab Creek at the foot of the Saddle Mountains.
Includes the Lenice-Nunnally lake chain, managed for quality fishing.
Sagebrush desert, rolling hills, cattail marshes. Good waterfowl habi-
tat. Known chiefly by hunters and fishermen. Dunes at the W end are
managed by the DNR for use by ORVs. They are prohibited in the WA
Wildlife Area, and trespass has been a problem.

Spring and early summer are the best times to visit. The prospective visitor should include Crab Creek as a side trip from the Columbia National Wildlife Refuge, Potholes Wildlife Area, and other sites in
the region. The secondary roads, such as those between Potholes
Reservoir and Crab Creek, offer good sightseeing with little or no traffic. The road from O'Sullivan Dam to Othello and Lower Crab Creek
Rd. W from Othello passes through fenced portions of the Columbia
National Wildlife Refuge. Good birding along the roadside. Beyond
Corfu the road is on a shelf cut into Saddle Mountain, providing a
good view of wetland and irrigated farmland below.

### Activities

*Camping:* Informal.

*Canoeing:* From bridge 5½ mi. E of Beverly to Columbia River. One S-
curve requires short portage.

### Nearby

Columbia Basin Recreation Areas (see entries this zone and zone 5).

## Headquarters

WA Dept. of Fish and Wildlife, Regional Office, 1550 Alder St. N.W., Ephrata, WA 98823; (509) 754-4624.

......................

## Lyons Ferry State Park

Washington Parks and Recreation Commission
1,282 acres.

SE WA, on Hwy 261 at the Snake River; 22 mi. SE of Washtucna.

The Park itself is not a natural area, but it offers access by boat to some interesting country. The property is leased from the U.S. Army Corps of Engineers. The Corps has 1,609 acres on the Palouse Canyon, which is managed as a natural area. The Park has 52,000 ft. of shoreline on the Snake River where it is joined by the Palouse River. This portion of the Snake is impounded by Lower Monumental Dam, forming a pool extending 29 mi. upriver to Little Goose Dam. The Snake River Gorge is here about 200 ft. deep, cut through a basalt plateau. Surrounding terrain is dry. Rolling hills with bluffs, lava outcrops, terraces. Vegetation is chiefly sagebrush and sparse grasses.

**Birds:** The impoundment is attracting increasing numbers of migratory waterfowl. No checklist. Species noted by manager: pheasant, chukar, meadowlark, killdeer, red-tailed hawk, eastern kingbird, goldfinch, great blue heron, northern shrike, dark-eyed junco, horned lark.

**Mammals:** Include marmot, coyote, porcupine, beaver, cottontail, mule deer.

## Activities

*Camping:* 62 sites.

*Fishing:* Steelhead, bass, catfish, crappie, perch.

*Swimming:* 428 ft. of beach.

*Boating:* 2 ramps.

## Nearby

Palouse Falls, scenic area. Falls drop 200 ft. into a canyon with vertical walls. Best when water is at full flow, spring and early summer.

**Headquarters**
WA Parks and Recreation Comm., Box 157, Starbuck, WA 99359; (509) 646-3252/(800) 233-0321.

## McNary National Wildlife Refuge

U.S. Fish and Wildlife Service
3,631 acres.

6 mi. S of Pasco on US 12, near Burbank.

The closing of McNary Dam submerged a number of Columbia River islands that had been important nesting habitat for Canada goose. Strawberry Island, in the Snake River just before it meets the Columbia, and the six Hanford Islands upstream from Richland in the last free-flowing section of the Columbia are a partial replacement. They are administered by the Refuge.

The mainland part of the Refuge includes 825 acres of marshes and open water, 750 acres of cropland, 1,359 acres of native grasslands. Cropland is used to produce cereal grains, corn, winter wheat, and alfalfa for waterfowl feed. Crops are also used by upland game birds.

Two public roads cross the Refuge, but there is no auto tour route. Most visitors take the 1-mi. wildlife trail, which circles the slough area.

Elevations from 330 to 500 ft. Precipitation is a scant 7 to 8 in., requiring that crops be irrigated.

**Plants:** Uplands: sagebrush, rabbitbrush, wheatgrass, cheat grass. Cattail and hardstem bulrush in marsh. A few cottonwood, willow, Russian olive.

**Birds:** Checklist available. Seasonally common or abundant species include great blue heron, black-crowned night heron, tundra swan, Canada goose, mallard, gadwall, pintail, green-winged and cinnamon teals, wigeon, shoveler, redhead, ring-necked duck, canvasback, lesser scaup, common goldeneye, bufflehead, ruddy duck, common merganser. Also coot, killdeer, avocet, northern phalarope, California and ring-billed gulls, Caspian tern, pheasant, mourning dove, burrowing and short-eared owls, 5 swallows, marsh wren, water pipit, 4 warblers, yellow-headed and red-winged blackbirds.

**Mammals:** Include black-tailed jackrabbit, cottontail, coyote, beaver, muskrat, raccoon, mule deer, silver-haired bat. Present but seldom seen: mink, weasel, kangaroo rat, pocket gopher, deer mouse, badger, river otter.

**Reptiles and amphibians:** Northwest fence lizard, salamander, bullfrog, leopard frog, Great Basin spadefoot toad, painted turtle, valley garter snake, bullsnake.

### Activities

*Hunting:* Refuge is best known for goose hunting. Also other waterfowl, pheasant.

*Fishing:* Bullhead, carp. Check regulations.

### Adjacent

Two Rivers and Peninsula Habitat Management Units (see entry this zone).

### Publications

Leaflet.

Bird checklist.

Hunting and fishing leaflet.

### Headquarters

U.S. Fish and Wildlife Service, P.O. Box 544, Burbank, WA 93323; (509) 547-4942.

........................................................................................

# Mount Baker–Snoqualmie National Forest

See entry zone 4.
Oak Creek Wildlife Area
Washington Department of Fish and Wildlife
89,023 acres.

From Yakima, NW about 23 mi. on US 12.

Between the Wenas Valley and Tieton River, bisected by the Naches River and Hwy 410. US 12 continues into the adjacent Tieton Ranger District of the Wenatchee National Forest (see entry zone 5), a busy resort area. Visitors should stop first at HQ, on the N side of US 12 about 2 mi. from Hwy 410. A good map of the Wildlife Area is on the bulletin board. Maps are sometimes available for distribution. Even with the map, though, we had difficulty finding several of the roads. Ask at HQ for route advice and information on road conditions. Roads are usually in their best condition in summer.

The W portion of the Wildlife Area, bordering on the National Forest, is mostly heavy ponderosa forest. To the E, trees are more scattered, open forest giving way to grasses. Slopes are moderate to steep, rising 500 to 1,500 ft. above the river valleys. Cottonwood, aspen, willow along the stream bottom. The Cowiche Unit, to the S, is on the South Fork of Cowiche Creek, along a county road. 1,440 acres. Open bunchgrass, sagebrush, rolling hills. Trout fishing; bird hunting; some deer.

The area is known for its large elk population, attracting many elk hunters. Many people visit the feeding stations at HQ, which may be used by up to 4,000 elk in severe winters.

The Tieton is a swift-moving shallow stream, popular for fishing. US 12, following the stream, has numerous turnouts. The Oak Creek and Bethel Ridge roads, which begin near HQ, continue into the National Forest; Oak Creek Rd. becomes Forest R. 140, linking with roads N of Rimrock Lake. Both are primitive roads, and checking their current condition is advisable. Bethel Ridge Rd. was closed by washouts when we visited, is closed during winter feeding of elk.

The Wildlife Area has several popular camping areas, but you are free to camp in almost any suitable place. Hiking is said to be good in the Cleman Mountain area, on the NE side of Hwy 410 but reached more easily from the Wenas Rd. N from Selah. In summer, we'd try the Bethel Ridge area first.

Information about plants, birds, and mammals of the area is not available, but species are much the same as those in the Wenatchee National Forest entry.

In hunting season, any Wildlife Area is best left to hunters. Spring is a good time to visit here, as soon as roads are dry enough for travel. Summer weather is a bit cooler here than in lower, drier areas to the E.

## Publication
Site map, not always available.

## Headquarters

WA Dept. of Fish and Wildlife, Regional Office, 1701 S. 24th Ave., Yakima, WA 98902; (509) 575-2740.

## Potholes State Park

Washington Parks and Recreation Commission
640 acres.

From I-90 at Moses Lake, SE about 2½ mi. on Hwy 17, then S 5 mi. on Sullivan Rd. Across bridge turn right and continue past dam to Park.

See Columbia Basin Recreation Areas entries, this zone and zone 5. The Park is just a convenient camping area on Potholes Reservoir, adjacent to the Potholes Wildlife Area and Columbia National Wildlife Refuge. Many visitors prefer to park their RVs for the night at one of the many Dept. of Fish and Wildlife boat-access points. Those who want a proper campground come here.

In odd contrast with the surrounding desert, the Park is landscaped with irrigated lawns and rows of poplars. Although the site is on the reservoir and has a beach, campsites are set well back, almost out of sight of the water. There are hiking and fishing access trails.

## Activities

*Camping:* 126 sites.

*Boating:* Ramp.

## Headquarters

WA Parks and Recreation Comm., 6762 Hwy 262E, Othello, WA 99344; (509) 364-2759/(800) 233-0321.

## Potholes Wildlife Area

Washington Department of Fish and Wildlife
38,588 acres.

From I-90 at Moses Lake, SE about 2½ mi. on Hwy 17, then S 5 mi. on Sullivan Rd.

The Desert Wildlife Area and the Columbia National Wildlife Refuge (see entries this zone) are adjacent; several other sites of interest are nearby. The area, described as channeled scablands, was waterless desert until the O'Sullivan Dam formed Potholes Reservoir. Countless sand dune islands dot the N half of the reservoir, creating unique habitats. Seepage has formed countless small lakes, ponds, marshes, and sloughs, and the area is now a major nesting, resting, and feeding area for waterfowl and shorebirds. A wildlife reserve at the N end has a winter population of 20,000 to 50,000 waterfowl.

At the S end of the lake are several launching areas where RV camping is permitted. However, this end of the lake is often noisy with racing motors. If you have a canoe, the far NW end of the reservoir is quieter and more interesting. Since the reservoir is about 10 mi. long, try one of the several access points coming in from Potholes Rd. on the N. Here are many quiet channels too shallow for power boats. RV camping is possible at most boat-access points. Since the reservoir is used for irrigation, water level drops in summer.

For fauna and flora of the area, see entry for Columbia National Wildlife Refuge.

### Activities

*Camping:* Primitive, at boat-access points.

*Hunting:* Waterfowl, upland game birds.

*Fishing:* Largemouth bass, black crappie, yellow perch, trout, bluegill, walleye. The lake is a popular fishing area.

### Adjacent

Potholes State Park and Columbia National Wildlife Refuge (see entries this zone).

### Headquarters

WA Dept. of Fish and Wildlife, Regional Office, 1550 Alder St. N.W., Ephrata, WA 98823; (509) 754-4624.

## Quincy Lakes Wildlife Area

Washington Department of Fish and Wildlife
13,508 acres.

On the Columbia River, W of Hwy 281, N of I-90. Access from Hwy 28 W of Quincy by Ancient Lake Rd., from Hwy 281 S of Quincy by Rd. 5 or Base Line Rd. Signs mention Evergreen Reservoir, Quincy Lake, Stan Coffin Lake, etc., rather than the Wildlife Area.

Several of the lakes can be reached by car over reasonably good dirt roads. But to appreciate the area fully, one must hike. Towering cliffs, sagebrush coulees, basalt pillars, and—if you hike—magnificent views from the rim of the Columbia River Canyon.

Within the Wildlife Area, high points give a view of great expanses of sagebrush broken by large, jagged lava outcrops. Some of the lakes are surrounded by lava bluffs up to 30 ft. high.

The area is maintained for waterfowl and upland wildlife and is an important link in the Columbia Basin chain. Canada geese, tundra swans, and many species of ducks are among those stopping for a time. On a summer visit, we saw a few Canada geese, grebes, coots, great blue heron, ring-billed gull, red-tailed hawk, canyon wren, chukar.

Many of the lakes are managed for trout fishing. Very large crowds of fishermen and -women gather during the early spring opening weekend. Both shore and boat fishing.

Hunters are busy here in the fall. For others, spring and early summer are good for visiting.

### Activities

*Camping:* Informal. Latrines at Evergreen.

*Hunting:* Waterfowl, pheasant, chukar.

*Fishing:* Trout, bass.

### Headquarters

WA Dept. of Fish and Wildlife, Regional Office, 1550 Alder St. N.W., Ephrata, WA 98823; (509) 754-4624.

## Sunnyside Wildlife Area

Washington Department of Fish and Wildlife
8,466 acres.

Sunnyside Unit: 5 mi. S of Sunnyside on Holiday Rd. Byron Unit: Along Hwy 22 approximately 5 mi. E of Mabton and 5 mi. S of Grandview.

The Wildlife Area consists of 4 main units, plus several other smaller areas. The Sunnyside Unit has 2,793 acres of continuous property along the Yakima River with approximately 13 mi. of river frontage. This unit includes Bridgeman Pond, Giffin Lake, and Morgan Lakes. The site is managed for waterfowl and upland game birds. The surrounding area is some of the most intensively managed agricultural land in the country.

6 ponds or lakes of varying sizes offer excellent nesting habitat in spring and resting areas for migratory waterfowl in the winter and fall months. Two of the lakes are located on the Snipes Unit, which has been designated a waterfowl reserve. 10,000 to 15,000 lesser Canada geese graze the area in winter and early spring.

The Byron Unit, a series of depressions and rolling hills with a series of ponds extending about 2 mi. (about 400 acres), also offers fine waterfowl nesting and brooding areas. Closed Feb. 1–Aug. 1 to protect the nesting waterfowl. Canada geese here in late winter and early spring.

The Rattlesnake Slope Unit is 7 mi. N of Benton City on the lower eastern slopes of Rattlesnake Peak. Horn Rd. is the E boundary and the only public access to the unit. Large stands of bunchgrasses with smaller patches of sagebrush and cheat grass. Game and nongame species are limited in this unit because of the lack of water.

*Camping prohibited.*

Birders find Wildlife Area interesting in spring and early summer. 8–10 mi. of service roads used for hiking, mountain biking, and horse riding.

### Headquarters

WA Dept. of Fish and Wildlife, Regional Office, 1701 S. 24th Ave., Yakima, WA 98902; (509) 575-2741.

# Toppenish National Wildlife Refuge

U.S. Fish and Wildlife Service
1,763 acres.

From Toppenish, 6 mi. S on US 97, then 1 mi. W from Refuge sign.

The Refuge is in the lower Yakima Valley in the heart of the Yakima Reservation. The Refuge has 3 units along Toppenish Creek and the Yakima River. The directions above are to the HQ area. A map available at HQ shows routes to other areas. Brushy creek bottoms, wet meadows, croplands, and sagebrush uplands. The Refuge is maintained for waterfowl, and up to 200,000 ducks are present winter and spring, a dense concentration for an area of this size. A wildlife observation point is at the Upper Toppenish Unit.

If you plan a visit, check the Refuge schedule. Some of the units are open year-round, while others are closed to the public Oct. 1–Feb. 28/29 to protect the wildlife.

Birding is said to be good in all seasons. Seasonally common and abundant waterfowl include mallard, shovelers, pintail, Canada goose, heron, gulls, egrets, terns. Raptors include hawks, bald and golden eagles. Songbirds. An estimated 1,500 ducks are raised each year.

Deer, muskrat, badger, and other mammals are also seen.

## Activities

*Hunting:* Limited to a few species in designated areas, from mid-Oct. to mid-Jan. Information at Refuge office. Yakima Indian Nation Reservation permits required.

*Hiking:* Self-guided viewing trail.

## Publications

Bird checklist.

Hunting leaflet with map.

## Headquarters

U.S. Fish and Wildlife Service, 21 Pumphouse Rd., Toppenish, WA 98948; (509) 865-2405.

## Two Rivers and Peninsula Habitat Management Units

U.S. Army Corps of Engineers.
3,000 acres.

Just S of Burbank, off US 395.

Adjoins the McNary National Wildlife Refuge (see entry this zone). The federal Refuge is on the inland side of US 395; the Habitat Management Units are on the other side, with about 7 mi. of river frontage. A major portion of the HMW is closed to vehicle access from Feb. 1 to mid-Oct.; entry on foot or horseback is permitted. A gravel road from Burbank extends into the HMW. A railroad embankment extends through its full length.

Wildlife on the Habitat Management Units include long-billed curlew, sandhill crane, white pelican, bald and golden eagles, and most species of North American waterfowl; also deer, raccoon, coyote, mink, badger; an occasional painted turtle.

Camping is not prohibited, but there is no campground.

### Activities

*Fishing:* Columbia River.

*Boating:* Launch sites on both Habitat Management Units.

*Hunting:* Goose and duck. Restricted to shotguns and archery. State hunting and fishing regulations apply. Check for specific site regulations.

### Headquarters

U.S. Army Corps of Engineers, Ice Harbor, Rural Rt. 6, Box 693, Pasco, WA 99301; (509) 547-7781.

## Umatilla National Forest

U.S. Forest Service
311,197 acres in WA; 1,091,283 acres in OR.

SE corner of WA. Access in WA by secondary roads only, chiefly from Asotin, S of Clarkston, on the ID border, and from Pomeroy and Dayton on US 12.

Forest map required.

The WA portion is in the Blue Mountains, which extend N from OR. A major part of the Wenaha-Tucannon Wilderness is in WA. Points of interest include Clearwater Lookout, 25 mi. S of Pomeroy, and Sunset Point, 30 mi. S of Pomeroy, both offering fine views. A number of Forest campgrounds are in this area. The road beyond Sunset Point goes to the edge of the wilderness area. See entry in Oregon zone 4.

### Ranger Districts

Pomeroy R.D., Rt. 1, Box 53-F, Pomeroy, WA 99347; (509) 843-1891. Walla Walla R.D., 1415 W. Rose, Walla Walla, WA 99362; (509) 522-6290.

## Umatilla National Wildlife Refuge

U.S. Fish and Wildlife Service
14,006 acres.

On the Columbia River, bounded by Hwy 14, E and W of Paterson.

About half of this Refuge is in OR. Since the two parts are separated by the river, each is an entry.

The Refuge extends along the river for about 18 mi., with two gaps. The portion E of Paterson is open to the public all year. Lands W of Paterson to Glade Creek are closed to public use Oct. 1–Feb. 28. Closing of John Day Dam inundated much waterfowl habitat, but it also created Paterson Slough, E of Paterson, now a fine place to observe wintering or migrating waterfowl. The Refuge includes a number of islands, sandbars and sandy shores, sloughs, marsh, cultivated cropland, and bits of sagebrush upland.

**Birds:** 189 species recorded (OR and WA units). Checklist available. Seasonally abundant or common species include pied-billed grebe, double-crested cormorant, great blue heron, tundra swan, Canada goose, mallard, gadwall, pintail, teals, wigeon, shoveler, goldeneye, bufflehead. White pelican is noted as occasional in fall, uncommon in winter, but we saw two dozen on the OR side in Aug.

Also seasonally abundant or common: northern harrier, kestrel, California quail, pheasant, coot, killdeer, greater yellowlegs, sandpipers, avocet, ring-billed gull, terns, rock and mourning doves, northern flicker, magpie, raven, crow, marsh wren, robin, cedar waxwing, western meadowlark, yellow-headed and red-winged blackbirds, northern oriole, cowbird, house finch, goldfinch, sparrows.

**Mammals:** Include black-tailed jackrabbit, cottontail, opossum, porcupine, muskrat, coyote, badger, beaver, raccoon, river otter, bobcat, mule deer.

### Activities

*Hiking:* A wildlife foot trail is located on the McCormack Unit. Hiking is permitted in all open areas.

*Hunting:* Waterfowl and upland game. Designated areas and special regulations, including required permit, obtained by mail application.

*Fishing:* River. Sturgeon, bass, salmon, steelhead.

### Publications

Leaflet with map.

Umatilla bird checklist.

Umatilla hunting information and map.

### Headquarters

U.S. Fish and Wildlife Service, P.O. Box 700, Umatilla, OR 97882; (541) 922-3232.

## Wahluke Wildlife Area

Washington Department of Fish and Wildlife
57,839 acres.

On both sides of Hwy 24, about 10 mi. S and W of Othello. From Pasco, N on Rd. 68 to Ringold, following signs.

This Wildlife Area adjoins the Saddle Mountains National Wildlife Refuge, which is on Nuclear Regulatory Commission land and closed to the public. The Wildlife Area is also on NRC land, but limited public use is permitted. Regulations are posted. Day use only.

On the S slope of the Saddle Mountains, extending to the Columbia River. Seep lakes have formed from waste water, attracting waterfowl and numerous shorebirds. The area is also noted for raptors. Bald eagle often seen in winter. 50,000 to 100,000 waterfowl can be seen in winter on the river reserve.

This is the last free-flowing stretch of the Columbia River. The White Bluffs on the river provide strong visual contrast with the generally flat terrain. On the S end of the site, on the river, are abandoned farms, now a hunting area.

### Headquarters

WA Dept. of Fish and Wildlife Regional Office, P.O. Box 1237, Ephrata, WA 98823; (509) 754-4624.

## W. T. Wooten Wildlife Area

Washington Department of Fish and Wildlife
14,120 acres.

From Clarkston, W on US 12 through Pomeroy. At Zumwalt, left on Tatman Mountain Rd. Go S to Blind Grade, then down Blind Grade to Tucannon River Rd. Turn left on Tucannon River Rd. S 1½ mi.

The road along the river is a northern entrance to the Umatilla National Forest (see entry this zone) and the Panjab Campground at the edge of the Wenaha-Tucannon Wilderness. In the spectacular Blue Mountains. Most of the Wildlife Area is on the E side of the river. The river valley is rugged, with sharp, steep ridges, talus slopes, broad-topped tablelands. N-facing slopes are timbered, S-facing slopes open and grassy.

A local HQ is at the N edge of the Wildlife Area. Beyond it, along the valley, are several small ponds. This is a popular fishing area in summer, and many people camp here rather than continue into the National Forest. But the Wildlife Area has enough backcountry to offer ample solitude. Tumalum Creek and Cummings Creek are possible routes.

The valley is a wintering area for elk. A few bighorn sheep may also be in the Wildlife Area. Also present: white-tailed and mule deer, black bear, snowshoe hare, cottontail, mountain lion, bobcat. Game birds include Rio Grand turkey, California and mountain quail, chukar, Hungarian partridge, pheasant, dove.

**Headquarters**
WA Dept. of Fish and Wildlife, Regional Office, N. 8702 Division St., Spokane, WA 99218; (509) 456-4082.

# INDEX

# About the Authors

The Perrys, long residents of the Washington, DC, area, moved to Winter Haven, Florida, soon after work on these guides began. Their desks overlook a lake well populated with great blue herons, anhingas, egrets, ospreys, gallinules, and wood ducks, plus occasional alligators and otters.

Jane, an economist, came to Washington as a congressman's secretary and thereafter held senior posts in several executive agencies and presidential commissions. John, an industrial management consultant, was for ten years assistant director of the National Zoo.

They have hiked, backpacked, camped, canoed, and cruised together in all fifty states. They have written more than twenty books and produced two dozen educational filmstrips on natural history and ecology.

Their move to Florida marked a shift from international to local conservation action, participating in county Sierra Club and Audubon groups and the Polk County Coalition for the Environment.